Scrolls of Love

Scrolls of Love

RUTH AND THE SONG OF SONGS

Edited by Peter S. Hawkins and Lesleigh Cushing Stahlberg

FORDHAM UNIVERSITY PRESS

New York / 2006

Library of Congress Cataloging-in-Publication Data

Scrolls of love : Ruth and the Song of songs / edited by Peter S. Hawkins
  and Lesleigh Cushing Stahlberg.—1st ed.
    p.   cm.
  Includes bibliographical references and index.
  ISBN-13: 978-0-8232-2571-2 (cloth : alk. paper)
  ISBN-10: 0-8232-2571-2 (cloth : alk. paper)
  ISBN-13: 978-0-8232-2572-9 (pbk. : alk. paper)
  ISBN-10: 0-8232-2572-0 (pbk. : alk. paper)
  1. Bible. O.T. Ruth—Criticism interpretation, etc.   2. Bible. O.T. Song of
Solomon—Criticism, interpretation, etc.   I. Hawkins, Peter S.   II. Stahlberg,
Lesleigh Cushing.
BS1315.52.S37   2006
222'.3506—dc22
2006029474

Printed in the United States of America
08 07 06   5 4 3 2 1
First edition

For John Clayton (1943–2003),
mentor and friend

CONTENTS

ILLUSTRATIONS

INTRODUCTION

Peter S. Hawkins and Lesleigh Cushing Stahlberg

Scrolls of Love is a book of unions. Edited by a Christian and a Jew who are united by a shared passion for the Bible and a common literary hermeneutic, *Scrolls of Love* joins two biblical scrolls (*megillot*) and gathers around them a diverse community of interpreters. It brings together the book of Ruth and the Song of Songs, two seemingly disparate texts of the Hebrew Bible, and reads them through a diversity of methodological and theological perspectives. Respectful of traditional biblical scholarship, the collection of essays moves beyond it; alert to contemporary trends, the volume returns venerable interpretive tradition to center stage. Moreover, *Scrolls of Love* expands the notion of commentary, adding visual art and literary interpretation to textual hermeneutics.

In juxtaposing these two very different biblical books, we find in them a common theme: love. In Ruth, love is tender, filial, loyal; between Ruth and Naomi, it is almost sisterly. But even when love manifests itself sexually, as between Ruth and Boaz, it is marked by gentleness and loving-kindness (*ḥesed*). By contrast, love in the Song of Songs is physical, erotic, at times frantic, and densely metaphoric in its expression. It is a sexual love that is entirely mutual, that emboldens both lover and beloved. Ruth is a model of agape, the Song of eros, and yet both make declarations of love that are unparalleled elsewhere in the Bible. The reader is moved by Ruth's promise to cleave to Naomi until death and by the female lover's assertion in the Song that she belongs to her beloved and her beloved belongs to her.

The careful reader, moreover, is struck by the fact that *female* voices utter both these vows. In their depictions of love, in fact, the two scrolls celebrate women. In their transmission of woman's words and their foregrounding of the woman's body—treating female flesh not as a danger to be regulated, but as a source of pleasure, solace, and power—the book of Ruth and the Song of Songs stand apart from the rest of the canon. Unlike what we find elsewhere in Scripture, the scrolls' women are full participants in the covenant. Furthermore, in these books, the understanding of covenant undergoes a sea change: In contrast to more traditional biblical theology, with its reliance on divine utterance, in Ruth and the Song of Songs, the divine is known primarily in the context of human relationships. The scrolls evoke an apparently secular world in which God is not present, but where the female perspective is predominant. Indeed, the Song contains no reference to God, and although the book of Ruth invokes the Lord, there is no theophany, no angelic messenger, and no evidence of the cultic life of Israel. God acts within and among people, not on them. These scrolls are not simply united by the theme of love; rather, they share an ideal of a love expressed by and for human beings that comes before the love of God.

Despite the fact that Jews and Christians share a common text in the Hebrew Scripture, the two communities have read their Bibles in isolation from one another, each in ignorance of the richness of the other's traditions of reading. As a consequence, the text that unites threatens to divide. *Scrolls of Love* brings the two traditions into dialogue, enriching established modes of interpretation with unconventional ones. The contributors assembled here were chosen on the basis of their professional renown and their established record on the subjects about which they write, but also because of their commitment to working in an interdisciplinary endeavor that is self-consciously interfaith. The result is a volume that sets rabbinic, patristic, and medieval readings alongside feminist, psychoanalytic, and autobiographical ones. It combines historical, literary, and textual criticism with a variety of artistic reinterpretations—woodcuts, papercut images, poetry, and fiction. Some of the works are scholarly, with the requisite footnotes to draw readers to further inquiry, to other books and thinkers. Others, however, deal only with primary sources; they lead readers to plumb the intricacies of the biblical text itself. Some are more reflective than analytic; they allow readers to see what it means to live intimately with Scripture. As a unity, the collection presents Ruth and the Song of Songs not only as ancient texts that deserve to be treasured, but as old worlds capable of begetting the new.

Reading Ruth

For Ellen F. Davis, the book of Ruth is "the still, small voice in the canon." Running against the notion that the important events of history "occur in war rooms or on battlefields or even on holy mountains," the book of Ruth situates history in the most unexpected of places, in the intersection of three seemingly ordinary lives. The reader watches as Naomi, Ruth and Boaz "help each other grow through and beyond the lamentably common tragedies that mark many, even most lives: for Naomi and Ruth, displacement, bereavement, childlessness, and poverty; for Boaz, some unexplained loneliness in an otherwise prosperous and respectable life." In her sermon, Davis proposes that people love this book because of the ordinariness of the characters. Most biblical narratives are "about the people who shape history, for better or for worse. Ordinary people show up in those stories only as occasional foils for the main, extraordinary characters." But Ruth is about minor figures, "people sort of like us—or people we might grow to resemble," should we order our lives according to *ḥesed*, to loving-kindness.

In "Beginning with Ruth: An Essay on Translating," Davis notes that her translation of the book of Ruth in *Who Are You, My Daughter? Reading Ruth through Image and Text* allows her English reader a view into the book's original language. In highlighting what happens during the transformation of an ancient Hebrew book to a contemporary English one, Davis illuminates both the ways biblical books are read and interpreted. She explores the ways that a translator might at once leave the biblical text open for interpretation and guide the foreign reader through the translated work. She asks, "What choices does a translator make, and what possibilities are obscured once those choices are made?" By pointing to questions such as these, Davis hopes to show how, through a translation, the Bible may be viewed with fresh interest and genuine curiosity.

André LaCocque sees the Book of Ruth as a subversive text that works against received notions of gender, nationality, and class. Taking seriously the socioeconomic issues that provide a backdrop for the text, he reads Ruth as a correction of the social and political boundaries set by Second Temple Judaism. In elevating *ḥesed* as a crucial theological principle, the Book of Ruth goes beyond Israel to the universal. The book champions the Moabite, that is, the archetypal "other" of the Tanakh, and offers long-awaited good news to the poor and disenfranchised—to the Ruths of the world.

Arguing against traditional understandings of Ruth as a historical short story or a covenantal novella, Nehama Aschkenasy contends that the book is at heart a comedy. Despite its surface sobriety, it bears all the markers of the genre—deceptions, misunderstandings, mistaken identities, and even stock comedic figures. Drawing on dramatic theory from Aristotle to Northrop Frye and making parallels to the comedies of Shakespeare and Molière, Aschkenasy reveals the narrative to be another reworking of classic types, with Boaz as the *senex*, the comic old man; Ruth as the *virgo*, the young and unavailable object of the elder man's romantic interest; and Naomi as the *servus*, who is both clever and scheming.

Reading Ruth's Readers

Judith Kates focuses her attention on *Ruth Rabbah*, an ancient compendium of rabbinic interpretation. She notes in the midrash a thematic preoccupation with the question of conversion: at its heart, Ruth is a narrative about a Moabite woman who becomes the ancestress of King David. Thus rabbinic readers consistently find in Ruth a model of the *ger tzeddek* (the righteous convert). In fact, it is through their reading of the narrative that the word *ger*, used in the Hebrew Bible to designate a stranger, gains its rabbinic meaning of "convert." The rabbis see in Ruth's vow to follow Naomi to Bethlehem not just her willingness to take on the yoke of the law, but also a full awareness of all the journeys, both physical and spiritual, to be found in Torah. Although the biblical law seems explicitly to forbid the inclusion of the Moabite in the congregation of Israel, the rabbis harmonize legal and ethical demands in their establishing a genuine halakhic ground for embracing the Moabite foreigner. They understand that, despite her Moabite origins, Ruth is brought under the wings of God because of her extraordinary righteousness and because she is the exemplar of *ḥesed*. She is the opposite of what Deuteronomy understands a Moabite to be; she is righteous, modest, and faithful, fully in keeping with all that the law enjoins.

Nehemia Polen looks at Ruth in the context of Jewish thoughts about the messiah. Drawing on Kabbalistic and Hasidic traditions, he reads the messiah as being born into a lineage of transgression and blossoming into light. Ruth as a Moabite is a product of Lot's incestuous union with his daughters. From this tarnished beginning comes the woman who will win the heart of the righteous Boaz and conceive a son, Omer, the great-grandfather of David, the forerunner of the messiah. As the Polish Hasidic master Zadok ha-Kohen says of the messiah, "the lowest will become the highest." Or, in Polen's interpretation, only an imperfect messiah can redeem an imperfect world.

Neither the figure of Ruth nor the book that bears her name has been central to the Christian imagination, yet she plays any number of parts in the drama of the tradition. She is the paradigmatic Gentile who makes her way into the assembly of Israel; she is the ancestor of David and hence of Christ; she is a figure of the church, and of the obedient soul; and more recently, she is a woman who modestly, but courageously chooses another woman and, through her, moves in faithfulness to God. Peter S. Hawkins wonders whether in the future, with feminist readings of the Scripture already asking us to notice so much that was once passed over, what other Ruths may yet come out of the Christian imagination.

Reimagining Ruth

Kathryn Hellerstein attends to the literary afterlife of Ruth in two Yiddish poets, Roza Yakubovitsh (b. 1889, d. 1944 in Auschwitz) and Itzik Manger (b. 1901, d. 1969 in Tel Aviv). The former, an observant Jewish woman, grounds her modern poetry in traditional Jewish texts, particularly as they were handed down to women in the popular 1620 compilation of classical sources, the *Tsenerene*. On the other hand, there is something distinctly modern, even emancipated, about Yakubovitsh's Ruth. The poet at once renews the ancient text and undercuts the rabbis' misogynist readings of it. Thus, unlike the biblical and rabbinic Ruth, who is obedient and modest, Yakubovitsh's Ruth is independent and frankly sensual. Just as Yakubovitsh places her Ruth in a Polish peasant's threshing barn, Itzik Manger sets his rewriting in an Eastern European landscape. Unlike his female counterpart, Manger was raised in an assimilated Jewish home; his father was a self-proclaimed bohemian who coined the term *literatoyre*. The word, which fuses "literature" and "Torah," reflects the Mangers' comfort with playing with biblical texts, even to the point of profaning the sacred. The eight Ruth poems Hellerstein presents show a strongly autobiographical slant as Ruth becomes a wanderer, displaced from Moab, whose return to the promised land is completely uncertain.

As a printmaker who also teaches at a Christian seminary, Margaret Adams Parker has long been aware of a special relationship between the printmaking medium and Scripture. Since her own art is often intimately involved with biblical texts, Parker has turned to the rich legacy of printmaking not only as a resource, but also for inspiration. In her essay, she sketches a history of the medium, looking in particular at the ways in which the book of Ruth has been visualized. She then situates her own woodcuts, which appear in Ellen Davis's translation and commentary *Who Are You, My Daughter?: Reading Ruth through Image and Text*, in this long-established tradition. She notes that many artists have "read" the story as a romance centered on a beautiful heroine, and so Ruth often appears as young and lovely. Both Davis and Parker found this reading of the biblical story unconvincing. Parker therefore chose "to picture Ruth as attractive enough for Boaz to find her interesting," but attractive "in the way of the women we see on the evening news, crossing national borders with babies on their hips and their worldly possessions on their heads." She sought to highlight "Ruth's beauty of character" to show what it might mean to look like a woman of valor.

Translating and Reading the Song of Songs

Chana Bloch reminds us that "although the Song was in all likelihood composed as a poem about erotic love, the rabbis read it as an allegory about the love of God and the people of Israel;" this reading, coupled with the attribution of the poem to King Solomon, helped the Song to enter the canon. Similarly, the church fathers' allegorical reading took the Song to be "a loving dialogue between Christ and his bride, the church." For the two millennia following the canonization of the Song, such religious interpretations of the Song prevailed: the Holy of Holies of the Holy Scriptures was consistently understood as describing the love between humans and God. While Jewish and Christian mystics remained open to the emotional intensity and raw passion of the Song, "allegories about the love of God or Christ imposed a severe constraint on the interpretive tradition." Together with Ariel Bloch, Chana Bloch was drawn to translate the Song to redress their sense that no English translation reflected the "unusual combination of sensuousness and delicacy that makes the Hebrew so captivating." Because the Song is riddled with unique words, the Bloch's task of translation proved a great challenge. As Bloch's essay illustrates, virtually every line presents some complexity, gives rise to a history of wildly divergent translations of the Song.

André LaCocque argues that "the Song contains erotic descriptions that neither ask for nor require justification." Unlike the other parts of the biblical canon, and the prophetic literature in particular, the Song celebrates sensual life. This eroticism is a deliberate subversion of the institutionalized mores of the Hellenistic era in which it was composed.

In LaCocque's reading, the subversiveness is compounded in his contention that the book's author is a woman, a person at the periphery of the androcentric religious life of ancient Israel. LaCocque's Song of Songs is highly iconoclastic, playing provocatively with such proscriptive or condemnatory sources as Genesis 3 and Hosea 3–4 in its celebration of physical love.

According to Ellen Davis, the most troubling question in Song of Songs scholarship is the work's genre. She points to contemporary scholars who see the book alternately as a parody of Torah, the prophets, and the sages; as a reflection of Canaanite cultic religion, representing a marriage ceremony between deities; as "soft porn"; as a venture into the "grotesque" that is toxic to readers; and as the most exquisite love poetry. The answer to the genre question depends on how one understands the book itself. Davis stands almost alone among contemporary biblical scholars in her conviction that the Song was correctly understood by the rabbis and church fathers who set the book within Israel's Scriptures. She believes with them that to read the book allegorically is not to misread it; for her, it truly is, "in large part, about the love that obtains between God and Israel—or, more broadly, between God and humanity." Whereas "LaCocque argues that the Song is the work of a poet who resolutely subverts the religious traditions of Israel, taking the praise that is elsewhere offered to God and transposing it so that the language of desire and gratitude is focused on her human lover," Davis, by contrast, contends that the Song "returns us to Eden with the intent of imaginatively healing the ruptures that occurred there: between man and woman, between humanity and God, between human and nonhuman creation."

Marc Brettler also bucks contemporary scholarship on the Song, which has argued that the work is a unified whole, written by a single author who is quite possibly a woman. Brettler regards these conclusions as pat, and points to Sa'adiya Gaon's famous dictum that the Song is "a lock without a key." He asserts that the argument for unity overlooks the wide variety of styles apparent in the scroll and that scholars who identify clear structures within the poem have imposed them upon the work. Further, he contends that we may never be able to gain full access to the Song, in part because the world of its authors is so remote to us and in part because their language may be deliberately ambiguous. In contrast to the theological readings of LaCocque and Davis, Brettler argues against the possibility of a consistent reading of the Song.

Reading the Song's Readers

Judith Kates take up Daniel Boyarin's proposal that in interpreting the Song of Songs, Rabbinic midrash finds or creates a "language of intimacy" that generates shades of emotion and relationship that lend warmth to the historical experience of the people of Israel. The *Song of Songs Rabbah* (likely finalized in the sixth century C.E.) responds to the biblical arc from Abraham to messianic redemption, focusing in particular on the narratives at the Red Sea and Sinai. Throughout the rabbinic corpus, the Song of Songs is used to explore the narratives of Exodus and Revelation; the whole history of Israel is an expansion of the Song of Songs, a story of the love between God and human beings. In Kates's reading, the rabbis "enlisted the passionate energy, the sensual specificity and richness, and the erotic power of the Song's language into their quest to articulate their deepest and most intimate knowledge of relationship."

Arthur Green argues that the Kabbalah emerged not only at the time of but also in direct response to medieval Spanish Catholicism. He sees in the Zohar's focus on the *shekhina*, a feminine aspect of God who acts as mediator between the world above and the world below, a reworking of Marian devotion. With mystics seeking to achieve union with the *shekhina* in order to bring about the union of the male and female within God, the Song of Songs comes to be read not in terms of male and female or God and Israel, but as a love song between God (male) and God (female). Whereas the keystone of Catholic eroticism is celibacy, for the Kabbalists it is sexuality. Not only is the married life an option, it is a necessity, if one hopes to attain union with God. The sexual union between husband and wife enacts the union of *shekhina* and God. In this sense, it may be said that Zoharic exegesis seeks to reread the entire Torah as an expanded version of the scriptural Holy of Holies, the Song of Songs.

In the early twelfth century, Honorious Augustodunensis offered a long and rhetorically virtuoso commentary on the Song of Songs. In the prologues to his line-by-line exposition of the text, Honorius placed the Song within the framework of universal history. E. Ann Matter translates for the first time in English the synopsis of his commentary and offers an explication of it. Honorius sees in the Song four brides of Solomon: the daughter of the pharaoh, the daughter of the king of Babylon, the Shulamite, and the Mandrake. Because Honorius inherited a perceived connection between the Song of Songs and the biblical Apocalypse, he is particularly concerned with this last figure, whom he sees as Synagoga and the ultimate bride of Christ. She, with her bridegroom, will usher in the Second Coming. Thus, in Honorius's reading, the love song of the Hebrew Bible becomes the love song of the millennium, Synagoga becomes Ecclesia, and the conversion of the Jews becomes the last sign of the End Times.

In exploring the sermons of Bernard of Clairvaux, Mark Burrows asks about the interplay between the sexual and the spiritual for the monastic reader. He considers whether the spiritual reading of the Song signals a loss of erotic integrity or whether it makes the spiritual erotic. Bernard, who read the Song as an occasion for the construction of monastic life, makes the strong claim that love is the principle speaker in the Song. He insists, however, that love's language is not one that all are able to hear, that it requires an education and a conversion. The Song, when read aright, leads the monk into an eroticized spirituality that serves as a counterbalance to "the confused world beyond the monastic imagination." In Bernard's view, the ordered, externally discernible monastic regimen was not, in fact, where the key to the monastic life was to be found. Rather, the monastic life was organized around an internal pattern, in the interior habits of reading. In his view, allegorical reading does not merely provide a hermeneutic tool, but reading is itself the very locus of monastic conversion. To ruminate on the Song of Songs is not to interpret a text, but to construct experience itself.

Margot Fassler considers the musical compositions of Hildegard of Bingen in light of her theological treatises, arguing that the medieval abbess's music always interacts with her religious writings. Fassler sees her compositions as part of her concerted program to expand the canon of religious writings and music for the explicit use of communities of religious women. Hildegard was most interested in the idea of a unique "female voice" for the rendering of praise to God. Her music, which she claimed to receive through divine inspiration, could be so feminine because it flowed through a woman and was created specifically for female singers. Furthermore, because she believed it was from and of God, she saw it as a direct representation of those aspects of the divine nature that are female. The Song of Songs provided Hildegard with the language of passionate union that she in turn made vivid for the life of virgin nuns. Hildegard pairs the Song with the apocalyptic supper of the Lamb in Revelation 14 to prepare her community for a face-to-face encounter with Christ in the Eucharist. In the *Ordo virtutum*, the nuns sang a transformed prophets' play in which the female virtues replaced the old patriarchy as agents leading the faithful to God. In giving female voice to consecrated virgins, Hildegard afforded her community an entry into the feminine aspects of the divine. Fassler thus sees Hildegard of Bingen as building a bridge from cloister to choir to altar.

Lino Pertile reminds us that in the Middle Ages, the "weakness" of the historical and literal foundations of the text allowed for the development of "an almost limitless polysemy." Each of the Song's words and sentences "offered scope for the endless exercise of intertextuality involving not only the Old and the New Testaments," but perhaps most importantly, the fathers of the church. In Italy, the Song was particularly important to the Franciscan spiritual milieu, the Joachimites, the mystics, the apocalyptics, and generally to the Christian thinkers who yearned for a return of the church to her pristine purity. Indeed, the Song of Songs was often read and commented on in association with the Book of Revelation, "with which it made an almost inseparable prophetic unit." These two texts together offer Dante powerful inspiration for the overall construction of his earthly paradise in *Purgatorio* 28–33, and, in particular, for the kissing scene between the giant and the whore in *Purgatorio* 32. Their kiss "is the perverse parody—the antithetical figure"—of the Song's opening words, "Osculetur me osculo oris sui." The importance of the Song should not be surprising, especially given its luxuriant commentary tradition. It provided Dante with "a polysemous narrative pattern in which his autobiographical and theological concerns, his personal anxieties, and social and historical beliefs were already synthesized in one integrated system."

Reimagining the Song

Carey Ellen Walsh tries to account for the joy she experiences whenever she returns to the Song of Songs. To her mind, joy comes out of the relationship the reader develops with the text. She speaks of attraction: she is not "merely looking at the Song's two lovers," but is "drawn into the process of desire itself." Walsh is helped in understanding this experience by the work of psychoanalyst Jacques Lacan, whose "exploration of the interstices of desire, language, and reading" illuminate the Song for her: "For Lacan, language is so communal that the distinction between the reader and the writer is blurred; both are caught up in its web. Whereas other perspectives offer diverse insight into the Song's characters, Lacan's psychoanalytic perspective is instead concerned to treat the text itself as analysand, to discern how it expresses desire." Paradoxically, it is not finally what the Song offers—its luxuriant images, its evocative descriptions—that gives pleasure. Rather, it is what the text withholds, the satisfaction it denies, the appetite it exacerbates, that keeps Walsh coming back for more.

As a classically trained biblical scholar suspicious of the current penchant for autobiographical criticism, with its elevation of the interpreter to the level of text, it is with chagrin that Carole Fontaine found herself speaking about the Song of Songs very much in the first person. Yet despite her scruples, she decided it was important to reflect on personal discovery. "We read in company, and when we read in good company, our readings grow and change, though never so as to achieve a final resolution. In this respect, reading itself is not unlike the elusive 'plot' of the Song. Furthermore, reading the Song is a lifelong event, and by sharing what matters to us with other readers, we are able to see it more clearly, differently." Fontaine notes that in a postmodern critical climate where "the eternal verities that used to be proclaimed by all senior scholars have been silenced by assaults on meaning," the autobiographical critical choice represents a different strategy. Subjective bias is accepted as inevitable, "for how can we read except through the lens of bias and personal experience?"

Jacqueline Osherow is a poet as well as a lover of Scripture. She brings to her reading of the Song of Songs a lifetime of intimacy with the Hebrew text and with the experience of chanting it. When chanting, she finds herself at first overwhelmed by the beauty of the sounds and then made aware that the sounds are having a directed effect: They are producing and conveying an elaborate array of multiple meanings. While she acknowledges that she often does not understand the literal meaning of the text, she is energized by her perception that the Song dares us to believe it means what we suspect it means. She sees in the Song's tantalizing obscurity the secret of its erotic power: It forces us to engage our own erotic imaginations.

Finally, Lesleigh Cushing Stahlberg turns to contemporary Jewish poetry that plays with the Song of Songs, reading it in light of the two levels of meaning of the scriptural text. In the post-Holocaust Israeli literature she considers, the quest for the beloved is all the more poignant because the beloved is at once a human figure and an absent God. She asserts that these poems can be read not merely as love poems, but as expressions of human desire for reunion with God.

PART ONE

Reading Ruth

"ALL THAT YOU SAY, I WILL DO": A SERMON ON THE BOOK OF RUTH

Ellen F. Davis

The first words of Ruth: "In the days when the judges were judging, there was a famine in the land." "The days when the judges were judging"—if you have read the seventh book of the Bible, then you know that it was a time of political chaos, with Philistine enemies pressing hard on Israel's flank, and the "national leadership" (if you can call it that) worse than a bad joke. Yes, early on there was Deborah, a great judge, but things deteriorated pretty steadily after that. By the end of the period of the book of Judges, when our story is set, we see the perpetually adolescent Samson, too preoccupied with his sexual misalliances to give proper attention to the people's needs, and also "Jephthah the Gileadite . . . a mighty warrior" (Judg. 11:1), who, during his six years in office, managed to stir up civil war, killing forty-two thousand Israelites, in addition to his own daughter. Of this grim period when the judges were judging, the biblical narrator comments caustically, "there was no king in Israel, and everyone did what was right in their own eyes" (17:6).

Against that background of deterioration and disaster on a national scale, the small domestic tale of Ruth, Naomi, and Boaz unfolds. "And after the fire, a still small voice" (1 Kings 19:12). Through all those burning events reported in the book of Judges, there isn't much of God's action to be seen—but rather Israelite murdering Israelite; women kidnapped, raped, killed; bodies piled high at the fords of the Jordan. Ironically, it seems, "in the days when the judges were judging," the action of God in and for Israel was gradually obscured, eclipsed. It was as Elijah experienced at Horeb: God's presence is not to be found in the events that break up rocks and mountains and nations. For YHWH was not in the wind, nor the earthquake, nor the fire. But "after the fire, a still small voice."

The book of Ruth is the *qol dᵊmammah daqqah* (1 Kings 19:12), the still small voice in the canon. It quietly refutes the great-man theory of history, the notion that all the really important events occur in war rooms or on battlefields or even on holy mountains. After all the machination of those great (or at least powerful) men in the book of Judges, it is an experience of grace to turn to Ruth and dwell on the small and not evidently earthshaking interactions between three quite ordinary people. We watch as they help each other grow through and beyond the lamentably common tragedies that mark many, even most lives: for Naomi and Ruth, displacement, bereavement, childlessness, poverty; for Boaz, some unexplained loneliness in an otherwise prosperous and respectable life. I think it is the ordinariness of the characters that explains why people love this story so. Everywhere else, the biblical history tells us about patriarchs and matriarchs, prophets and kings, people whose lives are marked from the get-go by blessing, anointing, a special calling from God, people who shape history, for better or for worse. Ordinary people show up in those stories only as occasional foils for the main, extraordinary characters. But this little story is not about movers and shakers. At most these three generated a low buzz in Bethlehem ("Is this Naomi?! Oy, has she lost her looks!"), a little eddy of local news for a few months ("Older man falls for younger woman. Pillar of the local community takes up with Moabite laborer without a green card"). Naomi, Ruth, and Boaz are people sort of like us—or better perhaps, people we might grow to resemble, if we should order our lives to that end.

And that is further reason to love this story, because it gives us hope and direction for ourselves and hope also for something beyond our own lives. The story gives hope, because it shows ordinary people helping each other grow through and beyond personal tragedy. And what opens up, through acts of generosity and mutual regard, is something far beyond their own small sphere, beyond what they could know or imagine. Probably none of them ever saw the grandbaby (the great-grandson, to be precise) whose name is the last word—literally, the last word—of their story. Yet what opens up through David is the future God intends for Israel. After the spectacular failures of the days of the judges, this itself is amazing: God still intends a future for Israel. The full story of that future isn't yet known to any of us, even now. We have read far enough and lived far enough beyond that promising end of Ruth to know that what lies beyond their story is an imperfect future, marked by sin and much suffering and punishment for sin. Nonetheless, it is a covenanted future; it is a future with God—and all of us here, Gentile Christians along with Jews, dare to believe that we have some share in the covenanted afterlife of the story of Naomi, Boaz, and Ruth.

If the book of Ruth stands in the canon as a gracious counter to the book of Judges, it also speaks a word of grace to times such as our own. In pondering Ruth again, I have come to see it somewhat differently than I did before. For me, at least, the difficult world situation at the beginning of this new century has revealed more deeply the need for Ruth, and what I want to suggest is that this little book is *torah* for socially and politically disordered times. Like the Israelites in the time of the judges, we are worn down and out by "great events" on a national and international scale. In this country, in Israel and Palestine, in Afghanistan and Iraq, in Africa, maybe in China, and also in the ecosphere, we are witnessing cataclysmic events that seem to offer only the most uncertain hope of a better and safer future for any of the people of God. And so, perhaps the *torah* of this book of Ruth is especially apt now, for its essential message is this: In a time of widespread disorder and personal loss, simple acts of mutual regard—the Hebrew word for that is *ḥesed*, the discipline of generosity that binds Israelites to one another and to God—acts of *ḥesed* can open up the future God intends. This is something considerably more than a sop to those who are discouraged by their inability—our inability—to see the way out of some fearful situations. For the future that this book begins to open has the broadest scope possible. It encompasses Jews and Christians, and through our communities, we believe, it points to the repair and redemption of the whole world. This little book of Ruth teaches us, more concisely perhaps than any other book of the Bible, what the Swiss theologian Karl Barth calls, in a lovely phrase, "the simplicity and comprehensiveness of grace."[1]

"The simplicity and comprehensiveness of grace"—yet the *credibility* of grace depends on its concrete expression.[2] The ultimate concrete expression of divine grace in this book is, of course, the birth of a child. Probably there is no miracle that so regularly and powerfully speaks of God's grace manifest in our world. The conception and birth of a child is powerful to move even the most spiritually inert parent or loving observer—it moves us, for a time at least, to some degree of inchoate wonder. Notably, in the whole four chapters of Ruth, we hear of only one direct divine action, and that at the very end: "YHWH gave [Ruth] a pregnancy" (4:13).

5

So God's action is clear only at the end of the story, but acts of *ḥesed* enter the picture and shape it from the outset. Listen to Naomi's very first words, addressed to Orpah and Ruth on the road between Moab and Bethlehem: "Go on, go back, each of you to her own mother's house, and may YHWH do *ḥesed* with you, as you have done with the dead and with me" (1:8). Ruth is indeed the still small voice in the canon; all its literary effects are subtle. This blessing by Naomi of her "bride-daughters" (*ḳallo-tēha*) affords the first delicate surprise in the book. *Ḥesed*, the foundational virtue of Israelite community and culture, enters the story from what is, biblically speaking, an unlooked-for direction: from the East, from Moab. You will recall that everywhere else in the Bible, Moabites are well known to be heathen no-goodniks. But here two young Moabite women are distinguished for their covenantal kindness toward their Israelite husbands, now dead, and their grief-ravaged mother-in-law. And God is called upon to take special note of these Moabite women—even to follow their example!

Ḥesed is the keynote of this book in a way that is distinctive in the Bible. Moses and the prophets often enjoin the practice of *ḥesed*, but Ruth's story is altogether *torat ḥesed*, the teaching of *ḥesed*, to use a phrase from the book of Proverbs (Prov. 31:26). Ruth's story teaches in the way only a great narrative can, by taking a quality, a virtue of which we often speak in the abstract, and then showing us what that quality looks like when it is concretized in life. Isn't it always the case that when a virtue assumes flesh, the effect is much more interesting than you expected? I think this is why Jews and Christians have traditionally loved to tell stories about holy and righteous men and women: because there is invariably a surprising angle to holiness or true virtue when you see it in a life—or in this case, in several intertwined lives.

Ancient hearers of this story would be surprised to see a Moabite modeling *ḥesed*, but I think we, who have no particular animus against Moabites, might be more struck by something else about Ruth: namely, by her generous regard for Naomi when she can so ill afford to be generous. She takes an incalculable and completely unnecessary risk: leaving home, over Naomi's objections, to accompany the old woman to Bethlehem, a small town where a foreign woman who does not clearly belong to anyone—a woman with a tattoo, as artist Margaret Adams Parker has imagined her—can be viewed only with suspicion, if not with outright hostility.

Looking hard at Ruth, we see that for all her courage and physical strength, for all her determination to protect and provide for the old woman whose life has been shattered, Ruth is herself extremely vulnerable. She is the vulnerable protector. In that role, she stands for countless women throughout history and around the world who, though living in precarious situations, take on the additional risk and struggle of caring for the very old or the very young or the sick or the permanently frail. As a model practitioner of *ḥesed*, Ruth teaches us something about covenant relationship that might not otherwise be clear, although I am convinced that many parts of the Bible point to it: that the real test of covenant relationship is how one vulnerable person treats another who is likewise vulnerable, or (by extension) how one people, one nation that is troubled, frightened, terrorized, takes the risk of recognizing its kinship with another vulnerable, beleaguered people.

What we see in the course of this story is that Ruth's practice of *ḥesed* moves others into the incalculable risk and joy of covenanted relationship. First the old, spent woman, Naomi, who has loved and lost two "boys," as the narrator poignantly calls her two dead sons ("yᵊladēha," 1:5). At the beginning of the story she is ready to be done with God and with life (1:13). Yet gradually she reinvests herself in another young life as she plots to secure the future, to secure a good husband for this foreign "daughter" of hers. Then Boaz, the well-to-do man ("'ish gibbōr ḥayil," 2:1) who seems to lack no comfort but that of love, finds himself unexpectedly in emotional debt to the woman who asks him to marry her. Boaz, like Ruth herself, is a vulnerable protector.

The quality of relationship that has grown between Ruth and Naomi, Ruth and Boaz, is revealed in one phrase uttered at two key junctures: "All that you say (to me),[3] I will do." Ruth says it first, when Naomi gives her instructions for the threshing floor night. Knowing that her reputation and therefore (in that small-town world) her whole life hangs on the success of Naomi's highly risky scheme, Ruth entrusts herself completely to the old woman's wisdom: "All that you say, I will do" (3:5). Shortly thereafter, when Ruth whispers to a startled Boaz, "Spread your wing [your cloak] over your maidservant," Boaz answers with the same words: "All that you say, I will do for you" (3:11).

It is a statement of complete trust and deference. It sums up *torat ḥesed* as we see it in Ruth, all the acts of mutual regard that bind these three: "All that you say, I will do"—each one recognizing the other's genuine needs, spoken or unspoken, and letting those needs determine her or his actions; "All that you say, I will do"—each one, knowing the situation is precarious, taking on the still-unmeasured burden of the other; each one accepting as wisdom the considered judgment of the other; "All that you say, I will do"—each one honoring the risk undertaken by the other; each tough, determined individual giving up the impoverished security of going it alone and entrusting the future into the hands of a now-beloved other.

I suggested that Ruth may be *torah* for disordered, even desperate times. If that is so, it must not be because it turns us away from concern for the public sphere, enclosing each of us in our own little domestic world. Rather, it must be because Ruth teaches us the quality of relationship that enables life with others to be decent, secure, even (dare we say it?) happy. Mutual deference to the genuine needs and the wisdom of the other—we know this is essential if our families, our congregations, our schools and offices are to be places of *shalom*, of well-being and genuine peace.

We know this to be true on a small scale; is it also true on a larger one? As we look beyond our immediate communities, it seems to me that our work here is one example of, or at least one opportunity for, mutual deference in a wider public sphere. When Jews and Christians agree to read Scripture together, that is a significant act of mutual deference, since we come together after a bitter and, for Christians, shameful history of violent disagreement about the texts that mark us as siblings and at the same time divide us. We have come together to read Ruth, knowing that we do not entirely agree on what even this little book might mean for our own communities and for the world. But we sing it, see it, pray and interpret it in each other's presence—exploring an almost unused model of peace, believing that there is grace in the endeavor, even daring to hope that it may orient us more surely to the covenanted future God intends for us all. Amen.

BEGINNING WITH RUTH:
AN ESSAY ON TRANSLATING

Ellen F. Davis

The first and altogether the most important thing I have to say about preparing my annotated translation of the book of Ruth is that I did not do it alone.[1] I did it with my first-year Hebrew students. Reading Ruth with beginning Hebrew students while I was, for the first time, preparing a translation for publication turned out to be a stroke of holy luck. The translation is substantially different and better because we were beginning together. As it turned out, I needed reading partners for the counterintuitive reason that the Hebrew of Ruth is so easy to read. In sharp contrast to the Song of Songs, probably the single most difficult book of the Bible to read and translate, this is surely the easiest. The text seems to be perfectly preserved, and the vocabulary and syntax are those of "textbook" Hebrew prose. But its very simplicity proved to be a snare for me. In my initial passes at a translation, I worked quickly and thoughtlessly, because I assumed I knew exactly what I was reading. It was only through working with my students that I began to discover what you might call the "productive difficulty" of a story that is crafted as finely as a Shaker chair. It took the eyes of beginning readers, who have the marked advantage of reading slowly and hesitantly—in other words, with humility—to show me aspects of its art that rightly give a thoughtful reader pause.

I remember my own experience, as a beginning student of Greek, of reading the Passion narrative in John. I found myself reading it through my buttonhole, as though I did not know perfectly well what would happen next, getting a fresh shock from every word as I looked it up: "sword," "spear," "thorns," "flogged," "broken," "pierced." Against all logic (it seemed at the time), I had slipped into the state of excited uncertainty that I now know is the common condition of second-semester students of biblical language. The remarkable *novum* of actually reading the Bible in the language in which it was written is the reward one reaps for sweating through the paradigm of the strong verb during that interminable first semester.

I always tell my Hebrew students, beginning or advanced, that I don't want them to "translate," if that means to them producing polished English prose. I want to hear how they make sense of the Hebrew. Better, I want to know how they hear the Hebrew making sense, and that is a somewhat different thing from mere translation. When they read in class, I want them to play with possibilities, as so often there is more than one way of rendering a phrase into English, and sometimes it is finally impossible to choose between two (or even three) equally good and completely different meanings. When they finally settle on a translation, I prefer that it be a "wooden" one—that it reproduce Hebrew idiom as closely as possible, even at the sacrifice of English elegance. I sometimes say, when proposing to or accepting from them some bit of English awkwardness: "If we were publishing a translation, we probably couldn't get away with this, but isn't this what it really says?"

In my annotated translation of Ruth, I have tried to reproduce for English readers something of the experience (and, I hope, the excitement) of my Hebrew students. I have also accepted a number of their suggestions. The result is that there is a degree of deliberate foreignness to the translation I offer; it does not allow the reader to forget for long that this story was not written in English. In the main, I would not agree with Ronald Knox that "any translation is a good one in proportion as you can forget, while reading it, that it is a translation at all."[2] For the record, I am not a translational purist, and if I were preparing an English version for use in public worship, I would for the most part want people to forget that they were hearing a translation. In that context, I would want listeners to hear themselves being immediately addressed by "the Word of the Lord."

However, there is no such thing as an all-purpose translation of the Bible. Mine is written not for large public readings, but rather for study. That is, it is written for the kind of setting from which it emerged, in which (ideally) a small group of people are gathered to read slowly, to dwell on a text that is admittedly foreign to them, even if they believe that it bears directly on their lives, and to talk about what they are reading. It is written for people who are willing to take the time to ponder the implications of curious word choices and follow a trail marked by the repetition of key words, that most distinctive feature of biblical style (although it is generally muted, and sometimes obliterated altogether, by assiduously inventive translators). In sum, I have tried to produce a translation that makes the best possible sense of the Hebrew, and is transparent to some characteristic elements of biblical style and diction, even if that means in some cases not making it all the way into idiomatic English.

A notable example here would be the word *kallah*, which appears immediately and recurrently: we see it four times in the first chapter (1:6, 7, 8, 22). *Kallah* designates Naomi's relationship to Orpah and Ruth; it is the Hebrew word for "daughter-in-law." Yet something is lost by translating it thus in English, for it is also the ordinary Hebrew word for "bride." For English speakers, "daughter-in-law" is a matter-of-fact acknowledgement of legal and familial status, sometimes bearing negative associations. "Bride," by contrast, is a word that connotes joy, hope, expectation, all perhaps mingled with trepidation. There is a special poignancy in the frequent appearance of *kallah* in the first chapter of Ruth, which begins with the death of three husbands. Therefore, I have chosen to translate the word as "bride-daughter," even though that means converting a word that was standard vocabulary for Israelites into an English neologism. The new term captures both the relational intimacy of "daughter" and all the hopes for a future that are implied by "bride." Yet in this first chapter, it serves to remind the reader that the two *kallot* (plural) whose lives are bound up with Naomi's are now, like her, widows.

A similar difficulty of finding an adequate English equivalent occurs with the extremely common word *ḥesed*, which denotes the quality that binds covenant partners in mutual devotion and the practical actions proceeding from that devotion. The book of Ruth as a whole gives narrative form and substance to the virtue of *ḥesed*. The very first words spoken in it celebrate the realization of that ideal in the past and seek its continuation: "And Naomi said to her two bride-daughters, 'Go, turn back, each woman to the house of her mother. May YHWH do *ḥesed* with you, just as you have done with the dead and with me'" (1:8). From a biblical perspective, the moral ecology of the world functions properly when God and humanity are engaged in the perpetual exchange of *ḥesed*. There is a quiet irony in the fact that it is these foreigners who are the model practitioners of *ḥesed*—and Naomi's implication would seem to be that her own God, though reputed to be "abounding in *ḥesed*" (Ex. 34:6), could stand to learn something from them.

The problem for the translator is simply that there is no single English word that conveys, to twenty-first-century ears, at least, the full theological freight of *ḥesed*. I quickly found proof of this by checking several recent and careful translations for three occurrences of the word, almost randomly chosen, one in each section of the Hebrew Bible:

For Ex. 34:6, one of the most important biblical statements about the nature of God and probably the most frequently cited use of *ḥesed* in the whole Bible, four translations offer three different renderings: "loyalty" (Everett Fox), "kindness" (both Richard Elliott Friedman and the Jewish Publication Society *Tanakh*), and "steadfast love" (the New Revised Standard Version).[3]

Both the New Revised Standard Version and the Jewish Publication Society's translation offer a different rendering for each of the three occurrences checked. The New Revised Standard Version reads "steadfast love" in Ex. 34:6, "kindness" in Mic. 6:8, and "loyalty" in Prov. 3:3. The Jewish Publication Society's translation reads "kindness" in Ex. 34:6, "goodness" in Mic. 6:8, and "fidelity" in Prov. 3:3.

All of these renderings are good in their individual contexts, but all are partial. I experienced this as a problem because, for reasons I will discuss below, I wanted to choose a single word to use in every occurrence. So which to use? "Steadfast love" might be taken to designate a feeling but *ḥesed* is more than that. Likewise, it is more than a personal quality ("kindness"), although that is closer. *Ḥesed* denotes a cultivated disposition, nurtured and manifested through concrete actions. In my meditation on Ruth, I call it "the *discipline of generosity* that binds Israelites to one another and to God."[4] That may preach, but it does not translate. Finally I settled on two related phrases: "good-faith" to denote the basic disposition (1:8), and "act-of-good-faith" for the ways in which it expresses itself in Ruth's life: first, in leaving behind all that was familiar and (relatively) secure for Naomi's sake; second (and greater in Boaz's grateful eyes), "in not going after the men-in-their-prime, whether poor or rich" (3:10)!

My third example of unidiomatic translation differs somewhat from the two already treated, as in this case the phrasing is uncommon in Hebrew as well as in English. In the famous threshing-floor scene, when Boaz reassures Ruth: "Do not be afraid. Everything that you say, I will do for you. For *all the gate-assembly of my people* knows that *you are a valorous woman*" (3:11).[5] The Hebrew phrase that I have rendered "the gate-assembly of my people" is literally "the whole gate of my people."

Among the standard translations, the renderings of New Revised Standard Version ("all the assembly of my people") and the Jewish Publication Society translation ("all the elders of my town") are typical, and they are correct in substance. Boaz is referring to the whole (male?) population of Bethlehem. But they gloss over the fact that his specific wording, found only here in the Bible, serves as a thumbnail sketch of public life in an Israelite town, where the chief gathering place was the open square inside the gate. It was a place primarily for men, the "elders," the adult male householders, who gathered to make decisions affecting the well-being of the community. The gate is where Boaz goes to confront the redeemer of undistinguished appellation ("Mister Whoever"), Naomi and Ruth's closest living male relative (by marriage), who has a prior claim to the family land—and, if he wishes, to marrying Ruth (4:1–12).

Women, too, had some presence at the town gate. Margaret Adams Parker, whose series of twenty woodcuts constitute the "other half" of my annotated translation of Ruth, has created a memorable image of the men sitting by the gate and the women gathered in a group a little distance off as a bent Naomi, supported by Ruth, hobbles into her old hometown. But often, perhaps, women's presence at the gate was a less direct one. Israel "in the days of the judges' judging" (Ruth 1:1) was a kinship-based, subsistence-level society in which both economic and social power resided primarily in the extended family unit, not in the government. Women worked alongside men as primary economic producers of the food and other goods needed by the household and as caretakers of domestic animals and of land. In such a decentralized social structure, the line between public and private spheres was drawn much less firmly than it would be later, in the period of the monarchy, when life became increasingly urbanized and power was centralized. Consequently, women exercised more social power, even if not in an "official" capacity. The book of Proverbs gives an extended portrait of 'eshet ḥayil,' "a valorous woman" (the currently popular rendering, "a capable wife,"[6] is highly reductionistic), a resourceful and industrious domestic manager who gives to the poor (Prov. 31:20) and teaches ḥesed (v. 26). The poem honoring her concludes "Let her works praise her in the gates!" (Prov. 31:31). In other words, let her be publically recognized for what she contributes to upbuilding the whole community.[7]

Note that in Boaz's words on the threshing floor there is a double echo of that poetic portrait in Proverbs. That echo, which we may assume to be deliberate, is particularizing: These are the only two people in Scripture to receive the accolade "a valorous woman." (The echo is more audible in the Jewish ordering of the canon, where the book of Ruth follows

Proverbs instead of Judges, as it does in the Christian Old Testament.)[8] Therefore the connection with Proverbs creates a distinctive perspective from which to view Ruth. The woman whose portrait concludes the book of Proverbs appears there as the fullest human representation of the divine—or at least, godly—quality of wisdom (31:26, cf. 1:7, 3:19, 9:1–12, etc.). The echoing phrases are meant to put us in mind of this ideal *Israelite* woman as we view Ruth the *Moabite* through the eyes of Boaz and "the whole gate-assembly" of Bethlehem. With the double vision induced by his words, we realize that the indigent foreigner, always potentially suspect in a tightly knit, kinship-based community, is now herself honored as one who upbuilds and sustains community.

Still we are not through with that one sentence spoken on the threshing floor. The phrase *'eshet ḥayil* creates one more echo, this one internal to the book of Ruth. When Boaz is first introduced by the narrator, we are told that he is *'ish ḥayil* (2:1)—"a man of considerble substance," as I translate it. *Ḥayil* is a common word that designates various kinds of power, including (and often) military force. When Boaz is first introduced, that seems initially to suggest that he is materially prosperous, a wealthy landowner, a fact that is important for his role in the story. But as the story unfolds, we see that the description is apt in more than one way; Boaz is also a person of considerable personal substance. So, with the words on the threshing floor, Boaz unconsciously confirms what must be in the mind of Naomi, who plotted this encounter that would seem to put Ruth so much at risk. It is not the case that Ruth comes to the threshing floor as nothing more than a poor powerless woman, hoping to appeal to the kindness and perhaps the need of a rich and lonely man. Rather, they meet as equals, this *'ish ḥayil* and *'eshet ḥayil*. Their "substance," manifested in each case in acts of *ḥesed*, makes each the best possible match for the other.

If it seems to us unreasonable for any writer to expect an audience to remember how a word has been used earlier and draw connections on that basis between two scenes or even passages in two different books, we need to remember that the culture of ancient Israel was primarily aural. Even though Israelites were composing sophisticated written literature as early as the tenth century BCE, throughout the biblical period, most people would have *heard*, rather than read, stories and other literary works. Therefore, attention was captivated and memory strengthened by repetition of a few words. Key nouns and verbs carry and develop a theme through and across long stretches of "text," establishing connections between scenes or passages that would at first seem to be unrelated, though both acquire greater depth when heard together. Sadly, the only experience of significant repetition familiar to most people in our culture is the way popular memory attaches to the repeated images and slogans of commercial advertising.

Because verbal repetition is so essential to the way the biblical writers make meaning, my own translation aims at verbal consistency; I almost always render a given Hebrew word or phrase with the same (or similar) English wording in each of its occurrences. This also gives my rendering of Ruth a slightly foreign accent to the ears of native English speakers. "Good" English style (by contemporary standards) tends to avoid repetition, probably precisely because we are not an oral and aural culture. Moreover, as we have seen with *ḥesed*, a given Hebrew word usually has a different range of usage than its nearest English equivalent, so the most natural translational choice is to use different words in different situations. But since the book of Ruth was not composed according to our literary standards, preserving the repetitions yields insight. Thus we come to know something of Ruth's character by noting her repeated action of "sticking" (*davaq*). First, she "stuck by" (1:14, commonly rendered "clung to") Naomi on the road out of Moab; later, Boaz and Naomi advise her pointedly to "stick with" Boaz's female workers in the field (2:8, 21, 23) and not with the males. The verbal repetition draws a line connecting Ruth's initial protective action toward Naomi with the elders' reciprocal concern for her, a young stranger, a Moabite in Bethlehem, who is perhaps more vulnerable than she perceives herself to be.

Preserving such repetitions is thus one way to restore "productive difficulty" to a translation. "Translation" in French is *traduction*. "Traduction," in (antiquated) English, is "willful misrepresentation." "Translation is treason," as one of my teachers used to say. The advantage of an *annotated* translation such as the one in *Who Are You, My Daughter?* is that it affords the translator an alternative to committing treason through showing what a text means. The truth is that any text worth translating with real care undoubtedly means more than one thing by what it says. George Steiner, who in this generation has probably reflected most carefully on reading and translating (and shown that those are not separate activities), says:

> We must read as thought the text before us had meaning. This will not be a single meaning if the text is a serious one, if it makes us answerable to its force of life. . . . It will not be a meaning . . . isolated from the transformative and reinterpretative pressure of historical and cultural change. . . . Above all, the meaning striven

toward will never be one which exegesis, commentary, translation, paraphrase, psychoanalytic or sociological decoding, can ever exhaust, can ever define as total. Only weak poems can be exhaustively interpreted or understood. Only in trivial or opportunistic texts is the sum of significance that of the parts.[9]

The conscientious translator cannot be fully satisfied even if every word choice, judged on its own, is satisfactory. The best translation of a "serious" text must somehow suggest to the reader that the text means still more than this present rendering can convey. In a large sense, the insufficiency of all "exegesis, commentary, translation," and so on requires that the transport lines of translation and commentary be kept running over the river of text. If we are wise, we will recognize that the communities that keep those lines running depend on the inexhaustibility of the text. But every translator of an important work runs up against particular instances of the text's resistance to total disclosure. In my own work with Ruth, I felt that especially as I sensed the text pointing to and delicately probing two areas: the ambiguity of relationships and the complexity of identity.

As so often happened, it was a student's question that made me aware of a complexity in the first few verses, which I would otherwise have read right past: "And [Naomi's sons] took for themselves *nashim mo'aviot*" (1:4). Maybe no one but a first-year Hebrew student would have thought there was anything to discuss in that line; *nashim mo'aviot* is the normal, indeed the only way to say "Moabite wives." What stopped my student is something he was still not *quite* used to: that normal word order in Hebrew is the noun followed by the modifying adjective. As a result, the reader or hearer knows the sons took wives just a millisecond before she knows what kind of wives they took. After all, they might have married other Israelites in exile, since presumably more than one family fled "famine in the land" of Canaan (1:1).

The identity of the wives is important, because Israel was an endogamous society, and the biblical writers especially disapproved of *Moabite* marriage partners. In Moses's farewell address, the teaching is explicitly given: "No Ammonite or Moabite shall come into the congregation of YHWH, even to the tenth generation. . . . Because they did not meet you with food and water on your way out of Egypt, and against you they hired Balaam . . . to curse you" (Deut. 23:4–5 Hebrew [3–4 English]). Of course, the violation of that prohibition in the lineage of King David is particularly noteworthy, and from a Deuteronomic perspective, particularly unfortunate.

So the very slow reader, or the very careful one (those two most often being the same thing), can see a small domestic drama played out in an instant of time, in the space of two words. And what my student wanted to know was, can we see special significance in that "normal" word order here? Instead of translating "Moabite wives," maybe we should translate in such a way as to preserve the shock that follows from that tiny moment of uncertainty: "They took for themselves wives . . . Moabites!" I am not aware that any translator has ever before taken that to be the meaning of the text—as, in the end, I decided to do. But the more I think about it, even now, I am increasingly convinced that that must have been part of the meaning of the story, from the very beginning. Granted, one would be unlikely to notice the word order on the page. But whoever wrote this story had doubtless *told* it, and probably had heard others tell some version of it, many times. And would not a sensitive storyteller naturally pause, however briefly and only half thinking about it, before uttering that telling word, *mo'aviot*, thus disclosing the fact on which so much of the story's poignancy and plot depend?

Naomi's words on the road from Moab to Bethlehem show that in her mind, at least, she and the two Moabite women are still foreigners to each other. As I read it, the story puts in our minds the question of the degree to which her sons' marriages may be a source of lingering bitterness for the ravaged old woman. Her words to her "daughters" suggest that her feelings toward them are strong and mixed:

Turn back, my daughters; go. For I am too old to have a husband. For if I said, "I have hope . . ." even if I had a husband tonight, and even birthed sons—would you then wait until they were grown? Would you hold back from having a husband? Don't, my daughters! For it is very bitter for me because of you [*mar li me'od mikkem*]. For the hand of YHWH has gone forth against me. (1:12–13)

The reader's perspective turns on the perfectly ambiguous statment *mar li me'od mikkem*. It is commonly translated "My lot is far more bitter than yours" (in the Jewish Publication Society version, similarly in the New Revised Standard Version), and that makes good sense. The younger women can begin again with new husbands and families (1:9); for Naomi, all such joy has passed. But the (equally possible) translation option I have chosen points to the truth that Naomi's lot and that of the young widows are not simply to be compared side by side. Their lots are joined, and that in itself is a source of bitterness—and very likely, for

17

more than one reason. Perhaps Naomi feels deep love for Ruth and Orpah, who may have been family to her for as long as ten years. (The narrative chronology is ambiguous on that point; see 1:4.) Therefore the possibility of an empty future for them adds immeasurably to her burden of grief. Or—even at the same time—she may feel bitter *toward* them: "For the hand of YHWH has gone forth against me." The death of Naomi's "boys" (1:5) is divine punishment for apostasy. Were it not for those Moabite women, notoriously seductive as they are (see Num. 25:1–18), Maḥlon and Kilyon would still be alive today!

Over all Naomi's objections, "Ruth stuck by her" (1:14). And gradually, something changes—in their relationship, and also in each of them. Through the life they share, each becomes different in a way that was previously unimaginable. As the women of Bethlehem recognize when they see Naomi holding Ruth's son "to her body," after so much loss and emptiness, she is being given life-against custom and all the odds: "May he be to you as one who restores life and supports your gray-headed-years. For your bride-daughter who loves you has borne him—she who is better to you than seven sons!" (4:15).

The change in Ruth is more subtly delineated, through a series of questions about her identity. The first two times a question is posed, it is clearly appropriate to the situation. When Boaz sees this stranger among his workers in the field (Margaret Adams Parker gives Ruth a facial tatoo, marking her as a non-Israelite), he asks, "To whom does this worker-girl belong?" (2:5). Maybe Boaz already finds Ruth attractive, but he seems to see her less as a person in her own right than as a member of a class or a family. He must place her in a social context in order to know who she is.

The second time the question of identity is posed, it is directly to Ruth. Boaz starts out of a sound (and slightly drunken) sleep to find "a woman lying at the place-of-his-feet" (3:8), and of course he blurts out the obvious: "Who are you!?" (3:9). More noteworthy on this occasion is Ruth's answer: "I am Ruth, your maidservant. Now spread your 'wing' over your maidservant, for you are a redeemer" (3:9). This is the first time any character in the book speaks Ruth's *name*, in contrast to a classifying description: "a Moabite worker-girl" (2:6), "my daughter" (2:8, 22; cf. 1:11–13). While Ruth ostensibly identifies herself as Boaz's subordinate—"your maidservant" (*'amah*)—in fact she is subtly presenting herself as a worthy marriage partner. On first meeting Boaz, she addressed him as "my lord," twice calling herself a "servant-girl" (*shifhah*, 2:13). Now she chooses a term that, while nominally deferential, is fully compatible even with high social standing.[10] Moreover, she does not hesitate to tell him exactly what to do. Ruth speaks as Boaz's equal, and the fact that he honors her here as *'eshet ḥayil,* "a valorous woman," shows that he takes her point.

For me as a reader and translator, these questions about Ruth's identity were simply too ordinary to be noticeable until I got to the third occurrence, when she returns from the threshing floor and Naomi greets her with the question "Who are you, my daughter?" (3:16). The fact that Naomi calls Ruth "my daughter" indicates that she is not simply uncertain who it is arriving in the dark, "before a person can recognize his neighbor" (3:14). Translations regularly change Naomi's query into something that seems to fit the context better: "How did things go with you . . .?" (the New Revised Standard Version), "How is it with you . . .?" (the Jewish Publication Society version). But in fact, the question makes sense just as Naomi poses it, if we look at the wider significance of this moment, as we can now appreciate it in light of all that has gone before. When Ruth went to the threshing floor to approach Boaz, she risked personal rejection and, far more devastating, social ruin. Instead, she was received with gratitude and the most profound respect. She who arrived in Bethlehem as an indigent and promptly went on the Iron Age equivalent of the public dole has now secured a future for herself and Naomi. In light of all that this young woman has endured and done, Naomi's question is exactly the right one: "Who are you now, my daughter?" If we have ears to hear, the question advises us to open our eyes and see what is before us: a woman who is independent yet bound in relationship; bold, physically strong, persistent; and yet she is gentle, putting the needs of the vulnerable other before her own. In a word, Ruth is a living picture of *ḥesed,* the good faith that binds humans in life-giving relationships with one another and with God. Beginning with Ruth, that is who every reader of Scripture, by the grace of God, might grow to be.

SUBVERTING THE BIBLICAL WORLD: SOCIOLOGY AND POLITICS IN THE BOOK OF RUTH

André LaCocque

It is essential that we read Ruth in light of a complex social environment that in many ways the book is reacting *against*. This means taking into account the status of women in ancient Israel and, more broadly, the ancient Near East. It also means considering the status of foreigners within these same surroundings. Both issues become especially intense in a tale whose title character is both female and foreign.

The Socioeconomic Environment

We cannot speak of a unified status for either women or foreigners in ancient history or throughout the vast expanse of the Levant. In general, however, it can be said that sociologically and religiously speaking, a woman's condition was marked by her dependency on men, especially in the realms of the cult and warfare. Phyllis Bird writes that a woman's primary contribution to the society came through her sexuality. In the context of a marriage, "her duty was to 'build up' [her husband's] 'house'—and his alone."[1] This lot closely resembled that assigned by custom and legislation in the surrounding nations, despite Israel's efforts to distinguish itself from them. The situation is all the more surprising because it creates a grave discrepancy within the revolutionary program of a nation liberating itself from the dictatorship of Canaan's feudal city-states: While Israel set herself free, her women remained unliberated in a patriarchal society.

Studies in socioeconomics shed light on this situation. Carol L. Meyers, for instance, describes the dismal conditions of existence during the Late

Bronze Age. Outbreaks of violence, epidemic maladies, threats of "famine, pestilence, and sword" (to quote the prophets) were such that a human couple had to produce twice as many children as might hope to survive. Mortality rates among females made "women in antiquity . . . a class of humanity in short supply."[2] Hence, the females, being relatively scarce, had to be protected and, in particular, to be kept from harm during war. Survival demanded reproduction. Specifically, Israel, with its need to *build* a nation, much depended on populating the land, as we read in Exodus 23:23–30. However, it is not entirely fair to say, as Bird suggests, that the women's sexuality was their exclusive or even defining contribution. Women actively participated in the chores of a land-based economy, and other factors occupy an important place in the complete picture: Women also made clothing and household goods, raised children, and cared for elders. We can concur with Meyers that it is "an irony of history [that] this tight channeling of female (and male) energies into domestic affairs, which was a liberating event in its own time," institutionalized female behavior "in ways that became limiting and oppressive to women."[3] The book of Ruth, as we will see, addresses this problem head-on.

As to the condition of the foreigner in Israel, it was by any standard rather enviable in comparison with the policy of other countries in the region. So, theoretically speaking, the fact that Ruth was a foreigner should not have played a major role in the story. But the situation is far more complicated by the fact that she was a Moabitess. This affected thoroughly her status in Israel: She belonged to a nation that represented perversion and destruction. Numbers 22 explains the origin of the perennial hostility between the two peoples. Moabitesses attempted to corrupt the Israelites coming from Egypt on their way to Canaan, and the king of Moab hired the services of a prophet by the name of Balaam to curse Israel. From that point forth, all references to Moab in the Hebrew Scriptures are uniformly pejorative (Deut. 23:2–6; Zeph. 2:9). Ezra 9:1 speaks of the "abominations" of the Moabites. Nehemiah 13:1 reminds the former exiles that "an Ammonite and a Moabite should never enter into the assembly of God." More pointedly, Nehemiah reviles those Israelites who married Moabite women (vv. 23–27).

It is against such a background that we must assess the paradox of Ruth. Although the book constitutes a protest against exclusivity, its emphasis upon the heroine's foreign origins is striking. Ruth is described as "foreign" or "Moabite" more than ten times in the mere four chapters of the book. In fact, the adjective "Moabitess" appears at least twice in connection with Ruth where the plot does not demand the title (2:2, 21). Given the Israelite curse upon her people, Ruth's coming to Judah is as fraught as it is unexpected.

We would expect Ruth's situation in Bethlehem to have been very uncomfortable, a cause for bitterness. Nonetheless, several times the narrative mentions her *ḥesed*, that is, her fidelity toward Israelites and, particularly, toward her mother-in-law, Naomi. Is this a show meant to earn her acceptance in a hostile society? Is she working to make people forget about her foreignness through the display of compensatory virtues? Far from it! She herself reminds others that she is an alien. She says to Boaz, *'anōkhi nōkhᵊrīah*, "I am a foreigner" (2:10). She speaks without arrogance or defiance, in all humility, but without abjection. She is not looking for a niche in the system or looking for a way to "pass." On the contrary, she creates considerable ripples wherever she goes. No one can ignore her. The harvesters tell Boaz right away, "She is a Moabite girl" (2:6), and until the end of the story, she will be an object of contention among her host people.

Why, then, is she in Judah? Oswald Loretz suggests that the object of the book of Ruth is to conserve the name of an Israelite family threatened by extinction. As a matter of fact, thanks to the intervention of Ruth, not only is the name perpetuated, it is even granted a brilliant future: from Ruth descends King David.[4] Loretz is right, but the means to this end are as important as the Davidic outcome. After all, the narrative was composed long after the reign of David. In Ruth, the thrill was elsewhere; it lay in securing the *conditions* for the coming of that king-savior, founder of the messianic dynasty. When one realizes this, one cannot escape the conclusion that the very accomplishment of the *Heilsgeschichte* depended upon an obscure Moabitess. The task of the reader, therefore, is to discover what that young woman did to ensure that history unfolded according to God's design. It is on this very point that the narrative invites us to reflect.

The Political Theme of Substitution

Just as the pregnancy of Tamar carried with it the threat of death, rather than vindication and justice, so Ruth's choice jeopardizes her until chapter four's denouement, when she marries the man to whom she had so bravely offered herself. Until the very end of the tale, then, Ruth is a potential victim to be offered on the altar of xenophobia and religious bigotry. It is no accident that the text credits her with extraordinary *ḥesed*—loyalty, steadfast love, goodness of heart, generosity. She can also stand in comparison in this regard to Abraham, whose offering of Isaac is also and above all his own crucifixion.

At the beginning of the tale, Ruth refuses to return to her "mother's house" and to start another line by marrying one of her own. She "clings" (*dābaq*, 1:14) to her mother-in-law and, in the most moving declaration of loyalty in the Bible, she tells Naomi, "Wherever you go, I shall go; where you stay, I shall stay; your people is my people, and your God is my god" (1:16). This is much more than a declaration of affection for Naomi. It is a disavowal of Ruth's own existence and fate and an appropriation of someone else's. As the rest of the story goes on to show, Ruth engages in a veritable substitution of personality. She makes possible for her mother-in-law what age and widowhood had made impossible. Naomi is restored in her reproductive ability and, by consequence, in her eligibility as heiress and matriarch. Let us not forget that Naomi's ability to have a child and heir meant the total abnegation of Ruth's pride, of her reputation, of her flesh and her blood. In her desire to perpetuate the Israelite family's line, moreover, Ruth stood to lose her own good name. This is most clear in chapter three, when she comes to the harvest threshing floor where Boaz is sleeping. In a striking parallel to Tamar's resorting to wiles and seduction to maintain the line of Judah, Ruth's nocturnal visit to Boaz makes her utterly vulnerable, exposes her to abuse. She lays herself open to the ancient Israelite assumption that one cannot expect anything different from a woman of Moab. "Like mother, like daughter," as Ezekiel says (16:44).

While the community around Ruth will not forget her Moabite identity, Ruth is willing to erase not only her ethnic roots, but also her very self. This effacement is particularly notable in light of the ways that other scriptural heroines rise to meet challenges. Contrast Ruth, for instance, with Judith. The two women represent quite different paradigms—Ruth is theological, Judith political. Ruth embraces Israel from without; Judith is its passionate defender from within. The odds against the women are formidable, though their stories are quite different: Ruth gleans at the fringes of Judah, whereas Judith penetrates like a sword into the heart of the enemy camp and beheads its captain, Holofernes. Yet in each case, the outcome justifies the heroine's means to her end. Ruth makes herself vulnerable on the threshing floor: She "sleeps with the enemy" and becomes a mother of Israel. Judith makes herself vulnerable behind enemy lines: She slays the enemy and becomes a champion of Israel. Ruth's choice of vulnerability, however, distances her story from the popular genre of epic, in which the reader wants to identify with strength and daring as opposed to loving-kindness and self-effacement.

This deviation from a literary norm highlights the difficult choices made by the teller of Ruth's tale. Against the odds, she created a heroine who refutes the prejudice against Moabites and presents an image of strength in vulnerability. The fact that the narrative works so beautifully reflects the mastery of the author. She succeeded in making Ruth and her self-effacement stir our imagination.[5] The teller of the tale also succeeded in making Ruth a heroic figure, although clearly not on the martial model presented by Judith, or before her, by Miriam, Deborah, or Yael. Ruth's heroism is of another kind. Apart from Ruth, Naomi would be without support, without property of her own, without purpose in life—dead wood. "Call me Mara [Bitter]," she says on her way back to Bethlehem. By bringing together "Jewess" and "Moabitess," the author joins mutually exclusive terms. She asks us to think the unthinkable, to enter into the world of paradox. In this respect, she is reacting most strongly against the socioreligious situation that obtained in the early Second Temple period.[6]

Written in the time of Ezra and Nehemiah, the book of Ruth is politically subversive in quite astonishing ways. In her desire to shock her Israelite readership, the author chose the most controversial and even repulsive character as her heroine: a woman from Moab. Moreover, as if it were not outrageous enough to have a Moabitess feed an Israelite—the Moabites were in part vilified because of their refusal of food and drink during the Exodus (Neh. 13:2)—the story has the sociopolitical tension introduced by the unwelcome presence of the foreigner be resolved by a levirate marriage to Boaz, pillar of the community and *gōʾel* (redeemer) of Elimelek's family.

The Social Theme of the Levirate Marriage

Nothing could be more far-fetched than the application of levirate marriage law to a non-Israelite. More than any other, this law is exclusively for inner consumption, because it is meant strictly for the perpetuation of a family name in Israel (see Deut. 25:5–10). Moreover, its application is purely a matter of moral obligation: It cannot be enforced by coercion, and noncompliance entails guilt and shame that would be experienced only within the covenantal community. In her extension of the law to include a Moabitess, the author of Ruth pushed at the limits of her culture. She would, however, push them only so far. It would have been customary for the woman to be married to spit in the face of the man who refused to fulfill his duty. Ruth, it should be noted, does not respond thus to "So-and-so" when he declines to serve as *levīr* for Mahlon. At the last moment, the Jewish author of the story shrunk from letting a foreigner humiliate an Israelite.[7]

Nonetheless, the argument of Ruth shakes the foundations. If Ruth the Moabitess finds her home in the community of Israel, if she is entitled to go through a levirate marriage with an Israelite *gō'el* and to be blessed by the elders with a formula putting her on a par with Leah and Rachel (4:11), then a most significant precedent obtains for *anyone* desiring to enter the assembly of Israel. Far from polluting the race, as Ezra and Nehemiah contended a foreigner would, this Moabitess brings forth the ancestor of the greatest king in Israel's history. Thus she becomes the agent for an overthrow of bigotry and racism. The curse on Moab is lifted. From now on, Moab is not any longer "those who did not meet the children of Israel with bread and water and hired Balaam against them that he should curse them," as Nehemiah 13:2 recalls. Rather, Moab provides the foremother of King David, forefather of the Messiah. This move from "Moab 1" to "Moab 2," so to speak, is well expressed by eighteenth-century Jewish commentator Moses Luzzato: "Through Ruth, the soul of David that was clothed in the shell of Moab, was freed from Moab. As the Scripture says: 'Who could produce purity from impurity?' [Job 14:3]. The Midrash answers: Only God."[8]

The Economic Theme of Redemption

The story of Ruth strikes at the root of profit-oriented systems. A concern for the bottom line is everywhere present in the background of the narrative. It is shared by all those who self-righteously raise questions about the coming of Ruth into the community and is most evident in the person contemptuously dubbed "So-and-so." For this one, what ultimately counts is profit. If the law of redemption (*ge'ullah*, see Lev. 25:25) can become a source of income, or, at least if it incurs no financial loss, so be it. Then the kinsman will buy back Naomi's field. But when "So-and-so" realizes that the business transaction "could imperil his own inheritance" (4:6), he quickly retreats and forfeits his responsibility. We should not think that "So-and-so" is an exception in the society described by the author; his designation *Pᵊloni 'Almoni* suggests that he is just one of the many. By contrast, Boaz stands out within the community of males and thus is the only man in Judah to be named by the author.

The Legal Theme of Obedience

The book of Ruth subverts from inside what it considers to be a tragic misunderstanding of Judean identity as reified by the reforms of Ezra and Nehemiah. The pair, to recall, had reaffirmed the legal ostracism of Ammonites and Moabites. One of the ironies of the book of Ruth is that Boaz marries Ruth *in obedience* to the Law of Moses, not in defiance of it. One can therefore understand the embarrassment of the rabbis, who were obliged to harmonize the frequent biblical excoriation of the Moabites, on the one hand, with the integration of Ruth into Israel as ancestress of David. But how to effect this harmony within the legal code? *Yebamot* 76b spells out the halakhic judgment as follows: "Ammonite, but not Ammonitess; Moabite, but not Moabitess" should be kept from entering the community.[9]

One better appreciates in hindsight the subversiveness of the book of Ruth thanks to the perspective provided by the halakhists. In Talmudic and midrashic commentary on the opening verse, the rabbis deeply resent that an Israelite family would desert their people to settle in Moab, a country notoriously antagonistic to the Jews. These sources also note that, although famine in the land of Judah constituted an extenuating circumstance for leaving Judah, no circumstance would be dire enough to permit the marriage of Elimelek's two sons to Moabitesses. Moreover, it seems that these women did not convert to Judaism; had they, Naomi would not have encouraged them to return to the idolatry of their mothers' homes.[10]

In their commentaries on the story, the rabbis accumulate halakhic implausibilities. They argue, for instance, that Ruth's marriage to Mahlon is invalid in the first place, which means that Naomi is not her mother-in-law and therefore Boaz has absolutely no obligation toward her. In their view, the whole tale is built on nothing. Eventually, the thirteenth-century Spanish Zohar book states in a spirit of conciliation that Ruth had converted prior to her marriage. Her name Ruth, a Jewish name, was given her at that point, as became customary in a ceremony of conversion developed much later. But then, what about Ruth's statement of faith and dedication to Naomi and her God in 1:16? The Zohar answers that it was a renewal of an earlier commitment.

Hesed, a major theme in the book, defeats legalism. *Hesed* is loving-kindness, graciousness, an outpouring of concern that expects no return. In the prophets' teaching, it transcends all ritual requirements; God tells Hosea, "I desire *hesed*, not sacrifice" (6:6, see also Mic. 6:8; Isa. 1:11–17; 58:6–7, etc.). In Nelson Glueck's definition, *hesed* goes beyond obligation.[11] Ruth herself is an exemplar of that "beyondness." We see her loving-kindness exercised first and foremost vis-à-vis Naomi; it is an attitude praised by Boaz, who tells Ruth, "I have been fully informed of all that you have done for your mother-in-law after the death of your husband; how you left your father and mother and the land of your birth and went to a people you had never known before" (2:11).

Ruth's *hesed* moreover, is infectious, as we see in the evolution of Naomi in the course of the story. In the beginning, she is embittered by what she views as the failure of the covenantal relationship. In her eyes, the death of her two sons has doomed the line of Elimelech. Her complaint, however, slowly turns to hope through an unexpected *peripeteia* brought about by Ruth (see 2:20). By the third chapter, she is so impressed with this turn that she advises her daughter-in-law to adopt an open-minded attitude toward events, urging her to let things with Boaz develop almost by themselves (see 3:4: "he will tell you what to do.") Eventually, it becomes clear that the Lord has remained faithful to the widow, and a chorus of Bethlehem women declare, "A son is born to Naomi!" (4:17).

The Theological Theme of *Hesed*

Significantly, the story of Ruth brings the reader to think first of human manifestations of *hesed* before realizing that steadfast love (fidelity, loyalty, generosity) is a divine attribute. Human *hesed* is an echo of divine *hesed*. Hence, the *hesed* of God materializes for Naomi by way of the *hesed* of Ruth the Moabitess. This makes of Ruth an exemplar not only for the people around her, but for generations to come.[12] Because Ruth shows *hesed*, everyone else in the story, barring "So-and-so," feels challenged to emulate her. Naomi, Boaz, the elders, the chorus of women, the people at the city gate—all are caught up in a tide of goodness that culminates in the praise both of God and Ruth.

Ruth's example is transformative. It inspires Boaz, for instance, to put love before money and property. It should be remembered that he is no obscure citizen, but rather one of the burghers of Bethlehem. Consequently, his marriage with Ruth cannot pass unnoticed. Furthermore, the betrothal is celebrated in the presence of the elders, no private affair accomplished in stealth. In addition, a chorus of women guarantees that the implications of the union are lost on no one. They constantly express feelings that are at odds with male reservations regarding the Moabitess. From the outset, they welcomed the arrival in Bethlehem "from the fields of Moab," disregarding the nationality of Ruth and the impure land that had claimed all of Naomi's kin. At the end of the narrative, they celebrate the good fortune of Ruth and Naomi.

Society is transformed. This portrait of social transformation is no small feat in the days of Ezra and Nehemiah, when the book was written. It was then that foreign women and their offspring were extradited from Judea. Whether or not the governors of Jerusalem had good cause for such an expulsion in the fifth century, the very sweep of the measure raises suspicion. To blame the ills of society on aliens reflects the evil inclination toward scapegoating those who are not the same. Just as the author of Ruth spoke out against the edicts of Ezra and Nehemiah, so did another woman: the prophetess Noadiah, who led a party in opposition to the gubernatorial reforms. That both voices of opposition were female should not be overlooked; gender solidarity may have played a role in such subversion.

The Theme of Behavioral Subversion

Sarcasm is not foreign to the author of the book of Ruth. In a Bethlehem characterized by law and order, to say nothing of moral rectitude, she places the heroine in a most risqué situation—her nighttime visit to the threshing floor of Boaz. In hindsight, we know that Ruth is destined to become the ancestress of King David; no obstacle, even the obvious one of personal reputation, will derail that achievement. And yet in the eyes of the establishment, the blemish on the Davidic line will be indelible. The Second Temple priestly writer, as well as the chronicler, zealously list respectable progenitors for the important families in Jerusalem. They revel in pedigree. Ironically, the author of Ruth not only offers suspect lineage for David, but also links his foremother to another woman of dubious repute. She sets Ruth in parallel with Tamar of Genesis 38; both women must use subterfuge to ensure that their lines are continued. They stand together with Lot's daughters as women who use their wiles to cohabit with reluctant men.

Harold Fisch compares these three daring stories: "Lot is deceived into cohabiting with his daughters; Tamar disguises herself as a prostitute;

Ruth comes secretly[13] to the threshing-floor."[14] Ruth, in fact, exposes herself to the same danger courted by Tamar—the subversion of moral imperatives for the sake of the superior goal of fidelity. Paradoxically, these women must risk unfaithfulness or indecency to fulfill their destinies. Already a member of the hated people of Moab, infamous for their immorality, Ruth is ready to pass for a loose woman and be shunned for fornicating. Ruth's foreignness brings her still closer to her predecessor, Tamar the Canaanite. But there is a difference between the two women's stories. While it is quite clear what took place between Tamar and Judah on the road to Timna, the author of Ruth leaves uncertain what actually transpired between Ruth and Boaz on the threshing floor. Boaz clearly respects the integrity of Ruth, and so the outcome of their shared tale is a redemptive recapitulation of the events of Genesis 38.[15]

From this perspective, the book of Ruth demystifies the Davidic dynasty, and subsequently the messianic line. Ruth shows that the greatest king in Israel's history, the glorious David, was far from having a divine or semidivine ancestry. In this regard, he stands in vivid contrast to other esteemed kings in the ancient Near East. Indeed, Tamar and Ruth, both foremothers of David, were dubious women. This fact was not lost on the evangelist Matthew, who opens his Gospel with a messianic genealogy that includes not only Tamar and Ruth, but also Rahab and Bathsheba. The four women appear in an otherwise male list: "Judah begot Perez . . . of Tamar . . . Salmon begot Boaz of Rahab; Boaz begot Obed of Ruth . . . David begot Solomon of Uriah's wife" (Matth. 1:3–5). This record is striking. The women mentioned all had tainted reputations, both for their perceived sexual impropriety and for their status as aliens. Only Bathsheba was an Israelite, although Matthew hastens to note her as "the wife of Uriah"—the Hittite, being married to one.

The Ethical Theme of the Feminine Unconventional

It is worth noting that when any society sets ritual purity as its ideal, it is women who suffer most. So it was in the fifth-century theocracy of Jerusalem, when the Judeans fell into the trap of misogyny under the guise of holiness. Suffice it to recall the vengeance of Ezra 10 when leader and people inveigh against the foreign women who have entered into the household of Israel by marriage. To restore good faith with the Lord means to expel foreign women and their children. The term for "foreign" (nōkhᵊrī) here, happens to be the one used by Proverbs to designate harlots. The divorce from those "whores" in Ezra 10:3 is referred to as an "expulsion." The nation is purging itself of its foreign women and their offspring; Ezra 9:2 and Mal. 2:15 show that racism and sexism go hand in hand. The former text speaks of "the holy race" (*zera' haqōdesh*) and the latter of "the divine race" (*zera 'elohīm*) that has been polluted by the presence of foreigners.

The chorus of Bethlehem women at the end of the book of Ruth clearly does not understand the marriage of Boaz and the Moabitess to be a pollution. Rather, they embrace Ruth and celebrate her child. The Midrash is sensitive to this celebration and notes that although it is a joyous moment for some, it is not for all. The midrash explains that the opposition to the marriage came from those who considered it a scandal and saw the outcome of the union as the fruit of forbidden mating.[16]

Nonetheless, for the women of the story, Obed is the joyful possession of Ruth and Naomi. They do not even mention Boaz who is strangely bypassed in the process of naming the child: "The female neighbors gave him a name and said, 'A son is born to Naomi.' They named him Obed" (4:17). In an affront to the establishment ideologues, the text goes on to declare, "Obed was the father of Jesse, the father of David." At last the long-awaited good news for the poor and disenfranchised—the Ruths of the world.

We can thus see that through Ruth, the social and political boundaries set by Second Temple Judaism are eclipsed. When one remembers the vitriolic diatribe of the prophet Isaiah against Moab in Isaiah 25—an oracle that Joseph Blenkinsopp calls "pornographic violence"—the later book of Ruth comes as a welcome correction.[17] Because Moab represents the category of the other in all its forms, Ruth's protest is valid universally and without respect for time. Stereotyping—a favorite term today is "profiling"—must be disavowed, for it sterilizes all manifestations of *hesed*. Much of the Hebrew Bible understands this. It was also grasped by Saint Paul, who gave the Corinthians a definition of love that leaves no room for profiling: "Love . . . bears all things, believes all things, hopes all things, endures all things" (1 Cor. 13:7). The Apostle may have had the example of Ruth in mind.

THE BOOK OF RUTH AS COMEDY: CLASSICAL AND MODERN PERSPECTIVES

Nehama Aschkenasy

More than any other biblical story or cycle of tales, the book of Ruth belongs to the dramatic genre. Structured as a series of short, eventful scenes animated by spirited, dynamic dialogue, it can be easily adapted for the stage. The conversation in the book of Ruth is either between two protagonists or between a protagonist and "chorus" (in the form of the women of Bethlehem, or the workers in the field, or the elders at the gate), but there are usually no more than two principal interlocutors in any given scene. The story's narrator possesses only limited omniscience, offering brief historical information and then retreating into the background. The storyteller intervenes periodically to provide pieces of information, more like a dramatist or a theatrical director setting the stage (season, time of day, backdrop) than like an all-knowing author privy to his or her protagonists' internal thoughts and feelings. The obvious difference between Ruth and classical or Shakespearean drama is that Ruth was meant to be read, not performed. By contrast, both Greek and Elizabethan audiences knew plays not from reading, but from watching a theatrical production. In this sense, the biblical story is different.

Scholarly consensus regarding the literary genre of the book of Ruth is that it is "a historical short story" or a novella written in prose, and, at times, in poetic prose.[1] Yet the predominance of dialogue and the clear division of the dramatic structure into different scenes allows us to view the book of Ruth as drama. Dialogue is the fiber of drama, the yarn that weaves the story; as in the best plays, in the book of Ruth it is dialogue that advances action and reveals character. The storyteller never comments directly on Ruth's loyalty or other meritorious qualities, nor is anything said about Naomi's gratitude to Ruth, her anxieties, or her somewhat devious plans. It is mainly through the dialogue that the various forms of conflict—the heart of the dramatic—are represented in Ruth. Drama has been defined as the representation of the protagonist in conflict—either with an antagonist, with the circumstances or fate, or with the self. The book of Ruth reveals all three forms of conflict, but concentrates mainly on the second, that is, on people in conflict with circumstances. One might argue that Naomi and Ruth are also in conflict with an antagonist, the Bethlehem community at large, which no doubt condemns Naomi for abandoning it in a time of famine and distress and is suspicious of Ruth for being an intruder, a member of a despised nation.

It is therefore appropriate to study Ruth in the light of theories of drama, both ancient and modern. The book can be illuminated through attention to Aristotle's *Poetics*, the classical practitioners of drama from Shakespeare to Molière, and modern theorists including Henri Bergson, Northrop Frye, and Dorothea Krook. In these contexts, we see that the book of Ruth meets the major criteria of the dramatic form: It fulfills Aristotle's requirements of unity of plot, of pyramidic structure, and of reversal of fortune and epiphany.[2] Except for its plot line, which, as in every comedy, moves from distress to happiness, the book of Ruth displays Aristotle's primary tragic elements. Ruth's author manifests kinship with Shakespeare and other dramatists in his understanding of comedy as verging on the tragic and with Northrop Frye in his conception of comedy as "the mythos of spring."[3] Furthermore, when Ruth is read in the light of Dorothea Krook's mapping of tragedy—which begins with an "act of shame or horror" and concludes with "affirmation"[4]—Ruth emerges as comedy in the deepest sense, that is, as tragedy in reverse. The book features the main components of tragedy, yet with a happy, rather than catastrophic denouement; it also offers scenes in which human frailty, trickery, the unexpected, and the incongruous all coalesce to evoke laughter and a sense of merriment. As to the nature of the dramatic resolution, as Frye suggests, in comedy, "the erotic and social affinities of the hero are combined and unified in the final scene," since comedy is "much concerned with integrating the family and adjusting the family to society as a whole."[5] Ruth marrying Boaz and bearing a son to carry her dead husband's name suggests that Elimelech's family, estranged from its people and seemingly severed from them forever (since all its males have died), has miraculously become reintegrated into Israelite history and society.

Given a woman-centered reading of Ruth, the dramatic dialogue emerges as a strategy granting women a clear and direct voice. In conjunction, the comic mode allows for an irreverent perspective on the elderly patriarch and thus on patriarchy. The book of Ruth elevates the female figures to the role of the *eiron*, the conscious creators of the comic spirit, rather than its victims. It is only one scriptural example of comedy resulting from the fooling of the patriarch, a recurrent biblical situation and a universal laughter-inducing motif representing the Bergsonian "inversion."[6]

Whereas tragedy is the mimesis of the ritual of death, charting the hero's journey from success to disaster, comedy, as Frye sees it, follows the reverse trajectory: It begins with disaster and ends with triumph. In comedy, the ending might be called "an anastrophe, a turning up rather than a turning down."[7] Significantly, the story of Ruth itself is placed within the context of the spring season. We are first told of the rapid succession of disasters occurring in Naomi's family and then take in the three widows' agonizing dialogues, spoken somewhere in the desolate landscape between Moab and Judah. Yet immediately after these bleak narratives, we enter Bethlehem, with its bustling town life and curious crowds. Here we are also informed cryptically that this is the season of plenty, the beginning of harvest time. Thus, the cycle of nature, leading from winter to spring, is paralleled by the cycle of the women's lives, which move from death and emptiness to rebirth and fullness of life.

We should also remember that Greek drama grew out of the worship of Dionysus, the god of fertility, and that the theme of fertility, both of the soil and of the woman, is pivotal to our biblical story. The book of Ruth begins with the land of Israel barren and fruitless, causing famine and forcing Elimelech's family to leave it, and ends with the celebration of the plentiful harvest. It opens with childless women who have no prospect of becoming mothers—Naomi because she is past her prime and Ruth because there is no redeemer in sight—and closes with Ruth giving birth to a son, thus making Naomi a grandmother and providing the necessary link in the family's once-broken genealogical line. Frye further notices that, especially in Shakespeare, the dying and reviving character is usually a female, thus strengthening our sense that there is something maternal in the comic world that brings to bear and nourishes the new order of comic resolution. Once again, this happens at the end of our story, where the two bereft and deprived widows are fulfilled, even reborn, through the birth of a male child.

Another element of comedy pointed out by Northrop Frye and others is the Saturnalia, named after Saturn, the Roman god of agriculture, which usually happens at a crucial juncture in the comic action.[8] The Saturnalia is a moment of chaos that is characterized by the breaking of all boundaries, by making merry, and by eating and drinking excessively. One of the participants leads the festivities, assuming the role of the Lord of Misrule. Traditional commentary on Ruth sees Boaz as a dignified, composed, and staid pillar of the community, but I want to suggest that in the course of a comic reinterpretation of Ruth, it is Boaz who plays the role of the Lord of Misrule. Without the spirit of unrestrained revelry that exists during the spring celebrations, when men become so intoxicated that they are unable to return home to their own beds and therefore must remain overnight in the open field, the scheme of Naomi and Ruth would never have worked. Indeed, Naomi must be acquainted with this harvest custom of reversal of normal behavior, knowing that the most respectable and disciplined citizen of the community becomes the leader of the celebration and loses control of his senses. The success of her daring plan depends entirely on this fact. We may remember that in the two earlier biblical stories that also revolve around the deception of the patriarch by women in order to keep the family alive—the Genesis tales of Lot and his daughters and of Judah and Tamar—the women depend on the patriarch's losing his clear-headedness and becoming aroused erotically, whether by wine, in the case of Lot, or by the excessive eating and drinking during the sheep-shearing festivities, in the case of Judah.[9]

As we follow the story and its division into distinct scenes, we should also remember Aristotle's argument that the artistic construction of the action, or the plot line, is the most important element in drama, which in fact means "action" in the Greek. For proper structure, Aristotle requires a tightly knit story in which all events are causally connected, reflecting a great conflict and an entanglement leading to a climax, after which there is a movement toward a denouement, or resolution. Underlying this dynamic movement are elements of mystery and suspense, an epiphany, and the reversal of fortune. This pyramid structure is evident in Ruth. The following scenes lead to a climax: Naomi departing from her daughters-in-law, Naomi and Ruth arriving at Bethlehem and being greeted by a chorus of the townswomen, Ruth in Boaz's field, Ruth returning to Naomi and telling her the good news of her encounter with Boaz, the two women feeling left alone again at the end of the harvest season, and Naomi instructing Ruth how to act following the harvest celebrations.

The scene of Ruth and Boaz at the threshing floor is the climax of the story because it is the culmination of all events preceding it: Naomi's complaint of being empty and her hopes to find a redeemer for Ruth, Ruth's restlessness and her venture into the field to catch Boaz's attention, and, of course, the elaborate plan concocted by Naomi to be implemented by Ruth. The event at the threshing floor is suspenseful because Naomi and Ruth have put their reputation at risk. If this maneuver does not succeed, if Boaz becomes upset and exposes Ruth as a loose woman, a stranger who has attempted to seduce and corrupt a pillar of the town, these women are doomed. Even if Boaz is not upset or vengeful and decides to send Ruth on her way, the women's plot has failed, and they are back where they started: destitute and hopeless. There is an element of suspense and tension here; as in Shakespearean comedy (for instance, when Viola presents herself as a man to Orsino and the community in *Twelfth Night* and is challenged to a duel), the situation in which the heroine finds herself could as easily have ended tragically. Yet since this is a comedy, the tragic potential is held at bay and eventually stunted, so that Boaz does not denounce Ruth and her mother-in-law, and instead, the story shifts gears at midpoint to reach a happy ending for its women protagonists. The climactic, tense moment at the threshing floor is followed by a series of actions taken by Boaz to untangle the plot, leading to the happy ending—the birth of a son to Ruth.

The structure of the book of Ruth further adheres to the Aristotelian unity of action: there are no secondary protagonists, nor is there a subplot mirroring the main plot. Reminiscent of Shakespeare's practice, in the biblical story, Aristotle's unity of time is somewhat relaxed: Although the story takes more than twenty-four hours to reach a climax and then a necessary resolution, the unity of time is still preserved because all events take place during the spring season, from the beginning to the end of harvest. The principle of unity of place is also somewhat relaxed, because the action shuttles from Naomi's home to the streets of the town, to the fields (where the law requires that the needy may glean), to the city gates, where the elders sit in judgment. This movement between the indoors and the outdoors is in line with the practices of Roman New Comedy and Shakespearean comedy, where the action moves between public spaces and private domiciles.[10] Yet it is the city that anchors the story. The family's saga begins and ends in Bethlehem. Moreover, the women of the town serve as the counterpart of the Greek chorus: They comment on Naomi's appearance at the start of the dramatic story, they imply the great change in her looks, and they resurface at the conclusion of the story to name the newborn and rejoice in the miraculous journey of the women from bereavement to redemption. Thus Bethlehem offers a unity of location.

Concentrating primarily on plays from the long history of Western tradition that are categorized as tragic or tragicomic, Dorothea Krook offers a modern theory of drama. A number of her observations reinforce my placement of Ruth within the dramatic genre, as well as my argument that Ruth as comedy is tragedy in reverse. Tragedy, says Krook, is triggered by an "act of shame or horror" that is followed by great suffering.[11] Such an act often happens before the present time of the play itself; for instance, Oedipus's killing his father and marrying his own mother happened many years before *Oedipus rex* opens. Despite their remove, these prior actions overshadow present-time events and determine the course of Sophocles' play. Likewise, although the biblical narrator does not comment on Elimelech's departure from Bethlehem, it is clear that this desertion, made years before the present time of the story of Ruth, is still considered horrendous, perhaps even unforgivable, in its lack of faith in Israel as the divinely promised land. The family's departure before Ruth properly begins casts a pall on the entire narrative. And while the sons' marriages to non-Israelite women are similarly narrated matter-of-factly, these unions contribute to the sense that the family offended God and therefore was punished by him. Thus, the first two dramatic elements mapped out by Krook are met in Ruth: the initial shameful act(s), and the suffering that ensues.

Naomi herself understands her predicament to be God's deliberate action against her, not as random catastrophe: "The hand of the Lord is gone out against me," she cries (1:13). As in Greek drama, the question of divine retribution arises in the dialogue between the protagonist and the chorus. Naomi says to the women of Bethlehem: "For God has testified against me / and Shaddai has pronounced evil sentence on me" (1:21). Even as she expresses her wretchedness, Naomi frames her present misery as part of an ongoing dialogue between her and God. At first we might consider these words as commonplace in a God-fearing culture, as a cliché also used by Naomi's contemporaries to describe their misery. We come to see, however, that this is not simply colloquial speech. Rather, it is a well-thought-out argument on the part of Naomi, whose rhythmic lament reverberates with echoes of the book of Job, thus endowing her plight with larger, even colossal, significance. Naomi's language, at once polemical and philosophical, evokes a vision of the divine court in which

God is both witness for the prosecution and judge determining the verdict. In this scene, Naomi imagines herself to play a major role—the accused. Elsewhere, I have argued that Naomi's sense of self-worth is revealed precisely in these words.[12] Although she proclaims her wretchedness through them, she also claims that God has singled her out for persecution, couching her grievances in the language of Job, thus placing her predicament in the venerable biblical tradition of a man challenging a wrathful God over his undeserved suffering. Yet within her personal complaint, Naomi also recognizes that she is paying for the grave violation that occurred in her family.

Krook suggests two additional facets of drama: one is the coming into heightened understanding, or epiphany; the other is the affirmation of life and the dignity of humanity (even in defeat, in the case of tragedy). The happy resolution of the book of Ruth cannot be attained apart from the manifold epiphanies that are enjoyed by each of the three main characters. Naomi's epiphany relates to her realization that her predicament is a consequence of a sin, not one committed by her directly, but one in which she participated as part of her family. This epiphany is followed by another, in which she sees that she needs to make amends and redeem both herself and her people. Therefore, in her attempt to lift herself and Ruth from the jaws of poverty and destitution, Naomi is looking for more than a material solution to their problems. She does not sell her property, for instance, or try to reactivate her land so that it can once again become productive and a source of profit. Rather, she looks for a redeemer, a *go'el*, for Ruth, who will provide more than just the comforts of a husband and a home. Her quest for redemption thus gives a spiritual turn to her search for material security and survival.

Not surprisingly, Ruth's epiphany is akin to Naomi's. As later becomes clear, Ruth could well have found material salvation through marriage to one of the local young men who have shown an interest in her. However, she realizes that to truly become one of the Hebrew people whom she so passionately wants to espouse, she needs to enter the community through the time-honored custom of levirate marriage. She must rebuild the family that has been devastated.

Finally, Boaz's epiphany, so important to the happy ending of the story, comes to him from Ruth herself. Here we find a reversal of traditional roles, for now the woman teaches the man, and not vice versa. This reversal is one of the comic sources of the story, akin to the student lecturing his teacher or the accused chiding the judge. It becomes clear that while Boaz shows compassion and charity toward Ruth when he first spots her among the poor in his field, he had already known about Naomi's arrival. He was not moved to help her, nor does he show further interest in the two women once the harvest season ends. When Ruth asks Boaz why he has singled her out for special treatment, she is not being just modest or grateful. She elicits from Boaz an admission that he had heard that Naomi and her daughter-in-law had returned and that he knows much more about Naomi and Ruth than his actions so far have shown. But if Ruth's question is meant to stir in Boaz a sense of responsibility, and perhaps even guilt, which would drive him to do more for her and Naomi than he has so far, she is not completely successful. Therefore, when the season of harvesting is over and the women are again alone and desolate, they need to resort to action.

It is during the nocturnal encounter between Ruth and Boaz, the tale's climax, that Boaz's education is completed and his long-awaited epiphany is finally achieved. Ruth designates Boaz as her "redeemer" although technically he is not. Ruth's choice of words and the nature of her argument are significant; she could simply ask Boaz to rescue her from misery or to save her honor because she has now been compromised. Rather, she evokes the levirate custom, making Boaz understand the spirit of the law, rather than simply its narrow meaning. Ruth wants Boaz to understand that she is not a charity case, but that she is looking to find a place for herself within the Israelites' religious and ethical structure. She therefore wishes to enter the Israelite family through the institution of levirate marriage. She makes Boaz realize that the law itself does not always cover all the cases confronted in real life. With Ruth's subtle help, Boaz broadens his conception of the levirate obligation to include not only the widow's brother-in-law, but also her more distant relatives. Ruth teaches Boaz a lesson in the humanitarian interpretation of the law, which he readily accepts. She also creates a new reality with the aid of language; by naming Boaz a "redeemer," Ruth makes him one. Once this knowledge finally dawns on Boaz, he proceeds to do the right thing for his two widowed relatives.

The women's subtle and clever use of language is a means of self-empowerment, of creating a happy reality for themselves out of a situation of hopelessness and emptiness. Their lexicon, especially Naomi's nuanced and creative use of Hebrew, sustains the suspense; the various dramatic elements come to light only in the full course of the play. The dramatic tension in the story's plot line concerns how these two women, shunned by God and community alike, will lift themselves out of their misery. But underlying all this is the question of how these women will find a redeemer, not just a protector. The concern is to revive Naomi's family through a male child who, legally and socially, will be regarded as her own natural grandson and thus preserve and renew the line of Elimelech. It is Naomi who initially introduces the way that the plot will unfold, although she does not do so directly, but through a very innovative use of rhetoric. Naomi uses the potential of words to send subliminal messages and create new realities.

Naomi is first heard when she pleads with her daughters-in-law to return to their mothers' homes. In two quite elaborate speeches (1:8–9, 10–13) she thanks them for their past kindness, urges them to leave her and turn back, and wishes them well. Her explicit argument is that she is past her childbearing years, that therefore the daughters-in-law cannot be redeemed by any son of hers. But Naomi's language, describing the improbable event of her marrying a man that very night and eventually bearing sons, is so outrageously exaggerated that it points to a subtext quite different from the point that is ostensibly being made. Naomi describes at length what cannot happen, but her elaborating on the impossible—that she will remarry and give birth to sons, that her daughters-in-law will wait for those sons to redeem them—points to hidden desires and hopes. While on the face of it Naomi rules out any possibility of her daughters-in-law remarrying within her family, her protestations create an imaginary world in which the unlikely might indeed come true; behind the language of seeming desperation lurks the vision of a potential miracle. Naomi's comically absurd scenario plants for the actors and audience alike an idea and a hope that it be realized.

While dismissing the possibility of a levirate marriage for Ruth and Orpah, Naomi in fact introduces the concept into both the tale and the consciousness of the reader. Moreover, to further build up her vision of the possible, to enhance her subliminal message, and to create a world out of the word, Naomi names the relationship between the two women using a term that technically does not denote the link between women whose husbands are brothers. Naomi tells Ruth to follow her sister-in-law, Orpah, who has finally taken Naomi's advice and headed back to Moab. But in the Hebrew, Naomi does not use the term "sister" or "sister-in-law"; rather, she calls Orpah *yebimtekh*, using the term *yebamah* to describe the familial relationship between the two women. In biblical Hebrew, the noun *yebamah* designates the childless widow in relation to her dead husband's brother. He is the *yabam*, or "redeemer," as it is usually translated, and she is the *yebamah*, the feminine form of the same noun. But nowhere in the Bible is it suggested that sisters-in-law are each other's *yebamah*. This should not be taken as a slip of the tongue, a careless mistake on the part of a distraught woman. Naomi has taken a liberty with the language, but in the process, she has created a new frame of reference within the tale by filling the dialogue with intimations of *yibbum*, levirate marriage, thus mitigating the language of the unattainable. Naomi creates a world with the force of her tongue, and the reader is left to wonder how the misnomer she uses will enter reality. Will a time come in which either of these two young women will indeed be rightfully called *yebamah*?

Naomi further creates suspense with regard to her own destiny in the short speech that she gives to the women of Bethlehem: "Call me not Naomi, call me Mara: for the Lord has dealt bitterly with me. I went out full, and the Lord brought me back empty; why then do you call me Naomi?" (1:20–21). The despairing tenor of these words does not conceal the power of their message: A person's name conveys the essence and the fortunes of the individual.[13] Naomi claims that her name, which means "pleasure," contrasts with her sorry reality and therefore that it should be changed to communicate the bitterness of her lot. Naomi is here in line with biblical tradition, which attributes great importance to names, but what she means is, of course, not that her name should be changed, but that her *reality* should be mended and altered to conform to her original name. Naomi's lament about her name is meant as a challenge to her own fate, a call to God to adjust her life so that it will once again reflect the true meaning of her name. Again, the reader is left to wonder how Naomi's impossible wish will become a reality.

Henri Bergson has suggested that the comic writer has a "bag of tricks" including discrepancies, deceptions, misunderstandings, mistaken identities, the unexpected, and stock comic types. In Ruth, it is possible to see in the three protagonists a variation of the conventional comic types featured in classical comedy as well as in later works, such as the plays of Molière. Boaz plays the *senex*, the comic old man; Ruth is the *virgo*, the young girl often inaccessible for a variety of reasons; and Naomi is the *servus callidus*, the clever slave, or the *servus delusus*, the crafty servant whose inspired planning and improvisation bring about the happy comic resolution.[14]

The discrepancy in age and status between Boaz and Ruth, reflected also in the marked differences in their linguistic styles, is rife with comic promise. The attraction that a young woman holds for an old man has often been used by dramatists and stage directors for its hilarious, farcical possibilities. When the older Boaz notices Ruth among the people in his field, it is because he finds the young woman interesting, unusual, or perhaps even attractive. Furthermore, Boaz's lofty rhetoric, imbued with the concepts of morality, goodness, and charity, contrasts with his inaction through most of the story. Boaz emerges as a pompous old man for whom talk is easy, but he is awkward and hesitant when it comes to interaction with a young woman that he obviously likes. In public, he praises Ruth for her good deeds, but he is reluctant or afraid for his good name to visit the women's home in private. Boaz's "comic flaw," the counterpart of the Aristotelian tragic flaw, is excessive concern with his public image. His inclination is to make grand public gestures on which he does not follow through. His flaw may also lie in his timidity with women, in his sexual shyness, which creates a comic discrepancy between his status as a wealthy, powerful figure and his diffidence in private with women. Ruth and Naomi use these weaknesses to their own advantage.

Additionally, Boaz's style seems stale and rigid: He uses a set format of greetings (addressing his workers with the conventional formula of "God be with you," to which they respond with "God bless you," 2:4) and customary blessings ("May God grant you due recompense"; "May your payment be full from the God of Israel, under whose wings you have come to seek refuge," 2:12). The old man sounds like a puppet repeating familiar formulae, rather than expressing his own original sentiments. This renders him mechanical, robotic, and therefore comical in the Bergsonian sense.[15]

In addition to the *eiron*, the creator of comedy, Frye distinguishes the *alazon*, the butt of it.[16] The *eiron*, according to Frye, may often be the heroine, who brings about the dramatic resolution through disguise or some other trickery. According to this description, Ruth is the perfect *eiron*. Frye also speaks of the *eiron* as "the type entrusted with hatching the schemes which bring about the hero's victory." Often a female confidant,[17] in the biblical story this type of *eiron* is Naomi. It goes without saying that in this comic scheme of things, Boaz plays the *alazon*.

In the very first encounter between Boaz and Ruth, the latter uses a playful, even teasing tone when she asks Boaz why he has singled her out. The old man embarks on a lengthy speech about how he has already heard of Ruth; his stilted, effusive language contrasts amusingly with Ruth's easy and straightforward tone. We can only imagine Boaz's young workers laughing and sneering at their old master behind his back. Ruth's strategy of gently embarrassing the old man who is so conscious of his status in the community culminates in the scene at the threshing floor. This is a classic example of the comic situation known as the "bed trick," or the fooling of the powerful male. The *alazon*, says Frye, is often the "heavy father" or a surrogate of this character (Boaz addresses Ruth as "my daughter") who often displays "gullibility." Frye further describes the *alazon* as a "man of words rather than of deeds."[18] As noted, Boaz often uses a highly rhetorical language, lauding charity and good works, and yet, as we have seen, he stays within the realm of speech, not that of deeds; it is the women who drive him to action.

The climactic moment in comedy is presided over by the spirit of chaos and loss of control, as in Shakespeare's *Twelfth Night* when Sir Toby Belch plays the role of the Lord of Misrule. Boaz undoubtedly becomes intoxicated, unsteady, and forgetful when he sinks into deep sleep. Here the situation can easily develop into physical farce as the old man, usually buttoned-up and proper, wakes from his drunken stupor disoriented and alarmed to find a strange woman at his feet in the open field. Ruth, on the other hand, is sober, controlled, and purposeful; she asks, in fact orders, the old man to "redeem" her. The comic possibilities envisioned by Bergson are numerous here. We find disguise, pun, comic repetition of verbal formulas, inelasticity of the body, and manipulation of one person by another so as to appear "as a mere toy in the hands of another." First, Ruth expands on her mother-in-law's initial plan. Naomi had instructed Ruth to wait for the man to speak when he discovers her, but Ruth says more than the man's question warrants. In response to Boaz's startled "Who are you?" Ruth not only identifies herself, but makes an almost audacious suggestion: "I am Ruth thy handmaid: spread therefore thy skirt [or wing] over thy handmaid; for thou art a near kinsman [or, a redeemer]" (3:9). A woman asking a man to marry reverses the norms of patriarchal society. It is inherently comic. In addition, I believe Ruth is somewhat mischievous when she repeats the ceremonious phrase that Boaz himself had uttered earlier—"under [God's] wings" (2:12)—and jokingly alters the overstated "God's wings" simply to "wings," the corners of Boaz's garment. She sounds buoyant and daring as she uses this verbal pun, making fun of the old man's grand, but shallow vocabulary. When Boaz regains his composure, he is still emotional and effusive; in a flowery speech he blesses Ruth and commends her profusely, perhaps to cover up his embarrassment and discomfort at her presence. When, in a theatrical gesture, he measures out a significant portion of barley and tells Ruth to hold up her apron so that he can fill it up (3:15), one can only imagine the farcical, even bawdy visual possibilities of Ruth returning home, her apron bulging provocatively. Furthermore, when Ruth exposes Boaz's legs—and, if legs are being used euphemistically here, exposing more than this part of the body—we inevitably laugh when, as Bergson suggests, "our attention is diverted to the physical in a person when it is the moral that is in question" and when a person is "embarrassed by his own body."[19]

Two conventional types are still missing in our appraisal of Ruth as comedy: the romantic young man, who wins the female protagonist at the end, and the comic scapegoat. In our biblical story, Boaz combines in himself two diametrically opposite comic figures: the old man absurdly interested in a younger woman and the object of the young woman's desire. His interest in Ruth is on the one hand ridiculous, but it is also reciprocated. He may try to cover up his embarrassment over her uninvited attraction, but the fact is that Boaz is the woman's romantic interest. Furthermore, in traditional comedy, the heroine is inaccessible to the male hero, either because there is another figure to overcome—a rival for her affections or some other "blocking figure" such as his own father (as in Molière's *The Miser*)—or because the woman is stigmatized socially (she is not freeborn, for instance).[20] Both factors are found in the book of Ruth: Boaz is aware of a possible rival, both in the form of a closer male kin who would have precedence if the question of *yibbum* ever came up and in the form of the local young men who, as he notices, have shown an interest in Ruth (3:10). Boaz is also held back by Ruth's disdained foreignness as a Moabite. Once we realize that Boaz unites two clashing figures of comedy, the preposterous old man and the romantic hero, we understand that the book of Ruth is highly unusual in its fusion of two distinct forms: the universal genre of comic romance and the biblical narratives' covenantal history.

Finally, Northrop Frye argues that comedy often includes a communal scapegoat and a ritual of expulsion whereby society purges itself of the spirit of chaos that has temporarily seized it. With moderation and harmony reestablished, a far better and well-integrated society emerges from the one we experienced at the beginning of the play.[21] We find evidence of this in Ruth in the scene that takes place at the city gate (4:1–12), which concludes the dramatic part of the book. Here we witness a public ceremony in which Naomi's male kin draws off his shoe, signaling that he wishes to excuse himself from performing the rite of *yibbum*, thereby "expelling" himself, if not from the community at large, then from his role as redeeming kinsman. This nameless man, humorously referred to as *Peloni 'Almoni* (So-and-So), quickly disappears. His departure ushers in the festivity in which the elders and the crowd gather at the gate to bless and embrace Ruth.[22]

I do not assume that the Ruth narrator was in any way acquainted with the genre of comedy as practiced by the Greeks, nor do I propose that the narrator had in mind a stage production when composing the tale.[23] I argue that comedy provides an undergirding to the story of Ruth, the scroll traditionally read in synagogue during the holiday of Shavuot in recognition of its links to the agricultural gifts offered at the Temple at this time. Yet just as we recognize the ancient harvest festivals within the biblical holidays of Sukkot, Pesach, and Shavuot, we catch glimpses of comedy behind the sober surface of the biblical tale. Ruth is a romantic comedy, rooted in the seasonal celebration of nature and its cycles and thereby connected to festivities outside the boundaries of respected society. It offers a humorous, perhaps rebellious critique of law, coated with a story of historical and covenantal significance to the people of Israel. Its comedic mode and voice have not been entirely suppressed.

We may read the comedy in Ruth in light of Freud's concept of humor, which sees in jokes and laughter-causing situations an emotionally liberating device, a mechanism for the release of pressures and the temporary lifting of the fear of authority. Thus, the humor in Ruth, especially in its deception of a patriarch, offers a topsy-turvy moment in which the woman is licensed to manipulate the powerful man and teach him how to behave.[24] We might also read comedy through Mikhail Bakhtin's Marxist lenses and thereby take in the subversive and the antinomian aspects of its intent to destabilize society with its rigid laws and its multiplicity of voices.[25] In these lights, the comedy in Ruth threatens to destabilize society by offering a voice to two minority groups. We have on the one hand the antiestablishment groups who, in the time of the tale's composition, fought against the likes of Ezra and Nehemiah for the acceptance of foreign wives.[26] On the other is the disenfranchised half of Israel, the women who are allowed in this story to assert themselves, to take the center stage, and to exercise an agency largely afforded to men in the biblical narratives.

A comedic reading of Ruth coincides with a feminist one, because it empowers women and exposes male weaknesses in a culture where this was unexpected. The reversal of accepted norms makes the book funny. Women are seen as the creators of the comic spirit, as able to transcend their private misery so as to take a broader view of existence. The comic potential of the Ruth story does not detract from the serious themes raised in the tale. On the contrary, at its best, comedy has always been serious business, pointing out the absurdities of the human condition, highlighting human frailty and folly, while at the same time delighting us with redemption of a happy ending.

PART TWO

Reading Ruth's Readers

TRANSFIGURED NIGHT: MIDRASHIC READINGS OF THE BOOK OF RUTH

Judith A. Kates

Unlike the skepticism they brought to other *megillot* (scrolls) such as Esther and the Song of Songs, the rabbis never questioned the sacredness of the book of Ruth. Without a doubt, as the Talmudic phrase would have it, this text was, *nᵊᵓemra bᵊruaḥ haḳodesh*—that is, spoken by means of the breath or by the spirit of holiness. The Talmud also ascribes its authorship to the prophet Samuel, who is understood to have written it in order to explain the ancestry of David (b. Baba Batra 14b).

Throughout the Talmud and early collections of midrash, we find commentary and reflection on this book. But here I will be paying particular attention to a coherently edited anthology we call *Ruth Rabbah*, a midrashic collection composed of verse-by-verse commentary, divided into eight chapters and introduced by a long proem or *petiḥa* (opening) that is connected thematically to the initial verses of the book.[1] *Ruth Rabbah* includes material found in the Jerusalem Talmud as well as in some earlier midrashic collections, such as *Pesiḳta d'Rav Kahana*; it reflects an awareness of certain motifs that we find explicitly in the Babylonian Talmud, giving it a plausible date of the sixth or seventh century CE. In the essay to follow, I dwell on a few of what I find to be its most compelling themes.

Let us begin with a comment offered on 1:8, the first words of direct speech to be found in this book, which is in fact composed largely of dialogue. Naomi says: "Turn back, each of you to her mother's house. May the Lord deal kindly [*ḥesed*] with you, as you have dealt with the dead and with me." The midrash glosses Naomi's use of the word *ḥesed*:

14. The Lord deal kindly with you (*ib.*)R. Hanina b. Adda said: The *ḳetib* is *ya'aseh*. He certainly will deal kindly with you. As ye

HAVE DEALT WITH THE DEAD, in that ye busied yourselves with their shrouds; AND WITH ME, in that they renounced their marriage settlement. R. Ze'ira said: This scroll [of Ruth] tells us nothing either of cleanliness or of uncleanliness, either of prohibition or permission. For what purpose then was it written? To teach how great is the reward of those who do deeds of kindness. (*Ruth Rabbah* 2:14)

The first comment relates to a textual phenomenon unusually frequent in the book of Ruth: The spelling in the received consonantal text (the *ketiv*) yields a meaning different from that of the spoken pronunciation accepted by the Masoretic tradition (the *k³ri*). The disparity between written and spoken text is frequently noted in *Ruth Rabbah*, leading to an additional panoply of meanings where there is already a multiplication of possible interpretation. In this instance, the traditional, received pronunciation would have it that Naomi speaks in the optative: "May the Lord deal kindly. . . . " She shows appropriate humility as a supplicant when she says "May God do (ya'as) *ḥesed* with you." Or perhaps we are meant to hear in this sentence a tentativeness regarding God's kindness, which would fit the state of painful separation from God as author of *ḥesed* that Naomi expresses so powerfully on her return to Bethlehem: "Do not call me Naomi, call me Mara, for Shaddai (the Almighty) has dealt bitterly with me. / I went away full, but the Lord has brought me back empty; How can you call me Naomi when the Lord has dealt harshly with me, when Shaddai has brought calamity upon me" (Ruth 1:20–21). On the other hand, if we consider the *k³tiv*, the letters of the text as written, we find not *ya'as*, "May God do *ḥesed*," but the future form *ya'aseh*. In this light, Rabbi Hanina sees the verse as a definitive statement—perhaps even a prophecy—about God; the speaker then foretells, "God will do *ḥesed* with you." There is no doubt about what is to happen.

Midrashic commentary on the next two phrases—"May the Lord deal kindly with you *as you have dealt with the dead and with me*"—also begins with what one might call technical details. Exactly to which acts is Naomi referring when she talks about the *ḥesed* her daughters-in-law have already enacted? In relation to *ḥesed* done "with the dead," R. Hanina specifies providing shrouds for them. In doing so, he recalls Talmudic statements that consider such care for the dead to be the defining example of *ḥesed*, a generous action that goes beyond obligation precisely because there is no possibility of reciprocity from the one cared for. In a similarly concrete vein, they read the acts of *ḥesed* performed by Ruth and Orpah "with me" as their generous renunciation of what a widow would be owed according to the terms of the *ketubah*, the marriage settlement written at the time of the wedding, in accordance with rabbinic law. (This reading, of course, requires that we forget an earlier midrash in *Ruth Rabbah* that notes that Ruth and Orpah, the Moabite daughters-in-law, had not converted. As a result, their marriage would not have been sealed with a *ketubah*, and they would not be owed any compensation at all.)

After commenting on such details, the midrash goes on to quote Rabbi Ze'ira and in so doing makes an unusually expansive, indeed inclusive, statement about the purpose of the book of Ruth as a whole. He says, "This scroll [of Ruth] tells us nothing either of cleanliness or of uncleanliness, either of prohibition or permission. For what purpose then was it written? To teach how great is the reward of those who do deeds of kindness." Employing the tone of an impatient halakhist asking why we need to spend time and interpretive energy on a text that apparently has nothing to teach us about the essential categories of the law, Rabbi Ze'ira offers a reading that invites us to see Ruth in the context of scripture as a whole. In that context, he offers a pious affirmation in harmony with what we might call a Deuteronomic theology; it is certainly one congenial to the rabbinic principle of *middah cᵊneged middah*, measure for measure. To see the book as "written to teach how great is the reward of those who do deeds of *ḥesed*" is to find in it an ethically comprehensible, divinely ordered world in which the blessings and sufferings of human beings can be clearly seen as rewards and punishments for deeds done.

Nonetheless, a surprisingly large amount of space in *Ruth Rabbah* is devoted to a theme that seems to me to challenge, if not subvert, that harmonious reading. From the first lines of the *petiḥa*, or proem, and all throughout the collection, the rabbis reflect on the difficulty of the project that Milton would later call "that enterprise of highest hope and hardest attempting . . . to justify the ways of God to Man."[2] The rabbis take with utter seriousness what might seem merely a historical marker in the first four words of the book—*vayᵊhi b'yimei shᵊfot hashoftim*, "in the days when the judges judged." They seize upon these words and the narrative to follow as opening up difficult questions of justice and justification. Although the *pᵊshat*, the literal reading of the text, is clear enough, the midrashim consistently read against the grain. They take *vayᵊhi*, "there was" (or "at the time that") to read *voi*, "alas" or "woe." Then they force the opening to shift from "in the days that the judges judged" to "woe to the day the judges are in need of being judged." Instead of what appears to be a remarkably spare reporting of facts at the opening of the book, written in language that is restrained to the point of utter neutrality, the rabbis attune us to signs of a world out of joint. For the midrash, the biblical text begins in a world of disorder and disruption, a world dangling over the abyss of transgression and breakdown. Yet it will be rescued by human *ḥesed*, leading to the promise of redemption, since the David who reigns over the midrashic reading of Ruth is the messianic descendant of David yet to come.

As in the comment by Rabbi Ze'ira explored above, midrashim on the opening verses of Ruth set the famine and departure from Bethlehem of Elimelekh and his family in the context of other apparently similar biblical narratives. (The rabbis claim, in fact, that there have been a total of ten famines in Scripture.) But the book of Ruth takes strange turns. In contrast, for instance, to Abraham's survival in Egypt during a famine, Elimelekh's escape from Israel to the neighboring country of Moab precipitates death and desolation. The rabbis seem impelled to explain the difference:

> Of the famine which came in the days when the judges judged, however, R. Huna said in the name of R. Dosa that instead of the normal produce of forty-two *se'ahs*, there were only forty-one. But we have learnt: A man should not leave Palestine unless two *se'ahs* [of wheat] cost a shekel? And Rabban Simeon b. Gamaliel said: When is this? When even then it is difficult to obtain, but if it is possible to obtain even one *se'ah* for a shekel, a Jew should not leave the land. But it has been taught: In time of pestilence and in time of war, gather in thy feet, and in time of famine, spread out thy feet. Why then was Elimelech punished? Because he struck despair into the hearts of Israel. He was like a prominent man who dwelt in a certain country, and the people of that country depended upon him and said that if a dearth should come he could supply the whole country with food for ten years. When a dearth came, however, his maidservant went out and stood in the market place with her basket in her hand. And the people of the country said, 'This is the man upon whom we depended that if a dearth should come he would supply our wants for ten years, and here his maidservant stands in the market-place with her basket in her hand!' So with Elimelech! He was one of the notables of his place and one of the leaders of his generation. But when the famine came he said, 'Now all Israel will come knocking at my door [for help,] each one with his basket.' He therefore arose and fled from them. This is the meaning of the verse AND A CERTAIN MAN OF BETH-LEHEM IN JUDAH WENT. (*Ruth Rabbah* 1:4)

According to this midrash, the fate of Elimelekh is a punishment, not, as we might think, for leaving the land of Israel unnecessarily, but for failures of leadership and of what we might call the moral imagination. The rabbis consider Elimelekh among the *gᵊdolei ha-medina*, the great men of the region, those to whom others look for guidance. He is one of the *mᵊfarn'sei hador*, translated here as "leaders." Avivah Zornberg points out, however, that the midrash uses a word for leadership whose root meaning is "to feed."[3] Elimelekh is supposed to nourish, to care for others, but his response to the imagining, not even the reality, of people coming to him with their needs is enough for him to close his doors and flee. Rashi captures this interpretation with a wonderfully evocative phrase in his commentary on Ruth 1:1. In his note about *vayelekh ish*, "and a man went," Rashi states, "he was rich and important and the leader [*parnas*] of the generation and he left the land of Israel because of *tzarut ha'ayin*, literally 'narrowness of the eyes.'" This phrase is an idiom for stinginess. But Rashi plays on the literal sense of a man shutting his eyes, closing himself off: "his eye was narrowed against the poor people who came to push him, therefore he was punished." As the rabbis read Elimelech, he was "The Man" of Bet leḥem—the house of bread—who made himself an inhabitant of *bet kᵊvarim*, the house of graves.

The midrashic narrative responds to the rabbis' pressing questions of justice. It is not enough to quote the phrase we hear so often in the book of Judges, "Every man did what was right in his own eyes." The deaths of Elimelekh and his sons—whom the midrash implicates in their father's failure by their continued residence in Moab, by their marriages to Moabite women, and by their failure to concern themselves with their wives' conversions—all reflect the disastrous disorder of a generation in which the judges, that is to say the leaders of the people, "are in need of being judged."

But what of the one who is left? In fact, the midrashic reading of Naomi, as Zornberg has taught us to see, reflects Naomi's own language of judgment and punishment in complex and deeply moving ways. Naomi, after all, is the character who, over and over again, uses the language of divine judgment and affliction: "It is far more bitter for me [*mar li*] than for you, for the hand of the Lord has struck out against me" (1:13); "Do not call me Naomi . . . call me Mara, for Shaddai has made my lot very bitter [*hemar . . . li*]. I went away full and the Lord has brought me back empty. How can you call me Naomi, when the Lord has dealt harshly ['anah] with me, when Shaddai has made it bad for me!" (1:20–21).

The rabbis expound:

CALL ME NOT NAOMI, CALL ME MARAH. Bar Kapparah said: Her case was like that of an ordinary ox which its owner puts up for sale in the marketplace saying, 'It is excellent for ploughing, and drives straight furrows.' 'But,' say the bystanders, 'if it is good for ploughing, what is the meaning of those weals on its back?' So said Naomi, WHY CALL YE ME NAOMI (PLEASANT), SEEING THE LORD HATH TESTIFIED AGAINST ME, AND THE ALMIGHTY HATH AFFLICTED ME (I, 21).

I WENT OUT FULL AND THE LORD HATH BROUGHT ME BACK EMPTY (*ib.*). I went out full with sons and daughters. Another interpretation of I WENT OUT FULL, is, I was pregnant. WHY CALL YE ME NAOMI, SEEING THE LORD HATH AFFLICTED ('ANAH) ME, AND THE ALMIGHTY HATH DONE EVIL TO ME. God has afflicted me with His Attribute of Justice, as in the verse, *If thou afflict* ('aneh) *him in any wise* (Ex. XXII, 22). Another interpretation of 'anah is 'testified' against me, as in the verse, *He hath testified* ('anah) *falsely against his brother* (Deut. XIX, 18). (*Ruth Rabbah* 3:6–7)

Midrashic play on the possible meanings of the root translated as "deal harshly" ('*anah*) opens the possibility that Naomi is not only afflicted, but that God, in particular, has testified against her, presumably giving testimony that she is guilty. And yet the midrash goes out of its way to assert that responsibility for the family's lot lay first with her husband and second with their sons. In other words, the sense of God as bearing witness against her entails what Zornberg calls the "Kafka situation," the sense of enormous, but unspecified guilt that reveals itself in her suffering and in the fact that her suffering is visible to all who see her. That her pain stems from her existential situation is already suggested by an earlier midrash on 1:5—"then Mahlon and Khilion died, both of them"—in which what happens to Naomi is compared first to the afflictions of Job, then to the plagues in Egypt, and finally to a skin disease called *tzara'at*. A rabbinic pun on the name of this last affliction, *tzara'at*, explains it as a quid pro quo, a response to those who *motzi shem ra*, that is, literally bring forth evil language or speak slanderously. The juxtaposition of these three analogies suggests that this moment in the narrative when, as the text has it, Naomi is "left, or bereft, of her two children and her husband" arouses anxiety. It cries out for some understanding: How can such disaster have engulfed this woman in a world that we expect to make moral sense? The midrashic comparisons raise the question of whether she is punished, like the *m^ətzor'a* or the Egyptians, and if so, for what reason? Or is it that she is being tried, like Job, and therefore generates an existential anxiety similar to the effect of the book of Job?

The specific midrash we are exploring here is framed by a formulation that is stunning in its starkness and empathy. On the verb *vatisha'er*, ("and she was left") which appears twice, once after each death, the rabbis make two comments. The first notes that "she became remnants [*sh'yarei*] of the meal offering [*minḥa*]," and the next that "she became remnants of the remnants." The nineteenth-century commentator on *Ruth Rabbah*, Rabbi Ze'ev Wolf Einhorn, the Maharzu, understands this sequence to be telling us that Naomi is now of no value whatsoever. After her husband's death, she was still a little something; but after the death of her sons, not even that modicum was left.

I prefer to read this midrash, however, with Zornberg—to see it not as a rabbinic observation from outside, but as an example of rabbinic empathy, an entrance into Naomi's experience of calamity as a personal and divine affliction. What is a remnant of the *minḥa* offering? She is a mere husk or, as Zornberg puts it, like the walking dead, emptied out, and yet suffering from that emptiness all the same. I am suggesting that the rabbis, in contemplating Naomi with their questions of justice in mind, see in her both a figure of suffering and a challenge to any simplistic notion of divine justice.

There is a second thematic preoccupation of the midrash to consider: the question of conversion. Ruth, after all, is a narrative about the other, about a particularly challenging other, when we think about the attitude toward the Moabites found in such texts as Numbers 22 or 25 or Deuteronomy 23. The midrash, well aware of those sections of the Torah, hears a loud, if implicit question: How could king David be descended from a foreigner, and a Moabite at that? In response, rabbinic readers insistently find in Ruth the paradigm of the *ger tzeddek*, the righteous convert. Their reading of the narrative embodies their transformation of the biblical word *ger* from its original definition, "stranger," to its rabbinic meaning, "convert." Naomi's efforts to persuade her daughters-in-law to leave her (1:8–14), culminating at the crossroads, are unveiled as stages in a tense and dramatic dialogue of conversion:

> TURN BACK, MY DAUGHTERS, GO YOUR WAY (I, 12). R. Samuel b. Nahmani said in the name of R. Judah b. Hanina: Three times it is written here '*turn back*', corresponding to the three times that a would-be proselyte is repulsed; but if he persists after that, he is

accepted. R. Isaac said: [It is written,] *The stranger did not lodge in the street* (Job XXXI, 32): A man should rebuff with his left hand, but bring near with the right. (*Ruth Rabbah* 2:16)

Rabbi Samuel b. Nahmani and Rabbi Isaac are boldly anachronistic when they find in the biblical text the specific gestures and movements of later rituals of conversion. But they also are quite sensitive in their registry of paradoxical nuance. Naomi's verbal "pushing away," charged as it is with the emotion of imagined alternatives for Ruth, opens up possibilities for her in the very moment when the older woman declares their impossibility. Although she does "rebuff with the left hand" she also "brings near with the right." The midrash reframes this subtle perception into the opening movement of what is for the rabbis the essential drama of an explicit conversion.

Even more radically, they transform Ruth's beautiful declaration of devotion, which appears in the text very much as a solo aria, into a duet, one that envisions what are, literally, the life-and-death consequences of Ruth's choice:

> AND RUTH SAID: ENTREAT ME NOT TO LEAVE THEE, AND TO RETURN FROM FOLLOWING AFTER THEE (I, 16). What is the meaning of EN-TREAT ME NOT? She said to her, 'Do not sin against me; do not turn your misfortunes away from me.' TO LEAVE THEE AND TO RETURN FROM FOLLOWING AFTER THEE. I am fully resolved to become con-verted under any circumstances, but it is better that it should be at your hands than at those of another. When Naomi heard this, she began to unfold to her the laws of conversion, saying: 'My daughter, it is not the custom of daughters of Israel to frequent Gentile the-atres and circuses,' to which she replied, 'WHITHER THOU GOEST, I WILL GO' (*ib.*). She continued: 'My daughter, it is not the custom of daughters of Israel to dwell in a house which has no *mezuzah*,' to which she responded, 'AND WHERE THOU LODGEST, I WILL LODGE' (*ib.*). THY PEOPLE SHALL BE MY PEOPLE (*ib.*) refers to the penalties and admonitions [of the Torah], and THY GOD MY GOD (*ib.*) to the other commandments of the Bible.
>
> Another interpretation: WHITHER THOU GOEST, I WILL GO: to the tent of testimony, to Gilgal, Shiloh, Nob, Gibeon, and the Perma-nent Temple. AND WHERE THOU LODGEST, I WILL LODGE: I shall lodge overnight with the sacrifices. THY PEOPLE SHALL BE MY PEOPLE, in that I will destroy all idolatry within me, and THY GOD SHALL BE MY GOD, to pay me the reward of my labour.

WHERE THOU DIEST I WILL DIE (I, 17) refers to the four forms of capital punishment inflicted by the Court, viz. stoning, burning, beheading, and strangulation. AND THERE I WILL BE BURIED; these are the two graves prepared by the Beth din, one for those who have suffered stoning and burning, the other for those decapitated and strangled. THE LORD DO TO ME AND MORE ALSO. Naomi said to her: 'My daughter, whatever good deeds and righteous actions you are able to acquire, acquire in this world, for in the World to Come, DEATH SHALL PART THEE AND ME.' (*Ruth Rabbah* 2:22–24)

In the first interpretation, the smooth, rhythmic flow of Ruth's crescendo, "Entreat me not to leave you," becomes an antiphonal call and response. Each of Ruth's "whither's" and "where's" is now an assenting response to Naomi's (very rabbinic) instruction in the laws and customs required of "daughters of Israel." This antiphonal exchange follows the Talmudic model of instruction for converts: at first a few specific laws, and then, if the convert is sincere, fuller instruction once the *ger tzeddek* has been brought inside.

A second interpretation, however, recasts Ruth's language in a different mode. Her apparently simple, basic declaration of loyalty contains, for the midrash, a full awareness of all the journeys, both physical and spiritual, to be found in Torah. She, like Israel's sacred center, will move from the desert Tabernacle to the Temple in Jerusalem, from idolatry to true worship, from a morally arbitrary religious universe to an understanding of the justice of God. At the end of this passage, Ruth is envisioned as taking on all the possible consequences of the Torah's laws, including punishment for transgression through the oath formula "The Lord do so to me and more also." In these revisionary interpretive movements, the midrashist carefully maintains the rhetorical structure of the actual biblical text. But at the end, he breaks up even that structure, transforming the subjunctive finale of Ruth's oath—"the Lord do so to me and more also"—into a final declarative instruction in Naomi's mouth—"My daughter, whatever good deeds and righteous actions you are able to acquire, acquire in this world, for in the World to Come, death shall part thee and me." The rabbinic voice gets the last word.

We can feel the pressure behind this midrashic reading when we take into consideration the sequel to Ruth's avowal: "When she [Naomi] saw how determined she was to go with her [*'itah*], she stopped talking to her, and the two of them went on [*vateilachna shteihem*] until they reached Bethlehem" (1:18). It would seem from this verse that Naomi responds to Ruth's incandescent declaration of loyalty with stony silence. It may be silent acquiescence, or a retreat into that dark emptiness she exposes on the return to Bethlehem. In Naomi's speeches to the women of the city, it is as if Ruth were simply not there. Yet the midrash insists on reading the text otherwise: "R. Yehuda bar Shimon commented: Come and see how precious in the eyes of the omnipresent are converts. Once she decided to convert, scripture makes her equal to Naomi" (*Ruth Rabbah* 3:5). What ultimately matters for R. Yehuda is the word *'itah*, "with her," followed immediately by the feminine plural—the two of them went. Despite Naomi's silence, Ruth has in fact joined her.

But this triumphant solution to the difficult question of foreignness is haunted by the possibility of transgression, the fact that David's great-grandmother may be anathema because of her particular ethnic origin. Deuteronomy 23:4 sounds like an unequivocal prohibition against the conversion the rabbis read into Ruth's declaration: "No Ammonite or Moabite shall be admitted into the congregation of the Lord. None of their descendants, even to the tenth generation, shall ever be admitted into the congregation of the Lord." Despite this statement, *Ruth Rabbah* alludes again and again to the *halakha shᵊnithadsha*, the *halakha* that was renewed, reenacted, or innovated. What *halakha* is that? *Ammoni vᵊlo ammonit, moavi vᵊlo moavit*—an Ammonite man is prohibited, but not an Ammonite woman; a Moabite man but not a Moabite woman.

The classic source for this creative reading reveals the urgency of this issue. In the Talmudic tractate Yevamot, which deals with forbidden and permitted marriages, a mishnah (8:3) states apodictically and thus without any justification: "An Ammonite man and a Moabite man are prohibited and their prohibition is eternal. But their females are permitted immediately." As part of the discussion of this mishnah, we find in the gemara the following commentary on that moment in I Samuel 17 when King Saul seems not to recognize the slayer of Goliath, David:

"Who is this lad?" (I Sam. 17.56)

Doeg then said to him: "Instead of inquiring whether he is fit to be king or not, inquire rather whether he is permitted to enter the community [of Israel] or not!" What is the reason? Because he is descended from Ruth, the Moabitess. He wanted publicly to proclaim him [unfit].

Immediately Amasa girded on his sword like an Ishmaelite and exclaimed: "Whoever will not obey the following ruling will be stabbed with the sword: This rule emanated from the Prophet

Samuel's Beth Din. An Ammonite [is unfit], but not an Ammonitess; a Moabite but not a Moabitess." (Babylonian Talmud, *Yevamoth* 76b, 77a)

This intriguing bit of Talmudic midrash suggests that the gendered reading of the verse in Deuteronomy should not be dismissed simply as an example of fancy rabbinic footwork undertaken to remove an embarrassing anomaly. Rather, it registers an anxious sense of precariousness in the whole Davidic enterprise—and for "Davidic," read messianic.

In one account of this "revived *halakha*" that appears in *Ruth Rabbah*, the midrash opens with a verse from the book of Chronicles (1 Chron. 2:17), a book that, according to *Ruth Rabbah*, was given only *lᵊhidaresh*—to be interpreted in the mode of midrash. When the rabbi comes to the name Yeter the Ishmaelite in David's extended family, he fairly explodes with the following insight:

> One verse says, *Ithra the Jesraelite* (II Sam. XVII, 25), while another verse says *Jether the Ishmaelite* (I Chron. II, 17). R. Joshua b. Levi said: '*Ithra the Jesraelite*' is the same as '*Jether the Ishmaelite*'. R. Samuel b. Nahman and the Rabbis [give different explanations]. R. Samuel says: He was an Ishmaelite yet you call him an Israelite? Indeed he was an Ishmaelite, but he entered the house of study and found there Jesse expounding the verse, *Look unto Me, and be ye saved, all the ends of the earth* (Isa. XLV, 22), and he became converted and he [Jesse] gave him his daughter to wife. The Rabbis say he was an Israelite, and yet you call him an Ishmaelite? Indeed he was an Israelite, but he girded on his sword like an Ishmaelite and he stuck it in the middle of the house of study and exclaimed, 'Either I will slay or be slain, until I establish this law publicly so that whoever annuls it I will behead him with this sword.' [Which law?] 'Ammonite but not Ammonitess, Moabite but not Moabitess.' (*Ruth Rabbah* 4:1)

I suggest that the tremendous energy invested in this "renewed" *halakha* is not simply generated by the force of a narrative that seems to connect the Davidic line to earlier transgressive acts, one of which involves the admission of a Moabite into the community. Rabbinic thought is generally concerned with issues of group definition and boundaries, and we see that concern reflected here. However, our passage does not focus only on ethnic boundaries, for the prohibition against the Ammonites and Moabites in Deuteronomy is explained in terms of ethics: "because they did not meet you with food and water on your journey after you left Egypt, and because they hired Balaam son of Beor . . . to curse you" (Deut. 23:5). The Moabites are, after all, descendants of Abraham's nephew Lot and therefore relatives, closer to Israel than complete outsiders; nevertheless, they represent the antithesis of the Torah's ethic of care for the weak and vulnerable. In their withholding of food and sustenance, they embody the opposite of *ḥesed*. The exclusion of Moabites would thus seem to be based on an ethical, as much as an ethnic rationale.

We might then argue that the book of Ruth teaches us that, despite her Moabite origins, Ruth is brought under the wings of God because of her extraordinary righteousness and because she is the exemplar of *ḥesed*, as Boaz himself testifies. *Halakha*, represented by the prohibition in Deuteronomy, is set aside because of her exceptional ethical qualities. The rabbis counter such an argument with their emphasis on a genuine halakhic ground for the embrace of the Moabite woman. They implicitly demonstrate that legal and ethical concerns can be harmonized. The midrash emphasizes without question her righteousness, modesty, and piety, but it also mobilizes an idea that, though never spelled out in *Ruth Rabbah*, is fully developed in the Talmud: Her conversion was perfectly in keeping with the law. Indeed, it was possible because of the law, or at least because of the law as understood by the rabbinic interpreters. The rabbis' Ruth then comes to teach not only the reward for deeds of loving-kindness, as Rabbi Ze'ira said. It comes to underscore the network of righteousness so powerfully present in this story—the interdependence of law and ethics, *halakha* and *ḥesed*.

DARK LADIES AND REDEMPTIVE COMPASSION: RUTH AND THE MESSIANIC LINEAGE IN JUDAISM

Nehemia Polen

Jewish tradition celebrates Shavuot as the festival of the Giving of the Torah, the anniversary of the time when, fifty days after the Exodus, God came down on Mount Sinai and spoke the Decalogue (the "Ten Commandments") to Israel. So it is that every year synagogue congregations take out the Torah scroll from the Holy Ark, place it on the reading table, and read from Exodus 19–20 as a public reenactment of that ancient covenantal proclamation. But just before that happens, another, much smaller scroll is opened and read: the scroll of Ruth.[1]

The significance of this smaller scroll claims my attention in this essay, but I want to reflect for a moment on the juxtaposition of these two public readings. The synagogue lectionary is designed to take the congregation through the entire Torah, the Five Books of Moses, once a year. The Pentateuch is divided into over fifty sections, each with its own conventional name that gives some hint of the basic topic: "In the Beginning"; "Noah"; "Get Thee Out [of Thy Father's House]"; and so on. But along with this weekly sequence from Genesis to Deuteronomy, there is another coordinated set of readings from the prophets, called the Haftarah. Each selection from the prophets is in some way related to the Torah reading, although the relationship is not always obvious or simple. Sometimes the prophetic reading carries the Pentateuchal narrative forward in time, sometimes it highlights the ethical teaching of the Torah selection, and sometimes it provides a counterpoint to the Torah reading, as when Leviticus 1–5 is followed by Isaiah 43:21–44:23, and the week after, when Leviticus 6–8 is followed by Jeremiah 7:21–8:3. The juxtapositions are provocative and meant to be so. But because they are part and parcel of one liturgy, the congregation hears verses such as "For I spoke not unto your fathers nor commanded them . . . concerning burnt offerings or sacrifices" (Jer. 7:22) not as a repudiations of the sacrifices of Leviticus, much less as a polemical denunciation of the law as a whole, but as something different.[2] Wisely, no attempt was ever made to encapsulate the message in a single formulation or aphorism, and there surely is enormous variation among listeners, interpreters, and periods of history. But in general, one may say that the words are heard as a challenge, as a call to reflection and deeper understanding. These readings open dialogue, rather than shutting it down.

While the reading from the prophets always follows the Torah reading, there are three occasions when a scriptural reading precedes the Torah lection: on Passover in the spring, with the Song of Songs; on Sukkot in the fall, with Ecclesiastes; and (as mentioned above) on Shavuot, with Ruth. In the tripartite division of the Jewish Bible, Song of Songs, Ecclesiastes, and Ruth fall in the third division, the "Sacred Writings." It is surely notable that these three short works, each of great interest in its own way, are chosen to precede the Torah reading on the three pilgrim festivals.

The connection between spring's holiday Passover, and Song of Song's passionate love is direct and unmistakable. It is also possible to discern the wisdom of pairing Ecclesiastes with Succot, the fall harvest festival: The celebratory joy and self-assured bounty of harvest time need to be tempered with a touch of Ecclesiastes' uncertainty and skepticism. But perhaps most intriguing of all is the reading of Ruth, which links Bethlehem with Sinai, Moab with Moses. And again, unlike the traditional Haftorot—which follow the Torah reading and remain ancillary to it—the reading of Ruth *precedes* the reading of Torah. It is as if to say the covenant of Sinai and the Torah of Moses are framed by—are to be understood under the canopy of—Ruth and her teaching.

It is not only in liturgical settings that Judaism creates seemingly unlikely neighbors. The entire genre of midrash involves revealing meaning by hurling texts at each other and observing the resultant trajectories and the energies released. As Michael Fishbane and others have reminded us, midrashic activity is traceable back to the Bible itself, which brims with intertextual allusions and delights in lexical plays and phonemic echoes in both prose and poetry.

In truth, the very embodiment of the Tanakh, the Hebrew Scriptures, as a physical artifact implies relationship. I hold a Tanakh in my hand, aware that I grasp a wide variety of genres and works: story and genealogy, creedal affirmation, ethical maxim, and joyous celebration. Bound in one volume are narrative, prophecy, prayer, wisdom, and law. In older times each work came written on its own scroll—scribal practice preserves this tradition even today—so the whole anthology would have been stored in a large pouch. I often wonder what these scrolls say to each other as they jostle about, rubbing shoulders willy-nilly. What does curmudgeonly Ecclesiastes say to pious, not to say the credulous Psalms? Do Job and Deuteronomy understand each other? How do Jeremiah and Ezekiel respond when approached by Song of Songs, all sultry and ready for a big hug? We know that some books were nearly excluded—or did they wish to opt out?—but in the end remained in the pouch. There were some works—Enoch and Jubilees among others—that did not make the cut.

I am personifying here, projecting human characteristics onto scrolls. But the reality is that behind each work stands a community, a group of devoted disciples who preserved, taught, and likely edited each of the scrolls, passing on words and voice and perspective for generations. Furthermore, the collection as a whole became the Scriptures of postexilic Judaism, the common ground of the people who gathered under the shadow of the Second Temple to pick up the pieces of the first one, who claimed the Bible as their living guide even though most of the events described in it already were of unimaginable antiquity in their own day.

When inviting guests to a dinner party, one can never predict which will hit it off, where the most scintillating conversation will arise, and who might exchange phone numbers or arrange a subsequent meeting. But if the party is to succeed at all, there must be some shared understanding. A basic trust undergirds the process of extending and accepting invitations, an implied pact between host and guests. Like all tacit understandings, this one probably cannot be brought to full articulation, but it surely includes the assumption that all participants will be open to camaraderie, discovery, and dialogue and that no one will prove an enduring embarrassment to anyone else.

This analogy should remind us that when speaking of a "canon," we are speaking of people as much as (perhaps more than) of books. As Rolf Rendtorff has put it, the postexilic Jewish community of returnees is:

> the community whose self-definition is expressed in the final form of the Old Testament canon. We have to think of a mutual relationship: through its handling of the texts passed down to it, the community builds up the way it sees itself; while in the process it often gives these texts a new interpretation, which is ultimately reflected in the final form of the text and the canon as a whole.[3]

All this means that there was always interchange and conversation between the subgroups that formed Second Temple Judaism and the books they held sacred. Because we are speaking of people more than books, perhaps it is time to find a term other than "canon," with its air of cold fixity, to describe the shaping of the Tanakh as Jewish sacred Scripture; we need a concept more open and capacious that can suggest the dynamic attractions and surprising alliances between books that attentive readers have always noticed. Whatever word we might come up with, one thing is certain: The Tanakh is a relational latticework that bestows a common frame of possibility for those who bear it as sacred.

This reminds us of other important features of the Tanakh: its fundamental mood of beneficence and hope, its bias toward growth and repair, its anticipation of the return of all things to their place and their dignity in God's good time. A deep optimism pervades the Hebrew Bible, despite repeated tragedy and trauma. This may be related to the experience of return from exile to Judea, which (quoting Rendtorff again) "Israel herself had obviously understood as God's Yes."[4] This disposition to optimism is heard with particular clarity at the close of the prophets, with the promise of Elijah's return and the restoration of "the heart of the fathers to the children, and the heart of the children to the fathers," and at the conclusion of the sacred writings—and thus the Hebrew Bible as a whole—with the proclamation to the Jewish exiles by the Persian king, Cyrus, encouraging those who wished to return to Jerusalem and rebuild their Temple: "the Lord his God is with him—let him go up."

This leads us to the book of Ruth itself—a work unmistakably modest in size, gentle in tone, brimming with blessing and with a glimmer of what later generations would call messianic hope. The web of intertextual allusions that readers ancient and modern have found between the Torah and Ruth—works so very different in character and size—might leave a beginning student surprised, yet the web is rich indeed, densely woven and firmly knotted. Some points of contact—with Deuteronomy and Leviticus, and most of all with Genesis—have been explored by previous writers; I hope to build on their insights. But let us begin by noting that Ruth stands at roughly a midpoint in the Bible's implied chronology. As we follow the biblical trajectory of time's arrow, the era "when the judges judged" stands about equidistant between the primeval age of patriarchs and matriarchs on the one hand, and the era that the Second Temple community would have experienced as *now*, the current age. Providing a welcome counterbalance to the bleak portrait of premonarchical Israel in the book of Judges, Ruth also forms a graceful arch with one foot in the era of primeval founders and the other in the "modern times" of postexilic restoration, cresting nobly in the days of Ruth, Naomi, and Boaz. The ten-step *tolᵊdot* genealogy with which Ruth ends—the only such genealogy outside the Pentateuch—creates a similar effect, suggesting the possibilities available for those who locate themselves in the arch's open space to find companionship and shelter, to hope, and to wait.

Modest in size as Ruth is, the book plays a surprisingly important role in the biblical schema. It is astonishing that the matriarch Leah, for all her centrality in the book of Genesis and later Jewish memory, is mentioned nowhere else in the Bible—except in Ruth. With Rachel, it is almost the same: After Genesis, she receives but two mentions in Jewish Scripture—plus here in Ruth. The pattern is similar for Judah's daughter-in-law Tamar: Other than a brief reprise in Chronicles, she appears only here, and it is much the same for Peretz. This should be a clue that the retrieval of lost names—*lᵊ-haḳim shem*, "to restore the name" (Ruth 4:5; in the felicitous translation of Ellen Davis)—is central to the message of Ruth. If, as noted above, the liturgical placement of Ruth on Shavuot suggests that her story can serve as a key to Moses's Torah, then perhaps an exploration of "restoring the name" would help us understand the nature of that key. Along the way, we also hope to gain a better grasp of Ruth's place in the development of Jewish messianism.

We begin our exploration with a rabbinic midrash from the classic period, roughly contemporaneous with the Talmuds, which already points to some mysterious divine plan in the puzzling events of the messianic line. Commenting on Genesis 38:1, "And it came to pass at that time, that Judah went down from his brethren," the midrash Genesis Rabbah (an early Palestinian midrash from about the fourth century CE) notes: "The tribal ancestors were engaged in selling Joseph; Jacob was engaged in sackcloth and fasting; and Judah was busy taking a wife. . . . And God was occupied in creating the light of King Messiah."⁵

When studying a midrashic text, is always important to note the biblical proof texts that frame the passage in question and shape its meaning. Here, along with Genesis 38:1, the midrash juxtaposes a prophetic passage, specifically Jeremiah 29:11, "For I am mindful of the plans that I made concerning you—declares the Lord—plans for your welfare, not for disaster, to give you a future and a hope." Chapter 29 of Jeremiah is the prophet's letter to those deported to Babylon in 597 BCE; he encourages them to build houses and raise families in exile and assures them that at the end of seventy years, God would fulfill his promise and bring them back to Jerusalem. So the sense of our midrash here is that at the very moment of apparent collapse—of fraternal betrayal and familial disaster—God was planning "a future and a hope." God was somehow involved in Judah's unfolding family saga and the establishment of the Judahite lineage with the birth of Peretz and Zerah, a story whose meaning would come to light centuries later, "when the judges judged" and that further provided the paradigm for Jeremiah's message of hope beyond destruction many centuries later still, in the exile and eventual restoration to Jerusalem.

This reading is reinforced by what follows directly in the midrash: " 'Before she labored she was delivered; [before her pangs came, she bore a son]' (Isa. 66:7)" Before their final oppressor was born, their first redeemer was born." That is to say, long before Israel was to suffer the imperial tyranny of Rome and the destruction of the Second Temple in 70 CE, the messianic line had already made its appearance with Peretz. The seeds of the final redemption already had been sown and would one day bear fruit. The linkage of Genesis 38 with Isaiah 66, moreover, makes Tamar, who was once mistaken for a harlot, the prototype for Jerusalem—the city stigmatized as a harlot by the prophet in Isaiah 1:21, but now to be restored and rebuilt. And the prophet's imagery of restored city as mother who gives birth without labor pains brings to mind the bereft Naomi, who at the end of the book of Ruth took the child Obed "and laid it to her bosom," the child of whom the neighbors said, "There is a son born to Naomi"—surely the exemplar of mothering without birth pangs. Here, as elsewhere, midrashic method reveals the meaning across biblical texts when they are read dynamically, read across arching spans of time, where the past foreshadows the future and the present fulfills the past. Neither exegesis nor eisegesis, this disclosure of the living convergence of text and community is itself a sign of enduring hopefulness.

The same midrashic collection also finds messianic significance in the story of Lot's daughters. On Genesis 19:31–32—"And the firstborn said to the younger: our father is old, and there is not a man on the earth. . . . Come, let us make our father drink wine . . . that we may bring life to seed of our father,"—Genesis Rabbah comments, "The verse does not say, 'so that we may bring a child of our father to life,' but seed of our father, meaning, seed destined to appear elsewhere, that is, King Messiah."[6]

The midrash continues by questioning how Lot's daughters obtained wine in the cave. One response was that the Sodomites had an abundance of wine, which they customarily stored in caves. But another midrashist,

Rabbi Yudan son of Rabbi Simon, taught that "they were given an experience of the Messianic Age, of which Scripture says, 'It shall come to pass on that day, that the mountains shall drip with sweet wine' (Joel 4:18)." So by entering the cave, Lot and his daughters had crossed into another reality, the world of final things and redemptive time. This is surely an intriguing view of what on the surface appears to be a most tawdry biblical episode.

The suggestion that the embarrassing liaisons of Genesis have some eschatological significance is found in the Babylonian Talmud, as well. At Sotah 10b, in an exploration of the episode of Judah and Tamar, the rabbis make the following comment: "'and Judah recognized [the signs] and he said, 'she is more righteous than I' (Gen. 38:25). The word *tzadkah*—she is righteous—was uttered by Judah, while the word *mi-meni* was interjected by a heavenly voice, by God, to say, 'it is I—these events are my hidden plan.'"[7]

These Talmudic and midrashic comments on the origins of the messianic line amount to little more than intriguing but undeveloped hints; in the vast corpus of rabbinic literature, this theme never receives sustained attention. A fuller exposition awaited the flowering of Jewish mysticism in the medieval period, in particular the Zohar, the Kabbalistic classic from the thirteenth century. The Zohar notes the similarities between the stories of Judah and Tamar and those of Ruth and Boaz and sees in them confirmation of its belief in the transmigration of the soul. Levirate marriage for the Zohar gives a second chance to souls that did not fulfill their mission during their first sojourn on earth.

> Tamar was a priest's daughter [the daughter of Shem, midrashically identified with Malkizedek, the king of Salem, priest of the Most High God]; it is inconceivable that she would have gone to fornicate with her father-in-law; she was in fact a most modest woman. Rather, she was righteous, and acted out of wisdom . . . she had knowledge, she saw wisely, she came to Judah to do kindness and truth [to the souls of Er and Onan].
>
> It was all from God. . . . There were two women from whom the seed of Judah was raised up; from those women came King David, King Solomon, and King Messiah. Those two women were alike—one corresponding to the other [*da ke-gavna de-da*], Tamar and Ruth—who had lost their prior husbands, and who worked to accomplish this thing—Tamar with her father-in-law [Judah], and Ruth with Boaz. (1:187b–188b)[8]

For the Zohar, then, Peretz and Zerah are reincarnations of Er and Onan, while Obed carries the soul of Ruth's dead first husband, Mahlon. Another Zohar passage comments on Boaz's words to Ruth, "Should you get thirsty, go to the vessels and drink (Ruth 2:9)": "If you are thirsty for a man, to establish seed in the world, then go to the vessels—go to the righteous, who are called God's vessels [see Isaiah 52:11], whom all the world will one day bring as a gift to King Messiah; they are indeed God's vessels, in whom God takes pleasure—they are broken vessels" (2:218a).

The notion of the righteous as God's "broken vessels" is evidently suggested by the repeated episodes of impropriety attending the establishment of the messianic line. These include not only the liaisons of Lot with his daughters and Judah with Tamar, but David with Bathsheba, mother of Solomon. In Zohar 3:71b-72a, we read: "From the *ḥutzpah* (brazenness) of the righteous woman Tamar, many blessings came into the world, as it is written, 'and she sat at *petaḥ 'Eynayim* (Gen. 38:14).' This is like Bathsheba, who was destined from the six days of creation to be the mother of King Solomon, so too was Tamar destined for Judah from the day the world was created."[9]

The transgressive behavior of Tamar was a *petaḥ 'eynayim*—the Hebrew can mean "opening of the eyes"—to new possibilities, as well as "opening of wellsprings"—of blessing and fruitfulness. Similarly, the episode of David's espying Bathsheba's bath was no accident, but the fulfillment of destiny. Is the Zohar suggesting that Bathsheba was not entirely innocent and unaware of the unobstructed view to the king's palace? In any event, the Zohar has made explicit what the Talmud and midrash had only hinted at—that the incest or adultery of the biblical heroes may have been part of a divine plan. And by pointing to a three-part correspondence: Tamar-Judah, Ruth-Boaz, and Bathsheba-David, the Zohar underscores the emergence of the messianic line from parallel transgressive episodes. Of course, Ruth does not commit incest or adultery. Yet, as Tikva Frymer-Kensky has noted, Ruth "does aggressively pursue Boaz, and comes to his bed in the middle of the night. . . . [She] does not consider herself bound by conventional mores when an important issue is at stake."[10] The *ḥutzpah* of women such as Tamar and Ruth opened eyes, opened wellsprings, breaking down barriers to blessing and redemption.

The Zohar's treatment of Tamar, Ruth, and Bathsheba grasps the lines of connection embedded in the biblical texts, lines that had only begun to be teased out by the Talmudic rabbis. By amplifying the intertextual reverberations, Zohar makes explicit what had been merely implied. This is consistent with the Zohar's contribution in general: Midrashic methods are raised to a new level of creativity and visionary sweep. All later writers on this theme were influenced by the Zohar's insights on Scripture and messianism. Yet for all the importance of the Zohar's contribution, it is also true that the Zohar initiated a process that eventually obscured the biblical heroes and heroines as actual characters, as personalities. In Kabbalistic theory, such figures as Tamar, Ruth, and Bathsheba, like Abraham, Isaac, and Jacob, become symbols of cosmic forces, of the *sefirot*—the manifestations of the divine on earth. At some point, therefore, the interest shifts from the actual lives (historical or literary) of the ancestors to these figures as avatars and finally as markers of an intradivine process. Kabbalistic texts are deeply interested in biblical narratives, but largely to highlight theosophical-cosmic processes and mystical doctrines such as reincarnation and the emergence of redemption from evil, light from darkness, and restoration from exile. So as the Zoharic teachings are taken up by subsequent Kabbalists, attention often shifts away from actual personalities toward theory-laden elaboration of these ideas.

This same tendency is evident in current scholarly writing, as well. In recent years, academic discussions on Jewish messianism have displayed little interest in David, even as a literary figure. Gershom Scholem's celebrated collection of essays *The Messianic Idea in Judaism* focuses on Kabbalistic notions of the redemptive process; Scholem barely mentions the biblical Ruth and David at all.[11] If any one personality dominates Scholem's concerns, it is that of Sabbatai Zevi, the messianic pretender whose movement engulfed all of world Jewry in 1666 and had a remarkable afterlife even following Sabbatai Zevi's conversion to Islam. Scholem is much interested in the Kabbalistic ideas that laid the groundwork for his career and the antinomian turn that they took as the Sabbatean movement developed. He writes of the anarchic element that entered messianic utopianism, out of which would emerge latent antinomian potentialities. Scholem points to one part of the Zoharic corpus where we find the idea that the entire system of Jewish law known as *halakha* is given in the shadow of the Tree of the Knowledge of Good and Evil in the Garden of Eden. But in the domain of the Tree of Life, there is only goodness, holiness, with no admixture of evil, no death, and therefore no need for restriction. In the time of messianic redemption, conceived as restoration of the state of Paradise, the time of universal holiness and purity, there will be no need or room for prohibitions or restrictions. This idea was taken up by Sabbatai Zevi and developed with even more vigor and insistence by his followers. The upshot was that the sign of belief in

Sabbatai Zevi as the true messiah was public transgression of traditional prohibitions, such as consuming nonkosher foods and eating on fast days. Many Sabbateans went further and argued that sexual restrictions such as the prohibition of adultery were abrogated in the messianic era that had arrived. As Scholem summarizes one Sabbatean author: "In the perspective of the paradisiac order of things where the Tree of Life has supplanted the Tree of Knowledge, even the biblical laws of incest—symbolizing the restraints of sexual morality—lose their unconditional validity. The laws of incest were imposed on Adam in this lower world, but in the higher world of 'asiluth there is no incest."[12] Playing out their antinomian dramas, the Sabbateans ransacked the texts of the Jewish tradition to find support for their ideas. Of course, the dark episodes in the Davidic lineage did not escape their attention. As Scholem summarizes:

> In order to accomplish his mission, the messiah would have to adopt "crooked" ways [because his soul comes from the mysterious place of tehiru, the cosmic void or vacuum]. It is not without reason that the origins and history of David, the founder of the messianic dynasty, were "crooked" by ordinary human standards: Lot's incest with his daughters (from which descended the ancestress Ruth the Moabite), Judah and Tamar, Boaz and Ruth . . . and [David's] lapse with Bathsheba. . . . Let no one, therefore, rashly cast aspersions at the Lord's Anointed [Sabbatai Zevi]. (*Sabbatai Sevi*, 819)

The Hasidic movement distanced itself from the antinomian excesses of Sabbateanism. Yet while working to avoid sectarian-heretical implications, it nonetheless drew upon the same basic store of Kabbalistic-Zoharic-Lurianic ideas in its own theology. Regarding the messianic idea, therefore, we find a similar notion of light coming from the darkness. The late nineteenth-century Polish Hasidic master, Rabbi Zadok ha-Kohen of Lublin, for example, writes in his *Tzidkat ha-Tzadik*:

> In the period leading up to the messianic advent, the main task is to extract the precious from the base (cf. Jer. 15:19). The redemption will emerge precisely from the place of lust and sin—by means of repentance. This is what the Talmud means when it says "The son of David will come in a generation which is entirely guilty" (Sanhedrin 98a). David is the archetype for the messianic soul because he showed how to make repentance into a life principle of sacrificial offering. The souls of people living in the era of the messianic advent will come from the feet [of Primordial Adam, the

universal soul]. . . . The Messiah himself is born from such a [lowly] place—you know what the Zohar says about Lot and his daughters: they are the source of the *yetzer ha-ra*, the evil inclination, and it's from there that the roots of the son of David grow. And just that is the realization of ultimate fulfillment—that the root of evil will be transformed to good. . . . At that time the lowest will become the highest. (no. 111)[13]

Once again, while this passage mentions biblical characters such as Adam, Lot, and David, its primary concern is to understand messianic redemption as a historical-theosophical process. One may conclude that while Kabbalistic and Hasidic authors were most astute biblical readers, acutely alive to patterns and allusions, their emphasis on theory limits their ability to shed light on the biblical characters as actual personalities. It therefore would be interesting to see what happens if we return to the Bible with the intertextual awareness of the midrash and Kabbalah, but bracketing the theoretical ideas of the Kabbalists.

Whatever one thinks of the doctrine of transmigration and the emergence of eschatological light from primordial evil, abstract ideas such as these seem not entirely at home in the biblical period. So the rest of this essay will attempt to explore the connections between Ruth and Genesis from a perspective immanent to the texts themselves. Our focus will be on names and people, on how reputations can be tarnished and redeemed by intergenerational dialogue and posthumous restoration. Because such developments are emergent, requiring trust and patience and collective memory, it follows that the Tanakh itself—the relational latticework spanning vast stretches of time—is itself one of the key actors in our drama.

Lot is hardly a heroic figure. It is not just that he allows himself to be intoxicated on two successive nights so that, stone drunk, he has sex with his own daughters. What was he doing in that cave in the first place? We recall that the town of Zoar ("tiny") was originally intended to be included in the destruction of Sodom and Gomorrah, but that Lot had pleaded that it be spared so that he could take refuge there. But we are told "now Lot went up from Zoar and settled on the mountain, for he was afraid to remain in Zoar, he dwelt in a cave, he with his two daughters" (Gen. 19:30). That is, his lack of faith in God caused him to abandon Zoar and hide in a cave, where he slipped into the compromising situation of the rest of the narrative. This is the same Lot who had earlier separated from Abraham and whose misadventure as a captive required

Abraham to rescue him. Let us recall that Lot is Abraham's nephew, several times called his "brother." Yet he and Abraham part from each other—Lot choosing to live in Sodom. As Genesis 13:10–11 tells us, "So Lot raised his eyes and saw the entire plain of the Jordan, that is was well-watered everywhere, before the Lord destroyed Sodom and Gomorrah, like the Garden of the Lord, like the land of Egypt, going to Zoar. So Lot chose for himself the whole plain of the Jordan, and Lot journeyed eastward; so they parted, one from his brother."

But parting from Abraham would seem to imply parting from the promise of blessing of Gen. 12:1–4, "and you shall be a blessing . . . through you shall be blessed all the families of the earth." In Abraham's own family there is a parting of the ways, his brother/nephew moving to Sodom, of all places. Recall that as Abraham returns from the rescue of Lot, he is met by two kings—the king of Sodom and the king of Salem. The king of Sodom says, quite abruptly and crassly, "Give me the people and take the possessions for yourself." (Gen. 14:21) But another king greets Abraham, as well. Malkizedek, the king of Salem, takes bread and wine and uses them to express greeting, thankfulness, and blessing. Genesis 12:1–4, which can be seen as the mission statement of Judaism, of all Abrahamic religion, begins to be realized in Salem. But, as we are soon to learn, the king and people of Sodom have taken their "Garden of Eden" and made it into hell.

Genesis 14 is actually a tale of two cities: Salem versus Sodom. Lot has separated himself from Abraham and the Abrahamic blessing and has aligned himself with Sodom. Then Ruth's actions and words, which occasion so many blessings throughout her story, are a return, many centuries later, to the Abrahamic blessing.

The intertextual allusions between Ruth and Genesis are bidirectional. A key word in the Ruth narrative is *yad'a*—"to know," which immediately evokes the usage of *yada/da'at* as "carnal knowledge "in Genesis. Boaz is introduced to us in 2:1 as *"u-le-Na'omi moda' le-ishah"*—"Naomi had a kinsman of her husband's." Later, when Naomi instructs Ruth on her night visit to the threshing-floor at 3:3, she says, *al tivad'i la-'ish,* "do not make yourself known to the man until he has finished eating and drinking." But all this should remind us of Lot and his two daughters—Genesis 19:33—"That night they gave their father wine to drink, and the older one went in and lay with her father; he **did not know** when he lay or when he rose—**ve-lo yad'a** *bᵊshikhvah u-vᵊkumah*. The usage here is ironic and mildly derisive—Lot knew his daughters carnally, mechanically, but without rising to conscious awareness or relationship. By contrast, while Boaz as well has eaten and drunk, *va-yitav libo*—his heart was merry—nevertheless, nothing carnal happens that evening. Boaz assures Ruth that he will act nobly, responsibly, but only after all legal issues have been addressed. "And now, my daughter, do not fear, whatever you say, I will do for you; for everyone at my people's gate **knows** that you are a woman of valor." To forestall any mischievous rumors, Boaz instructs, "Let it not be **known** [al yivod'a] that the woman came to the threshing floor" (3:14).

To sum up: Lot has carnal knowledge of his (actual biological) daughters but is oblivious; he has no higher-order knowledge. By contrast, Boaz delays carnal knowledge until the appropriate time, while he fully acknowledges Ruth's virtue and value as an individual.

Thus, Boaz redeems Lot, and Ruth redeems Lot's daughters, and if we were in any danger of missing any of this, the narrator winks at us—there is a rather arch reference to Lot at 3:7—"Boaz ate and drank and his heart was merry. He went to lie down at the end of the grain pile, and she came stealthily, uncovered his feet, and lay down." The Hebrew for the phrase "and she came stealthily"—va-teshev ba-**lot**— should give us a start. The Hebrew word lot, in the sense of secrecy or stealth, occurs but three times in Scripture, twice in the book of Samuel with reference to David and here in the book of Ruth. This gentle wink of the narrator's eye should not be missed.

Judah is mentioned in the very first verse of Ruth: va-yelekh 'ish mi-Bet Lehem Yehudah—"and a man went from Bethlehem of Judah/Judea"—of course Judah is here a geographic term, a name for a region within the land of Israel, but especially in light of the ten-generation genealogy at the end of the scroll, it is impossible not to think of the eponymous ancestor who stands at the head of the lineage.

In Genesis 38—the Judah and Tamar episode—we recall that Judah was trying to locate the woman he thought was a harlot, make payment of a kid from the flock, and retrieve his seal, cord, and staff. But his friend was not able to find her. Judah then says at 38:23: tikah lah, pen nihyeh la-**buz**—"Let her keep them, lest we become a laughing-stock." This last term is buz in Hebrew. Instead of Buz, however, Ruth enabled Judah's latter-day descendent to rise to the calling of Boaz—the man of courage and dignity.

This reading is strengthened by noticing other intertextual echoes between Genesis and the book of Ruth. Commentators as early as the midrash and as recent as Robert Alter have noted the centrality of the word haker—"recognize"—in various grammatical forms and usages in Genesis as a whole and especially in chapter 38. Similarly, in Ruth, in the initial meeting of Ruth and Boaz, Ruth says (2:10) "Why have I found favor in your eyes [le-hakireini], to take special note of me, to recognize me [vᵊʾanokhi nokhriya]—though I am a foreigner." And in 3:14, "she lay at his feet until the morning and arose before one man could recognize another"—bᵊ-terem **yakir** ʾish et reʿehyu. Judah at first does not recognize his own daughter-in-law and has sex with Tamar, whereas Boaz does recognize Ruth as a noble, compassionate woman and refrains from sex until the proper moment.

Finally, let us start to look at some broader patterns. We first meet Judah as the one who comes up with idea of selling his brother Joseph into slavery; then he has a rather squalid encounter with a harlot who turns out to be his own daughter-in-law, whom he almost has put to death by fire for a pregnancy which he caused. And yet, the whole point of placing Genesis 38 at this location is to establish Judah's turnaround, his *teshuvah*. In his role as family head and chieftain, when confronted with Tamar and her evidence, he could have easily said "I never had sex with that woman"; his acknowledgment of *tzadkah mimeni*—"she is more righteous than I"—rings through the millennia as an act of integrity, humility, and repentance. This sets the stage for the unfolding of the rest of the book of Genesis, and especially for Judah's breathtaking plea at Gen. 44:18–34, begging Egypt's viceroy to spare the life of Benjamin, his half-brother from Rachel, and to take himself—Judah—as a slave instead. This is a replay of the sale of Joseph twenty-two years earlier with Benjamin substituting for Joseph and with Judah reversing his role: Instead of selling a son of Rachel into slavery, he now saves his half-brother by offering himself. This is the perfect act of *teshuvah*, return, repentance. One can argue, then, that the real hero of the Joseph story is not Joseph, but Judah, and the inspiration for Judah's turnaround is none other than Tamar.

The process of redemption begun by Tamar is advanced by Ruth. She motivates Boaz to redeem Lot. This explains the prominence of *shov*— "return"—verbs in the book of Ruth. A particularly notable instance is at 2:6—Boaz has just noticed Ruth for the first time and asks about her identity. His servant replies, "She is a Moabite girl, who returned [*ha-shavah*] with Naomi from the fields of Moab." Commentators are puzzled by the fact that Ruth was not returning—she had never been in Judea before. But if regarded canonically, Ruth's presence was the return of Lot's family, Lot's progeny: the reunion of the Abrahamic family. So Boaz, like Lot, has indulged in drink, his heart is merry, and he too sleeps with a woman at his feet, but unlike Lot, Boaz is a *yodeʿa*—he knows who Ruth really is, he knows the right thing to do, and he knows when and how to do it.

All of this may explain in part why Judaism settled on David as the messianic precursor. We recall that there are some biblical strands where God alone acts as savior (see Exod. 14:30). If a human figure were deemed necessary, why not Moses, whom the midrash calls *moshi'an ha-rishon,* Israel's first savior? Why do Jews not pray for the return of Moses from occultation or for the emergence of a worthy scion from his lineage? The paradoxical answer seems to be that Moses is too close to perfection to do the job. Yes, he slew the Egyptian in Exodus 2:11–12, but commentators largely view the episode as a justified intervention to save the life of the victim, the Hebrew slave. Yes, he smote the rock in Numbers 20, but generations of readers have yet to figure out for sure exactly what the sin was. Moses apparently did not know, either, for he never apologizes for what he did (see, for instance, Deuteronomy 3:26).

Whatever flaws we may be able to discern in Moses, we sense that we already know them all; the FBI background search will not contain surprising new disclosures, no awkward revelations, certainly nothing with a whiff of scandal. Rectitude is wonderful, but what rectitude does not know is the yearning for redemption. For this reason, those whose story is painted only in bright colors could not serve in the role of re-deemer. It is rather the Judah-Peretz-Davidic lineage, with its emphasis on re-cognition (*hakarah*), appropriate knowledge (*yedi'ah*), and repen-tance (*teshuvah*), that could embody the notion of redemption emerging out of imperfection. It is this line which could sustain the notion of the redemption of humans as and by "broken vessels" in the Zohar's telling phrase.

Only an imperfect messiah can redeem an imperfect world and him-self as well. Judah's two-word *tzadkah mi-meni,* "she is more righteous than I," is excelled in brevity only by David's one-word cry of confession when confronted with his sin by the prophet Nathan—*hatati,* "I have sinned." This does not erase or remove the sin or even block its effects (as we might say today, its karmic consequences) from unfolding in the rest of the Davidic history. The child with Bathsheba dies, trouble in various forms strikes David's family *from within*—the rape of Tamar, the revolt of Absalom—but the royal line, the messianic line, continues through Solomon, son of David and Bathsheba, the same Bathsheba who in Chronicles is called Bat-Shu'a, the designation used for Judah's wife in Genesis 38.

The scroll of Ruth exemplifies the redemptive power of compassionate memory: "a child is born to Naomi . . . he shall be to you a restorer of life [*meshiv nefesh*]." This is not a messianism of muscularity, militarism, and conquest, but of redemptive compassion and revisioning—of spreading the corners or folds of the garment. This is why Ruth is the progenitor of the Messiah, because the Messiah is the ultimate *meshiv nefesh*, restorer of life and dignity when hope seems lost.

"To restore the name" need not be understood in the context of the transmigration of the soul, of reincarnation. To restore the name is to reach across the generations, and across the interpersonal divide, and at times across the divide between aspects or periods within one's own self, in active recognition, provoking true transformation. This is what compassionate redemption means.

And so, too, the "dark ladies" of my title. Lot's daughters do their deed at night, in a cave. Tamar covers herself with a veil and sits at the crossroads. Ruth comes from Moab, in the unstated shadow of Deuteronomy 23:4, " An Ammonite or Moabite shall not enter the congregation of the Lord." She, too, comes at night, in stealth. Although one could look at Lot's daughters, at Tamar, and at Ruth as four figures of the biblical demimonde, they return, through kindness and grace, to give and to receive blessing. And all of this is conveyed in echoes, in the dappled interplay of light and shadow, figure and ground, in eyes, in blessed gazes, and wellsprings.

At the end of the book of Malachi, the last of the prophets, we are enjoined to "Remember the Torah of Moses my servant; which I commanded him at Horeb for all Israel, decrees and ordinances." But then Malachi goes on to speak of Elijah,[14] the great day of the Lord, and the "restoration of the hearts of parents to children and children to parents." I would suggest that this last note—of return, reconciliation, of revisioning—alludes to the Torah of Ruth, the Torah of kindness, after Proverbs 31: *pihah pat-ḥah bᵊ-ḥokhmah, vᵊtorat ḥesed al lᵊshonah*: "She opens her mouth with wisdom, and the Torah of kindness is on her tongue." So the task is to remember both the Torah of Moses and that of Ruth, to read the Torah of Moses in light of the Torah of Ruth. That is why on Shavuot, the festival of first fruits, also the festival of the covenant, the giving of the Torah, we read the scroll of Ruth, the Torah of kindness, to prepare the way to receive the Decalogue itself as a Torah of kindness.

In the end, Ruth reminds us that nothing is more beautiful than friendship, that grace begets grace, that blessing flourishes in the place between memory and hope, that light shines most from broken vessels. What else is the Messiah about?

RUTH AMID THE GENTILES

Peter S. Hawkins

In the penultimate stanza of his "Ode to a Nightingale," Keats imagines that the bird's "immortal" music, consoling him in his quite mortal solitude, may also have been heard by "hungry generations" long before him:

> The voice I hear this passing night was heard
>> In ancient days by emperor and clown:
> Perhaps the self-same song that found a path
>> Through the sad heart of Ruth, when, sick for home,
>> She stood in tears amid the alien corn.[1]

Critics of the poem are surprised by this "unexpected allusion" to the Book of Ruth.[2] They conjecture that the poignancy of the young woman that caught his fancy—this stranger in a strange land, lost in the midst of someone else's abundance, alone with her tears and "sick for home."

What Keats critics fail to note, however, is that the tearful scene to which the poet alludes is nowhere to be found in the biblical book. The only occasions when Ruth is said to weep are the two times when Naomi urges her to return to her "mother's house" in Moab (1:8), to the place she comes from, where she is most likely to find a husband and reconstruct her former life. Rather than being "sick for home," as Keats imagined, the biblical Ruth wants only—and famously (1:16–17)—to leave "home" behind her: "Entreat me not to leave *you*," she tells Naomi, "where you go, I will go; where you lodge, I will lodge" (1:16, emphasis mine). She "clings" to her foreign mother-in-law (as a man is said to cling to his wife in Gen 2:24); she is "determined" to go with her to an otherwise unknown Judah. Furthermore, as soon as she and Naomi arrive in Bethlehem, Ruth hits the alien corn as if it were her native element. She has neither time nor reason to weep. Instead, she gleans a feast, finds a husband, is helped by the Lord to conceive a male child, and becomes the great-grandmother of a king.

How could Keats have gotten it so wrong? One can appeal, of course, to poetic license, the writer's freedom to transform any figure whatsoever into an avatar of his own "sole self." But clearly this is easier to do when the figure in question in some sense is up for grabs—not quite as free form as the unnamed "emperor and clown," but no household name, either. Keats could have his way with Ruth, so to speak, because she was, and is, a relative unknown "amid the Gentiles."

The book of Ruth, of course, is included in the Christian Old Testament, although not in the place accorded it in the Hebrew Tanakh, among the Writings (*Kethuvim*) and along with the other scrolls (*megillot*) connected with major feasts: the Song of Songs for Passover, Ruth for Pentecost or Shavuot, Lamentations for Tisha B'Av, Ecclesiastes for Sukkot, Esther for Purim. In the Christian liturgical year, by contrast, Ruth is not associated with Pentecost or indeed with any other feast, nor has she ever been "required reading" in the Eucharistic liturgy. In the Christian Bible—which in its first testament follows the ordering of the Septuagint—Ruth is positioned between Judges and 1 and 2 Samuel. Given this placement, the book offers a historical link between "the days when the Judges ruled" (Ruth 1:1)[3] and the Davidic monarchy that eventually issued forth from the union of Ruth and Boaz. For readers of the Christian Old Testament, therefore, Ruth provides an immediate and welcome alternative perspective on the often horrendous period of the Judges, when "every man did what was right in his own eyes" (Judges 21:25)—a warmly female antidote to the horrors enacted against the Levite's concubine (19:1–30) and the women of Shiloh (21:15–25). The book also suggests why David, when running for his life from King Saul, would have entrusted the safekeeping of his own parents to the king of the despised Moabites (1 Sam. 22:3–4): They were part of his own lineage.[4] Even though the genealogy that concludes Ruth traces a patriarchal line through Boaz—"Salmon [was the father] of Boaz, Boaz of Obed, Obed of Jesse, and Jesse of David" (4:21–22)—David's great-grandmother made him a descendant of Gentiles as well as of the Chosen People.

This fact did not escape Christian notice. At the very beginning of the Gospel of Matthew, and thus of the New Testament itself, Ruth makes her sole appearance in Christian Scripture as one of the Hebrew matriarchs in Jesus' family tree. Matthew begins: "An account of the genealogy of Jesus the Messiah, the son of David, the son of Abraham" (1:1). Matthew's use of such an "account" is part of his larger strategy to link Christian revelation to the Hebrew Bible and its distinctive ways—in this instance, to the succession of "begats" familiar to readers of Genesis or Chronicles. As in the Tanakh, Matthew uses genealogy to structure history into epochs, to suggest a collective personality for the one who is the end of the line, as well as to indicate God's providential hand at work in passing generations. Thus, Jesus, as son of Abraham, is heir to the patriarch's universal legacy ("through you all nations shall be blessed," Gen. 12:3) as well, in his identity as son of David, as heir to the Davidic dynasty's unique "scepter."[5]

It is precisely as an ancestor of David, and through David to Jesus as Messiah, that Ruth takes her place in Dante's fourteenth-century *Paradiso*. In the poem's penultimate canto, the pilgrim sees the blessed seated among the petals of the heavenly rose according to the spiritual hierarchy of their merits. This "candida rosa" (*Par.* 31.1) is divided into two *equal* parts. Half of the blessed are composed of the ancient Hebrews, beginning with Adam and Eve, all of whom looked forward to the coming of the one who, in the fullness of time, would strike the serpent's head (as promised by the Lord in the "protoevangelion" of Gen. 3:15). They all believed "in Cristo venturo," in a Christ who was yet to come (32.24). The other half of the heavenly city is populated by those who believed in a Christ who had already come, "Cristo venuto" (32.27). Poised at the midpoint between these two ranks of believers—at the turning point of the Testaments—is the Virgin Mary. Descending from her toward the center of the rose is a line of Hebrew women who are the matriarchal ancestors of Christ. Just below Mary we find Eve, Rachel, Sarah, Rebecca, Judith, and Ruth—or, as she is identified here in her relationship to David, as "colei / che fu bisava al cantor che per doglia / del fallo disse *'Miserere mei'* [she who was great-grandmother of the singer who, through sorrow for his sin, cried *'Miserere mei'* 32.10–12]".[6] Ruth is not merely a generalized foremother; she is quite specifically David's *bisava*, his great-grandmother.

Dante may well have chosen to privilege this matriarchal line because of what he found in the opening of the Gospel of Matthew, for a peculiar feature of the evangelist's reworking of Hebrew genealogy is his inclusion of women in what is traditionally a masculine preserve. And so, among the three sets of fourteen generations that Matthew constructs for the time between Abraham and Jesus, he names Tamar, Rahab, Ruth, "the wife of Uriah" (Bathsheba), and, at the end of the line, Mary. Each of these women is introduced as a partner with whom a father generates sons. Thus, "Judah [is] the father of Perez and Zerah *by Tamar*" (1:3), "Salmon the father of Boaz *by Rahab*" (1:5), "Boaz the father of Obed *by Ruth*" (1:5), and "David . . . the father of Solomon *by the wife of Uriah*" (1:6). In view of Jesus' divine paternity, however, the succession does not culminate in a father and his sexual partner, but rather in a *husband* and wife: "Jacob the father of Joseph the husband of Mary, of whom Jesus was born, who is called the Messiah" (1:16).

Early Christian commentators on Matthew recognized that the four Old Testament women conspicuous in the list of the Messiah's ancestors were not the obvious matriarchal choices—Sarah, Rebekah, Leah and Rachel—with their impeccable bloodline. They were also aware of slurs by those whom John Chrysostom (347–407) speaks of as "the Jews" who, "being of so unfriendly spirit towards Him," called into suspicion the virtue, not to mention the virginity, of Mary.[7] For these reasons, it became a point of honor among commentators on Matthew to draw attention to skeletons in the family closet—to insist that the Savior's foremothers were women who could be prostitutes (such as Rahab) or at least play the part when the occasion warranted (such as Tamar), women who had dubious ethnic origins (such as Ruth), or who were drawn into illicit sexual activity (such as Bathsheba). According to Jerome (ca. 340–420), "It should be noted that none of the holy women [of Israel] are taken into the Savior's genealogy, but rather such as Scripture has condemned, that he who came for sinners being born of sinners might so put away the sins of all."[8] John Chrysostom argues that Christ came not to escape our disgraces, but to bear them away: "it is not only because he took flesh upon him, and became man, but because he vouchsafed also to have such kinsfolk, being in no respect ashamed of our evils."[9] Likewise, no one's background should be held against him, for what matters is the disposition of the soul, one's pursuit of virtue: "For such a man, though he have an alien for his ancestor, though he have a mother who is a prostitute, or what you will, can take no hurt thereby."[10]

"Though he have an alien for his ancestor": With this aside, Chrysostom draws attention to an identity that is shared in one way or the other by all the Old Testament women in Matthew's genealogy. Tamar and Rahab were Canaanites; Ruth was a Moabite, a descendant of Lot's incestuous union with a daughter, and therefore of a people singularly reviled in the law on several counts—indeed, inadmissible to the assembly of the Lord "even to the tenth generation" (Deuteronomy 23:3–6). Although Bathsheba was undoubtedly an Israelite, "daughter of Eliam" and close to the royal court, she was also, as the genealogy names her, the "wife of Uriah"—who was, of course, "Uriah *the Hittite*" (2 Samuel 11:3, emphasis mine).

Matthew's tracing of a Gentile thread through the tapestry of the Chosen People—his looking back on a succession of aliens who went on to become central to the history of Israel—is one of the ways the evangelist establishes a mixed origin and identity for Jesus. On the one hand, he stipulates (on five occasions in his first four chapters) that this or that event took place in order to fulfill the word of a Hebrew prophet. On the other, his genealogy makes clear that the Gentile mission of Jesus and the early church developed out of a venerable matriarchy of non-Hebrews.

Ambrose (ca. 340–397) takes in the Gentile impropriety implicit in Matthew's genealogy and revels in it. He marvels at how the Jewish Boaz could have brought himself to marry a Moabite, wonders over how the Evangelist could admit a union between Jew and Gentile "which in the eye of the law was bastard." Wonder, however, quickly moves to delight:

> For this woman who was an alien, a Moabitess, a nation with whom the Mosaic law forbade all intermarriage, and shut them totally out of the Church, how did she enter into the Church, unless that she were holy and unstained in her life above the law? Therefore she was exempt from this restriction of the Law, and deserved to be numbered in the Lord's lineage, chosen from the kindred of her mind, not her body. To us she is a great example, for that in her was prefigured the entrance into the Lord's Church of all of us who are gathered out of the Gentiles.[11]

Note how many roles Ruth plays in this analysis. She provides an example of the outsider whom God brings into the fold, an example of one who leads a holy life quite apart from the doing of the law—of someone who demonstrates the superiority of mind over body, of spiritual life over bloodlines. Most important of all, Ruth prefigures "all of us who are gathered out of the Gentiles." Moabites become the New Israel of the church.

Like Ambrose, John Chrystosom also treats Ruth as a patron of those who are children of Abraham not after the flesh but according to the spirit. In his reading, Ruth is the bride of Christ, and Boaz a figure of the Lamb of God who redeemed his bride and restored her to life:

> See, for instance, what befell Ruth, how like it is to the things which belong to us. For she was born of a strange race, and reduced

to the utmost poverty, yet Boaz when he saw her neither despised her poverty not abhorred her mean birth, as Christ having received the Church, being both an alien and in much poverty, took her to be partaker of much blessings. But even as Ruth, if she had not left her father, and renounced household and race, country and kindred, would not have attained unto this alliance; so the Church too, having forsaken the customs which men had received from their fathers, then, and not before, became lovely to the Bridegroom.[12]

In an astonishing revision, Chrysostom turns the law of Israel ("the customs which men had received from their fathers") into the darkness meant to be left behind, along with idols, in Moab. Like Ruth, "we" must abandon Jewish "household and race" if we are to become "lovely to the Bridegroom" and be partakers "of much blessing."

What is only incipiently allegorical in Chrysostom's reading becomes full-blown allegory elsewhere as a New Testament or ecclesiastical interpretation provides a gloss on each figure in the story.[13] We see this perspective as early as Saint Paul who, writing to the Corinthian church about the Exodus, assures them that ancient history is as contemporary as they are, be they Jew or Greek. Why? "These things occurred as examples *for us*" (1 Cor. 10:6, emphasis mine). The Old Testament figure, in other words, is seen as "fulfilled" in Christian understanding and appropriation. Apart from the supersessionism that is more than implicit in all these accounts, be they by Paul or by the church fathers who followed in his wake, traditional Christian interpretations of Ruth tend to drain the biblical text of particularity, despite their relevance as "examples for us." With a kind of plodding predictability, characters become ideas, and individual stories are subsumed into a theological master plot that offers few surprises.

There is also an alarming amount of animus against the Jews, as in the popular and influential *Glossa ordinaria*. According to the *Glossa*, the famine that drove Elimelech and his family out of Bethlehem in the first place indicates "a hunger for the word of God since now the Law was marred through the agency of Jewish transmission."[14] Naomi is the voice of the synagogue, avowing the truth, but following error. She has become sterile, unable any longer to bear sons for God. Boaz is the church, who welcomes the Gentile Ruth; alternately, Boaz is a figure of Christ. In this latter role, he and his servants winnow the synagogue of the Jews where the barley of the law had been gathered, separating kernels of true nourishment from worthless chaff. Ruth, the daughter-in-law of the synagogue, marries Boaz, who was born of the synagogue but who, as Christ, rescues the law from what has become its barrenness. Thus, when we are told in 4:15 that Ruth proved to be more to Naomi than seven sons, we are to understand that those inferior seven represent "the multitude who were nourished in the doctrine of the Law of the Old Testament but who did not believe in the word of the Lord and immolated their sons and daughters to demons and finally killed Christ and persecuted the prophets."[15]

None of this anti-Jewish sentiment is to be found in the *De anima obediente* of Hugh of Saint Victor (1096–1141), a sermon most probably delivered to his fellow monks at the Abbey of Saint Victor. Here, no invidious comparisons are made between blind, superanuated Synagoga and the fair Ecclesia. Instead, Hugh's Ruth is simply presented as model of the obedient soul and as such as an inspiration both for individuals and for the church at large. In this reading, Naomi is interpreted as the ecclesiastical teacher and shepherd: When Ruth clings to her, she shows the virtuous soul's readiness to obey the commandments of a spiritual superior. Boaz is Christ, and his fields of grain represent the Holy Scripture—the barley of the Old Testament and the wheat of the New. The reapers who work their way through these fields are Christian exegetes and preachers. When Boaz warns Ruth not to stray from his harvest or to separate herself from his maidservants, we hear a charge to avoid heretical teachers and their books. Boaz's threshing floor and the winnowing of his grain suggest the work of Christ, not only to free his church from evil men, but also to liberate the faithful soul from corrupt thoughts, falsity, and a "carnal" understanding of the Scriptures. When Ruth goes to Boaz at night, removes the cloak from his feet and lies down next to him, we are presented, as it were through a veil, with the mystery of our redemption in Christ—his Incarnation in the flesh, the soul's humble plea for union with him, and the promise of an eternal resting together. The soul in no way presumes such familiarity with the Master unless she first sees her Boaz "gladdened with food and drink and in a bed of rest and peace"; that is, unless the soul partakes of Christ's food and drink, which are nothing other than the practice of virtue, the doing of God's will.

Hugh ends this sermon by asking his flock to take the book of Ruth to heart, so that they themselves might be transformed, as Ruth herself was, from Moabite to Israelite, from widow to bride:

> Let us abandon our native land and our gods by renouncing our old evils and the bidding of demons. Let us follow our Shepherd,

by imitating him in those things that he does. Let us cling to him truly by loving him; let us obey him by doing all the things that he has commanded us. Let us dwell with him in Bethlehem by conversing honestly with him in holy church. In Boaz's field let us gather and winnow the ears of wheat and let us bring them into our house by reading the words of the Savior, by reflection on them, by storing them in memory. . . . And let us finally go down into the threshing floor by humbling ourselves in the recess of our heart. Let us remove the cloak from part of his feet . . . by seeking in humble contemplation the mystery of our redemption. And let us cast ourselves down there until the end of his passion by asking humbly, again and again, to be united to him . . . at last to be joined to him in marriage and to taste the inward sweetness of the untouched bridal chamber and the glory of bliss in heaven.[16]

With this rhetorical flourish, Hugh completes his sermon by turning the book of Ruth into another Song of Songs.

The bridal chamber, or at least the occasion of a Christian marriage, is probably how most Gentiles now encounter Ruth. This does not mean that she is included among the holy women of the Hebrew Bible who are invoked in the nuptial blessing of both the Eastern Orthodox and Roman rites. In the latter, for instance, the priest says of the bride, "may she be the beloved of her husband, as was Rachel; wise, as was Rebecca; long-lived and loyal, as was Sarah."[17] Although not officially invoked by the nuptial liturgy, Ruth is nonetheless often a by-popular-demand presence through the reading of 1:16–17, usually in the sonorous King James version: "Entreat me not to leave thee, or to return from following thee: for whither thou goest, I will go; and where thou lodgest, I will lodge: thy people shall be my people, and thy God my God." I seriously doubt that the happy couples who choose this text for its romantic value have any idea that it was spoken by one woman to another, let alone by a daughter-in-law to her deceased husband's mother. There are others, however, who find the "same-sex" dimension of Ruth's clinging to Naomi a point worth making. The text has become a standard choice for same-sex unions and commitment ceremonies, as well as a biblical model for human love that flourishes outside the framework of patriarchy. In this light, the book of Ruth is seen (like the Song of Songs) as celebrating a deep "unconventional" love that stands apart from the reproductive goals of heterosexual marriage.

Christian interest in Ruth within the academy has developed precisely along these lines. In *God and the Rhetoric of Sexuality*, Old Testament scholar Phyllis Trible recalls rabbinic midrash when she judges Ruth's decision to set off with Naomi as surpassing Abraham's following of God's call to leave country, kindred, and father's house. After all, Ruth received no divine summons whatsoever, nor any promise of future blessing: "One female has chosen another female in a world where life depends upon men. There is no more radical decision in all the memories of Israel."[18]

Ann Ulanov, a Jungian analyst and professor of psychology and religion, argues in *The Female Ancestors of Christ*, "Ruth brings into patriarchy a new feminine capacity that is durable, tough, and tender, a love for the feminine in concrete attachment between women that gives itself to God."[19] Ulanov examines each of the four Hebrew women in Matthew's genealogy in terms of what they contribute, spiritually and psychologically, to the "Tree of Life leading to Jesus":

> Ruth foreshadows Christ the redeemer in her identifying with [Naomi,] the relict at the bottom of the heap, the remnant of the remnant. She allies herself with a single old woman who, in a patriarchal society, is without power or position. This is also what Jesus experienced—born in the muck of a stable, living his life with nowhere to lay his head, a constant example that God moves through the left-out and forsaken parts of us to bring wholeness to all.[20]

Ulanov is less interested in Ruth as a "blood" ancestor of Christ than she is in Ruth as a forerunner of the savior who not only identifies with the lowly but also becomes one of them. The *ḥesed* or "loving-kindness" that Ruth famously embodies, in other words, serves as a precursor to the Incarnation, God's *ḥesed* made flesh.

Both Trible and Ulanov offer a theological feminism that highlights how God is at work in a Scripture that explores (to quote Trible) "women in culture, women against culture, and women transforming culture."[21] Ulanov gives an explicitly Christian interpretation that, while not reducing the text to allegory, nonetheless highlights the foreshadowing and aftershadowing of Christ in this Old Testament story. Ruth becomes someone to emulate, not as Hugh of Saint Victor's obedient soul, but in the ancient tradition of the *imitatio Christi*, as a person who identifies with God's Way so as to "figure" Jesus in the world. Furthermore, she does this as a woman who, along with Tamar, Rahab, and Bathsheba, brings into the patriarchal inheritance of Jesus "the deeply needed elements of the left-out feminine."[22]

The "left-out feminine" is prominent in Joan Chittister's *The Story of Ruth: Twelve Moments in Every Woman's Life*. The title of the book capitalizes on the interest that many middle-aged Americans have in their own life "passages" (to recall Gail Sheehey's 1976 bestseller); it also implies, with its constant reference to a female "us" and a womanly "we," that the male reader might want to look elsewhere for guidance. Whereas for Ulanov Ruth is an *imitatio Christi*, for Chittister, she is a soul sister and her story "the spiritual Magna Carta of women":

> Ruth lives on in Hebrew Scripture to remind us that origin and destiny are not the same thing. Naomi lives on to call generation after generation of women to begin again, whatever our ages, to make life for ourselves, to refuse to wait for someone else to swoop down and make us happy, to fear nothing and risk anything that develops the dream in our own hearts, to learn to believe in ourselves as women, to find ourselves in one another and in that way to become more of value to the world around us than we have ever been before, to see ourselves as the carriers of the Word of God still to be said, still to be heard.[23]

Chittister attempts to redress the balance in Scripture, which is otherwise so heavily weighted toward the male. With the particular insights of a Roman Catholic nun, she wants to give the female underclass in her own religious tradition a chance to discover a Scripture in which, for a change, women discover both God and themselves on their own. The book of Ruth, then, becomes a liberation text for women—not exactly a song of Miriam about the destruction of Pharaoh and his horsemen, not a cry to arms such as was sung by Deborah (Judges 5) or Judith (Judith 16), but a kinder, gentler rally cry to "make a life for ourselves," "fear nothing and risk anything," "believe in ourselves," "dream in our own hearts," "see ourselves" as "carriers of the Word of God"—as *Theotokoi*, godbearers. After generations of Marian piety have stressed the Blessed Mother's impossible purity, passivity, and perpetual virginity, for many women, Mary has ceased to be plausible as a person, let alone an exemplary figure. Ruth, on the other hand, goes from rags to riches (not to mention to sex and motherhood) in "twelve moments." Her story suggests that, in God's grace, each of "us" can too.

Chittister's claiming of Ruth "for every woman" redresses another imbalance in the Gentile appropriation of the story. This has to do not with a male-dominated biblical world, but with the world of poetry written by men. By claiming the Ruth the Moabite for women, she counteracts (however unwittingly) the interpretation of the book of Ruth given by Victor Hugo in his much-celebrated 1859 poem, "Booz endormi" (Boaz asleep). In a text Marcel Proust celebrated as the finest poem of the nineteenth century, Hugo eliminates Naomi entirely, introduces Ruth only in the eleventh hour (and then heavily veiled on the nocturnal threshing floor), and in fact makes the tale entirely about "le vieillard," the old man. Poetic license strikes again. Whereas Keats gave us a homesick Ruth weeping "amid the alien corn," Hugo makes her merely an adjunct to the scene. Furthermore, at the poem's heart, it is Boaz who receives a prophetic vision: From his loins grows an oak tree, on whose lower branches "a king sang forth" and on whose upper limbs "a god died": "Un roi chantait en bas, en haut mourait un Dieu."[24] With the prospect of this genealogical tree growing out of his body, extending from himself to David and on to Christ, Boaz hesitates before the promised future. Like Sarah, he complains that he is too old to bear children; like Mary he asks, "How can these things be?":

> 'Une race naîtrait de moi! Comment le croire?
> Comment se pourrait-il que j'eusse des enfants?'

> A race of people born from me? How believe such a thing?
> How could it be possible that I should have children?

One could say that Hugo gives us a midrash: He tells the largely untold story of Boaz, presents us with a male genealogical tree such as later would be imagined to grow out of Jesse, and reminds us that men have babies, too. Thus the poet presents us with an androgynous Boaz, as much matriarch as patriarch. Or is this yet another example of the way the patriarchal imagination inevitably makes it all about "us" men—even the story of Naomi and Ruth?

In closing: Neither the figure of Ruth nor the book that bears her name has been central to the Christian imagination, yet she plays any number of parts in the drama of the tradition. She is the paradigmatic Gentile who makes her way into the assembly of Israel; she is the ancestor of David and hence of Christ; she is a figure of the church, and of the obedient soul; and more recently, she is a woman who modestly, but courageously chooses another woman and, through her, moves in faithfulness to God. Who knows in the future, with feminist reading of the Scripture already asking us to notice so much that was once passed over, what other Ruths may yet spring up "amid the alien corn" of the Christian imagination?

PART THREE

Reimagining Ruth

RUTH SPEAKS IN YIDDISH:
THE POETRY OF ROSA YAKUBOVITSH
AND ITSIK MANGER

Kathryn Hellerstein

Erich Auerbach famously characterized the direct discourse of the Hebrew Bible as serving "to indicate thoughts which remain unexpressed," in contrast to speech in Homer's *Odyssey*, which serves "to manifest, to externalize thoughts."[1] However, when the first speech occurs in the book of Ruth 1:8, Naomi, pausing on the road home back toward Bethlehem, in the land of Judah, addresses her widowed Moabite daughters-in-law in what seems to me a forthright way that makes her thoughts and feelings utterly explicit: "Go, return each of you to her mother's house; the Lord deal kindly with you as ye have dealt with the dead, and with me. The Lord grant you that ye may find rest, each of you in the house of her husband."[2] When the daughters-in-law protest and insist that they will follow Naomi back to her people, Naomi's speech grows stronger with irony to make clear to the emotional young women that she will not be able to provide them with husbands herself: "Have I yet sons in my womb, that they may be your husbands? Turn back, my daughters, go your way; for I am too old to have a husband" (1:12). Even if she had a husband who could give her future sons, and even if she were to become pregnant that very night, Naomi asks, "Would ye tarry for them till they were grown? Would ye shut yourselves off for them and have no husbands?" (1:13). Caring, ironic, pragmatic, Naomi speaks her mind and urges the young women to think of themselves in the way that she is thinking of their futures: "Nay, my daughters; for it grieveth me much for your sakes, for the hand of the Lord is gone forth against me" (1:13). This forthright dialogue sets up the book of Ruth's overarching irony, one that even the ironic Naomi cannot foresee: In the end, Naomi *does* provide Ruth with a husband and thus her own people with a future—a king and a messiah.

Perhaps it is this quality of direct, foregrounded speech that drew two Yiddish poets to write their own versions of the conversations between the characters in the book of Ruth. The first, Roza Yakubovitsh (born in Parshnits, Protsker Province, Poland, 1889, died in Auschwitz, 1944), is a now forgotten figure who published one slim collection of poems, *Mayne gezangen* (My songs), in Warsaw in 1924. The second, Itzik Manger (born in Czernowitz, Rumania, 1901, died in Tel Aviv, 1969), is one of the best-known of the Yiddish poets, famous for his *Khumesh lider* (Bible or Pentateuch poems) and *Megile lider* (poems based on the Scroll of Esther), published in Warsaw in 1935 and 1936. His sequence *Rut* (Ruth) was written in North Africa in 1940 and first published in *Volkns ibern dakh* (Clouds above the roof, London, 1942).

Unlike most modern Yiddish poets, Yakubovitsh lived most of her life in a shtetl, Kalish, rather than in one of the urban centers of Polish Jewish life and Yiddish culture—Warsaw, Lodz, or Krakow. An observant Jew, Yakubovitsh was unlike her literary contemporaries, most of whom entered the secular avant-garde or political worlds. And in contrast to the prevailing literary tendencies of the 1920s, Yakubovitsh composed a sequence of poems spoken by biblical women. One of these poems, "Rut" (Ruth),[3] presents the story of Ruth in the form of a dialogue between Ruth and Boaz on the threshing floor of a barn that could as easily stand in the Polish countryside as on the outskirts of ancient Bethlehem.

Yakubovitsh's poem opens with a description of Ruth's nighttime approach to the barn through the yet unharvested fields, but quickly shifts from scene setting to portraying the emotions and sensual interiority of the character:

Af boazes felder, gerirt farn shnit,
Royshn in nakhtiker shtilkayt di zangen,
A meydl-geshtalt, fun beyslekhem gegangen,
Kumt tsu tsum shayer mit langzame trit.
Tsi iz es a vintl, vos veyet, tsi zi,
Vos halt ayn dem otem, bay boaz tsu fisn,
A vintl iz kil, un rut, akh zi glit,
Un kumt tsu ir har, on zayn visn:

🕊

On Boaz's fields, stirring before the harvest,
The stalks murmur in night's stillness.

Walking from Bethlehem, a girl's figure
Approaches the barn with slow steps.
Whether it is a winnowing breeze or she,
Who holds in her breath at Boaz's feet,
A breeze blows cool, and Ruth, how she glows
And approaches her master, without his knowing:[4]

The poem collapses time in these lines as Ruth walks through uncut stalks to the barn where the harvested grain is threshed. It also shifts drastically from the distant view of the "girl's figure" (l. 3) to the immediacy of Ruth holding her breath at Boaz's feet (l. 6). In the syntactic structure "Whether . . . or" (*Tsi . . . tsi*), conflating the image of the breeze (*vintl*) with Ruth's breath (ll. 5–6), the poem joins the external and the internal. The setting and the character become indistinguishable from each other, even in the opposite actions of the breeze that blows forth to winnow and the woman who "holds in her breath." As the breeze "blows cool," Ruth "glows," and the contrast of temperatures heats up the sensual tension. With such devices, Yakubovitsh guides the reader into Ruth's point of view.

The poet furthers the emphasis on Ruth through dialogue. In the biblical text, Ruth enters "softly" and says nothing until Boaz, startled awake, speaks, asking, "Who art thou?" (Ruth 3:9) In Yakubovitsh's poem, however, Ruth speaks first:

Du host dayne yungen bafoyln in feld,
Zol kloybn dos meydl fun vos ir gefelt,
Un ikh hob in feld do geklibn, geklibn
Un bin do di nakht oykh geblibn!
Boaz, o har, far dayn gutskayt un tugnt,
Shenk ikh in feld dir mayn yugnt!

〽

—You ordered your young men in the field,
"Let the girl gather what she pleases,"
And here in the field I have gathered, gathered,
I have also stayed here all night!
Boaz, oh, master, for your goodness and fairness
Here, in the field, I grant you my youth.[5]

By having Ruth initiate the dialogue, Yakubovitsh gives this character an authority that she lacks in the biblical text. In Scripture, Ruth follows the instructions of her mother-in-law, Naomi, to wash, anoint, and dress herself and to go to the threshing floor. She is to keep herself hidden from Boaz until he finishes eating and drinking, and then, when he lies down, she is to "uncover his feet" and lie down herself until "he will tell thee what thou shalt do" (3:1–4). With the last clause and the following verse, the traditional text emphasizes Ruth's obedience both to her mother-in-law and to Boaz: "And she said unto her, 'All that thou sayest to me, I shall do'" (3:5). Whereas the biblical Ruth obeys and reacts, Yakubovitsh's Ruth simply acts. She reminds Boaz of the orders he gave to his harvesters to allow her to glean the barley in the fields (ll. 9–10) and states that, as a consequence, she has "gathered and gathered" (l. 11) and now has stayed the night in the barn (l. 12). Ruth does not wait for Boaz to tell her what to do, but, in return for his generosity in the field, grants Boaz her "youth" (ll. 13–14).

While the poem allows Boaz indirect authority through Ruth's account of her response to him, it diminishes the authority of Naomi, who merits only one mention (l. 18):

> Boaz shpringt oyf: o got unzer hiter,
> Dos bistu fun moav gekumen nisht lang,
> Vos kleybst in mayn gortn a zang nokh a zang.
> Vos blaybst tsu der nomin getrey!
> Unzer got shteyt dir bay, unzer got shteyt dir bay,
> Ikh shver dir, az morgn nokh verstu mayn vayb,
> Dervayl ober blayb do, farblayb!

(

> Boaz leaps up: "Oh, God our Protector,
> It's not long since you came from Moab,
> You, gathering sheaf after sheaf in my garden,
> Remaining true to Naomi!
> Our God stands by you, our God stands by you,
> I swear to you, tomorrow you'll become my wife,
> But meanwhile, remain here, stay!"[6]

As Boaz jumps to his feet and replies to Ruth, he frames his reiteration of her deeds—arriving from Moab, gathering sheaves, and remaining true to Naomi—with a threefold invocation of God the protector, who stands by Ruth (ll. 15, 19). Unlike the biblical Ruth, who followed Naomi in order to adopt her mother-in-law's home, people, God, and place of death (1:16–17), Yakubovitsh's Boaz perceives Ruth herself as already protected and accompanied by God. Promising to marry her the next day, he entreats her to stay the night.

Stripped of the Bible's concern with a kinsman's obligation to a widow and the protection owed her (3:12–13), Boaz's invitation to Ruth— "remain here, stay"—conveys an eroticism that comes out even more explicitly in the final stanza of Yakubovitsh's poem:

> Shtil vert es vider in duftikn shayer,
> Shtil ergets tsindt zikh un lesht zikh a fayer,
> Nor boaz, er rut nisht, fargeyn zol di nakht,
> Es vakht iber im do zayn glik, o es vakht,
> Tsefisns shteyt rut mit ir freyd, tif farborgn,
> Un vart afn morgn.

ᘰ

> Quiet again in the fragrant barn,
> Quietly, somewhere, a fire lights and expires,
> But Boaz doesn't rest—let the night pass away,
> His luck watches over him here, oh it watches,
> At his feet stands Ruth with her joy, deeply hidden,
> And waits for the morning.[7]

Yakubovitsh expands into a six-line stanza what the biblical text summed up in a single verse that took the action into the predawn darkness— "And she lay at his feet until the morning; and she rose up before one could discern another" (3:14a). Whereas the biblical episode concludes with Boaz's words to Ruth and his gift of barley (3:14b–15), Yakubovitsh's poem ends with the tableau of a sleepless Boaz and a joyous Ruth, waiting patiently and expectantly. The phrase *tif farborgn* (deeply hidden) refers ambiguously both to Ruth's joy and to Ruth herself, hidden from all but Boaz in the frame of the story, but revealed to the reader through Yakubovitsh's poem. By evoking the sensory experience of the characters in the quiet, fragrant barn, the stanza brings the reader into the interiority of both Boaz and Ruth. Both characters are poised on the brink of change as, suggestively, a fire ignites and extinguishes "somewhere" (*ergets*) (l. 23).

Yakubovitsh removes from the biblical characters any framework of societal obligation—Naomi's instructions to Ruth and the levirate laws that Boaz espouses—in order to portray with a recognizable modernity the man's and, especially, the woman's sensuality. With this emphasis, Yakubovitsh reaches out both to the conventions of modern literature and to the conventions of Yiddish devotional literature. Modern literature reveals itself in the shifting of the third-person narrative point of view from the long view of the landscape to Ruth's breathing and emotions, in the cropping of the narrative to focus on mood, in the characters' liminality, and in the poem's open ending. The conventions of Yiddish devotional literature come forth in the focus on the story's sexual implications.

As in her other poems about biblical women, Yakubovitsh reveals her knowledge of the *Tsenerene* (Go forth and see). This so-called "women's Bible" is Rabbi Jacob ben Isaac Ashkenazi of Janow's 1622 compilation of biblical texts and rabbinic commentary in Yiddish translation, a book so popular among Eastern European women that it went through at least two hundred and ten editions and is still in print today.[8] Within its combination of moralism, mysticism, legend, exegesis, and prayer, as well as in its direct appeal to the emotions and contemporary experiences of the seventeenth-century reader, the *Tsenerene* does not hesitate to comment on matters of sexuality. Thus, the *Tsenerene* presents a passage on the modesty of Ruth who, unlike the other harvesters, refused to stoop or bend over to glean the sheaves, but either sat on the ground or stood for fear that her bare legs might be seen.[9] In its commentary on Boaz and Ruth, the *Tsenerene* explains Ruth 3:7 in explicitly sexual terms: "Boaz ate and drank and his heart was happy within him (3:7), from Torah and prayer. He came to lie down at the edge of a pile of grain. Stealthily she came, uncovered his feet, and lay down. The Sages say that the words, *his heart was happy*, (. . . from *tov*—'good'), mean that after eating he felt desire for a wife, who is called *tov*, as the verse says: . . . *He who has found a wife, has found goodness (Mishlei 18:22)*."[10]

When Boaz awakens to find Ruth at his feet and "grows frightened,"[11] the *Tsenerene* quotes "Our Sages" as the source for the following dialogue: "He touched her head to see if she had hair. Then he said: 'This is no demon,' for a demon is hairless. 'Who are you?' he asked. 'A woman,' she answered. 'Have you a husband?' he asked. 'No,' she said. 'Are you clean?' he asked. 'I am clean,' she replied."[12] A passage about the evil inclination then follows:

> The Sages say that there were three in the world whom the evil inclination wished to seduce: one was Yosef, the second Paltiel, and the third Boaz. . . . In Boaz's case, too, the evil inclination came to

him, spoke to him the entire night, and said, "You have no wife and she no husband. Why did she come to the granary, if not because she wished a husband? It is no sin, for she is not married." Then Boaz swore, by God, that he would not touch her. In this way he conquered his evil inclination.[13]

Except for the passage about Ruth's fear of exposing her legs, the *Tsenerene* discusses the erotic elements in the book of Ruth from Boaz's point of view. His midnight questions to Ruth about whether she has a husband and is ritually clean, that is, not menstruating, suggest that Boaz is considering whether to have sex with her. The remark that Boaz feels for the hair on Ruth's head to make sure that she is not a demon stands out as a cruel comment on the *Tsenerene*'s women readers. Eastern European Jewish custom decreed that a bride shear or even shave her head after the marriage ceremony, so that no man other than her husband would be able to glimpse even a strand of her hair escaping from a wig or a scarf and thus become aroused to commit adultery. By commenting that demons, like married women, are hairless, the *Tsenerene* encodes a slur against its own readers, although they probably did not perceive the analogy that may leap out to us.

The subsequent story about Boaz resisting the evil inclination instructs the reader that a man should control his urge to have sex with a woman to whom he is not married. Because the *Tsenerene* addressed primarily a female audience, the author draws a more general moral from this story about resisting the temptation to sin:

Every person should learn from this that when the evil inclination tries to persuade him [sic] to sin, he should immediately swear not to commit that sin. Then the evil inclination will not argue further with him, for the man knows well that a vow is awesome and if he breaks it God will punish him with terrible pains. For this reason, in the Ten Commandments, God specified only that He would punish those who worshiped false gods and those who swore falsely, equating the two sins. But to foil the evil inclination, one may swear.[14]

By swearing not to sin, the author teaches, a person risks not only sinning, but also breaking the commandment not to swear falsely. The consequences of this double violation would deter one from giving in to the evil inclination.

This episode is followed by a number of rabbinic stories about shrewish or licentious women, all of which teach that "if a woman is pious, she is without peer, and if she is wicked, she is also unequalled."[15] Reading the section of the *Tsenerene* devoted to the book of Ruth, a young woman thus would learn an emphatic lesson about the limitations, the foibles, and the dangers of being female.

In her 1924 poem "Rut," Roza Yakubovitsh, who was familiar with the *Tsenerene* since girlhood, dramatizes Ruth's point of view in the erotic, emotional encounter with Boaz in order to reclaim the character for women readers. This effort may have been a belated response to the 1910 proclamation by the great Warsaw Yiddish writer I. L. Peretz that Yiddish poets should "go back to the Bible . . . the most reliable point" and thus infuse their works with "tradition" and "Yiddish and Hebrew" in order to write "as . . . human being[s]" who are "on a Jewish path."[16] Yakubovitsh interprets Peretz's call in two ways. On the one hand, she grounds the modern poem in the biblical story and the devotional sources in order to connect the experience of contemporary Jews with centuries-old traditions. On the other hand, she renews the ancient Hebrew texts and subverts the *Tsenerene*'s Yiddish translation of medieval rabbinic interpretation. Yakubovitsh's poem unbinds the story of Ruth from the misogynist presentation of the story in Yiddish to generations of women readers and allows it to be read in a modern light by *mentshn* (human beings) walking "a Jewish path."

In Warsaw, eleven years after Yakubovitsh's *Mayne gezangen* appeared, Itsik Manger published *Medresh Itsik* (Itsik's midrash), a collection of poems retelling the stories of the Hebrew Bible. Like Yakubovitsh's poems, Manger's secular midrash connected twentieth-century Yiddish poetry to the traditional texts that, since the Jewish Enlightenment, had been jettisoned by cultural moderns. Manger's 1935 *Khumesh lider* and 1936 *Megile lider* brought biblical characters to life as dramatic personae in an Eastern European Jewish landscape. In these works, Manger merged the folk forms of the ballad and the Purim *shpil* (play) with a modern sensibility. Like Yakubovitsh's poems of 1924, Manger's poems rework the stories and characters from both the ancient Hebrew texts and the Yiddish folk interpretations of those texts. And like Yakubovitsh's poems, Manger's poems have a twofold impact: First, Manger extracts from the sacred texts a literary tradition in which to ground his secular Yiddish storytelling. Second, he rewrites the religious and folk texts in modern forms that made even the most skeptical Yiddish secularist reconsider the deracination of Yiddish culture. Unlike Yakubovitsh, though, Manger was a flamboyant bohemian, and his poems immediately found a wide audience in the lively Yiddish literary scene in interwar Warsaw.[17]

Manger left Warsaw for Paris in 1938, but in 1940, after northern France fell into Nazi hands, he fled south to Marseilles and then boarded a ship that landed him in North Africa. There, it seems, he wrote the series of poems titled *Rut* (Ruth).[18] The series opens with a note that presents an essential bit of information: "This fragment of the long poem *Ruth* I dedicate to my sister Sheyndl and her friend, the weaver Volke Glozman. Two-thirds of this long poem, together with other manuscripts, was lost to me in the course of my itinerant wanderings."[19]

The editor of the critical edition of Manger's poems, Khone Shmeruk, corroborates this account, stating that after Manger wrote *Rut* in North Africa in 1940, the surviving "fragment" was first printed in London in 1942 in the volume *Volkns ibern dakh* (Clouds above the roof) and a decade later reprinted in *Medresh Itsik* (Paris, 1951), and in *Lid un balade* (Songs and ballads, New York, 1952). Like Manger's dedicatory note, Shmeruk's 1984 bibliographic note states that the Ruth poems we have today are only a portion of the original. In fact, though, the extant *Rut* poems convey the sense of a whole, for they center on the themes of leaving home, of living *in der fremd*—in the foreignness—and of longing to return home.[20]

Like Yakubovitsh, who placed her Ruth in a Polish threshing barn, Manger sets his rewriting of Ruth in an Eastern European landscape, where, along with the biblical characters, the trees, the river, and the wind speak Yiddish. The landscape and the characters are anything but traditional, and the titles of the eight poems indicate how freely Manger adapted the story of Ruth. In fact, these titles reveal as much about Manger's anxious preoccupation as about the book of Ruth: "Naomi Recites 'God of Abraham,'" "Naomi Speaks to Her Daughters-in-Law," "Naomi Cannot Sleep," "Orpah Cannot Sleep," "Ruth Cannot Fall Asleep," "Naomi Leaves the Village," "At the Fork in the Road," and "Orpah Says Good-Bye."[21] The themes of restlessness, insomnia, indecision, and leave-taking in these titles show how Manger avoids the certainty of the biblical Ruth, who successfully crosses over from her home in Moab to Naomi's in Bethlehem and from her Gentile origins to her adoptive religion and people. Instead, he focuses on Naomi, the displaced Jew, and Orpah, who returns to her Gentile home. Of the eight poems, four contain "Naomi" in the titles, two contain "Orpah," and only one contains the name "Ruth." Whether or not these poems are in fact a fragment of a larger work now lost to us or whether they constitute the whole of a projected sequence that Manger wrote between 1940 and 1942, the eight extant poems have an autobiographical feel.

It hardly matters if the sister Sheyndl and her weaver friend Volke Glozman were actual people or Manger's inventions in his dedicatory note to *Rut*, or what their fate was in 1940. Manger's *Rut* expresses the emotional tenor of an Eastern European Jew who has lost his home and, specifically, of a Yiddish poet who has lost his manuscripts, his poetry, and the place of his culture and language.

This sense of loss manifests itself in the absence of dialogue within these poems. Unlike Manger's earlier sequences, *Khumesh lider* and *Megile lider*, which are loud with verbal interaction between the characters and between the characters and the inanimate elements of their environment (trees, mills, mirrors, stars), the poems in *Rut* are strangely silent. Here one does not find the chatter, arguments, song bursts, soliloquies— the instruments of drama, performance, and human stories. Instead, one finds introspection, observation, memory, and insomnia. The characters' exchanges are brief and even incomplete. With the exception of the final poem, the characters lack the energy even to talk to themselves, much less to each other. The absence of Manger's characteristic dialogue seems especially strange when we recall the explicit and dramatic nature of the dialogue in the book of Ruth itself.

This lack of dialogue contrasts with Manger's overt concern with the act of speaking, evident in the titles of the *Rut* poems. Seven of the eight titles include verbs, three of which describe speech acts: "Nomi *zogt* 'got fun avrom'" (Naomi *recites* 'God of Abraham') (*zogt*, "says" or "recites"), "Nomi *redt* tsu ire shnurn" (Naomi *speaks* to her daughters-in-law) (*redt*, "speaks"), and "Orpe *gezegnt zikh*" (Orpah *says good-bye*) (*gezegnt zikh*, "says good-bye," "bids farewell"). While three of the other titles denote the inability to sleep, their repeated negation suggests the characters' liminal states of mind in which they talk to themselves—"Nomi *ken nisht shlofn*" (Naomi *cannot sleep*), "Orpe *ken nisht shlofn*" (Orpah *cannot sleep*), "Rut *ken nisht antshlofn vern*" (Ruth *cannot fall asleep*). And in the seventh title, "Nomi *farlozt* dos dorf" (Naomi *leaves* the village), the verb *farlozn* denotes the act of departure and connotes loss through its root *lozn* (to lose). Although the eighth title, "Afn sheydveg" (At the fork in the road), contains no verb, it names the act of choosing a direction. A brief survey of these eight poems shows us what Manger has to say about speaking.

In the opening two stanzas of "Naomi Recites 'God of Abraham,'" Naomi initiates a dialogue with God as her daughters-in-law listen. We hear her begin to recite the Yiddish *tkhine* (supplicatory prayer), "Got fun

avrom" (God of Abraham), uttered by women throughout Jewish Eastern Europe on Saturday evenings as the Sabbath departs:

Di alte nomi in mitn shtub
Sheptshet "got fun avrom,"
Di blonde shnurn nebn ir
Hern forkhtik un frum.

"Got fun avrom, groyse got,
der heyliker shabes fargeyt
un vi der shabes in fremdn dorf
azoy iz avek mayn freyd."

Old Naomi, in the middle of the room,
Whispers "God of Abraham,"
Nearby, her daughters-in-law, blonde,
Listen, pious and intent.

"God of Abraham, great God,
The holy Sabbath now departs,
And like Sabbath in this alien town,
My joy flees my heart." [22]

In the Yiddish prayer, a woman asks the "God of Abraham, Isaac,
and Jacob" to "protect Your people, Israel, from all evil" as "the beloved,
Holy Sabbath takes leave—that the coming week may arrive to bring
perfect faith" and salvation and that the coming week "arrive for kindness, for good fortune, for blessing, for success, for good health, for
wealth and honor, and for children, life, and sustenance, for us and for
all Israel."[23] Naomi, however, revises the prayer for her own purposes,
creating an analogy between the Holy Sabbath, isolated in the mundane
week, and her own isolation as a Jew "in fremdn dorf," in the alien or
foreign village. Naomi's discourse with God is private, for she prays in a
whisper, and her blonde—that is, Gentile—daughters-in-law have to listen hard to catch what she is saying. In the rest of the poem, Naomi
stands at the window and, watching the landscape darken, reflects upon
all that has happened—the deaths of her husband and sons, her gradual
affection for Orpah and Ruth, her loneliness. She decides that she:

Vet zikh shlepn un shlepn tsu fus,
Biz zi vet kumen keyn knaan

Un dortn vet der malekh-hamoves
Vern ir tsveyter man.

Will trudge and stagger, stagger and trudge
Until she comes to Canaan
And, there, the angel of death himself
Will become her second husband.[24]

The poem ends with the fragrance of hay and prayer permeating the night as Naomi continues whispering the prayer and her daughters-in-law listen.

The second poem, "Naomi Speaks to Her Daughters-in-Law," takes place on that same "end-of-summer night," as Orpah pours tea from a samovar for Naomi and Ruth. Manger personifies the night outside as "A shiksa in a shirt of stars" singing a song that "summons back / Love from the foreignness" (ll. 6–8). In the subsequent stanzas, the river, the wind, the road, the forest, and all the world join the night in its song, but "the three widows" cannot hear it. Instead, a thoughtful Orpah and a sad Ruth listen to tired old Naomi, who tells them of her intent to "set out for home / To my land, to find my grave / Where once my cradle stood" (ll. 22–24). She instructs her daughters-in-law to return to their parents' homes with her blessing. At the end of the poem, "Naomi falls silent" (l. 29), and the sounds of the oil lamp burning and the samovar humming fill the room as "the crown of grief" trembles above the three widows' heads (ll. 32).

The third, fourth, and fifth poems present the responses to the incomplete or unanswered dialogue of the first two. Each of these poems, in the form of an oblique dialogue, presents one of the widows reflecting upon where she will go the following day. In the third, "Naomi Cannot Sleep," the mother-in-law grieves over abandoning the graves of her husband and sons. As she contemplates her sorrow from her bed, Naomi hears the graves speak to her, demanding that she remain near them, rather than return to Bethlehem:

Di kvorim mogn un rufn zi:
"Nomi . . . mame . . . neyn!
Blayb do mit undz, blayb nebn undz,
Du torst, du vest nisht geyn.

"Nisht dortn vu s'shteyt dayn vig,
nisht dortn iz dayn heym,
nor do vu du host undz farshart
mit faykhter erd un leym."

꧇

The graves demand and call to her:
"Naomi . . . Mama . . . no!
Stay here with us, you must stay near,
You must not, you will not go.

"Not there, to where your cradle stands,
There is not your home.
But here, where you have buried us
Beneath damp earth and stone."[25]

Instead of answering the graves directly, Naomi addresses God, asking him to "Reveal the way to me: / Should I go or stay right here . . . ?" (ll. 26–27). Although God replies to her "without a voice" (l. 31), his revelation is verbal:

"Di toyte zenen shotns bloyz
vos tuen rak nor vey,
un got iz likht, iz eybik likht,
shtey oyf far tog un gey!

"Nisht bay di kvorim vakht dayn got
nor dortn bay dayn vig,
shtey oyf, mayn kind, ven s'togt der tog,
un gey aheym tsurik!"

꧇

"The dead are only shadows
That cause continuous pain,
And God is light, is always light,
Rise and go before dawn!

"Your God stands watch, not by graves,
But there, where you were born.
Rise my child, when the day dawns,
Rise, and go back home!"[26]

God's reassuring words that allow Naomi to sleep in Manger's poem contrast with the biblical Naomi's assertion that "the hand of God is gone forth against me" (1:14). The pattern of dialogue in the poem is one of displacement: The graves speak in response to Naomi's inner thoughts, but Naomi deflects the graves by addressing God, who answers her directly, although silently. This divine response resolves Naomi's dilemma and redeems her from the bitterness ascribed to her in the Hebrew text.

In the fourth poem, "Orpah Cannot Sleep," the dialogue is more direct and literal. Significantly, the most dialogue and speech occur in the poems centered on Orpah. Here, Orpah's old peasant father "speaks" to her in his letter, which she reads and rereads in her insomnia. Affectionately calling her by her Slavic nickname, the father summons home his "Orposya" with news from her home village: Her mother is old and sick, the cow has calved. He also provides juicy gossip, as well: Stashek the miller murdered his wife with an ax one night; "Anyusya, the blacksmith's girl" returned pregnant from the big city, to the sorrow of her parents; and "Itska the Jew" and his family caught Vazshne in the act of breaking the windows of their tavern (ll. 5–20). The most enticing bit of news, though, concerns "Antek, the writer for the court," whose conversation the father quotes directly:

"Yo, antek der shrayber fun gerikht
hot mikh anumlt opgeshtelt:
'gehert az orposyas man iz toyt
un zi hot fashpilt ir velt.

"'to zol zi kumen aheym,
shrayb ir, az ikh bin greyt,
khotsh zi hot gelebt mit a zshid,
zi tsu nemen vi zi shteyt.'"

౹ఓ

"Yes, Antek the writer for the court
Pulled me aside and said:
'Heard that Orposya's lost her world
Now that her husband's dead.

"'So let her come home, write her that
I am well prepared,

102

Although she has lived with a Jew,
To take her as she is.' "[27]

As Orpah wonders if her fate and good fortune lie with Antek, she gazes out the window at the moonlit cemetery and "weeps a final tear" (l. 36). In the father's letter, Manger emphasizes how fully a Gentile Orpah is through the Slavic names; through the repetition of the slur *zshid* ("Jew") to refer to the village tavern keeper and to Orpah's dead husband, Makhlon; and through the violence inherent in the everyday life of the peasant village. The contrast of these details of Orpah's hometown with Naomi's quiet Yiddish prayer in the first poem also underlines how alien the Moabite environment remains to Naomi, as well as the degree to which Manger has transplanted the desert story to the forests of Eastern Europe. As in the other *Rut* poems, Manger conveys the communication between the characters through indirect discourse. Antek's spoken marriage proposal comes to Orpah twice removed, mediated by her father's letter—a quote within a quote. Moreover, Orpah must infer the substance of the proposal through Antek's insults.

The parallel title of the fifth poem, "Ruth Cannot Fall Asleep," contrasts the situation of Ruth with that of Orpah. Ruth stands before the mirror, reflecting upon the effects for her of her mother-in-law's decision to return to Bethlehem (ll. 1–8). Unlike Orpah, who contemplates her options through the letter from home, Ruth recalls the terrible conditions under which she lived in her home village with her drunken father and abusive stepmother, where the landowner brutalized the serfs, including her own brother, and where the deranged Christian, Vasil, "announced to the marketplace / How Pan Jesus had blessed him / On the peak of the church mount" (ll. 9–20). As she trembles, the river calls to Ruth to "marry" him, that is, to drown herself:

"Kum, zay mayn rusalke, ruzshka kroyn,
Kum ver dos vaservayb

. . . .
Vestu hobn bay mir fun kol haguts

. . . .
Bay tog—dos gingold fun der zun
Un bay nakht—dem levone-shayn."

"Come, be my naiad, Ruzshka love,
Come be my water wife

. . . .
With me you'll have the very best

. . . .
By day—the fine gold of the sun,
And by night—the moon's bright beam."[28]

In the concluding stanza, Ruth resigns herself to suicide:

Rut hert un fibert. Yo, zi iz greyt.
Oyb di shviger nemt zi nisht mit,
Vert zi di rusalke funem taykh.
Un zi shmeykhlt troyerik un mid. . . .

Ruth listens and fevers, yes, she's prepared.
She smiles, tired and sad,
If her mother-in-law won't take her along,
She'll become the river's naiad.[29]

With the parallel speech acts of the river's marriage proposal to Ruth and that of Antek, the court scribe, to Orpah, Manger reveals the very different motivations these characters will have when they come to the fork in the road, where Ruth will decide to accompany Naomi and Orpah to return home. In Manger's version, Orpah has a future husband awaiting her in her father's village. Ruth, on the other hand, can choose either to follow Naomi to Bethlehem or to drown herself in the river. Manger knowingly sets his characters in contrast to the book of Ruth, where Naomi voices her persuasive arguments and Orpah and Ruth respond with dramatic immediacy. In the biblical book, the daughters-in-law, hearing twice Naomi's command that they turn back, "lifted up their voice and wept" (Ruth 1:9, 14). At Naomi's first command, both Ruth and Orpah protest in unison that they will return with Naomi to her people (Ruth 1:10). However, when Naomi reiterates her order, Orpah silently kisses Naomi and departs (Ruth 1:14). At this crucial moment, the only voice we hear is that of Ruth as she speaks her famous words of loyalty (Ruth 1:16–17). Whereas the Bible's Ruth articulates that she will give herself over to the land, people, and God of her mother-in-law, Manger's homeless Ruth chooses to go with Naomi in desperation and without speaking.

"Naomi Leaves the Village," the sixth poem, opens with roosters crowing, with the dawn trembling "like a big blue spider" on the village windowpanes (l. 4). At dawn, Naomi is still awake. She reflects upon the sleepless night, during which she heard the voices of the graves and the words of God, which she recalls in a direct quote (ll. 9–16). Naomi calls to Orpah and Ruth. The three women walk through and out of the Moabite village. Manger depicts this village as a Catholic village in Poland as the women pass the inn, the forge, the church, the bridge, and the cemetery until they reach the wide highway that leads to the horizon, beyond which lies "the Bible's land" (ll. 21–28). In stanzas 8 and 9, Naomi describes this biblical land, her homeland, as the place where the patriarchs lived, where almond trees blossom, where even the wind and the birds are pious, and where a holy song trembles above all the elements of nature. There, God can be found in an actual place, ("vu got iz af an emesn do"), rather than simply being imagined or dreamed (ll. 33–36). The poem ends with the image of the three women: As "Naomi smiles" at the thought of God in her homeland, Ruth sits "sad and pale," and "the wind plays with Orpah's hair" (ll. 37–40).

The opening three stanzas of the seventh poem quote the wind's song:

Afn sheydveg zingt der zumervint:
"di vegn zenen alt,
eyn veg tsum dorf, eyn veg tsu got,
der driter veg tsum vald.

"Der veg vos firt tsum vildn vald,
Dos iz der veg fun toyt.
Der veg vos firt tsum shtiln dorf,
Dos iz der veg fun broyt.

"Der driter veg vos firt tsu got,
Dos iz der veg fun freyd,
Vayl got iz freyd un iberfreyd,
Got iz eybikeyt."

At the fork in the road sings the summer wind:
"All the roads are old,
One to the village, one to God,
The third road to the woods.

"The road that leads to the wild woods,
That is the road of death.

105

The road that leads to the quiet village,
That is the road of bread.

"The third road that leads to God,
That is the road of joy,
Because God is joy and more than joy,
God is eternity."[30]

In this penultimate poem, unlike the second poem, in which none of the three widows could hear the songs sung by the night, the river, the wind, and the road, Naomi in fact hears and understands the wind's song, just as she had long ago, when she was a baby. She smells the freshly harvested hay and wonders why, at this juncture, when she finally feels alive again, she is on the brink of tears.

In the sixth stanza, Naomi announces to her daughters-in-law that they will have their final meal together at the fork in the road. Now we understand that the three roads listed in the first stanza will send the women their separate ways. Orpah will take the road to the village, Naomi will take the road to Bethlehem, and, the stanza suggests, Ruth will take the road to the woods and death. From the biblical story, the reader knows that Ruth will choose the road to God, along with Naomi, but here, as Manger's sequence draws toward its end, this outcome is not at all clear. In fact, we do not see or hear from Ruth again in the sequence. In the fifth poem, Ruth was uncertain whether or not Naomi would allow her to come along. At the end of the sixth poem, Ruth is "sad and pale" (l. 39). At the end of the seventh poem, Manger refuses to let either his Ruth or his readers to know what her fate will be.

Instead, the three women at the side of the road do not respond to the imprecations of the "old deserted mill" in the distance, which calls to them reproachfully (ll. 29–32). Neither do the women listen to the tired old lindens lining the road, whose "rustle" expresses the trees' longing to return to their own native habitat, the forest (ll. 33–36), where they will no longer have to shade the roads of humankind. As the summer wind has stated, these "wild woods" are also the place of death. With "pious" swallows fluttering above their heads, the women (ll. 37–40), sitting at the fork in the road, "mutely hold their feast" (l. 39). The imagery of these failed communications from the inanimate mill and trees to the women and of the silence among the women themselves emphasizes the futility of speech to change their fate.

In the eighth and final poem, "Orpah Says Good-bye," speech is the prerogative of Orpah alone. Naomi listens silently, while Ruth has simply vanished. In six of the poem's seven stanzas, Orpah explains why she will take the road that leads back toward her parents' village:

Orpa iz modne bleykh un sheyn
Beshas zi redt di reyd:
"Shviger, ikh hob aykh biz aher
Gegebn dos bagleyt.

"Dort hinter di volkns ligt mayn heym
Un khotsh azoy iz zi sheyn,
Un khotsh azoy iz zi eygn un noent
Un ahin tsu vil ikh geyn.

"Dort bentsht pan yezus mayn tatns feld
Un der mames geboygenem kop,
Dort torgt mayn kindhayt a royte shleyf
In ir blondn farshaytn tsop.

"Dort roysht dos vaser un murmlt der vald
Un der odler iz blutik un sharf,
Dort shpilt di libe un s'shpilt der toyt
Af eyn un der zelber harf.

"Dort hitn di verbes di breges fun taykh
Un di shtarke dembes dem veg,
Dort zenen di nekht vi kales farbenkt,
Un vi mutike mener—di teg.

"Dort, shviger, iz mayn dorf un mayn heym,
Dort hinter di volkns, dos land.
Zayt moykhl—ayer geyn aheym
Hot di eygene heym mir dermant."

Orpah is lovely and strangely pale
When she speaks these words:
"Mother-in-law, this is how far
I'm able to come with you.

"Beyond the clouds there lies my home,
And just because it's beautiful,
And just because it's familiar and mine,
That's where I want to go.

"There Pan Jesus blesses my father's field
And my mother's bowed head,
There my childhood wears a red bow
In her saucy blond braid.

"There, the waters rush in the murmuring woods
And the eagle is bloody and sharp,
There, love strums and death is played
On one and the same harp.

"There, willows guard the riverbanks
And strong oaks, the road,
There, nights are yearning like young brides,
And days like daring men.

"There, Mother-in-law, is my village, my land,
There, behind the clouds, my home.
Forgive me—your going home
Reminded me of my own home."[31]

In Orpah's monologue to Naomi, the most foregrounded speech in Manger's sequence, the predominant idea expressed is that of going home. The word *heym* ("home") is repeated five times, three of those times in stanza six, where Orpah admits that, when Naomi spoke earlier of going home to die, she began to think about going home to live. While the poem's forthright and explicit expression of Orpah's mind explains the subsequent action in the biblical narrative in which Naomi brings Ruth home with her to Bethlehem, this action does not take place in Manger's *Rut*.

The memories of the beauty and familiarity of village life that call Orpah home are the same aspects of life in Moab that have most alienated the listening Naomi in the previous poems. Orpah recalls her parents' Christian faith, expressed by "Pan Jesus" blessing her father's field and her mother's bowed head. These lines set up a contrast between Orpah's parental home, blessed by Jesus, and the home in Bethlehem where the God of the patriarchs awaits Naomi's return, earlier in the sequence.[32] The eagle of Orpah's home is "bloody and sharp" (l. 14), not "pious," like the eagle in Naomi recalls from Bethlehem.[33] Yet despite these differences between Orpah's village and Naomi's Bethlehem, the eighth poem expresses an ambivalent attraction to the Gentile place, with its natural beauty of rushing water and murmuring forests, willows and oaks, yearning nights and daring days. These positive images suggest that not only

Naomi, but also Manger feels regret about leaving behind the alien place, Moab/Poland.

Orpah's praise song arouses in Naomi, as well as in Manger's reader, her attachment to the foreign land she is about to leave. When Naomi responds to the emotion it awakens, she does so with a gesture and a thought, but, significantly, not with spoken words:

Orpa shvaygt, zi otemt tif.
Un nomi heybt oyf di hent:
Az voyl iz tsu dem vos geyt aheym
Nokh yorn zayn in der fremd.

🖋

Orpah falls silent, she takes a deep breath.
And Naomi raises her hands:
How nice it is for the one who goes home
After years in foreign lands.[34]

Although in these lines Naomi anticipates reaching her old home, Bethlehem, she has far to go, and we never see her arrive there in Manger's poem. These final lines convey an old woman's longing to return to her place of origin from the alien land to which she has grown accustomed. They also convey a longing on the part of the Yiddish poet, Manger himself. In 1940, Manger, having fled Poland for France and then France for North Africa, where he wrote these poems, was far from home. He could not return to Poland and would not for many years go forward to Israel.[35] Orpah's renunciation of Naomi and Naomi's isolation at the start of her journey home set an emotional tone that resonates with the situation of a Yiddish poet on the run from Nazi-occupied Europe.

This abrupt ending to the Yiddish retelling of the book of Ruth rings true when we ask what has happened to Ruth at the end of Manger's poems. Although Ruth frames the sequence with her name in the title, Manger has relegated her, the progenitor of King David and the Messiah, the source of the Jews' future political survival and anticipated salvation, the wellspring for national and sacred history, to silence. Which of the forks in the road she will follow—the road toward God, or the road toward death—remains unstated in Manger's 1940 Yiddish poem.

RUTH

Roza Yakubovitsh

On Boaz's fields, stirring before the harvest,
The stalks murmur in night's stillness.
Walking from Bethlehem, a girl's figure
Approaches the barn with slow steps.
Whether it is a winnowing breeze, or she,
Who holds in her breath at Boaz's feet,
A breeze blows cool, and Ruth, how she glows
And approaches her master, without his knowing:
   —You ordered your young men in the field,
   "Let the girl gather what she pleases,"
   And here in the field, I have gathered, gathered,
   I have also stayed here all night!
   Boaz, oh, master, for your goodness and fairness
   Here, in the field, I grant you my youth.

Boaz leaps up: "Oh, God our Protector,
It's not long since you came from Moab,
You, gathering sheaf after sheaf in my garden,
Remaining true to Naomi!
Our God stands by you, our God stands by you,
I swear to you, tomorrow you'll become my wife,
But meanwhile, remain here, stay!"

Quiet again in the fragrant barn,
Quietly, somewhere, a fire lights and expires,
But Boaz doesn't rest—let the night pass away,
His luck watches over him here, oh it watches,
At his feet stands Ruth with her joy, deeply hidden,
And waits for the morning.

RUTH

Itsik Manger

This fragment of the long poem *Ruth* I dedicate to my sister
Sheyndl and her friend, the weaver Volke Glozman. Two-thirds
of this long poem, together with other manuscripts, was lost to
me in the course of my itinerant wanderings.

Naomi Recites "God of Abraham"

Old Naomi, in the middle of the room,
Whispers "God of Abraham,"
Nearby, her daughters-in-law, blonde,
Listen, pious and intent.

"God of Abraham, great God,
The holy Sabbath now departs,
And like Sabbath in this alien town,
My joy flees my heart."

She walks slowly to the window:
Outside, the darkening mill.
She barely breathes with the stirring wings.
The evening wind is cool.

Elimelekh bought this mill,
And the mill ground bread,
Now her husband's in the Truer World
And both her sons are dead.

Now desolate, widowed in this town,
Alone with both daughters-in-law—
Orpah is wholesome, like rye bread,
Ruth, pious and beautiful.

Naomi recalls: Once, long ago,
These shiksas disgusted her,
But maybe it was decreed by fate—
That now she holds them dear.

They had adored those sons of hers,
Worked side by side in the field.
And paid their in-laws great respect
And honored them in this world.

Now they, poor things, are widows, too
And she—a widow alone.
For them, perhaps, the earth still has joy;
She, lonely as a stone,

Will trudge and stagger, stagger and trudge
Until she comes to Canaan
And, there, the angel of death himself
Will become her second husband.

Naomi whispers, and nearby
Her daughters-in-law obey—
The house is fragrant with her prayer,
Outside, with wind and hay.

Naomi Speaks to Her Daughters-in-Law

Orpah pours from the samovar
Three glasses of hot tea,
The first glass for her dear mother-in-law,
Whose head is white as snow.

Outside, the end-of-summer night,
A shiksa in a shirt of stars,
Bewitches and sings and summons back
Love from the foreignness.

And what she sings, the river repeats,
The wind in the field repeats,

113

The road repeats, the forest repeats,
The whole world repeats.

But the three widows in the house
Do not hear the sweet song.
Orpah is thoughtful, Ruth is sad,
And Naomi is tired and old.

Naomi raises her head and says:
"Listen, my daughters, listen,
What, as they say, can be the worth
Of an old and broken person?

"So, tomorrow, at the crack of dawn,
I will set out for home
To my land, to find my grave
Where once my cradle stood.

"And as for you, back home you'll go,
On your separate ways,
And may my blessing follow you,
Until you end your days."

Naomi falls silent. The oil lamp burns,
And the samovar hums.
And above the three widow heads
Trembles the crown of grief. . . .

Naomi Cannot Sleep

Old Naomi lies in bed
And cannot fall asleep,
In the window, good and gold,
Tremble three pious stars.

The same three stars she knew at home;
Why, then, are they strange?
And Naomi feels how her old heart
Grieves and grieves and grieves.

Here, under foreign stars,
She will leave graves behind.
Weeping over the graves, she laments
The ruin of her good luck.

Tomorrow at dawn, with help from Above,
She will go away forever.
Really? Truly? And suddenly
She's overcome with fear.

The graves demand and call to her:
"Naomi . . . Mama . . . no!
Stay here with us, you must stay near,
You must, you will not go.

"Not there, to where your cradle stands,
There is not your home,
But here, where you have buried us
Beneath damp earth and stone."

Naomi says fervently, "Righteous God,
Reveal the way to me;
Should I go or stay right here
Until the day I die?"

And Naomi hears the rustling wind
In the nearby apple trees,
And all of a sudden, without a voice,
God's grace is revealed.

"The dead are only shadows
That cause continuous pain,
And God is light, is always light,
Rise and go before dawn!

"Your God stands watch, not by graves,
But there, where you were born.
Rise, my child, when the day dawns,
Rise, and go back home!"

Naomi smiles. Outside the wind
Rustles in the apple trees.
She falls asleep, and above her
Trembles the grace of God.

Orpah Cannot Sleep

Orpah sits in her room at night
And yet again reads the letter.

Her father, the old peasant, writes,
She reads and breathes deeply.

"Orposya, little daughter, come home,
Your mother is sick and old.
Krasa the cow has calved
And everything is thank-God.

"Stashek, the miller, with an ax
murdered his wife at night,
Now he's in the 'clink.' Praise God,
We drag in a bit of bread.

"Anyusya, the blacksmith's girl, came back
From the city with a belly,
Her mother cries and the blacksmith drinks
And beats her into jelly.

"At Itsko the Jew's village tavern,
They knocked out all the panes
And Itsko himself with his household
Caught Vazshne in the act.

"Yes, Antek the writer for the court,
Pulled me aside and said:
'Heard that Orposya's lost her world
Now that her husband's dead.

" 'So let her come home, write her that
I am well prepared,
Although she has lived with a Jew,
To take her as she is.' "—

Orpah puts away the letter.
Antek calls her back,
Perhaps indeed, maybe with him
Is she decreed her luck?

She walks slowly to the window,
A strange ache in her heart.
The cemetery sleeps in the moonlight
And she weeps a final tear.

Ruth Cannot Fall Asleep

Ruth stands slender before the mirror
And combs out her blond hair.
The words that her mother-in-law spoke
Are all too painfully clear.

Tomorrow, that means, in several hours,
Old mother-in-law alone
Will return to her people and her god
And she, where will she go?

Home to the village where her father drinks
And her wicked stepmother swears,
Too long has that blond Marusya
Saddened and darkened her world.

Home to the village where the landowner beats
The serfs with an iron rod,
She remembers distinctly how her brother's flesh
Spilled out sweat and blood.

Home to the village where Vasil the madman
Announced to the marketplace
How Pan Jesus had blessed him
On the peak of the church mount.

She trembles. Outside, the river's rush:
"Come, Ruzshka, beloved, come!
I have divorced my old naiad
And you are pious and good.

"Come, be my naiad, Ruzshka love,
Come, be my water wife,
I have water roses for your hair
And for your body, pearls.

With me, you'll have the very best
Of all that you could dream,
By day—the fine gold of the sun,
And by night—the moon's bright beam."

Ruth listens and fevers, yes, she's prepared.
She smiles, tired and sad,
If her mother-in-law won't take her along,
She'll become the river's naiad.

Naomi Leaves the Village

In the village, the roosters crow
Early; the dawn trembles
On every pane of the sleeping village
Like a big blue spider.

Naomi's awake. She hasn't closed
Her eyes at all tonight.
For the rest of her life, however long,
She will remember this night.

This very same, late summer night
With stars, with grief, with tears,
With graves that call out, "Mama, stay"
And with the voice of the Lord,

"Arise, my child, before the dawn,
And go back to your home,
God does not sorrow over graves,
God exults where a baby's born."

She takes up her bundle. "Orpah! Ruth!"
"Mother-in-law, we're ready to go!"
Orpah, flushed, her hair loose,
Ruth, dressed in calico.

They walk. Here is the village inn,
Yanek the blacksmith's forge,
The little church with its green roof
Where a blind beggar kneels.

Here is the graveyard and the bridge
And here is the beaten path,
And there, where the sky touches the earth,
There is the Bible's land.

That is the land where the patriarchs lived,
The land where the almond tree blooms,
Where the wind and the eagle piously float,
And where the holy song trembles.

Above mountain and valley, above forest and field,
Above water, grass and trees,
Where God is in an actual place
And not only in your dreams.

Naomi smiles. God above lives,
And she is a child to him—
Near her, Ruth is sad and pale,
The wind plays with Orpah's hair.

At The Fork in the Road

At the fork in the road sings the summer wind:
"All the roads are old,
One to the village, one to God,
The third road to the woods.

"The road that leads to the wild woods,
That is the road of death.
The road that leads to the quiet village,
That is the road of bread.

"The third road that leads to God,
That is the road of joy,
Because God is joy and more than joy,
God is eternity."

Naomi harkens. Her heart understands
What the summer wind sings,
It's a long time since she heard his babbling
In her cradle, as a child.

She breathes deeply. In the field,
The scent of fresh-cut hay,
Why, then, does the fork in the road
Make her want to cry?

And Naomi says, "Listen, daughters, hear,
What has to be shall be,
We'll hold our final feast here
With rye bread and with wine.

At the edge of the road, they sit down
And feast, wordless and still.
In the distance, winking at them,
Stands the old deserted mill.

The good old deserted mill
Stretches out its arms:
—I served you faithfully for years,
Why would you do me harm?

By the road, the linden trees
Line up, tired and old.
They rustle now as always
Their longing for the woods.

By the road, the women sit
And mutely hold their feast,
And above the widows' heads
Pious swallows drift.

Orpah Says Good-Bye

Orpah is lovely and strangely pale
When she speaks these words:
"Mother-in-law, this is how far
I'm able to come with you.

"Beyond the clouds there lies my home,
And just because it's beautiful,
And just because it's familiar and mine,
That's where I want to go.

"There Pan Jesus blesses my father's field
And my mother's bowed head,
There my childhood wears a red bow
In her saucy blond braid.

"There, the waters rush in the murmuring woods
And the eagle is bloody and sharp,
There, love strums and death is played
On one and the same harp.

"There, willows guard the riverbanks
And strong oaks, the road,
There, nights are yearning like young brides,
And days like daring men.

"There, Mother-in-law, is my village, my land,
There, behind the clouds, my home.
Forgive me—your going home
Reminded me of my own home."

Orpah falls silent, she takes a deep breath.
And Naomi raises her hands:
How nice it is for the one who goes home
After years in foreign lands.

PRINTING THE STORY:
THE BIBLE IN ETCHINGS,
ENGRAVINGS, AND WOODCUTS

Margaret Adams Parker

It can be argued that printmaking in Europe grew up alongside the printed Christian Bible. The print's beginnings in Western Europe[1] coincided roughly with the development of the printing press and movable type. Indeed, the impact of the biblical print is in some ways analogous to that of the printed text. Just as the printing press made possible the broader dissemination of the Bible, the print made biblical images widely available. Likewise, translations of the Bible into local vernaculars made the text accessible to those who could not read the Latin Vulgate, just as the printed image "told" the biblical story to those many Christians who could not read at all. Even in our time, when universal literacy is taken for granted (if not actually achieved), the print has remained an important means of depicting biblical characters and the biblical narrative. This is true whether the picture appears separately from the text or alongside it.

As a printmaker who also teaches at a Christian seminary, I have long been aware of the special relationship between this medium and Scripture. Indeed, since my own art is often intimately involved with biblical texts, I've turned to the rich legacy of printmaking not only as a resource, but also for inspiration. I was therefore delighted at the opportunity to create a set of woodcuts to accompany a new translation of the book of Ruth by Ellen F. Davis. Depicting this complete narrative in prints has drawn me to look more systematically at the tradition of biblical printmaking, to approach the subject as an artist who is also a theological educator looking for ways to help her students think about art. This essay represents one way to consider biblical prints and offers insight into how my Ruth woodcuts fit into a long-established tradition.

The relationship between prints and biblical texts varies widely. While many illustrations are fairly literal, not all are faithful renderings of the scriptural narrative. Some prints feature biblical characters in distinctly unbiblical settings and guises: The biblical text never describes Mary as the Virgin of Mercy, sheltering tiny humans beneath her cloak, nor does it depict the Christ child carried on the shoulders of a giant Saint Christopher. Other prints juxtapose disparate biblical scenes to make a theological point, rather than merely to illuminate the action. For instance, fifteenth-century illustrated editions of the *Speculum humanae salvationis* (The mirror of human salvation) illustrate the harmony of Old and New Testaments by printing side by side such scenes as Melchizedek making offering to Abraham, the Passover lamb, the manna in the desert, and the Last Supper.[2] Studying this material, I have found it interesting and helpful to categorize each print by pondering its original purpose. Needless to say, this is an exercise that relies more on speculation than on scholarship, since for many prints we have little or no written documentation. The purpose of this imaginative exercise is to stimulate our thinking about how a print functions, rather than to create neat categories. We can sometimes learn a good deal from our conjectures.

In my speculative exercise, I divide biblical prints into four categories: devotional, didactic, narrative, and interpretive (where the primary purpose seems to have been the artist's desire to explore and understand the biblical text.) These categories, of course, are not mutually exclusive; one print may fit into several categories.[3] For instance, the fact that a print's primary focus is to convey the action of a narrative does not preclude its having devotional or didactic uses. In this essay, I will look at prints in each category from the first three centuries of Western printmaking (the fifteenth through the seventeenth) before I turn to examine more contemporary works.

The earliest prints—woodcuts from the beginning of the fifteenth century—were, for the most part, devotional images that depicted characters and scenes drawn from Scripture or from the lives of the saints. Their primary function was to provide a visual focus for individual prayer. Most of these images were printed and sold as individual sheets, termed single-leaf woodcuts. One woodcut block could print an almost unlimited number of images; moreover, these images could be mass produced on paper, a material that was by this time relatively inexpensive.[4] As a result, Christians for whom a painting of Mary or a sculpture of Jesus was an unattainable luxury could afford an image printed on paper. Such devotional prints were sold at shrines, at monastic foundations, and even at fairs.[5] Travelers or pilgrims purchased them as souvenirs, bringing them home to affix on the doors or walls of their houses, to sew into their clothing, or even to paste inside the lids of their alms boxes and strong-boxes.[6] Most of the prints that survive today (and given the fragility of paper, it is amazing that any are left) were preserved within prayer books. There they served as an aid to devotion and offered a silent appeal to the protective powers of the saint who was depicted.

In figure 1, *The Madonna and St. Bridget* (ca. 1480–1500), the saint is identified by her pilgrim's staff, bag, and hat—all references to her journey to Jerusalem. The picture also includes the coat of arms of her native Sweden. Bridget kneels in front of Mary, who in turn kneels before the newborn Jesus. In her *Revelations*, Bridget recorded the life of Christ as revealed to her in visions by Mary.[7] This woodcut records the revelation in which Mary, while kneeling in prayer, with her golden locks cascading about her shoulders, miraculously gives birth to her son.[8] The German inscription reads: "Thus Mary showed St. Bridget how Jesus was born." In the background, we see a convent of Saint Bridget's order. One can easily imagine a pilgrim visiting a Brigittine convent and purchasing such a print. In doing so, he or she would also be invoking Saint Bridget in an appeal for the Virgin's protection.

Didactic images used the biblical text to provide elementary Christian instruction. These prints typically drew parallels between Old and New Testament stories, a tradition begun by the Gospel writers themselves and continued in such commentaries as Gregory of Nyssa's *Life of Moses*. Unlike devotional prints, which were sold singly, didactic images were bound into volumes such as the fifteenth-century best sellers the *Biblia pauperum* (the Bible of the poor), the *Canticum Canticorum* (The song of songs), and the *Speculum humanae salvationis*. These books provided minor clergy, who were often scarcely more literate than those they served, ideas for their homilies;[9] lay people may also have used them for their own religious instruction.

Figure 2 presents one such didactic image, a page from a fifteenth century *Biblia pauperum*. This particular edition has a Latin text and was printed ca. 1465–70, probably in the Netherlands; other editions were available in German. Here the central scene shows Jesus fasting in the wilderness. He is confronted by a grinning devil, who holds out stones that he offers to turn into bread. In the background, visible behind the rocky crags of the wilderness, the dome and towers of Jerusalem point to Satan's third temptation of Christ. In the scene on the left, Jacob holds out a bowl of food to his brother Esau. The famished Esau, identified by his bow as a man of the hunt, has been tricked into surrendering his birthright in exchange for Jacob's food. In the scene on the right, Adam and Eve, who stand on either side of the Tree of Knowledge, cover their nakedness with fig leaves and hold up apples taken from the tree. The serpent, twined around the tree, gazes at Eve with a satisfied look. The texts related to these images cite the Old Testament passages they depict. They also connect these scenes to Christ's temptation so as to underscore theological links between the testaments. In the earliest examples of such volumes, called block books, both words and images were carved on a block of wood.[10] Later editions of the *Biblia pauperum* combined woodcut images with moveable type,[11] but the same images appeared again and again, printed either from the original blocks as they were carried from city to city or from copies of the original. The artisans who created the blocks seem to have had no concern for originality or, of course, fear of copyright infringement.

Narrative images accompanied the actual biblical text and were closely tied to the narrative. New translations of the Bible produced at the time of the Protestant Reformation reflect a widespread desire to read Scripture. Although this resulted in dramatic increases in literacy in Protestant countries, there still seems to have been a market for illustrated Bibles. Numerous translations were published with accompanying illustrations; no doubt these pictures provided a break in the page of text, and the lively images of selected dramatic scenes made the text easier to understand.[12] Illustrations of this kind depicted the narrative for its own sake, rather than presenting theological concepts, as had the *Biblia pauperum*, with its juxtaposition of the testaments.

Figure 3 is a woodcut illustrating Genesis 22, Abraham's near-sacrifice of his son Isaac. The image is taken from the Koberger Bible, a translation in High German published in Nürnberg in 1483. The volume is folio-sized and, as in the unillustrated Gutenberg Bible, the text in the Koberger Bible appears in two vertical columns per page. The woodcuts were made from the same blocks used for the Cologne Bibles of 1478 and 1480, which had each offered the biblical text in a different Low German dialect.[13] In figure 3, as in many medieval woodcuts, paint has been added to the prints by hand. The woodcut depicts two episodes from the story, a convention popular in medieval paintings. On the right, Abraham and Isaac set off on their journey. Isaac is bent under the weight of a load of kindling; Abraham carries a sword and a firepot. He also wears a distinctive headdress designating a male Jew in medieval Europe. Above and to the left, an angel stays Abraham's sword (quite literally) while the ram stands patiently waiting to the side. The landscape in the background features a distinctly North German walled city, a windmill, and a stream (complete with swan) in the verdant foreground. Significantly, the image offers no hint of the common theological interpretation of Isaac's sacrifice as a "type" for Christ's. In the *Biblia pauperum*, for instance, the image of Isaac carrying the wood is one of the Old Testament prints used to gloss the central New Testament image of Jesus carrying his cross. In the Koberger Bible, by contrast, the image is entirely narrative.

All these early fifteenth-century prints were woodcuts, in part because the medium is among the simplest of printmaking techniques. In printmaking's earliest European incarnation, woodcuts provided easy and cheap reproduction, first for printing fabric and later for playing cards and religious images. (We might consider the woodcut block the Xerox machine of its day.) The artisan who carved the blocks was likely to be either a member of the carpenter's guild[14] or of a religious order. He would never have claimed for himself the status of artist or thought to sign his own work. Beginning with a plank of wood on which an image had been drawn—in most cases by another hand—the artisan carved away any areas that were to remain uninked. He then rolled ink across the surface of the block and placed the block against a piece of paper, applying pressure to transfer the image to the paper. In this early period, the woodcut print was characterized by simple outlines, with large open areas that were often hand colored. The hardness and grain of the block's wood seemed to impose a limit on the complexity of design.

With the development in the mid-fifteenth century of metal engraving as a medium for printmaking, images could be created with finer line and more sumptuous detail. The engraver (who was likely to be enrolled in the more prestigious goldsmith's guild) gouged fine lines and other marks into the flat surface of a metal plate. The ink was thus pulled out of the lines, rather than off the surface, as with a woodcut. Only a limited number of prints could be pulled from an engraved plate, and consequently, engravings were more costly than woodcuts. Whereas the latter were mass produced for a wide public, engravings seem to have been created for a more discriminating audience.[15] But as with the woodcut, there was no concept of originality: The artist felt free to copy from other prints, from manuscript illustrations, or from painted or sculpted images. Such borrowing also took place in the other direction: Tilman Reimenschneider's relief sculpture *Noli me tangere*—depicting the meeting between Mary Magdalene and the resurrected Jesus—reproduces in carved wood Martin Schongauer's engraving of the same subject.

Figure 4, Schongauer's *Nativity* (ca. 1470–75), illustrates engraving's capacity for subtlety and great delicacy, in contrast to the bolder, cruder woodcuts of the period. Schongauer was from the generation of print-makers who began to claim status as artists, rather than artisans, and he accordingly signed his prints with his initials. He displays his skill through an extensive vocabulary of fine marks that delineate stones, foliage, the skins of the shaggy cow and donkey, the folds of Mary's garments, and Joseph's disheveled hair. The medium is also capable of great expressiveness. Here Mary gently contemplates the holy infant, while Joseph gazes tenderly at his wife.

How does this particular image fit into our categories? Obviously, it depicts the events of the narrative—along with such additional details as the cow and donkey, which had accrued to the narrative over time—but it was surely made with devotional intent. The medieval church was devoted to Mary; churches and shrines were filled with her images, often depicting her in many different manifestations. One small parish church in Kent, for instance, had at least four images of Mary: Our Lady of the Assumption, of Pity, in childbirth, and with Saint Anne.[16] In contrast to the austere, dignified Mother of God from Byzantine art, the late-medieval Mary was tender and sweet, someone to be adored, to approach for intercession.

A generation after Schongauer, Albrecht Dürer removed printmaking completely from its roots in the artisan class. Dürer was the great artist of the northern Renaissance. He was a painter and printmaker, a well-traveled, educated man, a prominent and prosperous citizen, a favorite of princes. Although he did not cut the blocks himself, his designs raised the woodcut to an amazing level of intricacy, and his skill as an engraver was unparalleled. He sets *The Prodigal Son* (1496), figure 5, in surroundings familiar to any North German. Indeed, his contemporaries so admired his rendering of the farm buildings that they often copied the print.[17] Dürer shows the prodigal, kneeling with bare feet, his clothes tied up to avoid the muck of the pigs. Head tilted and hands clasped, he is clearly at the moment in the parable when he repents, saying: "I will get up and go to my father and I will say to him, 'Father I have sinned against heaven and before you'" (Luke 15:18).

How might we classify this print? We know that Dürer was a passionate advocate of Luther and his attempts to reform the church. He was also, interestingly, the godson of Anton Koberger, who printed the Koberger Bible. Even so, the artist remained in the Roman Catholic Church and often depicted quintessentially Catholic devotional themes. This image of a moment in the biblical story—transposed, it is true, into Dürer's time and place—seems to me to be more clearly devotional than narrative. Any young German man might gaze at this curly-headed prodigal and visualize himself at the moment of penitence.[18] Furthermore, the engraving has the same meditative tone as the devotional series that were a major focus of Dürer's work as a printmaker: He completed three print cycles on Christ's Passion, as well as another one on the life of the Virgin.

Moving to the seventeenth century, we encounter Rembrandt, whom many would single out as the greatest printmaker (indeed the greatest artist) of all time. Rembrandt's primary medium was etching, which had been developed almost a century earlier as a swifter method of creating lines on a copper plate. Etching employs the action of acid on copper to bite lines and marks, which are then printed in the same way as in an engraving, by leaving the ink in the lines rather than on the surface of the plate. Rembrandt typically relied on etching to bite his image onto his plate, touching up with engraving and drypoint.[19]

To my mind, Rembrandt is the foremost example of an artist who illustrates Scripture in order to understand it for himself; his prints fall in the category I have termed "interpretive." Many of his paintings, prints, and drawings deal with biblical scenes. In his early works, he quite clearly mined the text for those dramatic moments that might call particular attention to his prowess as an artist. But in his later years, it is clear that he probed the text, concerned to set the story in the context of ordinary human life, always searching for ways to portray the intimate connections between God and humanity. His continual engagement with the biblical text is particularly clear in his drawings. We see him tackle the same scene over and over, sometimes returning to it across the span of his lifetime. There was no market for these drawings in Rembrandt's day. Yet in these rapidly drawn, sometimes fragmentary sketches, it is as if we are privy to the artist's personal meditations on Scripture. They are the visual equivalent of a theologian's notes in the margins of her Bible.

The Return of the Prodigal Son is one of the stories that haunted the artist's imagination. He treated the subject at least nine times.[20] The first of these depictions was a double portrait of himself and his young wife; here the artist is in the guise of The Prodigal wasting his inheritance in riotous living. At the end of the sequence is a 1669 painting that art historian Kenneth Clark called "the single greatest picture ever painted."[21] Rembrandt's etching in figure 6 is one of the earliest treatments. It dates from 1636, but like his more mature work, it grapples with the text in human terms. We see the prodigal so battered by the elements that he reminds us of the urban homeless who sleep on heating grates or take refuge in doorways. His garments are in shreds about his waist, exposing his emaciated torso. How great was the son's pride, that he was reduced to such a state before asking his father's forgiveness. Rembrandt's unblinking depiction of filth and desperation makes Dürer's image look theatrical by comparison. A true disciple of the Renaissance, Dürer was convinced that only a beautiful human form could depict appropriately the great biblical figures.

The reunion between father and son is the focus of Rembrandt's print. The father, a frail and stooped figure, bends over his son with an expression of anguish. Three servants stand by, their eyes averted. We gauge the intensity of this reunion by the fact that they cannot bring themselves to intrude upon so poignant and intimate a moment. Kenneth Clark describes the scene as "almost unbearably moving."[22] Here, as in all Rembrandt's great biblical works, we are not just shown the literal meaning of the story, but are pulled past it into the essence of the story: This father and this son refer us to God's forgiving love for humankind.[23] As a result of Rembrandt's intense desire to understand the story, the etching fits into all four of our categories: The print illustrates the parable, teaches us the story's meaning, and may even summon us to prayer.

From these early biblical prints, we now jump forward to the twentieth century. Perhaps surprisingly, many of the great artists of this period took on biblical subject matter. Among them were a number of major German artists: Ernst Barlach, Max Beckman, Käthe Kollwitz, Gerhard Marcks, and Emil Nolde. All of them made art independent of the authority and patronage of the established churches, expressing their personal responses to the text. Like them, German-born illustrator Fritz Eichenberg also worked outside the sponsorship of the church. Naturalized as an American citizen, Eichenberg became involved with the Catholic Worker movement in New York through his friendship with social activist Dorothy Day. One of his most famous images was *Christ of the Bread Lines*, a drawing produced for Day's newspaper *The Catholic Worker*. In a line of hungry, stooped, and ragged figures stands Jesus, identifying quite literally with the plight of the poor.

Eichenberg shows this same sympathy with the downtrodden in his *Lamentations of Jeremiah* (1955), the wood engraving in figure 7.[24] The prophet, his hands shackled and his head extended in grief, stands mourning over a mother and her children. These wan figures call forcefully to mind not just the destruction of ancient Jerusalem, but also the ravages of twentieth-century Europe. What category might we choose for Eichenberg's print? It can stand both as an illustration of a text and a meditation on the plight of the dispossessed; perhaps by extension, it can also be a devotional print. But I think I must, in the end, classify it as didactic. Eichenberg always seems intent on teaching us, or reminding us, that God stands on the side of the poor and broken. Like Rembrandt, Eichenberg draws us into the scene, but his commentary is more explicit, and therefore more narrow. Rembrandt's print elicits a wider range of reactions: We note not just the poverty of The Prodigal Son, but also the father's generosity and the servants' hesitation, and the complexity of the whole suggests far more than God's identification with the downtrodden.

As we explore depictions of the biblical story in prints, we note that the tradition is alive and well in the present day. In 2000, the well-known American illustrator Barry Moser produced a complete set of engravings for the entire Bible.[25] These pictures accompany the King James Bible and are available not only in mass-market format, but also in a limited-edition typeset version with original wood engravings. Like the Koberger Bible, this recent illustrated Bible is printed in a large folio size with the text in double columns. As is the case in the earlier Bible, Moser's engravings enliven the pages of text and underscore visually the drama of a character or scene. And they are clearly narrative in intent. We see this in figure 8, where Jonah appears in the water against the backdrop of the whale.

Two other artists who are currently producing biblical prints are Sandra Bowden and Edward Knippers. Both were founding members of Christians in the Visual Arts (CIVA), an organization of artists, galleries, and institutions. Both see their image making as a reflection of their faith. In figure 9, Knipper's 1993 etching *With His Stripes*, he alludes to Isaiah 53:5, a prophetic text that Christians have long associated with Christ. In illustrating "And with his stripes we are healed," the artist thrusts Christ's beaten figure toward the viewer: The stripes of the title, placed between bound hands below and lowered head above, fill the frame of the print. Knippers describes this work as both narrative and didactic. In a different vein, Figure 10 shows Sandra Bowden's collagraph[26] *In the Beginning*. Here, the Hebrew letters that spell "God created" (Gen. 1:1) emerge from the rest of the Genesis text to take shape as a celestial body. Bowden makes an image out of text; she creates a wordless evocation of the primal moments of creation, thus offering a meditation on the relation between word, image, and creativity.

This relation between word and image has influenced not only my reading of Biblical prints, but also my creation of them. I have long made biblical prints, but my participation in a two-year project with Old Testament scholar Ellen Davis provided the opportunity to explore a biblical text in a sustained way. In our book *Who Are You, My Daughter? Reading Ruth through Image and Text*, we translate and illustrate an annotated edition of the book of Ruth. In her translation, Davis attempts to adhere as closely as possible to the original text, that is, to find an English that—however awkwardly at times—sounds like Hebrew. I, too, sought faithfulness to the text, providing woodcuts that did it justice.

We intended, in other words, to start from scratch, which is not always easy with a book as familiar as Ruth. Looking at illustrated versions of the text, it is evident that many people have read the story as a romance centered on a beautiful heroine. ("Gorgeous foreign widow catches eye of wealthy landowner.") Ruth often appears young and lovely, dressed fashionably—even alluringly—for the hard work of gleaning. Both Davis and I found this reading of the biblical story unconvincing. The text itself underscores Ruth's plight: She is widowed, subsisting in a foreign land with her destitute mother-in-law, singled out in Judah as a foreigner by the local people, and working daily under the hot sun. I have therefore chosen to picture Ruth as attractive enough for Boaz to find her interesting, but I imagine that she would look less like a cover girl and more like the women we see on the evening news crossing national borders with babies on their hips and their worldly possessions on their heads.

I have tried to focus on Ruth's beauty of character by making her hands a significant feature. Thus we see her work with her hands, "talk" with her hands, carry burdens and eat with her hands. In figure 11, I depict her reaching out to Naomi as she declares, "So, I'm going to go to the fields and glean." And with this focus on hands, there is a quite wonderful linguistic allusion. In Hebrew, Ruth is described as possessing *hayil*—valor. As such, she calls to mind the *'eshet hayil*, the woman of valor in Proverbs 31:10–31.[27] It is this woman who "works with willing hands" (31:19), who "opens her hand to the poor, and reaches out her hands to the needy" (31:20). It is also this woman who, like Ruth with Naomi, "provides food for her household" (31:15). With the one text following the other so closely in the Hebrew canon, the reader can hardly fail to note the intertext.

Our concern for the textual and historical integrity of the images sometimes created challenges and motivated me to alter my original designs. For instance, when Davis found early twentieth-century photos of the actual pass from Israel into Moab (modern-day Jordan), I changed my drawings, which had featured a dramatically different terrain, to incorporate the actual landscape into the print. Later, I searched for a means to identify Ruth as a foreigner, to set her apart visually in the same way that the text singles her out six times as "the Moabite." I decided to distinguish her from the Israelite women by giving her a marker no Jewish woman would have had: a tattoo across her forehead. Because Jewish law expressly prohibits tattoos, a woman who bore such marks could never be accepted as a member of the community.

Along with historical details, I was also interested in the universal human truths in this very human story. Like other astute observers of human appearance—I think of doctors, therapists, and clergy, for instance—artists know that how a person carries her body often reveals her state of health and mind. In my own work, I want not only the face, but also the body to tell the story, and my Naomi is the strongest evidence of this intention. At the beginning of the tale, she stands bereft, closed in upon herself (figure 12): Her head is bowed, her arms crossed over her breast. She stands with this same posture two other times. In figure 13, we see her closed in on her body as she faces a daughter-in-law who will not return to her own mother's house (1:15–18). This is a scene that is usually interpreted as a tender moment between the two women, but Davis believes it is more a moment of tension. I picture Naomi holding herself the same way once more as she and Ruth limp exhausted through the gates of Bethlehem. It is only as she gazes wonderingly at the bounty Ruth has gleaned from Boaz's field that she begins to relax, and her change in posture indicates a change of mind. So, at the beginning of chapter 3, when she seizes the initiative and sends Ruth out to the threshing floor, her gesture (in figure 14) shows her new attitude: She reaches out with *her* hands to encourage the younger woman. Finally, when Ruth's baby is given her to hold, she again closes her arms, this time not around her misery, but around her grandson (figure 15).

Using the categories I described above, how would I classify my Ruth woodcuts? I did not intend them to be didactic; nor would I call them devotional, even though some viewers might find the image of the widowed Naomi, for instance, a stimulus to prayer for the bereft, in the same way as Eichenberg's *Jeremiah* might elicit prayers for the downtrodden. Without hesitation, I would consider these images narrative. And like my mentor and model, Rembrandt, I have found that making these images has enabled me to explore the meaning of the text and the human implications of the story. I know far more about these characters from having "lived" their story as I depicted it.

I have written a great deal at the beginning of this essay about the ways that printmaking allowed biblical images to be widely available. It pleases me to think that my Ruth prints now appear in book form and so are easily obtainable at relatively little cost. In these ways, I stand in a venerable popular tradition. The prints in this book are, of course, reduced in size and duplicated in ways that any medieval artisan would find astonishing. Nonetheless, my original woodcuts were made exactly as medieval prints were made: My tools, materials, and methods are essentially unchanged from those of the fifteenth-century woodcut carver. I find this physical link between their work and mine thrilling. And I venture to hope that my prints, like those of my many forebears, will urge others to explore the narrative more closely, will teach us truths drawn from the text, and will even, perhaps, move us to prayer. May these prints have something to say to modern-day readers of the Bible, even if they don't sew the images inside their clothing.

Figure 1. *The Madonna and St. Bridget*, ca. 148?–1500. Courtesy of National Gallery of Art, Rosenwald Collection, Washington, D.C.

Figure 2. Jesus fasting in the wilderness, from a *Biblia pauperum*, ca. 1465–70. Courtesy of Library of Congress, Rare Book and Special Collections Division, Rosenwald Collection.

Figure 3. *Sacrifice of Isaac*, from the Koberger Bible, 1483. Courtesy of Library of Congress, Rare Book and Special Collections Division, Rosenwald Collection.

Figure 4. Martin Schongauer, *The Nativity*, ca. 1470–75. Courtesy of National Gallery of Art, Washington, D.C.

Figure 5. Albrecht Dürer, *The Prodigal Son*, ca. 1496. Courtesy of National Gallery of Art, Rosenwald Collection, Washington, D.C.

Figure 6. Rembrandt, *Return of the Prodigal Son*, 1636. Courtesy of
National Gallery of Art, Washington, D.C.

Figure 7. Fritz Eichenberg, *The Lamentations of Jeremiah*, 1955.
Used by permission of the Eichenberg estate.

Figure 8. Barry Moser, *And the sea stopped raging*, 2000. Courtesy of R. Michelson Galleries.

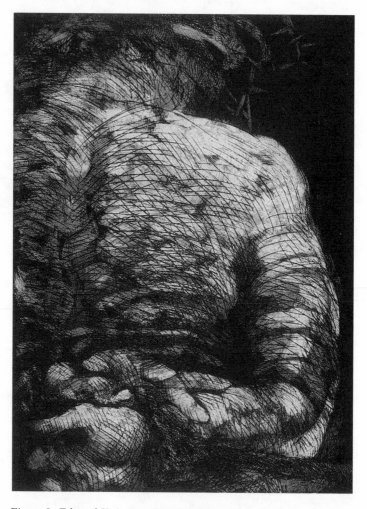

Figure 9. Edward Knippers, *With His Stripes*, 1993. Courtesy of the artist.

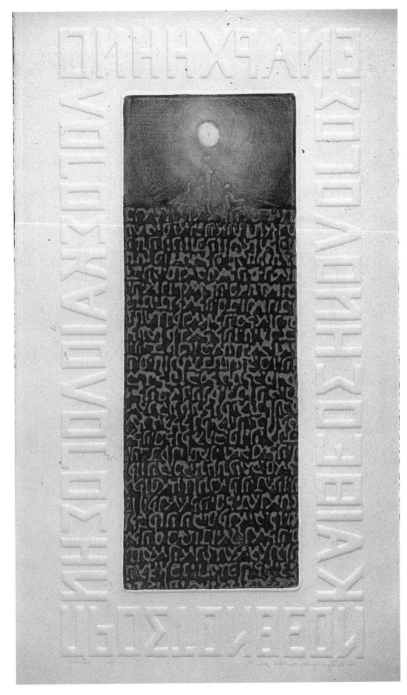

Figure 10. Sandra Bowden, "*In the Beginning*," 1978. Courtesy of the artist.

Figure 11. Margaret Adams Parker, *And Ruth the Moabite said, "So, I'm going to go to the field and glean,"* 2002. From *The Ruth Portfolio*. Courtesy of the artist.

Figure 12. Margaret Adams Parker, *And the woman was left without her two boys and without her husband*, 2000. From *The Ruth Portfolio*. Courtesy of the artist.

Figure 13. Margaret Adams Parker, *And Ruth said, "Don't press me to leave you,"* 2000. From *The Ruth Portfolio*. Courtesy of the artist.

Figure 14. Margaret Adams Parker, *"Now wash up, and anoint yourself, and put on your best dress, and go down to the threshing floor,"* 2002. From *The Ruth Portfolio*. Courtesy of the artist.

Figure 15. Margaret Adams Parker, *And Naomi took the child and held him to her body*, 2002. From *The Ruth Portfolio*. Courtesy of the artist.

PART FOUR

Translating and Reading the Song of Songs

TRANSLATING EROS

Chana Bloch

"Kiss me, make me drunk with your kisses! Your sweet loving / is better than wine."[1] The great love poem that begins with these words does not follow the conventional romantic plot: boy meets girl, boy and girl get acquainted, boy proposes marriage. That the two are already intimate is clear from the very first words of the Song of Songs. Love, not marriage, is what they propose, and the woman, who is called the Shulamite, does most of the proposing. She, in fact, is the one who issues that first urgent invitation. If she declares that his loving is better than wine, we may reasonably conclude that she has tasted it.

The lovers praise each other's bodies in knowing detail: her breasts, belly, navel, thighs; his loins and thighs. The Shulamite pictures the two of them lying together: "His left hand beneath my head, / his right arm / holding me close" (2:5). They describe their lovemaking with images of eating and drinking: "Honey and milk / are under your tongue," he says (4:11); "I would give you spiced wine to drink, / my pomegranate wine," she muses (8:2). She imagines her lover as an apricot tree and remembers: "In that shade I have often lingered, / tasting the fruit" (2:3). When she invites him, "Let my lover come into his garden / and taste its delicious fruit" (4:16), he answers in the perfect tense:

I have come into my garden,
my sister, my bride,
I have gathered my myrrh and my spices,
I have eaten from the honeycomb,
I have drunk the milk and the wine. (5:1)

The Hebrew verbs *ba'ti, 'ariti, 'akhalti, shatiti*, "I have come, I have gathered, I have eaten, I have drunk," indicate a completed action and make it clear that the couple's love has been consummated.

I have begun with these examples in order to establish the temperature of the Song, which rises at times to 120 degrees in the shade. What I am saying may seem perfectly obvious, though it is far more obvious in the Hebrew text of the Song than in the long history of exegesis and translation, where the temperature drops precipitously. It is not hard to understand why. Although the Song was in all likelihood composed as a poem about erotic love, the rabbis read it as an allegory about the love of God and the people of Israel; this interpretation, along with the attribution to King Solomon, helped the Song to survive the final cut of the canon makers. The Church Fathers in turn read the Song as a loving dialogue between Christ and his bride, the church. Once the Song became part of the Holy Scriptures, it demanded exegesis befitting its holiness, and for two thousand years, religious interpretations of one kind or another prevailed.

It is true that the mystics, Jewish and Christian, remained open to the intensity and passion of the Song, to its emotional power, but for the most part, allegories about the love of God or Christ imposed a severe constraint on the interpretive tradition—what my collaborator and co-translator Ariel Bloch calls the "pious bias" of biblical exegesis. To name just one example: The rabbis identified the Shulamite's breasts with Moses and Aaron ("As the breasts are full of milk, so Moses and Aaron filled Israel with Torah"),[2] and Christian expositors identified her breasts with the Old and New Testaments. If the Song can be aphrodisiac in its effects, commentary of this sort is the very antidote to desire. Exegetes and translators commonly presented the young lovers as chaste, yearning for one another from a respectable distance, though in doing so they were ignoring the plain sense of the Hebrew. This "pious bias" continues to be felt in contemporary translations of the Song, even in versions that present themselves as erotic, because readings and misreadings tend to get passed down uncritically from one generation to the next.

I am not saying, of course, that the task of the translator today is simply to turn up the heat. The language of the Song is at once voluptuous and reticent, an effect that is achieved through the medium of metaphor. Sexuality is evoked by metaphors such as the vineyard and garden, mountain of myrrh, hill of frankincense, the sweet fruit of the apricot tree. The Shulamite describes her lover as a shepherd pasturing among lilies (2:16, 6:3); he describes her as a fountain in the garden, a well of living waters (4:15). The invitation I just quoted—"Let my lover come into his garden / and taste its delicious fruit" (4:16)—is characteristic both in what it asserts and what it leaves unexpressed. The suggestive language of metaphor enhances the Song's eroticism, suffusing the entire landscape with eros.

Language that is too explicit violates the spirit of the Song. Here is how a distinguished scholar cranked up the heat in his translation: "Your vulva [is] a rounded crater; / May it never lack punch!" (7:3).[3] The sexual organs are never explicitly named in the Song, though they are of course suggested many times over. This translation, with its three howlers, illustrates how important it is to be sensitive to questions of style. By "crater" this scholar meant a mixing bowl, and by "punch" he meant spiced wine, though it seems he did not stop to think about the associations of those words in English. But "vulva" takes the prize. The word *shorerekh* means "your navel," not "your vulva"; in any case, the anatomical term "vulva" is barbaric, given the elegantly evocative language of the Song. Our translation reads:

> Your navel is the moon's
> bright drinking cup.
> May it brim with wine! (7:3)[4]

Ariel Bloch and I were drawn to translate the Song because we felt that no available English translation fully conveyed the unusual combination of sensuousness and delicacy that makes the Hebrew so captivating. The task we set ourselves—to decipher exactly what the Hebrew text was saying and to embody that reading as richly as possible in English poetry—proved to be more challenging than we had anticipated. The Song is one of the most enigmatic books in the Bible, far more obscure than a reader of English might suppose. In fact, there is hardly a line that does not present some difficulty, and no other book of the Bible has provoked such wildly divergent interpretations.

Why is it so hard to translate the Song? The difficulties arise in part from the compactness and concentration of the form. While the narrative prose of the Bible is fairly straightforward and accessible, biblical poetry is compressed and elliptical, sometimes to the point of being unintelligible. Also, the language of the Song is very often obscure, with an unusually high proportion of *hapax legomena* (words occurring only once), as well as an abundance of rare words and constructions. A *hapax* is very frustrating for the interpreter: Even where the context provides some clues, it is hard to establish the meaning of such a word. Thus lines such as "King Solomon built an *'appiryon*" ("pavilion," 3:9) or "your *shelachim* are an orchard" ("branches," 4:13) or "a king is caught in the *rehatim*" ("thicket," 7:6) must finally remain a riddle. But even apart from these rare words, there are plenty of other challenges.

I came to the Song after translating works of contemporary Yiddish and Hebrew literature—stories by Isaac Bashevis Singer, poems by Jacob Glatstein and Abraham Sutzkever from Yiddish, books of poetry by Dahlia Ravikovitch and Yehuda Amichai from Hebrew. As might be expected, I found that it is more difficult to translate poetry than prose and considerably more difficult to translate an ancient text than a contemporary one. If you have a question when you are translating a living author, you can often get the answer straight from the source's mouth. When you are translating an ancient text, however, there is no author to consult. And as I discovered, there are many more questions than answers. In translating the Song, I was fortunate to have Ariel Bloch, an expert in Semitic languages, as my collaborator.

One of the major challenges facing a contemporary translator is to find the proper register in English, neither too formal and stylized nor too breezy and colloquial—language that is fresh, urgent, and passionate, yet at the same time dignified. The most impressive English translation of the Song is that of the King James Version (1611); this magnificent poem, with its rich textures and resounding cadences, has been justly beloved by generations of readers. But significant advances in biblical scholarship during the past four centuries have shown many of its readings to be in error, including some of the best-known verses, such as "Stay me with flagons, comfort me with apples" (2:5) for *samkhuni ba-'ashishot, rapduni ba-tapuchim,* or "terrible as an army with banners" (6:10) for *'ayummah ka-nidgalot'* And its language is often dated, such as "I am sick of love" (2:5) for *cholat 'ahavah 'ani,* or the unfortunate "My beloved put in his hand by the hole of the door, and my bowels were moved for him" (*me'ay hamu 'alav,* 5:4). The heightened diction of the King James Version was conceived for liturgical purposes and was already somewhat archaic in the seventeenth century; thus it would be inappropriate in a contemporary translation. Finally, the Song in the King James Version is very stately and formal; it scarcely reflects the fact that this is a poem about young lovers—indeed, very young lovers, probably just past the age of puberty. Our aim, apart from fidelity to the meaning, was to convey the heat, the speed, the intensity of the original.

There has been a lot of debate about how free a translator ought to be. Since most readers of English today do not know Hebrew, Ariel and

I committed ourselves to be as faithful as possible to the text—that is, both its letter and its spirit. Where we differ from earlier translations, we are—more often that not—closer to the original. We worked from the Hebrew, digging down inch by inch, as much as possible without preconceptions, trying to puzzle out the meaning of each line and looking to other parts of the Bible for help in deciphering rare words. I say "digging down" advisedly, since translating an ancient text is truly a work of excavation.[5] We resolved to pay attention to every nuance of the text, and we found that even the smallest details could make a difference in sustaining or inhibiting the erotic mood. Let me offer a few examples.

In the opening verse (1:2), *tovim dodekha mi-yayin*, the word *dodekha* means "your lovemaking"; outside of the Song, *dodim* occurs only three times in the Hebrew Bible, always with the same unambiguous meaning. In the Book of Proverbs, a married woman seduces an innocent young man: "Come, let us drink our fill of *dodim* [*nirveh dodim*], let us make love all night long, for my husband is not at home" (Prov. 7:18; cf. Ezek. 16:8, 23:17). This sense of the word is found also in the allegory of the unfaithful wife in Ezekiel 16:7–8, where God addresses Jerusalem: "Your breasts were well-formed. . . . I saw that you had reached the age of lovemaking ['*et dodim*]," and in 23:17, another passage about the "whorings" of Jerusalem: "The Babylonians came to her into the bed of love [*mishkav dodim*], and defiled her with their lust." Given these uses of *dodim*, we may be quite certain that the word also refers to sexual love in the Song. Most translations, however, render *dodim* in the opening verse as "love," which is imprecise just where precision is required. Since the initial verse sets the tone for the entire poem, it is important to establish immediately that *dodim* means an activity, not just a state of mind. Hence we chose the verbal noun "loving": our translation reads "your sweet loving is better than wine."

On the other hand, "love" is the proper translation of *dodim* in the Shulamite's invitation in 7:12–13, where the context makes its meaning perfectly clear: "Come, my beloved, / let us go out into the fields / and lie all night among the flowering henna. . . . There I will give you my love."[6] Here too, translators have often evaded its implications. For example, in 7:12 the phrase *nalinah ba-kefarim* literally means "let us pass the night among the henna bushes." This has been rendered "Let us *lodge* in the villages" (KJV, RSV)—as if "passing the night" were simply a matter of finding proper accommodations. The dictionary definition "lodge" is possible, of course, but again, it misses the point.

The Shulamite's *tsammah* (4:1) is usually taken to be her "veil," although medieval Jewish commentators Rashi and Ibn Ezra understood the word to mean "hair." In our commentary, Ariel spells out how he deduced that "hair" is the more probable reading.[7] But most translations, from the Septuagint on—the King James Version is a notable exception—have the young woman hiding her charms behind a veil like a proper virgin. The Shulamite looks rather different—and so does the entire Song, in consequence—if *tsammah* refers not to a veil but to her wild flowing black hair, described more fully in the following verse: "Your hair like a flock of goats / bounding down Mount Gilead" (4:1, 6:5) and later on in the poem: "the hair of your head / like royal purple" (7:6).

Let me note also, while I am speaking about virgins: In the Shulamite's first speech, the King James Version translates ʿal-ken ʿalamot ʾahevukha (1:2) as "Therefore do the virgins love thee." But the word ʿalmah does not imply virginity here any more than it does in that famous verse in Isaiah 7:14: *Hinney ha-ʿalmah harah, vᵊ-yoledet ben, vᵊ-karat shemo ʿImmanu ʾEl,* "A young woman is pregnant, and she will give birth to a son, and will call him Immanuel." In the Septuagint, ʿalmah was translated *parthenos,* which can mean either "young unmarried woman" or "virgin." As for the interpretation of *parthenos* as "virgin" in the Christian tradition, one could hardly find a better example of the impact of translation—or rather, mistranslation—on theology and human history.

Some verses in the Song give no indication of who is speaking. Who, for example, says, "Catch us the foxes, / the quick little foxes / that raid our vineyards" (2:15), or "Then I went down to the walnut grove" (6:11), or "My vineyard is all my own" (8:12)? In each case, we deduced the speaker from clues in the context, and our reasoning may or may not be convincing. But where the lovers address one another, it is clear who is speaking, since Hebrew distinguishes between masculine and feminine in the second person.

In one of the lovers' dialogues, there is an abrupt shift of speakers that has eluded most translators. The young man is telling the Shulamite how she once appeared to him, and he reveals his erotic fantasy about her:

That day you seemed to me a tall palm tree
and your breasts
the clusters of its fruit.

I said in my heart,
"Let me climb into that palm tree
and take hold of its branches.

And oh, may your breasts be like clusters
of grapes on a vine, the scent
of your breath like apricots,
your mouth good wine—"

In the middle of the verse, the Shulamite interrupts and finishes her
lover's sentence:

That pleases my lover, rousing him
even from sleep.

I am my lover's,
he longs only for me,
only for me. (7:8–11)

There is no doubt that she is the speaker at this point: twice she calls him
dodi, "my lover," a masculine noun and her favorite epithet for him.
Translators who assign the entire speech to the man are obliged to emend
the word *dodi* or even to delete it. But there is no reason to depart from
the Hebrew text; the Shulamite's playful interruption beautifully renders
the way in which lovers complete one another's thoughts. This intimate
little scene—I imagine it as a form of pillow talk—is one more example
of the poet's sophisticated artistry.

Rare or obscure words in the Song are problematic, of course, but even
the simplest words can be far from simple. Consider *bet ha-yayin* (2:4).
Every student of elementary Hebrew learns that *bayit* means "house" and
yayin means "wine"; thus *bet ha-yayin* means "house of wine." But what
does "house of wine" mean? Here it is our knowledge of the cultural
context that is deficient. Is *beyt ha-yayin* a place in which wine is drunk,
a wine cellar, a vineyard, or a hut in the vineyards where the watchmen
rest and refresh themselves? Or perhaps, metaphorically, is it a place
where the lovers meet to make love? Among the translations we looked
at, "bower of delight" seemed rarefied and Spenserian; "banquet hall"
suggested either English nobility or bar mitzvahs in the Bronx, and "tavern" seemed too crude, too low-life. Translations of that sort tend to be
limiting and reductive. By translating *bet ha-yayin* as "house of wine," we
allow for various metaphorical possibilities, in keeping with the spirit of
the Song.

When the lover speaks of the Shulamite's *salmah* ("Your clothes hold
the scent of Lebanon" 4:11), or when she says that she has taken off her
kutonet ("I have taken off my clothes" 5:2), we weren't entirely sure what
she was wearing, but the real problem was how to convey whatever it

was in English. "Cloak" and "mantle" seemed too old-fashioned, "gown" too formal, "robes" too regal, "tunic" too Greek, "dress" too contemporary; "smock" makes her sound like an artist, "garment" evokes the International Ladies' Garment Workers Union. These terms are too time bound, too culture bound; they convey nuances that are alien to the Hebrew, and are constricting, in the way that illustrations in a book often limit rather than stir the imagination. As a teacher of poetry workshops at Mills College, I am always urging my students to greater specificity of expression. But sometimes, in fact, the more general word is the one that works best. In these two verses, I settled on the word "clothes" because it leaves something to the imagination.

A translation is an interpretation, and it involves choices at every turn. In a poetic translation—as opposed to a scholarly one—sound and rhythm are crucial elements; they are part of the sensual experience for the reader. In choosing between alternatives, we were particularly attentive to the music of the poem. The Hebrew of the Song is rich with assonance and alliteration, as the following lines suggest:

Nofet tittofnah siftotayikh kallah
dᵊvash vᵊ-chalav tachat lᵊshonekh
vᵊ-reach salmotayikh kᵊ-reach lᵊvanon. (4:11)

Sometimes it is possible to duplicate the effects of the Hebrew fairly closely; in our translation these verses read:

Your lips are honey, honey and milk
are under your tongue,
your clothes hold the scent of Lebanon. (4:11)

But since it is not always possible to echo the sound of the Hebrew in situ, we used alliteration and assonance wherever we could, for example:

They beat me, they bruised me,
they tore the shawl from my shoulders,
those watchmen of the walls. (5:8)

Let me conclude by looking at two verses from the Song. "Stay me with flagons, comfort me with apples" is the well-known King James translation of *samkhuni ba-'ashishot, rapduni ba-tapuchim* (2:5). But *samkhuni* and *rapduni* are not verbs of feeding, as is commonly assumed; they are, rather, verbs of upholstery. The image here is one of spreading a bed as a prelude to an erotic encounter, as in the words of the seductive woman in Proverbs 7:16–17, "I have decked my bed with linen, perfumed my bed with myrrh." Our version reads: "Let me lie among vine blossoms, / in a bed of apricots!"

Apricots? Some readers of our translation have objected: "Put the apples back in the Song of Songs!" Reading the Song as a poem about paradise regained, they demand "an apple for an apple"—though of course there is no apple in the Garden of Eden story, simply the generic "fruit." The word *tappuach* means "apple" in modern Hebrew, and it has usually been translated as "apple" in the Song, but botanists argue that it more likely refers to the apricot, a fruit that is abundant in Israel and has been since biblical times.[8] The apple tree is not native to Israel and was introduced comparatively recently; moreover, its fruit in the wild state is small, hard, and acidic. The apricot, on the other hand, is soft, golden, fleshy, and fragrant.

The last line of this verse, *cholat 'ahavah 'ani*, is translated in the King James as "I am sick of love." In the King's English of the seventeenth century, that would have meant "stricken by passion"; in colloquial English today, "I am sick of love" means "Leave me alone, I've had enough!" Some translators try to salvage this phrase by putting a patch on it—"I am sick *with* love"—but to my ears, that does not sound like contemporary English. "I am faint with desire," one of the possibilities we considered, sounds too effete, too Victorian. I can still remember the day when, after months of wrestling with this verse, the word "fever" occurred to me: "I am in the fever of love." I felt so high that I dashed out the door and ran four miles. I suppose that is what it means to be in the fever of words!

The most enigmatic verse in the Song—and perhaps the most erotic, as well—is 6:12. One scholar renders this "Unawares I was set / In the chariot with the prince," and another "I am beside myself with joy, for there thou wilt give me thy myrrh, O noble kinsman's daughter."[9] These are actually translations of the same lines. This verse is filled with difficulties, the most perplexing of which is *'ammi-nadiv*. Since the Masoretic text of the Song is very reliable, Ariel found it necessary to emend only this single verse. Reversing the order of those two words yielded the phrase *nediv 'ammi*, which occurs in the Psalter (*'im nedivey 'ammo*, Psalm 113:8).[10] This led him to interpret the phrase as "the chariot of the most noble of my people," "the most noble of chariots."[11] We took "chariot" to be an erotic metaphor for the Shulamite's body. In 6:11–12, a lyric of mutual seduction, the young man goes down to the walnut grove hoping that the moment is ripe—and there, to his surprise, the Shulamite anticipates and rewards him. Our translation reads:

Then I went down to the walnut grove
to see the new green by the brook,
to see if the vine had budded,
if the pomegranate trees were in flower.

And oh! before I was aware,
she sat me in the most lavish of chariots. (6:11–12)

Earlier, I characterized the translator of an ancient text as a kind of archaeologist. I actually had some experience of archaeology years ago as a volunteer at Masada, and I can still remember the tremor of excitement I felt at uncovering something two thousand years old—as it happened, a silver coin and a piece of purple cloth. I often felt that excitement as Ariel and I worked on our translation of the Song. I have no idea what happened to the coin and the cloth; they are probably buried for good in some museum drawer. But the text we labored to uncover has enjoyed an active afterlife. It is recited at weddings, at Passover Seders, in the synagogue. In the spring of 2002 it brought us the gifts of music and theater. "Song of Songs," a cantata for soprano and tenor, chamber orchestra and chorus, by Jorge Liderman, was performed by the San Francisco Contemporary Music Players along with the Chamber Chorus of the University of California at Berkeley. Liderman's setting, with its rich orchestration and its lively syncopated rhythms, captures the erotic intensity of the text and its air of youthful wonder. "Come, My Beloved," an adaptation of the text for the stage, conceived and directed by Naomi Newman of A Traveling Jewish Theatre, brings together the erotic and the spiritual interpretations—a young couple's sexual awakening and an older woman's search for union with the divine—so that they interact, finding parallels and striking fresh sparks. Both works reflect the varied moods of the Song—passionate, tender, playful, yearning, exuberant— and celebrate the power and joy of human love in a fitting contemporary idiom.

Immersed in the text through these powerful new renditions, I could almost be forgiven for imagining that the new millennium might usher in an era of love and joy. Yet I have only to glance at the daily headlines to know otherwise. I can't help thinking of one of Shakespeare's sonnets on mortality: "How with this rage shall beauty hold a plea? . . . O, how shall summer's honey breath hold out / Against the wrackful siege of batt'ring days?" Those questions take on new meaning in a time of terror and devastation. It seems best, then, to conclude with a prayer: May the life-affirming spirit of eros in the Song prevail over the dark forces of thanatos that threaten us all.

"I AM BLACK AND BEAUTIFUL"

André LaCocque

In *Romance, She Wrote: A Hermeneutical Essay on Song of Songs*,[1] I argue that the Song contains erotic descriptions that neither ask for nor require justification. In vivid contrast to the prophetic writings, in which eros is employed only in condemnation, it affirms, even revels in, sensual life. In fact, the Song's eroticism is deliberately subversive in its challenge to the institutions of the Hellenistic era (ca. 333–175 BCE), the probable time of its composition. I take it that the book's author is a woman and that this female authorship adds to its polemical celebration of "free" love, that is, love that is quite independent of social wont. I reject outright all attempts to view the Song—as has been done most recently by Tremper Longman—as a wedding libretto.[2] Contrary to the consummation represented in a marriage feast, the lovers' quest for one another is endless and only momentarily satisfied. Their love is on the fly, with not even a single encounter taking place inside a house. Lovemaking is repeatedly upset and thwarted. The shepherd must flee; his beloved cannot come to him; the two unite only for short moments; they are granted no rest, dependable routine, or enduring peace. The pair meets by night, endangered by "city watchers," guardians of morality on the lookout for delinquents or sexual outlaws. Their caresses take place under the starry sky, their tryst in woods outside the city limits. In 5:5–6, the woman's bedroom almost becomes their love nest, yet the customary marriage bed is shunned by her fugitive lover: "I sought him, but did not find him; I called him, but he gave no answer" (5:6).

Nothing in the Song bows to convention. At one point, the Shulamite actually boasts about her loss of virtue (1:6). The author has only scorn for the custom of exchanging goods between families busy marrying off their children. Again and again, she enjoins, "do not wake up love before it is ready" (2:7; 3:5; 5:8; 8:4). Nor does she have any patience for mercenary concern over bride price or dowry: "If one offered for love all the wealth of his house, it would be utterly scorned" (8:7).

In short, the Song of Songs is highly iconoclastic, particularly when it is engaged in provocative intertextual play with such proscriptive or condemnatory sources as Genesis 3 and Hosea 3–4. The most nonreligious text among all biblical documents, it is also the most irreverent. As Francis Landy writes, "it cocks a snook at all Puritans. Yet it points to something essential in holiness: the dream of justice and universal peace of which Israel is the bearer."[3] Indeed, the Song takes human love to its most elevated theological heights, making it, in effect, a song of paradise.

This dialectical quality of the Song—its simultaneous play with flesh and spirit—can place its readers in a highly paradoxical bind. Its inner workings can be traced, I think, as follows: In a first move, the author "defigurativizes" the language that the prophets typically use in describing the vertical relationship between God and Israel. In other words, she restores eros to the horizontal plane of love where it is naturally enjoyed between lovers. It is on this plane that her refiguration must be read, for, in a second move, the author extols physical love, which she clothes in metaphors drawn from the realms of nature, courtship, luxury, eroticism—all of which the prophets and sages by and large found objectionable. In summary, language has come full circle. It begins on the horizontal plane of daily parlance, where the prophets found it in the first place; it moves then to the vertical plane via a radical ad hoc metaphorization; finally, it returns to the horizontal by means of a poetic reclamation and refiguration. If only this were the end of the process. Unfortunately, tradition has turned the iconoclasm of the Song into a standard piece of wisdom literature, one that claims to be written by the greatest master of the genre. As we are told in the superscription, it is "The Song of Songs, which is Solomon's" (1:1).

This attribution should have been sufficient to make the Song orthodox and canonical, but apparently it needed something more to bring it into line. And so a thoroughgoing allegorization of the text obliterates eros in favor of an altogether disincarnate agape. From the second century CE, the book has traditionally been read, mutatis mutandis, as an allegory of the mutual quest of God and humanity. By this means, the female author is dispossessed of her property, which becomes the possession of scribes, sages, and church fathers.

No modern reader can entirely bypass this centuries-old interpretation, anymore than she can ignore the obvious intent of the poem to celebrate the human and sensual. And it is precisely with this tension between the text itself and the abstractive ways it has been read that our quandary lies. I am arguing in the face of postmodernism's disdain for the notion of authorial design and am challenging a strict "canonical" reading. I am also advocating a Barthian distinction between the terms "religious" and "theological." Karl Kerenyi speaks of the religious as "the primordial threat to man"; it comes between God and humanity, taking "the place of that which is irreplaceable."[4] We can find no better illustration of this intrusive religious process than by looking at the hermeneutic history of the Song of Songs. We must retrieve a largely lost sense of the *subversive* dimension of the biblical text in order to note how it prevents customs and established mores from becoming taboos and keeps the Bible itself from becoming an idol.

Such was the object of *Romance, She Wrote*, in which I perused the whole poem, demonstrating how in passage after passage the author borrowed from established traditions of her people, sometimes conforming to those traditions, but even more often contradicting them. For instance, whereas the writer of Genesis 3:16 has God declare to Eve, "Your desire is to your husband and he, he shall rule over you," the author of the Song empowers woman, when she exclaims, "His desire is for me" (7:10). While Leviticus 26:12 says, "I became your God and you became my people," the Song daringly transposes this divine-human relationship to the plane of eros and cries out, "My beloved is mine and I am his"(2:16). In Exodus 33, Moses is moved by the desire to see the glory (i.e., the face) of God. In response, God "put [Moses] in a cleft of the rock" and shielded him with a hand (33:22). By way of clear imitation of this scene, but with an irreverence bordering on blasphemy, the Song has the lover say to his beloved, "O my dove, in the clefts of the rock, in the covert of the cliff, let me see your face!" (2:14).

With so many examples of precisely this kind of echoing, the text reveals itself to be an entirely intertextual creation. It must be remembered, moreover, that intertextuality blazes a two-way street. This means that the Song and its provider texts are always interacting, recreating each other in the process. On the one hand, the Song must be read with narrative and prophetic figurative discourse in mind; on the other, the narratives and oracles must be reread in the new light shed by the Canticle. In such a rereading, apparently misogynistic texts like Genesis 3 or

Hosea 2, which invoke shame and punishment on women, are counter-balanced by the Song's unabashed celebration of the female body and its desires. Without such cross-reference within the canon, we would run the risk of perpetuating a grave injustice. The intent of these texts is no doubt to liberate humans from delusion and sin, but the texts themselves need to be liberated.

The Song provides this liberation: it is a key that can unlock the Torah and prophetic texts, opening them to life-giving interpretation. A case in point is offered by Song of Songs 1:5–6 (NRSV):

> I am black and beautiful,
> O daughters of Jerusalem,
> like the tents of Kedar,
> like the curtains of Solomon.
> Do not gaze at me because I am dark,
> because the sun has gazed on me.
> My mother's sons were angry with me;
> they made me keeper of the vineyards,
> but my own vineyard I have not kept!

As is well known, the alternative reading of "black *and* beautiful" is "black *but* beautiful," a variant that has been a point of contention among scholars. Which is it, then, "and" or "but"? To resolve this question, we have to keep in mind the paradigmatic nature of the Song: It does not speak of particular or historical individuals. "He" and "she" remain anonymous—"the Shulamite" is a title, not a name (*shubî, shubî, ha-shulam-mîth*, "turn, turn, O Shulamite," 7:1). Furthermore, the poem unfolds without a distinct *Sitz im Leben*. There is no plot or development toward a conclusion, for the Song has neither beginning nor end. Rather, it is, as I have suggested, a "ritornello."[5]

It is futile to wonder, therefore, if the speaker is saying that she herself is black *but* beautiful, that is, black although a tanned country girl who has spent her days exposed to the elements. The poem takes us at random to the country and to town; the lover is at will a king or a shepherd; the beloved girl is at times shunned by city damsels as a sort of peasant and at times bedecked with jewels like a rich lady. As to the color of her skin, she is sometimes black, but also as white as a lily of the valley or a lotus (2:1). The maidens call her fairest of women (5:9; 6:1): Seen in this way, she is as resplendent as the dawn, as the moon, as the sun. (In 6:10, the moon is called *lebanah*, the white one!) Likewise, her hair is black like a flock of goats (6:5); it is also said to be purple (7:5). Her voice is soft (2:8) and charming (4:3), her tongue flows milk and honey—like the Promised Land itself!—yet she is also fearsome, "terrible as an army with banners" (6:4,10).

The same "inconsistency" is found with regard to the shepherd-king. In 5:10, he is both *ṣaḥ we-'adôm*, white and red or ruddy. So David is described in 1 Sam. 16:12, "he was ruddy, and had beautiful eyes, and was handsome"; likewise, in Lamentations, the young courtiers of Jerusalem before the city's fall, were "purer than snow, whiter than milk; their bodies were more ruddy than coral and their hair like sapphire" (4:7). As with the female beloved, we cannot determine the color of the male lover's hair. His ruddy complexion suggests that it might be auburn. And yet in 5:11 we are told that his head is pure gold, and then, surprisingly, that his locks are black like a raven.

In short, consistency plays no role in these descriptions, whose purpose cannot be to tell what he or she "actually" looks like. Instead, raven black or coral pink refer us to other texts within Scripture and thereby link the lovers of the Song to contexts that have nothing to do with erotic dalliance. In this instance, I am thinking of a parallel text with both philological and ideological kinship—Numbers 12:1. This passage also concerns a woman, but takes an altogether different evaluative tack. As in the examples I offered above, the Song reverses the negative assessment in the Torah text by replacing it with one that is an entirely positive. In so doing, the poem again proves itself to be irreverent, iconoclastic, and subversive.

The provider text from Torah that I am proposing here presents Miriam and Aaron speaking angrily to Moses "because of the Cushite woman whom [Moses] had taken, for he had taken a Cushite woman," *'al 'ôdôth ha-'ishshah ha-kushîth 'asher [Moshe] lâqaḥ kî 'ishshah kushîth lâqaḥ*. Then, abruptly, their discourse seemingly deviates to move on to another subject, Moses' alleged claim that YHWH speaks to him exclusively. Miriam and Aaron accuse Moses of arrogance in contradiction to another text that, by way of aside, refers to him as "a very humble man," *'îsh . . . 'ânâw me'od*, more than anyone on the face of the earth (Num. 12:3).

Be this as it may, it is clear that the Moses's interracial marriage provides Miriam and Aaron with the excuse for complaint. We do not know if the Cushite woman is, as tradition has it, Zipporah herself. What is clear, however, is that Miriam and Aaron blame Moses for ritual uncleanness due to his "becoming one flesh" with the black Cushite. In doing so, the man who talks with God "face to face" (Num. 12:8) reveals his all too human weakness and enables them to dislodge him from his pedestal.

But does he need to be humiliated? We have already been told that Moses is the most humble of men and does not himself claim any special privilege. Miriam and Aaron, therefore, are wrong in their accusations, and Miriam, the instigator of the whole affair, is punished. She "become[s] leprous, as white as snow" (12:10), whereas Moses's disparaged wife, the Cushite, is raven black.

The negative valuation of blackness, here signified by Miriam and Aaron's denigration of the Cushite, represents the establishment view in Israel. In the seventh century BCE, with Egypt under the sway of Nubian or Sudanese southerners, Isaiah prophesizes against Cush:[6] "They [Judeans] will be dismayed and confounded because of Cush, their hope, and Egypt, their adornment." One can comprehend this longstanding antipathy. As mentioned in the Table of Nations (Gen. 10), Cush (Ethiopia)— like Mitsrayim (Egypt), Put (Libya), and Canaan—is also a descendant of Noah's accursed son Ham.

Against this background of texts that place a negative judgment on Africa or that treat a black woman with contempt, the Shulamite proudly declares herself to be black and beautiful. Her blackness is by no means a flaw, but rather adds to her attractiveness. Consequently, if the shepherd of the Song turns to the "black and beautiful" shepherdess, it is hardly evidence of the weakness of his fleshly self, but only of his good "sense." Beauty triumphs, and with it, love itself.

The homebound "daughters of Jerusalem" in the Song represent the social prejudice against Cush, personified in Numbers 12 by Miriam and Aaron. They shun the swarthy woman as belonging to a lower social class. Their judgment, however, is baseless; so, too, the rash condemnation of the Shulamite as a loose woman in chapters 3 and 5 by any number of bystanders. But in order to recognize the truth, one must turn away from prejudice and share with the Shulamite and her shepherd the elation of a love that transcends mere convention.

In Song of Songs 1:5, the woman's blackness is compared to the tents of Kedar and, further, to the curtains of Solomon. The latter similitude is evident; Exodus 26:7 and 36:14 specify that the Tabernacle's curtains were made "of goats' hair." But the motif of the tents of Kedar is more obscure. Nomads, descendants of Ishmael, erect these dwellings. But why would *these* tents be chosen for comparison, apart from their dark color? The root of the word "Kedar" means to become black, even dirty (see Job 6:16; Jer. 8:21; 14:2). We know that these tents, like the curtains of the Tabernacle, were made from goat hair. If the etymological root of "Kedar" was the basis of the simile in Song 1:5, or if the point is darkness alone, then there is no necessary connection with the sacral curtains of the Tabernacle. This is not the case, if we remember how Exodus 26:14 speaks of the *yerîôth ha-'ôhel*: "You shall make for the tent [of meeting] a covering of tanned rams' skins." These curtains were to cover the Ark so as to form a veritable tent over it—hence its designation as an *'ohel*, the same term used for the nomadic dwellings of the people of Kedar.

It is one thing to compare a dark lady's appearance to desert tents. It is quite another to compare her to the Tabernacle's décor. Is this simply poor taste, or is it deliberate defiance of the religious establishment?

The apparent irreverence turns out to be even more extensive. The author's simile involves three terms: the Shulamite's skin, the skin curtains of the Tabernacle, and the skin tents of Kedar. The bringing together of the latter two terms, however, is nothing less than outrageous, for the tents of Kedar come under Jeremiah's scathing attack. In an oracle, the prophet urges Israel to "Rise up, advance against Kedar! Destroy the people of the east! Take their tents [*ôhôleyhem*] and their flocks [*ṣ'onam*],[7] their curtains [*yerîôtheyhem*], all their goods" (Jer. 49:28–30). Evidently, Kedar is no idyllic place in the eyes of the Israelites. Their tents and curtains do not look like awesome drapes. How can they be equated with the tent of meeting, with the curtains of the Temple of Jerusalem? The priests of the time must have been filled with rage.

Whereas comparisons to the Temple can only be favorable, the female lover is self-conscious about her blackness. Her assertion, "I am black and beautiful, O daughters of Jerusalem, like the tents of Kedar, like the curtains of Solomon," is followed immediately by the injunction, "Do not gaze at me because I am dark."

We ought not to understand this darkness as a mark of her shame. Rather, ever assertive, she is in effect saying, "Do not look at me as one who is swarthy, do not be fixated on my blackness! For, if I am dark, it is because my brothers [*b'ney 'immî*], in their anger [*niharû bî*], have sent me into the country and set me [*sâmunî*] as a guardian of the vineyards [*notérah 'eth ha-ḵerâmîm*]."

Several aspects of this self-description must be highlighted. First, it is clear that the woman's brothers are to be blamed for her darkness. Second, they are *b'ney 'immî*, something like "my very brothers, the sons of our common mother," a phrase we also see in Deuteronomy 13:6, which warns against being lured into idolatry by close family members. In the Hebrew Bible, brothers are usually designated as offspring of a common father, (*beyth 'ab*), but here they are linked by a common mother, (*be'yth 'ém*). Does this indicate a deceased father, as Franz Delitzsch has argued?

It is true that no fathers are mentioned in the Song, but it would be presumptuous to say that the Shulamite and her lover have none. Israelite society attributed authority over girls to fathers and brothers, especially over their sexuality. It is clear that the combined absence of any *'ab beyth 'ab* (pater familias) and the ineptitude of the brothers—alongside the favorable treatment of the mother throughout the book (see 3:4; 6:9; 8:2)—all serve the subversive purpose of the author.

We learn that the "sons of her mother," the appointed guardians of her morality, have sought to keep their sister in line. Fearing her spirit of independence, they "were angry with [her]" and "made [her] keeper of the vineyards" (1:6), no doubt in order to isolate her from the temptations of the city, to keep her out of trouble. Assuming the Köhler-Baumgartner lexicon's parsing of *niharû bî* is correct,[8] this verb—"to be angry"—appears only one other time in Scripture, in Jeremiah 6:29. There, the root is associated with smelting: "The bellows blow fiercely, the lead is consumed by the fire; in vain the refining goes on, for the wicked are not removed." But Marvin Pope is probably right when he sees here a niphal form of the root *hary*, as in Isaiah 41:11 and 45:24, with the sense of "to burn, be angry."[9] The figurative burning of the brothers fits well the actual burning of the maiden's skin by the sun. Furthermore, Isaiah's declarations provide an intriguing backdrop to our Song of Songs text. Isaiah 41:11 says, "Yes, all who are incensed against you [feminine, *ha-nèôhèrîm bak*] shall be ashamed and disgraced"; Isaiah 45:24b adds, "all who were incensed against Him [*kôl ha-nèhèrîm bô*] shall come to Him and be ashamed."

The audacity in the wording of Song 1:6 is clear. The girl likens herself not only to the Israel of Isaiah in 41:11, but also to the God of Isaiah in 45:24b. She understands herself to be righteous. And although her brothers see her as having disgraced them, she is proud of her defiance. They have entrusted her with the care of the family vineyards, and she has upheld their commission. However, the one vineyard she has not kept is her own (1:6):[10] Though cloistered from the city, she has nonetheless known a love that is as strong as death. There is no one able to defeat it.

In *Romance*, I showed the deep influence of the first chapters of Hosea on the Song of Songs, whose author steadily reverses the expressions and metaphors of the prophet. The Lord commands Hosea to take "a wife of whoredom"; this wife as prostitute functions as a trope for Israel, who "commits great whoredom by forsaking the Lord" (Hosea 1:2). In sharp contrast, the whole concept of whoredom is subverted in the Song. Defiantly, the Shulamite gives the appearance of being a loose woman (see, e. g., 1:6 here, or 3:1–5 and 5:2–8), but she upsets all the conventions. Her love, in contradistinction to Gomer's, is true; rather than being a source of shame, it is gloriously proclaimed.

In Hosea 2:14, the very elements we have been dealing with in Song of Songs 1:6—the vineyard, the woman, and righteous male anger—occur as well. In this case, however, they are negatively connoted. The vineyard is cursed: "I will lay waste her vines and her fig trees, of which she said, 'These are my pay, which my lovers have given me.' I will make them a forest, and the wild animals shall devour them" (NRSV 2:12). The righteous indignation is YHWH's, and it is directed against a people who have deserted him. He is the husband, they the wayward wife. He is the vintner, they the unruly vine. As in the Song, the motifs of husbandry both in marriage and vine keeping are intertwined: "The poetic choice of setting the dramatis personae in a pastoral environment and of depicting them as shepherd and vineyard keeper is not foreign to the author's general purpose of imitating the traditional metaphoric roles of God and Israel."[11] Just as God is vexed by Israel's idolatry, so is Hosea distraught over Gomer's waywardness. Gomer/Israel has not kept its own vineyard and has to be punished accordingly: "I will punish her for the festival days of the Baals, when she offered incense to them and decked herself with her ring and jewelry and went after her lovers and forgot me, says the Lord" (Hosea 2:13). The Shulamite, however, is untroubled by the perception that she has strayed. Over against the prophetic censure that she critiques throughout the Song, she proudly trumpets her own sexuality. Her vineyard is her own; it is under no one else's control, especially not the guardians of public morality.

Thus, what the Song does on every level—literary as well as moral—is revalue Hosea. Whereas in Hosea 2:3 God wrathfully turns Israel into a desert, the Shulamite, we are told twice, comes up *from* the desert (3:6; 8:5). While Gomer is decked with rings and jewels to allure new lovers, the Shulamite's jewelry is for the benefit of her beloved alone. Although Gomer is ever looking for partners with whom to commit adultery, the Shulamite's quest is strictly for the one whom her soul loves (3:1). And in Hosea, YHWH is the one who takes the initiative from start to finish, in the Song, the woman is the driving force.

There are three distinct conclusions that may be drawn from this close reading. First, the Song's elaborate intertextual reverberations suggest a highly literary culture: The Song of Songs is no popular legend. The author has produced a highly sophisticated polysemic construct; it is written for an enlightened public knowledgeable in the literature of Israel and the surrounding cultures. An aspect of this sophistication is the frequency of double entendres throughout the book. Given its refinement, its complex enjoyment of its own literary power, the work's classification as wisdom literature and its ascription to Solomon make aesthetic good sense.

Second, the phenomenon of intertextuality in Song of Songs is indicative of a protocanonization. The Song is in dialogue with what would have been traditional texts, that is, "classic" texts that bear the weight of authority and maintain ongoing currency. As Frank Kermode notes, such texts "can be more or less immediately relevant and available, in a sense contemporaneous with the modern reader."[12] All of this—self-conscious literary play, recourse to authoritative texts in startlingly new ways—points to a late date for the composition of the Song.

Third, the Song of Songs is a subversive text. It appropriates the negative female models found in Genesis 3 and in Hosea, where female sexuality is tied to male dominion ("your desire shall be for your husband and he shall rule over you," Gen. 3:16) or viewed as promiscuous and base ("their mother has played the whore," Hosea 2:15). Instead, the author establishes woman as the proper object of male desire and celebrates desire itself. The canon contains other subversive works contemporary with the Song: One thinks of Job, Jonah, Ruth, Esther, and Qoheleth. Whereas it has proven too easy to domesticate these works, to forget how they each undermined the wisdom of their day, the Song, by contrast, has never been fully tamed. It remains highly contentious. Not even the superscription imposed by a scribal zealot could turn it into a product of the wisdom establishment.

READING THE SONG
ICONOGRAPHICALLY

Ellen F. Davis

Among the most important questions for biblical interpreters to ask is the question of genre: *As what* are we to read this text? In the modern period, it was Hermann Gunkel who brought that question to the fore. As he demonstrated, the issue confronts us as soon as the opening pages of Genesis.[1] Do we read this as history (cum science) or as myth, as something that happened at a certain time—history, or as (citing the description of myth offered by the Roman historian Sallust) "something that happens over and over again"?

When it comes to interpreting the Song of Songs, determining the answer to the genre question seems to me to be the most vexed issue in modern scholarship on the book. Is the Song a parody of Torah, prophets, and sages (André LaCocque),[2] or is it a reflection of Canaanite cultic religion, representing a marriage ceremony between deities (Marvin Pope)?[3] Is it "soft porn" (David Clines),[4] a venture into the "grotesque" that is toxic to readers (Fiona Black)?[5] Or is it rather exquisite love poetry that deserves to be matched and rendered into accessible language by the best efforts of contemporary poets (Marcia Falk, Ariel and Chana Bloch)?[6]

What all of these genre identifications (and a number of variations on them) share is the assumption that the Song is in the canon because the rabbis who voted it in had no idea what they were reading. Almost all these interpreters would say that the rabbis did the right thing for the wrong reason, because they thought the Song was about the love between God and Israel. (Although Clines and Black would agree that this was the reason for its canonization, they would of course disagree that its inclusion was "the right thing.") As far as I know, I am almost alone among contemporary biblical scholars in my conviction that the Song was correctly understood by those who accorded it a place among Israel's Scriptures. In other words, I believe that it really is, in large part, about the love that obtains between God and Israel—or, more broadly, between God and humanity.[7]

The fullest articulation of my view is found in my brief commentary on the Song;[8] below I will give some details of my interpretation. However, this present essay sets forth an idea that has come to me since I completed my commentary, namely, that the Song is an iconographic text. Before I explain what that means, I will briefly trace how I came to this notion, because I think it shows something of the unique complexity—I might even say "mysteriousness"—of interpreting the Song. Perhaps it even shows the fruitfulness of disagreement about this most difficult of all biblical books.

The idea that the Song is iconographic came to me through reading and teaching André LaCocque's hermeneutical study of the Song, *Romance, She Wrote*, which was published just about the time my book went into production. I now ask my students to read the two books together, because they throw into high relief the current debate over genre. Our approaches are in several ways strikingly similar; in terms of method we are, I believe, closer to each other than to other scholars. Both LaCocque and I consider the Song of Songs to present the greatest hermeneutical challenge in the Bible, and our books are more detailed hermeneutical statements than full commentaries on the Song. Both of us treat the Song as a literary whole, arguably the work of a single poetic imagination. Both of us choose the same methodology, intertextuality, based on our observation that the Song's most prominent literary feature is the extraordinarily high incidence of words and phrases that echo other parts of Scripture and yet in their creative reuse here become imbued with fresh and unexpected meaning.

In sum, both LaCocque and I agree, against most modern commentators, that the Song has a familial relationship with the rest of the biblical books; it is not the foundling in the canon. We suppose that an Israelite poet created the Song in direct response to what she[9] already knew as sacred Scripture—but with what intent? In answering this question, we differ completely. LaCocque argues that the Song is the work of a poet who resolutely subverts the religious traditions of Israel, taking the praise that is elsewhere offered to God along the "vertical axis" and transposing it onto the "horizontal axis" so that the language of desire and gratitude is focused on a human lover. I think the Song returns us to Eden with the intent of imaginatively healing the ruptures that occurred there: between man and woman, between humanity and God, between human and nonhuman creation. So where LaCocque hears deliberate irreverence, rebellion against the tradition, I hear adoration—that is, prayer—in a distinctly traditional mode. Where he repeatedly asserts the poet's intent to be "iconoclastic," I see a style of theological reflection I have recently come to call "iconographic"—and for that term I am indirectly indebted to LaCocque and his antithetical way of viewing the text.

I return to Hermann Gunkel because I believe that what he taught us about genre identification, now more than a century ago, clarifies the difference between LaCocque's and my readings and perhaps sheds some light on the general problem of interpreting the Song. As every student of Scripture is told, Gunkel identified three criteria for identifying the genre of a piece of biblical literature: first, *Sitz im Leben*, the presumed place the text occupied in ancient Israel's life (frequently, since Gunkel favored the Psalms, in its cult); second, formulaic language, words or phrases that seem to serve a fixed function within various texts (e.g., "Thus says YHWH," the messenger formula that introduces prophetic speech); and third, the somewhat elusive criterion of *Stimmung* ("tone")— what kind of note or responsive chord a text strikes. Is this psalm a lament, an appeal for God's deliverance, or part of a hymn, a statement of confidence in God's ability to deliver? If we are honest, we must admit that such distinctions are often drawn on the basis of ambiguous evidence.

With these three criteria, Gunkel gave modern readers of the Bible the chance to learn a virtue that was highly prized by its monastic readers from Augustine through the Middle Ages: humility in interpretation. If we consider the criteria closely, it is evident that reading a text well involves more than mastery of linguistic "hard data" (criterion number two). It also involves a large measure of historical imagination: *Sitz im Leben* is not something you can excavate; it has to be imaginatively (re)-constructed—although the imaginative element has not been sufficiently acknowledged, especially in the earlier, more confident period of historical criticism. Further, good reading involves subjective judgment, in the discernment of *Stimmung*.

Looking at the difference between André LaCocque's reading of the Song and my own, it is evident how important is the element of subjective judgment. With respect to Gunkel's first two criteria for genre identification, we would seem to concur entirely: first, that the *Sitz im Leben* for this work was not some oft-repeated public ceremony (e.g., a wedding, either human or divine), but rather a poet's extraordinary imagination; and second, that the chief datum for interpretation is "formulaic language," which is recontextualized here in wholly surprising ways. Indeed, LaCocque and I comment on many of the same words and phrases and trace them to the same scriptural sources. So it is only on the point of *Stimmung* that we part ways, and yet as a result, there is probably not a single verse of the Song on whose interpretation we would agree.

What are scholars who presume to interpret the Song for others to infer from this? *Not* that "it's all relative" anyway and there is no right and no wrong interpretation—of this book, at least. In this case, LaCocque and I cannot both be right. (We might both be wrong.) Differing interpretations might in some cases be complementary. For instance, although I differ from the medieval allegorists, I see my reading as congenial with theirs on most of the essential points. (I confess to doubt that they would agree with me that a reading that includes a sexual dimension is congenial with theirs.) However, LaCocque and I disagree fundamentally about what to read the Song *as*, and yet neither of us has succeeded in persuading the other. At one time—even recently, before the conference that generated this volume—I would have regarded this as a failure either of our persuasive powers or of our open-mindedness. I now think such disagreement goes with the territory of interpreting this book, and more so with this than with any other in the Bible. 'Twas ever thus, since the rabbis first debated its inclusion in the canon, and it will remain so as long as the Song is read as Scripture. Why? Because for the Song, *Stimmung*—that elusive element whose identification depends on our subjective judgment—is everything.

While emphasizing subjectivity in the interpretation of the Song, I would also acknowledge that one can reasonably speak of probability and plausibility in developing a hermeneutical argument. In each case where I propose to trace a line of thought connecting the poet of the Song with earlier biblical writers, I ask myself whether it is likely that an ancient poet would have thought like this, and, further, would have expected at least some readers (or hearers) to "track" her. I try to hang the heaviest weight of my intertextual arguments on verses that I can assume predate the Song and would have been well known, not only to the poet, but to her audience; wherever possible I draw multiple strands connecting an earlier tradition to the Song. A reader should use these criteria to judge my commentary, as well as LaCocque's work.

In sum, while one can and should make judgments about probability with respect to interpretation of the Song, subjectivity is a more important element here than with most other biblical books. From this I would not infer that we should give up trying to persuade one another of the merits of our distinctive views; that is, after all, what scholars and teachers are obliged to do. Rather, by frankly acknowledging the importance of subjective judgment, we might gain in the practice of humility. My view is not the only one that can reasonably be argued, and certain factors predispose me to it. Concretely, then, I suggest that the practice of interpretive humility might begin with each of us identifying, as best we can, what factors in our personal histories conduce to a certain interpretive style. I think it must surely be the case that, while every dedicated interpreter of the Song is likely to insist upon the special character of this book, our readings of it in each case bear a strong family resemblance to our readings of other biblical texts. So, I end these prefatory remarks by noting that I am a catholic Christian—a moderately high-church Anglican, to be exact. Long familiarity with and love of the liturgy has bred in me an affinity for monastic theology in both its medieval and its modern expressions. Partly as a result, I read the Bible with a strong theocentric bias. Like the monastics—and in contrast to many Protestant interpreters—I see the central focus of the Bible as revelation of God's character, desire, and involvement with the created world. The undeniable biblical concern with fulfillment or salvation of the human person seems to me related and subordinate to that primary revelation. These biases are reflected in the reading of the Song that follows.

An Iconographic Text

In my own short commentary on the Song, I followed Harold Fisch in likening the Song to a dream that moves from one scene to another without logical transition.[10] As I have indicated, André LaCocque's notion of iconoclasm indirectly suggested to me another comparison, which I have come to prefer to the dream. It seems to me that the way the Song functions within Scripture bears some similarity to the role of an icon or iconostasis in the Eastern Church. I identify four characteristics of icons and iconostases that, in my judgment, are closely paralleled in the Song.

First, the icon is a window opening between two worlds: the world of history and ordinary sense perception, on the one hand, and on the other, the transcendent realm we designate as "heaven," "eternal life," "the kingdom of God." We live now in the first of those worlds, and the icon provides Orthodox Christians, at least, with a point of orientation toward the second. The icon is an image of this world, but it is far from naturalistic. Rather, it shows us our world as seen in the light of God's glory. It affirms that our historical, sensible experience is the basis for our experience of God, yet at the same time it suggests that the features of what we call "reality" are suppler than we generally suppose.

A second point of comparison: The iconic image does not reflect "universal human experience," if there be such a thing. It is a tradition-laden image that comes from a theological imagination formed in the traditions of Israel and the early church. The icon is "written" to provide orientation and effect reorientation for those immersed in that tradition. To those outside, its style of representation may be peculiar and only minimally intelligible.

Third, the iconostasis, the screen of icons that is the dominant architectural element of an Orthodox church, is a montage of more or less independent images, although all are anchored by the image of Christ, flanked on either side by the Virgin and the Baptist. The other images may be thematically connected (great saints, for instance), but to my untrained eye, it seems that the richest iconic montages—in my slight experience, Saint Catherine's Monastery in the Sinai and Saint George's Monastery in the Wadi Qelt—reflect, if not random juxtaposition of images, then at least loose governing principles. In their composite beauty and spontaneous unity, they resemble pieces in a kaleidoscope. One might imagine that the assemblage of icons mirrors our fragmented experience of God in this world at the same time that it shows the church straining and praying toward the One "in [whom] all things hold together" (Col. 1:17). Further, it guides the church in its prayer.[11]

A fourth element of comparison: The architecture of an Orthodox church represents schematically the Temple in Jerusalem. Within that design, the iconostasis marks the boundary between the main sanctuary and the priestly precinct, where the Holy Mysteries are celebrated. Ideologically speaking, then, the iconostasis is the point of entry into the Holy of Holies.

I believe that each of these four aspects of the function of icons and iconostases finds a parallel in the canonical function of the Song: the Song mediates between historical, sensible existence and transcendent experience; it is an imaginative expression shaped by prayer and the theological traditions of the Bible; it witnesses to our fragmentation and yet offers glimpses of a higher unity; and, as Rabbi Akiba famously declared, "All the Scriptures are holy, but the Song of Songs is the Holy of Holies."[12] In what follows, I will suggest that the connection between the Song and the Temple is real and precise, albeit metaphorical.

These several parallels suggest that the Song may be a verbal analogue and forerunner of the Byzantine icon. This comparison implies that the Song is essentially a mystical text, a text that emanates from religious vision and invites—even requires—prayerful reading. It implies further that there is a direct line of thought connecting the poet who wrote the Song to its later theocentric interpreters, both Jewish and Christian. As noted above, I do not share the currently widespread assumption that the Song entered the canon as a result of a happy misreading on the part of the first-century rabbis. I am convinced that the rabbis correctly judged the genre of the Song and heard a message that did not deviate widely from the theological vision of the poet who gave us the Song in its present form. (Parenthetically, I would allow that the Song had ancient secular antecedents and even relatives. I am persuaded by Michael Fox's argument for resemblance between the Song and the love poetry of Ramesside Egypt—the Nineteenth and Twentieth Dynasties, 1305–1150 BCE.)[13]

If the Song is read as an icon, then its anchoring image is, of course, the garden. All modern commentators have observed that the garden is both the lovers' haven and a metaphor for the woman's body (e.g., 4:12–5:1; 7:8–9 Heb., vv. 7–8 Eng.). My own view of the Song depends upon the significance of the garden for the Israelite religious imagination. What is crucial is that, in terms of both historical order (dating the Song to the Persian period) and canonical ordering, the garden of the lovers is the third important garden in the Bible. Both the second and the third gardens are related to the first, to Eden. The second garden is the Temple, which, as both its décor and its hymnody show, is the stylized Garden of God. The columns of the Temple were crowned with lilies and festooned with hundreds of pomegranates (1 Kings 7:18–20), symbols of fertility and life. Its great gold menorah was shaped like an almond tree in full bloom (Exod. 37:17–24). The walls were carved and gilded with palm trees and flowers and cherubim, those guardians of Eden. Lions lurked under the lavers, along with more cherubim and oxen (1 Kings 7:29). The inside of the building smelled like the woods; the whole building was lined with cedar, and "not a stone was seen" (1 Kings 6:18). On that dry stony hill in Jerusalem, Solomon had created a second Lebanon, the majestic and myth-laden mountains of the North. The whole Temple was a sensuous and at the same time a spiritual triumph over what would seem to be the limits of nature and geography. A poet making pilgrimage to the Temple exclaims ecstatically:

How precious is your covenant-love [*ḥesed*],
O God, and human beings—
in the shadow of your wings they take shelter!
They are drenched with the rich fare of your house,
and you let them drink from the torrent of your Edens [or:
   "delights"].
(Ps. 36:8–9)[14]

Thus, pilgrimage to the Temple was conceived as a return to Eden, to life as it was meant to be, at least for a few days each year. But the story of the second garden, like the first, ends with exile. So I believe that the third garden of the lovers takes up the story line that proceeds from the other two and effects—or envisions—a resolution of the abiding problem of humanity's exile from the Garden of God. Of course, the cause of exile, as we see in Genesis, is disobedience. Torah and the prophets consistently address the problem in terms of sin and Israel's refusal to listen to God, which eventually led to that second exile, from Jerusalem to Babylon. But the Song opens up a new (though not contrary) way of looking at the problem, and this in my judgment is its great theological contribution to the canon. The Song speaks not of obedience and disobedience, but in terms of intimacy and its threatened loss.

Loss of intimacy is exactly what happened in Eden. Eden was the place where God was most intimate with humanity. Witness God "taking a walk in the garden in the breezy part of the day" (Gen. 3:8), obviously expecting to have the humans for company, and calling out—"Where are you?"—when they do not appear. There is good reason to imagine that God intended to impart wisdom to humanity on those walks, little by little. But when Eve and Adam disregarded God and tried the direct route to "knowledge of good and evil," the immediate result was not literal death. Rather, it was distrust breaking into the relationship between God and humanity. It was blame erupting between man and woman (Gen. 3:12) and the onset of a long-term imbalance of power between them (Gen. 3:16). It was a curse on the fertile soil and enmity between the woman's seed and the snake's (Gen. 3:15, 17).

Viewed from the inside—as we are most profoundly touched by it—the exile from Eden represents the loss of intimacy in three primary spheres of relationship: between God and humanity, between woman and man, and between human and nonhuman creation. Correspondingly, the Song uses language to evoke a vision of healing in all three areas. More accurately, it *reuses* language from other parts of Scripture; verbal echoes explicitly connect the garden of the lovers with the two earlier gardens. (Unsurprisingly, descriptions of Jerusalem and its Temple find far more echoes in the Song than do the first few chapters of Genesis. As the paucity of direct references to Eden throughout the Bible shows, the second version of the Garden impressed itself more vividly on the Israelite imagination than did the first.) If, as I believe, the language of the Song resists systematic interpretation, that is because it is constantly moving among these different spheres, in each of which we can experience a profound connection with one who is other than and unlike ourselves. Following the Song's quicksilver movements makes interpretation at once difficult and compelling. In my judgment, the characteristic weakness of both traditional and modern commentaries is their confinement of the Song's meaning to a single sphere of relationship, be it divine-human (the allegorical tradition) or male-female (most modern interpreters).

The poet of the Song understood that the well-being of our world—not just of the individual person, but of the world as a whole—depends upon the human capacity to cultivate intimacy, indeed, love, in all three areas. Desire for such intimacy may be glimpsed at various points in Scripture. The Prophets and the Psalms in particular hold out the vision and hope of it. But the Song goes far beyond all previous texts in evoking the ecstasy of desire *fulfilled*, of intimacy realized in every aspect of human relationship.

Here I will point briefly to three moments in the poet's evocation of the time of fulfillment. The first is the woman's repeated references to her lover by the awkward circumlocution "['*et*] *she'ahavâh nafshî*," "the one whom my whole-being[15] loves"—a phrase that is hardly more idiomatic in biblical Hebrew than in English. The phrase appears five times, beginning in 1:7, and then repeated four times in rapid succession in the search scene in chapter three (vv. 1–4). The recurrence must be more than a slip of the tongue. Curiously, however, despite this repetition, the phrase does not well fit its context. The woman asks the city guards: "Have you seen the one whom my soul loves?"—a description obviously inadequate for its ostensible purpose of filing a missing person's report. Who could ever recognize a stranger on the basis of it? Yet in fact there is One whom we can recognize from that description. For the repeated phrase clearly recalls the Shema: "You shall *love* the Lord your God with all your heart and with all your *whole-being* and with all your *intensity*" (Deut. 6:5). In echoing what both Jewish and Christian traditions acknowledge to be the most important commandment in Torah—and in echoing it so awkwardly that the phrase sticks out like a jagged edge and catches our attention—the poet affirms indirectly that at last the commandment is being fulfilled in our hearing:

> On my bed at night I sought the one whom my whole-being loves;
> I sought him but could not find him.
> . . . .
> . . . I found the one whom my whole-being loves!
> I took hold of him, and I will not let him go. (3:1, 4)

Another evocation of the time of fulfillment occurs in 2:3–4:

> Like an apricot[16] among the trees of the wood,
> so is my darling among the lads.
> In his *shade* I delight and I sit,
> and his fruit is sweet to my palate.
> He has brought me to the *house of wine*,
> and his *banner* over me is love.

In our respective commentaries, both André LaCocque and I spend considerable time exploring the interactions between this passage in the Song and the fourteenth chapter of Hosea. There, at the end of the mostly unhappy love story of Israel and God, Hosea envisions a future day when Israel will at last return to her own God. The prophets frequently castigate Israel for consorting with false gods "under every green tree" (e.g., Jer. 2:20, 3:6, 3:13; Ezek. 6:13, cf. Deut. 12:2). Hosea offers the counter-image; Israel's own God consents to appear as something like a sacred tree:

> I will heal them from their turning away.
> I will *love* them *generously*. . . .
> . . . .
> They will again *sit* in his *shade*
> . . . and *blossom* like the *vine*,
> and his *remembrance* [i.e., fragrance] will be like the *wine* of
> Lebanon.
> . . . I myself will be like a luxuriant cypress;
> from me will come your *fruit*. (14: 5–9 Heb., 14:4–8 Eng.)

I have highlighted the words in Hosea that appear in the Song, many of them in the lines just cited from chapter two. LaCocque argues that the poet is working iconoclastically, desacralizing the sacred image: The (male) paramour provides the protection that once was sought from God.

181

By contrast, my iconographic reading of the passage suggests that the poet of the Song knows Hosea's dream and shares it—or better, that the poet of the Song puts Hosea's future vision in the present tense. The time of fulfillment is here: "He has brought me to the *house of wine*, / and his *banner* over me is love."

The NRSV renders that last line: "his intention toward me was love." But in fact, the Masoretic Text is unproblematic and readily intelligible in light of the similar image in Ps. 20:6 (Heb., v.5 Eng.): "In the name of our God [may] we set up our banners."

In both cases, this military symbol denotes protection of the one beneath it. Furthermore, the banner suggests vindication in the face of fierce opposition. Multiple moments in the Song attest to the fact that the lovers face hostility from forces that come from outside the garden. But for a time at least, *amor vicit omnia*; love *has* conquered all.

I have emphasized that the poet of the Song shows fulfillment of the desire for intimacy, and yet the note of yearning persists in the Song from the first line until the last.[17] Whatever the poet of the Song knows about fulfillment, it serves to make her less satisfied with the present than confident of the future. In other words, she holds the firm, wild hope of the prophet or the mystic. Yet she, like the other biblical writers, is a realist. One of the surprises in the Song is that we see the lovers' peace disturbed, not only by external opposition, but also by the momentary failure of desire. This is evident from the night scene in chapter five, where, because the woman hesitates too long to open the door to her lover when he knocks, he leaves. The way the poet describes the moment is intriguing: "My darling thrust his hand from the opening, / and my guts churned for him [*ûme'aî hamû 'alav*]" (5:4).

This churning would seem to be as obvious a reference to sexual excitement as any in the book. If so, it is not a simple reference. Both LaCocque and I note that the language of this scene comes from Jeremiah 31:20. The prophet uses the nearly identical phrase to describe God's pained yearning for the lost "child" Ephraim, that is, the Northern Kingdom of Israel. Despite our common recognition of the quotation, predictably, we diverge in interpretation. LaCocque sees this as an expression of a "defiant" eroticism that usurps the language of God's affection for Israel.[18] My own reading suggests that this unforgettable phrase is being used in its original sense, to speak of the love between God and Israel. But now it is used with a twist; here it signifies reciprocity. In Jeremiah, the phrase bespeaks God's longing for the beloved. In the Song, it suggests that "the woman" (Israel) is yearning in return. In other words, the churning guts convey the sense that at long last, God's love for Israel is requited; the divine-human story has finally ceased to be tragic. It is true, of course, that this time she has responded too late, but we cannot deny that the desire is now fully kindled, and (in the context of the Song's vision, at least) its flame never flickers again.

I have focused in this essay on the Song as an icon that portrays the healing of the relationship between God and Israel—or, taking the perspective from Eden, God and humanity. My commentary has attempted to show how the Song points also to healing in two other realms of relationship: the sexual and the ecological. With respect to the former, the Song contributes to the canon a strong affirmation not only of equality, but also of profound mutuality between the woman and the man. Phyllis Trible showed long ago that the Song corrects the imbalance of desire and power resulting from the disobedience in Eden.[19] Thus, God's stern warning to Eve—"Your desire will be for your husband, but he will rule over you" (Gen. 3:16)—is transmuted into the Shulamite's jubilant "My darling is mine, and toward *me* is *his* desire!" (7:11 Heb., v.10 Eng.). The use of the rare word *teshûqâh* for desire (which elsewhere appears only once, in Gen. 4:7) assures that the echo and inversion will be heard by those whose ears are attuned to biblical language.

The case for the healing of the rupture in the ecological realm is admittedly the hardest to make. It seems to me that in this matter the Song offers us only glimpses, probably because ancient Israel was not so troubled or endangered as we are by the broken relationship between human and nonhuman creation. The gist of my argument in the commentary is this: The prophets see the earth or the land of Israel languishing, sometimes shaking and dissolving, under the pressure of God's anger over human sin (e.g., Isa. 24:1–20, Jer. 4:23–26). Correspondingly, they envision a time of faithfulness in which the land, the whole earth, will flourish along with the people (e.g., Isa. 35:1–10). It is striking that the Song most clearly depicts not two gorgeous human beings, but rather a gorgeous land,[20] an idealized form of the land of Israel, in fact, newly lush with bloom and bursting with animal life:

> Now look, the winter is over,
> the rain has passed, taken itself off.
> The blossoms have appeared in the land;
> the time of melody has come,
> and the voice of the turtledove
> is heard in our land. (2:11–12)

The poet seems to share the intuition or mystical insight of earlier Israelite poets; along with the prophets, one might note the psalmists who produced texts such as Psalms 65, 72, and 85. They all saw something that most of us, it seems, do not: The condition of the earth itself is the first and best index of the state of health of the relationship between God and humanity. I believe that this dimension of the Song is one that we, perhaps more than earlier generations, might be ready to receive as God's word, because we need it so badly. I must admit that I have wondered what insight or intuition arose in a much earlier generation to yield the enigmatic rabbinic saying that anyone who treats the Song lightly (as a drinking song) "forfeits his place in the world to come and will bring evil into the world and imperil the welfare of all humankind."[21] This is a surprisingly global statement. Perhaps the medieval rabbis sensed that the Song has power to counter the depraved images of self and world that go far back in human history and have led to our present tragedy and crisis.

In this essay, I have argued that one important function of iconlike text within the canon is to depict the healing of the deepest ruptures in our world, a healing envisioned only fleetingly by the prophets and psalmists. But I do not wish to end without saying that I am never less sure of my ground as a biblical interpreter than when I am speaking—or more properly, stammering—about the Song. My uncertainty is itself indicative of what I would take to be the second indispensable contribution that the Song makes within the canon of Scripture, namely, to suggest the importance of the inarticulate within our religious experience. The Song sounds strong notes of jubilation and adoration. This adoration is not wordless (else we could not hear it at all), yet the words explain absolutely nothing. Instead, they celebrate, intrigue, confound. They do not make plain; they offer nothing that translates into simple prose. In this respect, the Song stands, within Christian tradition at least, as the counterpart to the liturgy; they are the two great vehicles of what is ultimately inarticulate experience. Andrew Louth comments perceptively: "It is not without significance that inarticulateness about what is deeply important is characteristic of the child whom we have to be like if we are to enter the kingdom of heaven."[22] Hebrew Scripture likens us more often to a lover in our relationship with God, and the Song reminds us that at the limit of experience, lovers fall silent, or babble more or less incoherently.[23] The Song, then, draws "a margin of silence" around the Scriptures as a whole; it creates a space where we who read and dare to interpret them do not have to know just what to say.

UNRESOLVED AND UNRESOLVABLE: PROBLEMS IN INTERPRETING THE SONG

Marc Brettler

The statement that best encapsulates the problems of the Song of Songs is the simile attributed to Sa'adiya Gaon, the head of the Babylonian Jewish community in the tenth century: "It is like a lock whose key is lost or a diamond too expensive to purchase."[1] The double simile is odd, since we typically discard locks whose keys we have lost, and certainly do not consider them to be fine diamonds. Yet, it is a perfect description of the Song: Its magnificence is well recognized, yet it refuses to be un-locked (though many have claimed to have found its missing key).

In focusing on the "unlockability" of the Song, I do not mean to sug-gest that the book is totally *na'ul* (locked) or *khatum* (sealed), to draw on the words of 4:12. Almost all modern scholars would agree on several key facts that are crucial for interpreting the Song. Their common view of the poem would stand in contrast to that of the medieval Jewish scholar Abraham ibn Ezra (1092/93–1167) who, in his introduction to the Song, speaks of it as Solomonic, holds it to be allegorical in the manner of Isaiah's song of the vineyard in Isaiah 5 or of the unfaithful wife in Ezekiel 16, and notes that it absolutely may not (*vᵊkhalilah khalilah*) be understood as a song of desire (*khesheq*), that is, as a secular love poem.[2] Modern scholars would reject all three of these assertions, and with good reason.

The Song cannot be Solomonic. The word *'appiryon* ("palanquin"?) in 3:9 is most likely Persian,[3] and the language of the book at several points resembles rabbinic Hebrew, suggesting a late date.[4] The mention in 6:4 of Tirzah, a northern capital in the ninth century, must also be post-Solomonic.[5] It is well known that the Song of Songs 1:1 uses *'asher* as the relative pronoun "of," the common form of the pronoun, while the rest of the Song without exception avoids *'asher*, using *sh* instead. The latter form is common in postbiblical Hebrew and in the very early Northern Hebrew Song of Deborah.[6] Thus, even if we must assume, as ibn Ezra did,[7] that the *l* of of *lishlomo* "of Solomon" is meant to indicate authorship—an assumption not so easy to grant, given the six or seven references to Solomon in the third person[8] in the Song—it is very likely that the superscription in 1:1 is secondary to the Song.[9] Taken together, this evidence suggests that there is no reason to take the Song as Solomonic, while there are good reasons to view it as post-Solomonic, and at least in part, postexilic (after 586 BCE).

Nor should the Song be understood as originally allegorical, as ibn Ezra suggests. Here he is following a very rich earlier tradition, evident in his statement: "And do not be surprised that [Solomon] compared Israel to a bride and God to her lover, for this is what the prophets do." Certainly ibn Ezra is correct that the husband-wife or the two-lover allegory is found in the Bible a sufficient number of times, especially in prophetic literature, to make us certain that it was relatively well known in ancient Israel.[10] However, to mix the language of the two great exegetes Sa'adiya and ibn Ezra, all of the allegorical passages identified by later interpreters contain a key indicating outright that they are allegorical. For example, the parable of the vineyard in Isaiah 5, a parable that has significant verbal similarities to the Song—note the opening verse's *dod* (beloved) and *qerem* (vineyard)—explicitly notes: "For the vineyard of the Lord of Hosts / Is the House of Israel, and the seedlings he lovingly tended / Are the men of Judah." Hosea 3:1, also cited by ibn Ezra, is similar: "The Lord said to me further, 'Go, befriend a woman who, while befriended by a companion, consorts with others, just as the Lord befriends the Israelites.'" In contrast to these and other passages, there is no key in the Song to suggest that it should be understood as anything other than literal. In fact, as is well known, with the possible exception of 8:6—*'esh shalhevetyah*, "flashes of fire, a raging flame" (NRSV), but "a very flame of the Lord" (JPS)[11]—God is totally absent from this book.

Stated differently, biblical authors use a variety of methods to mark various works as allegories. The Song has none of these marks and thus should not be seen as a work that was originally allegorical. The interesting question—a question that has many implications for the nature of the canon—is whether the allegorical understanding antedates or postdates the book's entry into the canon. Canonization, however, is a very complex and unclear process,[12] and I doubt that the question of when and how the Song entered the canon is answerable.[13] In any case, it is a question that belongs more to a volume on canon formation than to a series of papers on the variety of interpretations of the Song.

Ibn Ezra's final contention—that *vᵊkhalilah khalilah lihyot shir ha-shirim bᵊdivre khesheq*, "the Song of Songs may certainly not be considered among works of desire"—is also incorrect. This view can be dismissed rapidly—which Carey Ellen Walsh does when she opens her volume, *Exquisite Desire*, with the line "The Song of Songs is a depth charge into the nature of desire itself."[14] Although the Hebrew root *khesheq* ("desire"), the root used by ibn Ezra, never appears in the Song, we do find the even stronger noun *teshuqah*, ("deep desire", "longing"), in 7:11: "I am my lover's, and his deep desire is for me."[15] The previous verses (7:9–10), which depict the female lover as a stately palm, express desire even more explicitly: "I said: Let me climb the palm, let me take hold of its branches; so your breasts may be like the clusters of grapes, your breath like apples."[16] The Song is indeed about desire.

Unfortunately, showing that ibn Ezra is wrong and claiming along with many other modern scholars that the Song is post-Solomonic, non-allegorical, and about desire still leaves tremendous interpretive space for the Song and does little to resolve many of the book's fundamental difficulties. Ibn Ezra's clear positions, which typify medieval Jewish interpretation of the Song,[17] should not be replaced by new secular interpretive orthodoxies. Stated differently, what might be viewed as an emerging consensus concerning some of the interpretive issues of the Song is incorrect, or at least premature and problematic. More specifically, I would suggest that the following issues present significant problems, and, especially when considered together, make the interpretation of the Song more difficult than most commentators and interpreters acknowledge:

First, it is doubtful that the Song is a unity, and thus interpretations that speak of "the Song" and treat it as a whole are problematic.

Also, during the last decade, there has been a great deal of discussion of gender and the Song, and many scholars have suggested that a woman wrote the Song. Perhaps if we could show that it comes from the world of ancient Israelite women, we would have a key that would offer us interpretive clues. However, I believe that this claim should not be made.

Finally, most literature is fundamentally ambiguous—this is especially true of poetry. Trying to evaluate the extent of ambiguity within the Song is particularly difficult and provides yet another impediment to understanding.

The question of the Song's unity is one of the most complex issues in biblical studies. This is so, I believe, because so many different notions of unity exist among scholars and because there has yet to be a clear theoretical discussion about unity in general, about whether we assume unity until disunity is proven or vice versa, and about the extent to which a particular single author might vary vocabulary or style.[18] Certainly, some of these issues have been discussed concerning specific books, but I know of no satisfactory general discussion that could bear on the Song and its composition. In addition, there has been too little discussion of the interaction of centrifugal forces, that is, on those forces that pull away from the center, and centripetal forces,[19] that is, those that suggest a movement toward a center. How do these forces interact, and which is the more powerful? Equally ambiguous is the term "cohesion," which I and others in biblical studies often use to describe unity on the editorial level.[20] However, the meaning of this term has also not been explored sufficiently. For these reasons, the following comments should be viewed as tentative.

Two main centripetal arguments are used by scholars who view the Song as a unified whole: the one concerns the structural unity of the Song, and the other repeated motifs and vocabulary within it. Arguments concerning structural unity are often quite complicated and cannot be fully examined here; I have already offered a general critique of these types of arguments elsewhere.[21] The classic exposition of the Song's structure was offered by Cheryl Exum in 1973, who offers the following structure based on repetitions and inner-Song connections.[22]

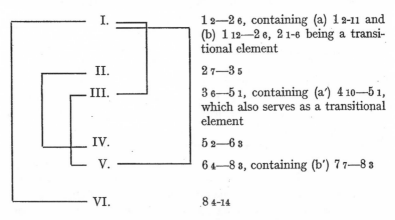

Figure 1. Structure of the Song of Songs. Chart by J. Cheryl Exum, "A Literary and Structural Analysis of the Song of Songs," *Zeitschrift für die Alttestamentliche Wissenschaft* 85 (1973): 77.

She recognizes the implications of the strong structures she adduces: They suggest "a unity of authorship" and prove "untenable the theory that the Song is an anthology or collection."[23] However, her theory depends on the same presumption shared by other such theories of structure, and this is the weakness of her argument. The textual units she sees as parallel are often of quite different size; these parallels are based on verbal and stylistic similarities that are not exclusive to the units and may be found elsewhere as well; and the final structure of the work that is suggested is so very complex that it is hard to imagine that an author could have intended it. More recently, scholars have offered more simple, alternative structures, indicating that they do not find hers compelling.[24] Indeed, Exum has acknowledged that she no longer agrees with the structure she posited and no longer sees the Song as a strong unity in the developed fashion she had once proposed.[25]

Exum's essay began a trend that has not abated, as other scholars have modified her structure, finding new structures that allegedly point to the structural integrity, and thus the unity, of the Song. These structures are typically chiastic, having an ABCC'B'A' structure.[26] Some, but not all of these scholars are from conservative backgrounds and/or teach at conservative institutions, and it is not impossible that their search for chiasms that suggest unity and textual integrity is influenced by religious factors. For example, William Shea's 1980 attempt, "The Chiastic Structure of the Song of Songs," follows a pattern that I have elsewhere called "chiasmania"[27] and is problematic because the sections that are viewed as chiastic are of different sizes, and often the similarities noted between chiastic units are thematic and too vague. In addition, Shea does not consider dissimilarities between units that he finds to be parallel, nor does he consider what David Wright calls "chiastic interference," when other units that are not part of the parallel share the same theme or key terms.[28] Shea's structure is thus highly problematic, and his conclusion that "the Song of Songs is unified structurally" is not compelling.[29]

A more recent example of a chiastic patterning was suggested by David A. Dorsey in 1990.[30] It is open to the same critiques of Exum and Shea adduced above—its units are not of equivalent size, and, like Shea's version, it often uses too broad thematic notions to determine patterns. For example, the opening and closing units are connected as *"Opening Words of Mutual Love and Desire"* and *"Closing Words of Mutual Love and Desire."*[31] The fact that three different scholars who argue for the unity of the Song find three different chiastic patterns within it should raise a red flag.[32] Perhaps the Song is not a unified, chiastic work.[33] Instead,

various chiastic structures may be found by picking up on particular occurrences of one phrase or theme or another, since the Song is so highly
repetitive. Clear examples of chiasm do exist in the Bible and in ancient
literature. Verses such as Genesis 9:6, *shofekh dam ha-'adam ba-'adam
damo yishafekh*—"Whoever sheds the blood of human, by a human shall
his blood be shed"—are certainly chiastic.[34] But I am skeptical concerning
the extent to which chiasmus was a significant structuring device of large-
scale literary units. More significantly, I do not believe that there is a
single, compelling chiastic structure for the Song that would suggest its
unity.

The other, nonstructural types of argument for the unity of the Song
are equally problematic. In a 1979 article, "The Unity of the Song of
Songs,"[35] Roland Murphy, the prolific author on wisdom literature and
on the Song, suggests that the refrains, themes, and repetitions of words
and phrases provide "evidence of love-experiences that continually repeat
themselves. This constitutes an argument for unity."[36] Michael Fox takes
a similar position in his 1985 commentary. He asserts, "In fact, however,
there is no reason to posit an editor to explain the Song's cohesiveness
and stylistic homogeneity. The most likely explanation of these qualities
is that the Song is a single poem composed, originally at least, by a single
poet."[37] But is this so clearly the case?

The first piece of evidence cited by Murphy is that "refrains" of adjuration appear in 2:7, 3:5 and 8:4; the existence of such refrains suggests
uniformity of authorship.[38] However, these three verses are not all identical. While 2:7 and 3:5 both read: "I adjure you, O daughters of Jerusalem,
by gazelles or by hinds of the field: Do not wake or rouse love until it
please!" 8:4 reads: "I adjure you, O daughters of Jerusalem: Do not wake
or rouse love until it please!" Thus, 8:4 is shorter than 2:7 and 3:5, lacking
"by gazelles or by hinds of the field," and it uses a different expression to
express the negative "do not"—"*mah . . . umah*," rather than "*'im . . .
ve'im*."[39] It is unclear why a single author should vary a refrain in this
fashion. These verses thus incorporate significant stylistic differences and
suggest centrifugal, rather than centripetal forces.

Similarly, the presence of two extended dream sequences, beginning
in 3:1 and in 5:2, is seen by some as a unifying factor in the Song.[40] Yet
there are significant differences of various types between these two units.
Both have the unifying phrase "I sought him, but did not find him" (3:1,
3:2; 5:6). However, the Hebrew reflects dialectical variation—3:1 and 3:2
read *biqqashtiv velo' m^ətza'tiv* (the first person form of the verb *b.q.sh* and
m.tz,' to seek and to find, each with a third-person masculine singular

suffix), while 5:6 reads *biqqashtihu velo' mətza'tihu* (the same verb forms, with a variant form of the third-person masculine singular suffix).[41] It is highly unlikely that a single author would use both the *-tiv* and *-tihu* forms with the same verbs. Furthermore, the style of these two dream sequences is quite different. The first is very tight and repetitive; it not only repeats "I sought him, but did not find him," but also gives a three-fold designation for the male lover, calling him "the one whom I so totally love," *'et she'ahavah nafshi.* This powerful phrase is absent in the sequence beginning in 5:2 and surprisingly appears only one other time in the Song (1:7); a more unified composition would have a more even distribution of the phrase. The opening of 5:2 is characterized by both rhyme and rhythm—*pitkhi-li 'akhoti ra'yati yonati tammati*—but this cadence is absent in chapter 3.[42] Although a single author or editor may use a variety of styles, the diversity noted here is extreme and seems to go beyond the variation expressed by a single author. Finally, although the tone of the "unified" Song is often characterized as idyllic, and certainly 3:1–5, where the female lover finds her man and they live happily ever after (3:4), fits an idyll, the dream sequence that begins in 5:2 does not. The latter is full of violence and unhappiness, perhaps even culminating in a gang rape: "The watchmen who guard the town found me; they hit me they bruised me, they stripped off my mantel from me, those who guard the walls" (5:7).

This last scene is atypical of the Song as a whole. Certainly, if we begin with a strong presupposition of the Song's unity, the discontinuities between the two dream sequences may not alone disabuse us of this view. I wonder, however, why we should begin with such a presupposition of unity in the first place; the Song is, after all, a biblical composition.[43] We should assume a neutral stance. In this case, the variety of stylistic, linguistic, and thematic evidence concerning the differences in the dream sequences is evidence of strong centrifugal forces: Rather than moving us toward a text with a center, they thrust us outward to a diversity of authors.

Many recent scholars have suggested that the wide range of repetitions in the Song suggest its unity. However, these similarities are because the material incorporated in the Song is generically similar, representing the love-song tradition in ancient Israel, perhaps even reflecting a single branch of that tradition. Especially when compared with other biblical literature, the language in the Song looks to be all of a piece. The following analogy expresses the nature of the Song. Imagine someone familiar with only Baroque art going to see an Impressionist exhibit at a museum.

It would be easy to see how she might assume all the works were done by the same artist—the same subjects recur (fields of flowers, haystacks, sunsets); the same brushstrokes are visible throughout; and a very modest palette predominates. This apparent unity is a result of all the pieces coming out of the same movement within the same time period. A closer analysis, however, would distinguish the Renoir from the Monet, the Cezanne from the Degas, even if the curator of the exhibit, like the editor or editors of the Song made *some* attempt to create a coherent experience. In the same way, the editor(s) of the Song were working with a collection of generically similar material and created an intelligently constructed anthology[44] or collection—biblical editors were not, as some earlier scholars believed, total hacks.[45] But the Song is not a strong unity, and when read carefully, its centrifugal forces strongly pull against the centripetal ones.

The arguments for the unity of the Song are summarized in the introduction to the translation and commentary by the Blochs:

> And one might imagine, too, that its unity and consistency were the work of a redactor who collected love poems of others, stringing them together with refrains and repetitions and multiple cross-references. But it is equally plausible, and rather more attractive, to assume that the Song was the work of a poet—one who, as so often in the Bible, would have found it perfectly natural to incorporate quotations and adaptations of material already in circulation. Indeed, if a redactor was responsible for shaping the poem as we now have it, then he or she was a literary artist of the highest caliber, and fully deserves to be called a poet.[46]

They go on to note that "apparently the biblical poets had a more flexible notion of unity and structure than many scholars have recognized."[47]

Unity and disunity, however, should not be seen as the only two possibilities, but rather complete authorial unity, versus complete editorial disunity should be seen as opposite poles on a continuum. The Song is somewhere in the middle. The Blochs's observation that "the biblical poets had a more flexible notion of unity and structure" is confusing—I am unsure how we might determine if this is true, and even whether biblical poets thought much about issues such as unity. Finally, it is unclear why the assumption of unity is "more attractive"—if this is a scholarly judgment, it is not backed up by evidence, and if it is an aesthetic judgment, it is unclear why this particular aesthetic is compelling.

A final example of disunity is found in the waṣfs, the physical descriptions of the lovers.[48] As is well known, the waṣfs beginning in 4:1 and 6:4 have many significant similarities; they both note of the woman, for example, "Like a pomegranate slice is your brow/cheek behind your veil/hair" (4:3b and 6:7).[49] This repetition constitutes strong evidence for the unity of the song. However, scholars, especially those espousing the unity of the Song, tend not to dwell on the small differences between these two waṣfs. For example, 4:2a reads "Your teeth are like a flock of shorn [sheep] climbing up from the washing pool," while 6:6a states "Your teeth are like a flock of ewes climbing up from the washing pool." In chapter 4, the animals are *keʿeder haqqᵊtzuvot*, shorn sheep, while in chapter 6 they are *keʿeder ha-rᵊkhelim*, ewes. Similarly, 4:1 ends with sheep that streamed down from Mount Gilead—*shegalᵊshu mehar gilʿad*—while in 6:5, they have streamed down simply from (the) Gilead—*shegalᵊshu min ha-gilʿad*. Additional variations exist between these two waṣfs. These dissimilarities serve no purpose in the development of a plot[50] in the eight chapters of the Song and argue against the work being written by a single author or poet or even being brought together as a unity by a single editor—these variations, like those found in adjuration, show no pattern. Instead, they are precisely the types of variants seen when the "same" poem is recited by different oral poets.[51] The Song is much better viewed as an anthology of poems. This means that it should not be read as a whole and that we should not say "the Song means." In addition we may not speak of the Shulamite as the female protagonist of the book.[52] This graceful woman of 7:1—called "O queenly maiden"—may not be the same woman mentioned in other compositions that were redacted into the "unified" Song; this woman may be many women.

Both the waṣfs describing the woman (or women) and the issue of unity lead us to the second issue I want to touch on: the possibility of female authorship of the Song. Athalya Brenner's *Feminist Companion to the Song of Songs* contains a section discussing this, with several articles that advocate female authorship for the Song as a whole.[53] My conclusions about authorship, however, suggest that this discussion should be refined, since it is possible that part of the Song was written by a woman and part by a man, or, following Brenner and van Dijk-Hemmes, that the Song may contain both male and female voices.[54]

The idea that the Song is a female composition was first suggested in a modern Hebrew book from 1957 by S. D. Goitein, the noted scholar of the Cairo Genizah.[55] He suggests that "the Song was composed in honor of King Solomon by a young woman, daughter of a nobleman (*nadiv*),

who was brought to his court in order to adorn his parties by her singing."[56] That specific suggestion is unacceptable, since it assumes both a
Solomonic date for the Song and the song's unity; these assumptions have
been criticized above. Goitein believes that it is a female composition
because the woman does most of the talking; there are three waṣfs to the
woman compared to one to the man; the Song's "way of life" is feminine,
referring, for instance, to the maternal house (3:4; 8:2); and it mentions
various groups of women.[57] Many of these reasons are repeated by subsequent scholars, often with more caution. For example, Athalya Brenner,
though noting that in well over half of the Song the women is speaking,[58]
remains tentative, noting "My personal guess is that passages such as
1.2–6, 3.1–4, 5.1–7 and 5.10–16 are so essentially feminine that a male
could hardly imitate their tone and texture successfully."[59] However, she
does not explain this judgment. Others are less cautious. Very recently,
Carey Walsh viewed the Song as "the voice of a desiring woman,"[60] while
a bit earlier, André LaCocque summarized his argument for female authorship of the Song in a book called *Romance, She Wrote*.[61]

It is difficult to evaluate many of these arguments, since we know very
little about the differences between what men and women would have
composed in antiquity. We do not even have a clear notion concerning
(male) literacy in Israel.[62] The arguments for a female voice need to be
counterbalanced by those assuming male authorship. David Clines reads
the book as a male fantasy.[63] In a review of Fox's *The Song of Songs and
the Ancient Egyptian Love Songs*, Jack Sasson makes a related point worth
considering: "Written mostly by males, erotic poetry indulges a male's
fantasy, wherein females are made to seek out lovers with the determination that is supposed to be stereotypical of the male."[64] There is evidence
for a male voice for at least parts of the Song that deserves attention. For
example, the man recites three waṣfs about the woman (4:1, 6:4, and 7:1),
but the woman recites only one to the man (5:10). Furthermore, the waṣf
about the man is quite static, turning him into a powerful statue,[65] while
those of the women are more typically dynamic and highly sexualized,
perhaps suggesting male perceptions of a woman. To reverse Brenner's
observation concerning various sections that reflect a/her female perspective, my (male) guess is that a man more likely wrote the highly sensual-
ized conclusion to the waṣf about the woman in 7:9, "I said: Let me climb
the palm, let me take hold of its branches; so your breasts may be like the
clusters of grapes, your breath like apples." Similarly, I think it doubtful
that a woman would write in this fashion of the violence in 5:7—"The

watchmen who guard the town found me; they hit me they bruised me, they stripped off my mantel from me, those who guard the walls."[66]

As in the argument against unity, technical Hebrew issues may also suggest that the current consensus is wrong. Hebrew typically has two forms of the second person plural pronominal suffixes: *-khen* (or *khena*), which is feminine, and *-khem* (or *khema*), which is masculine.[67] Yet the adjuration formula, addressed to the (feminine plural) daughters of Jerusalem—whomever they might be—is always found as *etkhem* rather than *etkhen* (2:7; 3:5; 5:8; 8:4). Indeed, the form *etkhen* is never attested in biblical Hebrew. The use of the masculine form *etkhem* instead is acceptable biblical grammar, since here as elsewhere, the masculine form may take over. Might we not, however, expect the female form to be preserved in literature written by women?

This list of objections should not suggest that the Song in its entirety should be viewed as a male composition. One of the advantages of reading the Song as an anthology is the possibility of ascribing sections to male authors and others to female ones. Some of the criteria developed by Goitein and others may be employed, though tentatively and with caution. Certainly the Song is very unusual when compared with most other biblical compositions, but these anomalies should not be automatically explained by assuming female composition. In fact, parts of the Song show significant similarities to Proverbs,[68] a work considered by all to come from the male world of the wise.

The extent to which gendered writing exists in any civilization is a difficult theoretical question.[69] Add to this the real problem that we have no clear female compositions from ancient Israel and so have nothing from which to extrapolate directly. Given the postexilic date of the Song as a whole, the best points of comparison may be from the Greco-Roman world, where we have Jewish works that we know were written by women, and we thus can begin to outline some of the differences between male and female compositions.[70] Most significantly, works that we believe were composed by women are interested in the small details of the women's world.[71] Sections of the Song fit this pattern, especially those that mention the *bet 'em*, mother's house (3:4; 8:2) rather than the expected, normative *bet 'av*, father's house.[72] Others show interest in the female conflict between a/the women lover of the Song and the *bᵊnot yerushalayim*, the "daughters of Jerusalem."[73] In any case, it is noteworthy that based on the criteria just adduced, the book of Ruth is a much stronger candidate for female authorship. Unlike the Song, which has as its focus the relationship between a man and a woman, Ruth is predominantly

concerned about the relationship between two women. Within the biblical corpus, the two main women of Ruth are complex, developing characters—more so than any woman/women in the Song.[74] Thus, although we
should not speak of the *entire* Song as a female composition, it is reason-
able to suggest that *parts of it* were either written by a woman or embody
a woman's voice. Unfortunately, it is not always easy to determine which
parts these are.[75]

The final point on which I believe the emerging consensus to be wrong
concerns ambiguity and the Song. Although several studies have emphasized various types of ambiguity in the Song,[76] I do not believe the topic
has been covered adequately, nor have the problems of ambiguity been
explored sufficiently. A complete exploration of this issue would involve
almost every verse of the Song. Instead, I will focus on two types of
ambiguities in the Song—those concerning possible sexual imagery and
those that prevent us from determining whether the love of the song is
ultimately fulfilled or unfulfilled.

Most cultures have a rich sexual slang.[77] There is no reason to believe
that ancient Israel was different; indeed, Ezekiel 33:31 suggests that the
people came to the prophet with the expectation of hearing "erotic" or
"bawdy" talk (*ʿagavim*).[78] But due to the highly selective nature of the
Bible, we know little of ancient Israelite sexual practices[79] or sexual slang.
For example, to the modern reader, it looks as if Song of Songs 2:3—
ufiryo matoq lekhiki, "And his fruit is sweet to my mouth"—might refer
to oral sex,[80] but we do not know if fellatio was (widely) practiced in
ancient Israel.[81] We do not even know if *peri*, "fruit," could refer to semen
in any register of Israelite diction.[82] Similarly, in the complex dream sequence beginning in 5:2, the male lover is depicted as "knocking" (*dofeq*).
Certainly in English, various words from "knock" (e.g. the idiom
"knocked up") are related to sexual intercourse,[83] but was this true in
Hebrew as well? If this usage did exist, an interesting ambiguity would
arise in this unit: It would be unclear whether the male lover were knocking to come in at the door of the female lover's home or at her body's
"door." Again, the nature of preserved ancient Israelite literature does
not allow us to determine whether this ambiguity is modern only or
existed and perhaps was even intentional on the part of this section's
author.[84] Given that much sexual slang is oral or is preserved in ephem-
era, it is unlikely that we will recover any additional evidence that will
help us determine the extent of this slang in the Song.

A much more significant ambiguity is found in the final verse of the
Song. It is thus especially frustrating, since that verse may be assumed to

offer an important interpretive key to the "unified" text that it concludes. The verse (8:14) reads: *Berakh dodi udᵊmeh lᵊkha litzvi 'o leʿofer ha-'ayyalim ʿal hare vᵊsamim*, "Make haste, my beloved, and be like a gazelle, or a young stag upon the mountains of spices" (in the NRSV). The first ambiguity is lexical—should the first word, *berakh*, be rendered "flee"? This is the typical meaning of the root, sometimes used in military contexts,[85] and is reflected in several translations, including Falk's "Go; go now."[86] Rendered thus, the verb suggests that the female lover is telling the male, perhaps playfully, perhaps not, to scram, that she has no interest in him. Not all love poems have happy endings; the Song would then be like an Old Babylonian dialogue that ends with "Your love means no more to me than trouble and vexation."[87] However, both the New Jewish Publication Society translation, *Tanakh*, and the Blochs translate this as "hurry," thereby emphasizing the speed, rather than the fact that *berakh* typically expresses separation.[88] The translation is no trivial issue: Are the lovers together or separate at the poem's end? Or perhaps, are they at a middle point, as indicated by the Blochs—separated, but anticipating their next tryst? [89] Or is this text quite clever in being intentionally ambiguous? The real question is: How may readers interested in the historical-critical mode differentiate between intentional ambiguities of clever, talented authors and ambiguities that we perceive due to our lexical ignorance?

The second, intersecting ambiguity of the verse concerns the last words, and the identification of the *hare vᵊsamim*, "hills of spices," to which the male lover is supposed to *berakh*. Are these some faraway location? Or should these be identified with the *hare vater* of 2:17? These hills or mountains are also difficult to specify. They are not unambiguously "hills of spices": the King James Version calls them "the Mountains of Bether," the New Revised Standard "the cleft mountains." Some scholars have suggested, especially given that the root *btr* (the root of *vater*) means "to cleave," that these mountains refer to the woman's breasts,[90] which according to 1:13 are the home of a sachet of myrrh.[91] If we accept this latter allusion, then the lover is fleeing or hurrying *to the woman*, not away from her.

Such striking ambiguity is not unique to this passage: Requited versus unrequited love is a recurring problem for the Song. As I have discussed elsewhere, the dream sequence beginning in 5:2 has all the same ambiguities.[92] Song of Songs 5:4 reads: *dodi shalakh yado min ha-khor umeʿay hamu ʿalav*. A literal translation might be: "My lover sent his hand toward/away from the hole and my innards seethed within me." The problems are legion: *Shalakh* usually is "to send to," yet it is here complemented by the preposition *min*, "from." Is the hand a hand, or a euphemism for the penis, as is the case elsewhere in the Bible?[93] And is the hole the door's keyhole or the woman's vagina?[94] Finally, we cannot tell why the lover's innards are seething—from pleasure or regret.[95] Just as in 8:14, we have no way of determining whether the love has been consummated or frustrated. And just as in 8:14, it is unclear if this ambiguity is ancient and intentional or modern and unintentional.

The preceding remarks, which focus on problems inherent to the Song, on what we should not say about it, are intended to be cautionary. Perhaps in this time even more than in recent periods, we like to have a sense of certainty. This is as true of biblical interpretation as it is of other aspects of our lives. However, certainty should not be based on ignoring important evidence in the Song—evidence that the work is composite and not completely coherent, that its authorship is not wholly feminine, that it is so full of ambiguities—intentional or not—that it may never completely be unlocked. Pointing out these problems has two functions: It serves as a warning for interpreters of the Song—ancient as well as modern—who attain interpretive closure by picking up only on certain of the text's clues, while ignoring others, and it serves to explain why there is such a rich interpretive tradition around the Song. Finally, I would hope that pointing out simultaneously both these problems and the richness of the Song helps establish the truth of the thousand-year-old judgment of Sa'adiya: The Song "is like a lock whose key is lost or a diamond too expensive to purchase."

PART FIVE

Reading the Song's Readers

ENTERING THE HOLY OF HOLIES:
RABBINIC MIDRASH AND THE
LANGUAGE OF INTIMACY

Judith A. Kates

In the midst of a Mishnaic debate about the canonical status of the books of Ecclesiastes and Song of Songs (*M. Yadaim* 3:5), a debate couched in the Mishnah's halakhically technical terms of whether or not these books "render the hands ritually impure," we hear an impassioned outcry from Rabbi Akiva: "God forbid!—no man in Israel ever disputed about the Song of Songs [saying that] it does not render the hands ritually impure, for the entire world is not worth as much as the day on which the Song of Songs was given to Israel; for all the Writings are holy, but the Song of Songs is the Holy of Holies."[1] For my purposes, two details of Rabbi Akiva's language here are crucial: The Song of Songs "was given" to Israel on a day, precisely the same language characteristically used by the rabbis for the revelation of the Torah. Like the Torah, this book was given to Israel, an equivalence that transforms what sounds like hyperbole into thoughtful description. Second, through the morphological echoing of the phrase "song of songs" in his evaluation—song of songs; holy of holies—"Song of Songs" becomes more than a title. It is also a declaration of supreme worth, as we hear in one midrashic explanation of the phrase (*Song of Songs Rabbah* 1:1, 11) "the best of songs, the most excellent of songs, the finest of songs."

But Rabbi Akiva's implied comparison takes us further than mere hierarchy. His language for the Song—*kodesh kodeshim*—summons the physically destroyed, but textually (and therefore imaginatively) present and potent innermost core of holiness, guarded and secret, yet both containing and radiating outward the most intense manifestation of the presence of God in the midst of the world: the Holy of Holies at the core of the sanctuary in Jerusalem. According to Rabbi Akiva, then, the day on which the Song of Songs was given to Israel creates, as Marc Hirshman puts it, "a day of entry into the most inner sanctum—the Holy of Holies."[2]

It seems to me no accident that this view of our book and the language in which it is expressed are attributed in the Mishnah to Rabbi Akiva. Known in rabbinic and later scholarship as the *darshan*, the midrashist par excellence, he, according to Talmudic traditions,[3] claims that every word, even every syllable and crownlike point that decorates the letters in the Torah scroll yields multiple fruits of meaning. God's language is bursting with meanings not apparent to the literalist reader, like the pomegranate whose hard, smooth outer skin conceals a bounteous store of juicy, invigorating seeds, an emblem of abundance and variety. For Rabbi Akiva, the devoted expounder of midrash, to speak of Song of Songs as a pathway into the Holy of Holies suggests a way of understanding rabbinic midrashic readings of the Song, or at least a very large proportion of such rabbinic midrash.

To read as the midrashist reads means to experience Scripture as an interwoven texture of texts. We can pick up a thread anywhere in sacred texts and it will lead us—by creative juxtaposition, by plays on sounds, by flowing from one possible meaning to another in the semantic range of a root, or by conceptual analogy—to see new possibilities of meaning, or as the *darshan* has it in *Song of Songs Rabbah*, to penetrate and to link together (*ḳodeach vᵊchorez*) the language of the Torah.

The phrase comes from a midrash on Song of Songs 1:10: in the Bloch translation,[4] "Your cheekbones, those looped earrings, that string of beads at your throat." As the rabbis seem to hear it, the verse reads "Your cheeks are lovely with circlets, your neck with pearls." "Cheeks" in the midrash suggest speech: "the cheeks are made only for speech."[5] In the following midrash, they mean Speech with a capital S—that is, Torah:

> when they were linking up the words of the Pentateuch with those of the prophets and the prophets with the Writings, and the fire flashed around them and the words rejoiced as on the day when they were delivered from Sinai. For was not their original delivery from Mount Sinai with fire, as it says, *And the mountain burned with fire unto the heart of heaven* (Deut. IV, 11)? Once as Ben Azzai sat and expounded, the fire played around him. They went and told R. Akiba, saying, 'Sir as Ben Azzai sits and expounds, the fire is flashing round him.' He went to him and said to him: 'I hear that as you were expounding the fire flashed round you.' He replied:

'That is so.' He said to him: 'Were you perhaps treating of the secrets of the Divine Chariot?' 'No,' he replied. 'I was only linking up the words of the Torah with one another and then with the words of the prophets, and the prophets with the Writings, and the words rejoiced as when they were delivered from Sinai, and they were as sweet as at their original utterance. And were they not originally delivered from Sinai in fire, as it says, *"And the mountain burned with fire"*?'[6]

The author of this midrash understands the loveliness of the beloved's cheeks to refer to "her" (the community's) way of "speaking Torah." "Her" version of Torah language is, in fact, midrash—the quintessential rabbinic reading and teaching practice, "linking up the words of the Torah with one another and then with the words of the prophets and the prophets with the Writings." For this *darshan*, however, the process of creating midrash cannot be described as simply an intellectual enterprise, a disengaged "inquiry" into the meaning of the Torah's verses (as one of the senses of the root DRSH would suggest). Rather, with his uncanny imagery of "fire flashing" around the rabbis as they expound, he presents the midrashic enterprise as the experiential equivalent of the revelation at Sinai: "the words rejoiced as when they were delivered from Sinai."[7] Midrash offers a way into the intense pleasure and nourishment of the original encounter between God and Israel: The words "were as sweet as at their original utterance." Language is the essential medium of that encounter. Even the visual imagery, the fire that, in Exodus and Deuter- onomy, marks the meeting of divine and human, here becomes an effect of language, specifically the language of midrash as the rabbi "sits and expounds," *yoshev vᵊ*doresh.

Why would we find such a metamidrash, a reflection on the nature of midrash in the midrash on *Shir hashirim*? The rabbis' reading practice of linking texts with texts, of finding meaning by discovering correspon- dences or hermeneutic links between prophets and Writings and Torah, leads, as we see in the midrash about Ben Azzai, to the possibility of "recreating a new event of revelation," to quote Daniel Boyarin,[8] who has developed an argument about the rabbis' readings of Song of Songs that I have found persuasive. I would suggest that the presence of this midrash, specifically in a collection of midrashim on the Song of Songs, reflects the fact that, for the rabbis, the texts of the Writings, and especially Song of Songs, provide, in Boyarin's words, a "series of readings in figurative language of the text of the Torah."[9]

The consequence that I want to emphasize of this intertextual practice is that these figurative readings of the Torah provide "powerful emotional and axiological realizations of the narrative situations described mimetically in the Torah itself."[10] Boyarin proposes that the rabbis understand Song of Songs as the functional equivalent of a *mashal*—a parable or extended metaphor—through which we experience emotional and relational dimensions of the narratives in Torah (that is how I understand his term "axiological"). He also argues in detail for distinguishing this mode of reading from the allegorical reading of an Origen or Philo or of medieval Jewish interpreters. To quote just one sentence in this vein: "For the midrash, the correspondences are not between things seen and their hidden or inner meanings, but between texts and the historical contexts in which they were produced or to which they apply, [between] texts and other texts."[11]

The rabbis, of course, take Solomon to be the author of the Song of Songs, but what is more interesting, at least to me, is that Solomon as the author of the Song becomes for them "the very prototype of the Rabbinic reader."[12] At the beginning of *Song of Songs Rabbah*, we find a series of *meshalim*, or parables, that explicitly address the role of Solomon's texts as interpretive tools:

> Rav Nachman gave two [parables]: It is like a great palace with many entrances, and all who entered it would lose the way to the entrance. A wise man came and took a rope and attached it to the entrance, and all would enter and exit by following the rope. Thus until Solomon came, no man could understand the words of Torah; but once Solomon had come, all began to understand the words of Torah. Rav Nachman gave another version: Like a thicket of reeds, and no man could enter into it, and a wise man came and took a sickle and mowed, then all began to enter and exit by way of the mowed [path]. So Solomon. Said Rabbi Yose: It is like a basket full of fruits, which had no handle, and it could not be carried, and someone wise came and made for it handles, and it began to be carried by its handles. So until Solomon came, no one could understand the words of Torah, but once Solomon had come, everyone began to comprehend Torah. R. Shila said: It is like a pot of boiling water, which had no handle to carry it, and someone came and made it a handle, and it began to be carried by its handle. R. Hanina said: It is like a deep well full of water, and its waters were cold and sweet and good, but no one could drink of them. Someone

came and provided a rope [tied to] a cord, a cord [tied to] a cord, and he drew from it and he drank. Then all began to draw and drink. So from word to word, from mashal to mashal, Solomon comprehended the secret of Torah, as is written, "The meshalim of Solomon, the son of David, King of Israel" [Prov. 1:1.]—by virtue of his meshalim, Solomon comprehended the words of Torah.[13]

Each *mashal* creates a different model of the hermeneutic task, some more perilous, others more benign. But in all of them, the verses offered by Solomon are what is essential to gaining access to something precious and necessary for life. When the midrash uses as its "punch line" the first verse of Proverbs (which in Hebrew uses *meshalim*, a word meaning "parable," as well as "proverb"), it clearly is referring to everything that Solomon is understood to have written. I would call attention especially to the last image of "a rope tied to a rope, a cord tied to a cord," so that everyone could drink the cold, sweet, and good waters of the deep well. The metaphor suggests not only the imagery of Torah as *mayim chayim*, "living waters," but the picture of Ben Azzai and Rabbi Abbahu, each of whom *yoshev vᵊdoresh*, sits and makes midrash by tying together the Writings and the prophets and the Torah so that the words become sweet.

In the brief scope of this discussion, I want to take up Boyarin's proposal that rabbinic midrash finds in or creates by means of the Song of Songs a language that generates dimensions of emotion, of relationship— what I would call a language of intimacy—in narratives of the historical experience of the people of Israel. In the later midrash *Song of Songs Rabbah* (finalized probably in the sixth century CE), the whole trajectory from Abraham to messianic redemption enters the midrashic reach, although its primary focus is on the narratives at the Red Sea and especially at Sinai. In earlier Tannaitic collections (*Mekhilta* and *Sifre*), we find the Song of Songs deployed in the exegesis of the narratives of Exodus and Revelation. I will be confining myself to just a few examples in which the rabbis create an intertextual texture of verses to unfold the fullness of Israel's experience at the Red Sea and at Sinai.

In *Song of Songs Rabbah*, chapter 2:14 of the Song ("My dove in the clefts of the rock, let me hear your voice") generates the following midrash:

The one of the house of R. Ishmael teaches: In the hour in which Israel went out from Egypt, to what were they similar? To a dove which ran away from a hawk, and entered the cleft of a rock and found there a nesting snake. She entered within, but could not go in, because of the snake; she could not go back, because of the hawk which was waiting outside. What did the dove do? She began to cry out and beat her wings, in order that the owner of the dovecote could hear and come save her. That is how Israel appeared at the sea. They could not go down into the sea, for the sea had not yet been split for them. They could not go back, for Pharoah was coming near. What did they do? *"They were mightily afraid, and the children of Israel cried out unto the Lord"* [Exod. 14:10], and immediately *"The Lord saved them on that day"* [Exod. 14:30].[14]

The already figurative address to the beloved as a dove in unspecified clefts of an unlocated rock by a speaker whose need to hear her voice comes from his general condition of desire here is given a full and fully affective narrative. It becomes a story of fear, anguish, and desperate need on the part of the unprotected dove, whose search for shelter yields only greater fear and need. Her voice becomes a cry for help and a call to the speaker, now understood in the narrative as the one who built the dovecote and has been, until now, her protector. The speaker's address to her reflects his desire to be called upon so that her reaching out to him can generate response itself, as well as protection. The verse in Song of Songs becomes a specified, located narrative full of affect, albeit in a darker emotional tone than we would hear from the surrounding verses in the Song itself.

At the same time, we hear in the verses from Exodus a full, detailed narrative unfolding of the inner, emotional experience of the children of Israel. I would underline the word "children" here. The usual formula for "the people" takes on real poignancy and suddenly departs from mere formula in this midrash as we experience with them the utter helplessness and literally crying need of their entrapment at the edge of the sea, an experience that we do not have when we read the laconic phrase in Exodus, "they were mightily afraid." The poetic text, the Song, is assumed to refer to a narrative context in the Torah. But that context is itself transformed by the infusion of the imagery and affect of the poetic language.

In a parallel text from the earlier midrash, the *Mekhilta*, attributed to the school of the same Rabbi Ishmael, a verse-by-verse midrash on the book of Exodus, it is the verse in Exodus that is interpreted through the same *mashal*, the same parable, of the dove caught between the hawk and the snake, with the same intensity and poignancy of feeling generated by the narrative.

They were mightily afraid, and the children of Israel cried out unto the Lord [Exod. 14:10]. *Stand still and see the salvation of the Lord* [Exod. 14:13]. To what were the Israelites at that moment like? To a dove fleeing from a hawk, and about to enter a cleft in the rock where there is a hissing serpent. If she enters there is the serpent! If she stays out there is the hawk! In such a plight were the Israelites at that moment, the sea forming a bar and the enemy pursuing. Immediately they set their mind upon prayer. Of them it is interpreted in the tradition: *"O my dove that art in the clefts of the rock let me hear thy voice."*[15]

But we also see that this particular narrative—a story of a dove, a rock, a call—may have been suggested by the *darshan*'s understanding that Solomon's verses offer the way into a deeper understanding of the Torah text; so "of them, it is interpreted in the tradition" (a phrase that always refers in the *Mekhilta* to a verse in the prophets or Writings), "O, my dove that are in the clefts of the rock, let me hear your voice."[16]

The interweaving of the Song and the narrative in Exodus creates a dynamic of emotion and relationship that flows both ways. The interweaving of the poetic text with the prose of Exodus creates a fully realized narrative, filled with intensity for us as readers, allowing us to become participants in this moment of terror and salvation. It also implies a relationship of mutual need in this crisis at the Red Sea. God wants to hear our voice, a dimension of the relationship totally submerged in the language of Exodus until illuminated by the verse from Song of Songs. The narrative of the Red Sea, as we hear it in Exodus 14:30 and 31—"So YHWH delivered Israel on that day from the hand of Egypt; Israel saw Egypt dead by the shore of the sea, and Israel saw the great hand that YHWH had wrought against Egypt, the people feared YHWH, they trusted in YHWH and in Moshe his servant" is a narrative of power, of fear, in the sense of both terror and awe, and of trust. In the midrash it is transformed, I would say deepened, into a narrative of terror, entrapment, and helplessness, but also of love, of mutual calling out and response, of need and desire. The Song's verse in this midrashic transaction is not translated into abstraction. Rather, the midrashic reading gives it specificity and location in a way that allows us to hear a darker, perhaps more intense emotional valence in its figures.

The best-known midrashic interpenetration of Song of Songs and Exodus and one that is developed with tremendous variety in *Song of Songs Rabbah* is the interpretation of the Sinai narrative, building on the metaphor of marriage already deployed in prophetic books from Hosea to

Second Isaiah. I offer just one example, a midrash on Song of Songs 1:2, "Let him kiss me with the kisses of his mouth":

> R. Johanan interpreted the verse as applying to Israel when they went up to Mount Sinai. It was as if a king wanted to marry a wife of good and noble family, so he sent an envoy to speak with her. She said: 'I am not worthy to be his handmaid, but all the same I desire to hear from his own mouth.' When the envoy returned to the king, he was full of smiles, but he would give no clear report to the king. The king, who was very discerning, said: 'This man is full of smiles, which would show that she consented, and he does not give any clear report, which would seem to show that she said that she wants to hear from my own mouth.' So Israel is the woman of good family, Moses is the envoy, and the king is the Holy One, blessed be He.[17]

Rabbi Johanan is fully aware of the Sinai narrative in Exodus, in which God speaks through thunder and fire and Israel responds in terror and awe of the voice ("You speak to us," they said to Moses, "and we will obey; but let not God speak to us, lest we die." Exodus 20:16). Indeed, other rabbis in this section of *Song of Songs Rabbah* (1.2:2) debate whether they withstood their terror for the duration of all the commandments, or only the first two. Yet here that narrative becomes an exquisite love game of a bride, vibrant with the tension between modesty and desire, and a groom, eager in his own desire, yet loving, intuitive, and sensitively responsive. The midrash transforms revelation into what the rabbis call it, *matan Torah*, the giving of the Torah. But the dialogic nature of the Song leads them to a further transformation—the narrative becomes a drama of giving *and* receiving, a *conversation* between lovers.

In the midrash, the rabbis clearly respond to the Song as dialogue—as not only dialogic in form, but as partaking of a shared vocabulary of praise, desire, and passionate engagement. These literary perceptions are embodied in midrashim in which the language of the Song at 2:16, "I am my Beloved's and He is mine," allows the rabbis to unveil a theology of complete mutuality, of reciprocal love and service between God and Israel:

> He is my God and I am His nation. He is my God,—*I am the Lord your God* (Ex. 20:2). I am His people and nation, as it says, *Attend unto Me, O My people, and give ear unto Me, O My nation* (Isa. 51:4). He is as a father to me, and I am as a son to Him. He is as a father

to me: *For You are our Father* (Isa. 63:16); also, *For I am become a father to Israel* (Jer. 31:9). I am as a son to Him—*Israel is My son, My firstborn* (Ex. 4:22), and again, *You are the children of the Lord* (Deut. 14:1). He is a shepherd to me—*Give ear, O Shepherd of Israel* (Ps. 80:2). I am to Him as a flock—*And you, My sheep, the sheep of My pasture* (Ezek. 34:31). He is to me as a keeper—*Behold, He that keeps Israel neither slumbers nor sleeps* (Ps. 121:4). I am His vineyard, as it says, *For the vineyard of the Lord of Hosts is the house of Israel* (Isa. 5:7). He fights for me against those that challenge me, and I fight for Him against those that provoke Him. He fights against those that challenge me, since He slew the firstborn of Egypt, as it says, *For I will go through the land of Egypt* (Ex. 12:12), and further, *And it came to pass at midnight, that the Lord smote all the firstborn* (Ex. 12:29). I fight against those that provoke Him, since I sacrificed the gods of Egypt. God said, *And against all the gods of Egypt I will execute judgements* (Ex. 12:12), and I sacrificed them to Him, as it says, *Lo, If we sacrifice the abomination of the Egyptians before their eyes* (Ex. 8:22) and also, *They shall take to them every man a lamb, according to their fathers' houses* (Ex. 12:3). He said to me: 'Let not mingled wine be wanting,' as it says, *Your navel is like a round goblet, wherein no mingled wine is wanting* (S.S. 7:3), and I said to Him, 'You are my well beloved friend, let Your kindness never be wanting,' as it says, *The Lord is my shepherd, I shall not want* (Ps. 23:1). R. Judah b. R. Il'ai said: He sang of me, and I sang of Him; He extolled me and I extolled Him; He called me, 'My sister, My beloved, My dove, My perfect one,' and I said to Him, 'This is my beloved and this is my friend.' He said to me, *'Behold you are fair, my love'* (S.S. 1:15), and I said to Him, *'Behold you are fair, my beloved, yea pleasant'* (S.S. 1:16). He said to me, *'Happy are you, O Israel, who is like unto you'* (Deut. 33:29), and I said to Him, *'Who is like unto You, O Lord, among the mighty'* (Ex. 15:11). He said to me, *'And who is like Your people, like Israel, a nation one in the earth'* (2 Sam. 7:23), and I declare the unity of His name twice daily, saying, *'Hear, O Israel the Lord our God, the Lord is one'* (Deut. 6:4). When I require anything, I seek it only from His hand, as it says, *And it came to pass in the course of those many days that the king of Egypt died . . . and God heard their groaning . . . and God saw the children of Israel* (Ex. 2:23–25).

And when He required anything, He sought it only from me, as it says, *Speak unto all the congregation of Israel, saying* (Ex. 12:3).

When I required something, I sought it only from His hand, as it says, *And when Pharoah drew nigh, the children of Israel lifted up their eyes,* etc. (Ex. 14:10). And when He required something, He sought it only from me, as it says, *Speak unto the children of Israel, that they take for Me an offering* (Ex. 25:2).[18]

Both the form of the verse in the Song of Songs, "I am my Beloved's and He is mine," with its rhythm of modulating repetitions, and the vocabulary of mutuality, of shared experience in different keys, generate a traversal of Israel's history and practice through the interweaving of texts. The midrash begins with a series of images and their proof texts in which the relationship of God and Israel is figured, not surprisingly, as one of caretaker and those cared for—God and nation, father and son, shepherd and sheep, keeper and vineyard. The metaphors connect divine and human in a field of shared experience, but the theologically conventional hierarchy of strength and activity remains undisturbed. Through each image, we perceive the power and love of God exercised on behalf of the needy, expectant human community.

But when the *darshan* shifts from images of the perennial, transhistorical relationship ("He *is* as a father. . . . I *am* as a son"—in Hebrew, these are noun clauses with the verb "to be" understood) to active verbs summoning the great events of Israel's history, he also, more daringly, creates a language of equality ("He [fights for, helps] me. . . . I [fight for, help] Him"). The foundational events, the contest with Pharaoh and the gods of Egypt, the first Passover night in Egypt on the cusp of liberation, the miracle of the Red Sea, all become evidence of mutual love and service enacted by God and Israel for each other. The inauguration of the Passover sacrifice of the lamb, for example, here represents more than obedience to a command. Rather it is transformed to evidence of Israel's powerful battle on behalf of God against the Egyptians' object of worship. Their recitation of the *Shema*, the declaration of "the unity of God's name" twice daily, similarly becomes one side of a mutual declaration of love for a unique object of devotion. At the end of the midrash, the *darshan* creates a vocabulary of shared need ("When I required [needed] something. . . . When He required [needed] something"). The people's cry for help to God on the shore of the sea, which might seem the quintessential moment of God's powerful activity on behalf of an utterly helpless human community (as in the midrash about the dove in the cleft of the rock), is balanced against God's expression of need, fulfilled by their building him a dwelling place (the reference to Exodus 25). Through this texture of interwoven texts, the midrash constructs a stunning composition in the form of theme and variations in which the relationship of reciprocal and reciprocated love becomes the theme song of God and Israel.

One final example: To me, at least, an astoundingly bold midrash from *Song of Songs Rabbah* on 3:11. In the Blochs' translation:

> Come out, O daughters of Zion
> and gaze at Solomon the King!
> See the crown his mother set on his head
> on the day of his wedding,
> the day of his heart's great joy.

Almost always in this midrashic collection, references to Solomon or King Solomon (*Hamelech Shᵊlomo*, in Hebrew) are taken to be references to *hamelech shᵊhashalom shelo*—"the king of whom or from whom is *shalom*, peace." This midrash then, takes the king who is crowned by his mother on the day of his wedding to be God:

> *The crown with which his mother crowned him.* R. Johanan said: R. Simeon b. Yohai asked R. Eleazar b. R. Jose: 'Have you perhaps heard from your father what is the meaning of *The crown with which his mother crowned him?*' He replied, 'Yes.' 'How did he explain it?' he asked. He said: 'By a parable of a king who had an only daughter of whom he was exceedingly fond, so that at first he called her "daughter", till not satisfied with that he called her "sister", and still not satisfied with that he called her "mother". So the Holy One, blessed be He, loved Israel exceedingly and called them "daughter", as it says, *Hearken, O daughter, and consider* (Ps. 45:11); till not satisfied with that he called them "sister", as it says, *Open to me, my sister, my love* (S.S. 5: 2); and still not satisfied with that He called them "mother", as it says, *Attend unto Me, O My people, and give ear unto Me, O My nation—[u-le'umi]* (Isa. 51: 4), where it is written 'ul'immi' ('and to my mother').' R. Simeon b. Yohai rose and kissed him on his head, saying, 'Had I come only to hear this explanation from your lips, it would have repaid me.'[19]

The narrative frame of the midrash involves two generations of the students of Rabbi Akiva: Rabbi Shimon bar Yochai, portrayed in Talmudic literature as one of the most intense and fiercely devoted of Rabbi Akiva's students, and Rabbi Eleazar, the son of Rabbi Akiva's student, Rabbi Jose. In the Torah study of this circle of intimates, the verse bursts

through the boundaries of its setting (the spectacle of a wedding ceremony) to ramify into a drama of a passion in search of a metaphor. The
"king" in the *mashal* loves (*chabᵊvah*) his "daughter" beyond all bounds
(*yoter midai*—"more than enough, too much"), with an intensity that explodes all conventional possibilities of articulation. Yet according to Rabbi
Yose, that same intensity of God's love for Israel creates a yearning for
expression. But at each rung on the ladder of metaphor, the abundance
and power of God's feeling encounter the limitations of the language of
human relationship and push the lover onward into metaphors of ever-
increasing intimacy: in a more literal translation, "he could not move
from, be satisfied in, his love of her until he called her." The *darshan*
implies that only the relationship of mother and child (who have been
literally united, part of each other) can come close to adequacy.

Such a metaphor may resonate harmoniously in the context of the
Song, where the female lover's longing for blissful union with her beloved is best fulfilled when "I brought him to my mother's house, / To
the chamber of her who conceived me [*horati*]" (3:4, 8:1, 2, 5).Yet the
tension created by midrashic manipulation of the verse from Isaiah may
also suggest the endless stretching required to find even approximate
expression of that boundless love. And the embrace of metaphors of such
potentially transgressive force (a king's daughter who is also a sister/
bride, and even more daringly, a mother, opening up the possibility of an
image of a mother for God) pushes us into an awareness of a love that
breaks all boundaries:

> For love is as fierce as death,
> its jealousy bitter as the grave.
> Even its sparks are a raging fire,
> a devouring flame." (8:6).[20]

This remarkable midrash attributed to the "school" of Rabbi Akiva gives
us a taste of what it means to call the song's poetry of passionate love,
kodesh kodashim—the "holy of holies." But we should also note that, as
this midrashic collection has been stitched together, this reading of the
verse appears in the context of the people's making of the *mishcan*, the
Tabernacle, and later the *bet hamikdash*, the Temple, "so that I [God] may
dwell in their midst" (Exod. 25:8) and in the context of their whole-
hearted acceptance of the Torah at Sinai. Perhaps the editor or editors
perceived in Rabbi Shimon's passionate response to Rabbi Eleazar's
teaching more than the emotional intensity of the Akivan circle. Does he
see in this midrash a way to articulate the sense that the people, as it

embodies God's desire through enactment of Torah, gives birth to God in the world?

To read Biblical text with the rabbis means to see the canon as an organism, a living body whose parts are interdependent, and to endow the whole with capacities impossible to find in separate parts. The Song of Songs allowed the rabbis to read the history of Israel as a love story, to read the Torah as a dialogue of love between God and human beings. They enlisted the passionate energy, the sensual specificity and richness, and the erotic power of the Song's language into their quest to articulate their deepest and most intimate knowledge of relationship. They thus unveil a relationship of mutuality, expressed in need and desire, but also in fulfillment—moments of fulfillment in the past, hopes of permanence in the future. In the midrash, erotic language is religious; religious language is erotic. Or as Rabbi Akiva tells us, speaking the Song's language opens up the Holy of Holies, gives us entry into the heart, in both senses of the word. We "penetrate" to the core, to the heart of the Torah, and unveil its language of heartfelt emotion.

INTRADIVINE ROMANCE:
THE SONG OF SONGS IN THE ZOHAR

Arthur Green

The Zohar is the great medieval Jewish compendium of mysticism, myth, and esoteric teaching. It may be considered the greatest work of Jewish literary imagination in the Middle Ages. Surely it constitutes one of the most important bodies of religious texts of all times and places. It is also a lush garden of sacred eros, filled to overflowing with luxurious plantings of love between master and disciples, among the mystical companions themselves, between the souls of Israel and the *shekhinah*, God's lovely bride, but most of all between the male and female elements that together make up the Godhead. Revered and canonized by generations of faithful devotees, the secret universe described by the Zohar's authors serves as the basis of Kabbalistic faith, both within the boundaries of Judaism and beyond it, down to our own day, one that has seen a significant revival of interest in Kabbalah and its teachings.

Written in a lofty combination of Aramaic and Hebrew, the Zohar was first made public around 1300. As the contemporary reader of the original encounters it, the Zohar is a three-volume work constituting some seventeen hundred folio pages, ordered in the form of a commentary on the Torah. The first volume covers Genesis, the second Exodus, and the third completes the remaining three books of the Pentateuch. In addition to these volumes is Zohar Ḥadash (the New Zohar), a collection of materials omitted from the earliest mid-sixteenth-century Zohar editions, but later culled from manuscript sources. Here we find partial commentaries on Ruth, Lamentations, and the Song of Songs.

For our purposes, it is interesting to note that the chief speaker and purported author of the Zohar, Rabbi Simeon ben Yoḥai, was a leading disciple of Rabbi Akiva, the earliest figure associated with the allegorical reading of the Song of Songs. The third-century Mishnah records Akiva as denying that there ever had been controversy as to whether the Canticle was to be included within the Biblical canon, since "all the Scriptures are holy but the Song of Songs is the Holy of Holies." The Zohar, composed a millennium later than Akiva's work, stands fully within that tradition. One might say that it was written under the spell of the Song of Songs, for the Canticle is quoted and commented upon with great frequency within its pages and is present everywhere in allusion and echo.

In the Jewish exegetical context, interpretation of the Song of Songs is one of the chief ways through which individuals and generations expressed their relationship with the loving God. Despite its being repeatedly tamed in the name of historical and collectivist allegory (the nation of Israel as beloved, etc.), the tremendous passion of the book has remained available to those over the ages who sought to convey such intense love in religious devotion. The Canticle itself, we might say, became the "locked garden" of which it speaks, opening itself to those whose hearts longed to dwell by its streams and to be intoxicated by the spices of its perfumed gardens. Ultimately the Song of Songs comes to represent not merely a single text, but a wide-ranging network of religio-erotic metaphors. The influence of the Canticle on the Zohar and on the Kabbalistic tradition as a whole is not limited to specific comments on that work or quotations from it, although these, too, abound in the Zohar's pages. It extends into the echoes and allusions mentioned above, into the entire metaphor of sacred courtship and marriage as used to describe the relationship between God and the holy community of his faithful.

The Zohar represents the apogee of a process that had been developing for a hundred years or more before its writing. I refer to the emergence in writing of Kabbalistic secrets and the attempt to interpret various aspects of Jewish Scripture and tradition in accord with the symbolism contained within them. Among the very first works of Kabbalistic exegesis were commentaries on the Song of Songs, including one by Rabbi Ezra of Gerona (now available in English translation), a lost commentary by Rabbi Moses of Burgos, and, contemporaneous with the Zohar, a commentary by Rabbi Isaac Ibn Sahula of Guadalajara.

Kabbalah represents a radical departure from any previously known version of Judaism, especially in the realm of theology. While Kabbalists remained loyal followers of normative Jewish praxis as defined by *halakha*, the theological meaning system that undergirded their Judaism was entirely reconstructed. The image of God that first appears in *Sefer ha-Bahir*, to be elaborated by several generations of Kabbalists until it achieved its highest poetic expression in the Zohar, is a God of multiple mythic potencies, obscure entities called *sefirot*. These elude precise definition, but are described through a remarkable web of images, parables, and scriptural allusions. Together, these entities constitute the divine realm; "God" is the collective aggregate of these potencies and their inner relationship. The dynamic interplay among these forces is the essential story of Kabbalah, the true inner meaning, as far as its devotees are concerned, both of the Torah and of life itself.

The *sefirot* constitute the subject of nearly all Kabbalistic discourse, including that of the Zohar. They exist in neither time nor space. They represent an inner divine reality that is prior to these ways of dividing existence, although both are derived from it. The word *sefirah* as "number" represents a high level of metaphysical abstraction. The existence of *sefirot* indicates a certain multiplicity or multifacetedness within the divine unity, a tentative "many" within the absolute One. This means that the oneness of God has a dynamic side; it is a oneness that is not simple and undifferentiated, but teeming with energy, life, and passion. There are even tensions and forces that pull in opposite directions within this unity, so that *yiḥud ha-shem*, understood previously as the *proclamation* of God's oneness, now comes to mean *effecting* the unity of God, bringing the *sefirot* together in harmony, so that a single energy may flow through them and unite them.

The *sefirot* are described by multiple layerings of symbol terms, which collectively constitute the secret language of Kabbalah. I have argued elsewhere that from a functional point of view, the *sefirot* are, in fact, nuggets of symbolic association. By far the richest network of such associations is that connected with the tenth and final *sefirah*. As *malkhut* ("kingdom") it represents the realm over which the King (the sixth *sefirah*, *tif'eret*, or the "blessed Holy One" of rabbinic tradition) has dominion, sustaining and protecting it as the true king takes responsibility for his kingdom. At the same time, it is this final *sefirah* that is charged with the rule of the lower world; the blessed Holy One's *malkhut* is the lower world's ruler.

The last *sefirah* is also called the *shekhinah*, an ancient rabbinic term for the indwelling divine presence. In the medieval Jewish imagination, this appellation for God had been transformed into a winged divine being, hovering over the community of Israel and protecting it from harm. The *shekhinah* was also said to dwell in Israel's midst, to follow the people into exile, and to participate in their suffering. In the latest phases of midrashic literature, there begins to appear a distinction between God and his *shekhinah*, partly a reflection of medieval philosophical attempts to assign the biblical anthropomorphisms to a being lesser than the Creator. The Kabbalists identify this *shekhinah* as the bride, spouse, or divine consort of the blessed Holy One. She is the tenth *sefirah*, therefore a part of God included within the divine ten-in-one unity. But she is tragically exiled, distanced from her divine spouse. Sometimes she is seen to be either seduced or taken captive by the evil hosts of *sitra ahra*—the "other," evil side of being. Then God and the righteous below must join forces in order to liberate her. The great drama of religious life, according to the Kabbalists, is the protection of the *shekhinah* from the forces of evil and joining her to the holy bridegroom who ever awaits her. Here one can see how medieval Jews adapted the values of chivalry—the rescue of the maiden from the clutches of evil—to fit their own spiritual context.

In the midrashic tradition, the *shekhinah* identifies with the sufferings of the community of Israel and dwells in its midst. Nevertheless, there is a clear distinction maintained between the two. The *shekhinah* is the presence of God; *kenesset yisra'el* is the collective body of the Jewish people. Sometimes this community of Israel is indeed depicted as a hypostatic entity, standing in God's presence and engaging in dialogue with him. But this partner in dialogue is always other than God, representing his earthly beloved. In what is surely their most daring symbolic move, the Kabbalists combined these two figures, blurring the once obvious distinction between the human community of Israel and their divine protector. They claim that the *shekhinah* *is* the community of Israel; *kenesset yisra'el* becomes another term for the tenth *sefirah*. Poised precisely at the border between the divine and the lower worlds, she is at once the this-worldly presentiment of God and a heavenly embodiment of Israel, her faithful people below.

The identification of the *shekhinah* and *kenesset yisra'el* enabled the Kabbalists to annex the entire midrashic tradition regarding the relationship of God and Israel and to declare it their own. Particularly, the rabbis' reading of the Song of Songs as a love dialogue between God and Israel makes it the key text for understanding the inner unity of God as the love between male and female. The implication for Jewish faith of this dramatic shift cannot be overstated. The essential relationship that Judaism comes to depict is now an inner divine one. The eros here is not the love and union between God and Israel or God and the soul, but between male and female forces within God. The earthly community of Israel remain God's partner and beloved people, but now he and they (the

217

Kabbalists in particular) share in the task of restoring cosmic oneness, of bringing the divine male and female face to face with one another. Through this union, lights might shine throughout the universe, and the waters of life might flow through it to nourish and sustain all the worlds below.

As the female partner within the divine, the tenth *sefirah*—the *shekhinah*—is described through a host of symbols that is derived both from the natural world and from the legacy of Judaism. The symbols are classically associated with femininity. The tenth *sefirah* is the moon, dark on her own, but receiving and giving off the light of the sun. She is the sea, into whom all waters flow; the earth, longing to be fructified by the rain that falls from heaven. She is the heavenly Jerusalem, into whom the King will enter; she is the throne upon which he is seated, the Temple or Tabernacle, dwelling place of his glory. She is the Ark of the Covenant, a symbol that takes on particularly sexual association since "covenant" (*brit*) in Judaism is especially associated with the act of circumcision. The tenth *sefirah* is a passive-receptive female with regard to the *sefirot* above her, receiving their energies and being fulfilled by their presence within her. But she is a ruler, the source of life, and font of all blessing for the worlds below, including the human soul. The Kabbalist sees himself as a devotee of the *shekhinah*. This does not mean that she may ever be worshipped apart from the divine unity. Indeed, this separation of the *shekhinah* from the forces above was the terrible sin of Adam that brought about exile from Eden. Nonetheless, it is only through her that humans have access to the mysteries that lie beyond. All prayer is channeled through her, seeking to energize her and raise her up in order to effect the sefirotic unity. The primary function of the religious life, with all its duties and obligations, is to rouse the *shekhinah* into a state of love.

All realms outside the divine proceed from the *shekhinah*. She is surrounded most immediately by a host of non-material beings. Sometimes these are depicted as angels; they are the maidens who attend the bride at the marriage canopy. These figures inhabit and rule over many different realms or "palaces" of light and joy. Such a picture seems tailor-made for exegesis of the Song of Songs: Daughters of Jerusalem, queens and concubines, and all the rest of the Canticle's host provide perfect scriptural settings for a Judaism in which the *hieros gamos*, the mystical/erotic union of the divine male and female, takes such a central role.

As will be obvious by now, there is a strong erotic element in Kabbalah and especially in the Zohar. The frank and uncensored use of bold sexual language for talking about the inner life of God is a major part of the

Zohar's legacy, found throughout the later mystical tradition. Such phrases as "to arouse the feminine waters" or "to serve God with a living limb" have become so much a part of the conventional language of later Kabbalah that one almost forgets how shocking it is that the act of worship is being described in terms of female arousal or male erection. How did it happen that such unbridled eroticism was permitted to enter the domain of the sacred? How, especially, could this have happened in an era and within a devotional circle that was at the same time so very conservative, even extreme, in its views of sexual temptation or transgression?

Use of erotic language to describe the relationship between God and Israel was well known already in Biblical times, as witnessed by several of the prophets, especially Hosea. In the rabbinic imagination, the chief vehicle for this all-important metaphor was the Song of Songs, read allegorically as the love and marriage between God and the community of Israel. This collectivist reading of the Canticle dominates the midrashic tradition. Its importance was underscored, moreover, by the fact that the church, from the time of Origen, adopted a parallel interpretation in which Christ and *ecclesia* were the lover and beloved of the Song. This Christian allegory was an important tool of supersessionist theology, with the church now claiming to be the maiden chosen for divine delight. The Jews, whose rejection by God seemed so obviously confirmed by their historical plight, had every reason to hold fast to the faith that God was their true lover, the one to whom they cried out even in his seeming absence: "On my bed at night I sought him whom my soul loves," knowing in faith that "here he stands behind our wall, peering through the lattice-work, gazing through the windows."

In the twelfth and thirteenth centuries, there was a great shift in the reading of the Song of Songs from a collectivist to an individualist allegory. The Canticle now came to be seen as a song between God and the soul, a reflection of the new emphasis on individual quest and personal pilgrimage in the religious life of the era. In Christianity, this was the development of an old tradition, and it especially flourished at the hands of Bernard of Clairvaux and other Cistercians. The Jews were slow to follow this trend and the few attempts at it were not great successes. The individual Jewish reader (typically a noncelibate male) did not easily see himself as the bride or female beloved of God.

Instead, the Jews developed another reading, one that was to reshape Jewish devotional life in a basic way. If the male Jewish reader could not wax passionate about the erotic relationship between himself and the essentially male figure of God, what was needed was a female presence, inserted between these two males, with whom both could have that passionate relationship. This is exactly what the Kabbalah did in placing the female *shekhinah* at the end of the sefirotic chart or as the gatekeeper between the upper and lower worlds. The inner unity of the Godhead was now seen, as we have already noted, primarily in erotic terms, with the union of "the blessed Holy One and His *shekhinah*" being the central focus of all devotional life. But Israel, too, as the devoted children, servants, and bridal attendants of the *shekhinah*, served as "awakeners of her desire to unite with the Holy King." They did this by cultivating their own love for the divine bride in their devoted lives of Torah study and in performance of the commandments, including that of holy union with their own wives, an earthly representation of the union above.

Where did the Jews get this idea of a female intermediary between themselves and God above? It seems all too obvious that this is a Jewish adaptation of the cult of the Virgin Mary, very much revived in the Western church of the twelfth century, especially in France and Spain, where Kabbalah also first emerged. Marian piety permeated the culture of Western Europe in this age: The dedication of cathedrals to the Virgin, roadside shrines, passion dramas, music and art of all forms glorified her role. The Jews were surely witness to this and must have found themselves of two minds about it. On the one hand, it confirmed their worst impressions of Christianity as pagan, idolatrous, and polytheistic. But there was also something beautiful and tender about the spirituality associated with it that could not be ignored. The Jews, whose culture knew no glorification of virginity or celibacy, adapted the female channel of worship to suit their own needs. The notion that there is a divine (or quasi-divine) female presence poised at the entranceway to the divine realm, one who loves her children, suffers with them, and accepts their prayers to be brought up before the throne of God, is shared by the Marian and Kabbalistic traditions. Clearly the latter, which developed in the century following the great Marian revival, is influenced by the former.

Once the female aspect of divinity was in place, without the Christian insistence on virginity, otherwise repressed erotic energies could find expression in the spiritual life and strivings of the Kabbalist. In practice, the Zohar's authors represent an especially strict halakhic viewpoint on all sexual matters, one that continued in Kabbalistic circles for many centuries. But the gates were thrown wide open to the rarified, only lightly masked, erotic fantasy to fuel the intensity of religious passion.

The Kabbalist's self-image as *tzadik*, the "guardian of the covenant," was at the same time an image of male potency. His task was to direct the aroused power of his *kavvanah*, or spiritual intention, toward the *shekhinah*, thus stirring the female waters within her so that she arouses the *tzadik* above (the ninth *sefirah*) to couple with her, filling her with the flow of energy from beyond in the form of his male waters, the lights from above as divine semen. As she is filled, the fluid within her in turn overflows to the lower world, and the earthly *tzadik* receives that blessing. Here the paradigm is of a fully coital expression of sexual union, seemingly closer in some ways to the religion of South India than to the virginal, celibate piety of Christian monks.

But the immediate influence that helped to stir these new energies within Judaism was indeed Christianity. If we look again at the Kabbalistic chart, especially at the elements highlighted within it by the Castilian Kabbalah, we may see a further parallel to the Christian structures of faith that so characterized this era. *Tif'eret*, or the blessed Holy One, stands at the center; this is the essential figure of the male deity, the God of the Bible and Jewish tradition. He is flanked on the right and left by *hesed* and *din*, compassion and judgment. This triad of *sefirot* is completed by *malkhut*, or the *shekhinah*, at the lower end of the Kabbalistic chart. Together, these four constitute a whole, represented by such symbols as the four directions, the four species of Sukkot, the three patriarchs plus King David, and so forth. These are all Jewish symbols of great antiquity. But if we look at this chart *structurally*, we cannot help but notice that it constitutes a trinity, with "God the Father" at the center, flanked by two others, with the female "below" them serving as intermediary between heaven and earth, bearer of prayers to God above and birth chamber of divine blessing as it flows into the world. Because of the Second Commandment, forbidding graven images, Jews were held back from any concrete expression of these structures beyond the occasional diagram and chart. But imagine what such Kabbalistic images might have looked like in stained glass. There we would have found something very close to the image world of medieval Christianity.

It should be emphasized that these tremendous importations of spiritual structures were carried out in a subtle and highly creative way, so that the connections were far from obvious, perhaps even to the Kabbalists themselves. Anything more than this would have labeled them heretics and enemies of Judaism, precisely the opposite of their goal, which was to strengthen Judaism in the face of its all-powerful and dangerous rival. It was in part because they were themselves so affected by the attractiveness of Christianity that the authors of the Zohar set out to create a Judaism of renewed mythic power and old/new symbolic forms. Far from being crypto-Christians (as they were thought by the Christian Kabbalists of the Renaissance), they are seeking to create a more compelling Jewish myth, one that would fortify Jews in resisting Christianity.

One example of the Jewish challenge to Christianity is the marriage relationship posited between God and the *shekhinah*, or the Holy Spirit. By contrast to Jewish life, the culture of Christian Spain was highly monastic. The thirteenth century, when the Zohar was written, marks the great heyday of both Dominican and Franciscan spirituality. In addition to influencing the religious life of the surrounding culture, these orders played a great role in socioeconomic life. Judaism, of course, had no tradition of monasticism or of glorified celibacy. Jewish pietists who shared in some of the other-worldly and ascetic values of the monkish life must have been impressed by the great monastic establishments, however. In sharp contrast to the Christian glorification of celibacy, the Zohar insists (albeit with meager support from earlier Jewish sources) that an unmarried man is merely half a person: The *shekhinah* does not dwell apart from the wholeness of male/female union. When a man is away from his wife, the Zohar tells us—whether he is traveling on the road, busy studying Torah with his companions, or kept from her because of menstrual impurity—the *shekhinah* joins to him, becoming his female spiritual companion. She does so, however, only because he has an earthly female partner to whom he will return. Anyone who lacks a wife cannot expect to be joined to the presence of God. In thirteenth-century Castile, this insistence on the spiritual necessity of marriage can best be understood as a frontal attack on Christian monasticism. Abstinence from marriage, claims the Zohar, does not free one for devotion to God, as the monks would have it; indeed, celibacy makes it *impossible* for one to experience the presence of the Holy Spirit.

The Zohar thus draws marital life into the framework of the celestial romance. Marriage saves a man from the fate of being "half a body" and grants man and woman entrance into the secret of God's nuptial embrace, earthly husband and wife assuming the roles of *tif'eret* and *malkhut*. Just as the divine male mediates between the Upper and Lower Mothers, gathering the blessing of *binah*, the third *sefirah* or "Upper Mother," and sowing it into the fertile and receptive field of *malkhut*, so, too, does the husband stand between two female presences, the *shekhinah* and his wife. For the Kabbalist, conjugal intercourse must be conducted in the light of the intradivine romance. When husband and wife focus their consciousness and desire upon the celestial union, their lovemaking is a dramatic enactment of cosmic realities. Human intercourse is grounded in a divine event and functions as its terrestrial expression. Such a union of earthly male and female, it is promised, will bring about the birth of pure and holy children.

Although verses from the Canticle are quoted with great regularity throughout the pages of the Zohar, there are two sections within the text where the treatment is most concentrated. One of these has already been mentioned: the so-called Zohar to the Song of Songs in Zohar Ḥadash, which has never been translated into English. Ranging over some thirty tightly printed pages in the current edition, it in fact contains homilies to the first ten verses of Canticles 1, with the greatest attention given to the first two verses. The other section, smaller, but of great importance, appears in Zohar 2:143a–145b in the midst of the portion *Terumah*, containing prescriptions for the building of the wilderness Tabernacle. The tabernacle is the prototype for the Jerusalem Temple, erected by Solomon, purported author of the Song of Songs. The figures of Moses and Solomon are seen as parallel to one another: the greatest of prophets and the wisest of men. Each was the author of a famous song, Moses's at the Red Sea and Solomon's Canticle, and each directed the building of a dwelling-place for the *shekhinah* on earth.

The ascription of bridal imagery to both Tabernacle and Temple has roots in ancient Judaism. The clever misreading of *kelot* ("completed"), spelled defectively, in Numbers 7:1, "On the day when Moses *completed* ["bride"] erecting the tabernacle" to refer to *kalat Moshe*, the Tabernacle or Torah as Moses's bride, is well known. The Song of Songs itself, according to traditions ascribed to various second-century authorities, records a conversation between God, Israel, and the angels during the lifetime of Moses. According to some, this took place in the Tabernacle or "tent of meeting" described in Exodus. Solomon only recorded and perhaps gave final poetic form to a dialogue that had taken place much earlier. But the Zohar prefers a divergent rabbinic opinion, one claiming that "the day the Song was given" was in fact the dedication of the Jerusalem Temple. At this moment in human history, there was utter convergence between the worlds above and below, when God as *sh'lomo*, the king of peace, and the earthly *sh'lomo*, Solomon, the king, could both be acclaimed as speakers of the Song.

Despite earlier rabbinic approbation for this view, it presents the Zohar's author with difficulty. He seems to be placing Solomon on a higher rung than Moses, the one who is clearly "lord of all prophets" and whose encounter with God was never equaled. Elsewhere in the Zohar, as throughout Jewish literature, it is Moses who most embodies the sublime vision. The Zohar is sensitive to this unspoken criticism. In terms of prophecy, the author admits, Moses indeed knew no equal. But when it comes to the poetic muse, matters are somewhat different. Moses's song—that of the sea—was still concerned with matters of this world; he was thanking God for Israel's deliverance from a very real enemy and singing in praise of his miraculous deeds. As we read in Zohar 2:144b–145a:

> But King David and his son Solomon spoke a different kind of Song. David sought to arrange the maidens and to adorn them along with the Queen, to show Queen and maidens in all their beauty. This is his concern in the psalms and praises; it was they, Queen and maidens, that he was seeking to adorn. When Solomon arrived he found the Queen adorned and her maidens decked out in beauty. He then sought to bring her to the Bridegroom and to bring Him under the canopy together with His Bride. He spoke words of love between them so that they be joined as one, so that the two of them form a single one in the wholeness of their love.
>
> In this did Solomon rise high in praises, above all other humans. Moses was wedded to the Queen in this world below, so that there be a whole union among the lower creatures. Solomon brought about the complete union of the Queen above, first bringing the Bridegroom under the canopy and only afterwards joyously inviting both of them into the Temple he had built.
>
> Blessed are David and Solomon his son for having brought about the union above. From the day God had said to the moon: "Go and diminish yourself! (Hullin 60b)" she had not been fully coupled with the sun until King Solomon came forth.

Moses the prophet still needs to bring the *shekhinah* into the lower world. He has a people to worry about, a people wandering the wilderness, who need assurance that God is indeed in their midst. The prophet's concern is his flock. Solomon, the mystic hierophant, can afford to be utterly selfless; it is not of his own love that he speaks, or even the love of earthly Israel for her God. He is the attendant, or better, the officiant, at the union of divine bridegroom and bride. He offers his song as an epithalamium, a gift to the sacred couple, intending nothing more or less than to fill all the universe with his freely given words of love.

The spiritualized reconstruction of the ancient Temple and the vener-
ation of Temple-centered piety may also have to do with the Zohar's
attempt to compete with the grand edifices and elaborate, incense-filled
ritual drama offered by the religion of the surrounding culture. The great
Temple to the *shekhinah*'s presence on earth, the reader is reminded, was
not the latest cathedral erected in Castile of the Reconquista, but the only
true Temple, that of the holy city. In another key passage (*Zohar Hadash*
62d–63a), the Song of Songs is identified with the underground channels
or furrows (called *shittim*) that run under the Temple Mount, into which
flowed the sacrificial blood and the wine of libations. These *shittim*, according to old Jewish lore, date back to creation itself. In this spirit, the
Zohar reads the opening word of Genesis, *bereshit* as *bara shit,* "He created the channel." But now the underground channels are uplifted and
identified with the inner divine channels, the *sefirot*. As such, they are
both singular and plural, *shit* and *shittim*. Alas, the channels are closed
off in our day because of the curled snake, identified with the evil urge
or the demonic forces, that now sits atop them. One day, however, God
will remove that coiled figure. Now, suddenly, the Zohar switches from
cosmogony to graphology: When the curved, snakelike line on the left
side of the latter *tav* in *shit* and *shittim* is removed, the letter becomes a
resh, and the words reveal themselves as *Shir ha-shirim*, the Song of Songs.

Alongside the glorious memory of Temple piety, the Song of Songs is
often related by the Zohar to its own favorite act of contemporary religious practice, the study and interpretation of Torah. The Zohar stands
within the long tradition of Jewish devotion to sacred study as a religious
act. The Torah itself commands its faithful to "contemplate it day and
night," traditionally taken to mean that the study and elaboration of the
Torah is ideally the full-time obligation of the entire community of male
Israelites. This community viewed the Torah as an object of love, and an
eros of Torah study is depicted in many passages in the rabbinic *aggadah*.
Based on ancient images of feminine wisdom, the Torah was described
as the daughter and delight of God and as Israel's bride. Study of the
Torah, especially the elaboration of its law, was described by the sages as
courtship and sometimes even as the shy, scholarly bridegroom's act of
love, the consummation of this sacred marriage. The midrash on the
Song of Songs, compiled in the seventh or eighth century, devotes a large
part of its exegesis to discussion of the revelation at Sinai and the delights
of both God and the sages in the study of the Torah.

The Zohar is well aware of these precedents and expands upon them.
The Kabbalists' literary imagination links the gardens of eros in the Song

of Songs, the *pardes* or "orchard" of mystical speculation itself, with the mystical Garden of Eden, into which God wanders each night "to take delight in the souls of the righteous." The description of Paradise in Genesis—"a river goes forth from Eden to water the garden, whence it divides into four streams"—and certain key verses of the Canticle—"a spring amid the gardens, a well of living waters, flowing from Lebanon"—are quoted endlessly to invoke the sense that to engage in mystical exegesis is to dwell in the shade of God's garden. Even more: The reader comes to understand that all of these gardens are but reflections of the true inner divine garden, the world of the *sefirot*, which in the tradition that runs from *Sefer ha-Bahir* to the Zohar is described as lush with trees, springs, and ponds of water.

The Zohar is devoted to the full range of religious obligations that the Torah places upon the community of Israel. Still, it is fair to say that the central religious act for the Zohar was the study and interpretation of the Torah. Again and again, Rabbi Simeon waxes eloquent in praise of those who study the Torah, especially those who do so after midnight. They indeed take the place of the priests and Levites of old, "who stand in the house of the Lord by night." Those who awaken nightly to study the secrets of the Torah become the earthly attendants of the divine bride, ushering her into the chamber where she will unite at dawn with her heavenly spouse. This somewhat modest depiction of the Kabbalist's role in the *hieros gamos*—the role we have see applied to Solomon as well— does not exclude a level of emotional/mystical experience in which the Kabbalist himself is also the lover of that bride and a full participant in, rather than merely an attendant to, the act of union.

> Torah in the Zohar is not conceived as a text, as an object, or as material, but as a living divine presence, engaged in a mutual relationship with the person who studies her. More than that, in the Zoharic consciousness Torah is compared to a beloved who carries on with her lovers a mutual and dynamic courtship. The Zohar on the portion *Mishpaṭim* contains, within the literary unit known as *Saba de-Mishpaṭim* a description of maiden in a palace. Here the way of the Torah's lover is compared to the way of a man with a maiden. Arousal within Torah is like an endless courting of the beloved: constant walking about the gates of her palace, an increasing passion to read her letters, the desire to see the beloved's face, to reveal her, and to be joined with her. The beloved in the nexus of this relationship is entirely active. She sends signals of her interest to her lover, she intensifies his passionate desire for her by games

of revealing and hiding. She discloses secrets that stir his curiosity. She desires to be loved. The beloved is disclosed in an erotic progression before her lover out of a desire to reveal secrets that have been forever hidden within her. The relationship between Torah and her lover, like that of man and maiden in this parable, is dynamic, romantic, and erotic. (Melila Hellner-Eshed, *Ve-nahar yotse me-ʿEden: ʿal śefat ha-ḥavayah ha-misṭit ba-Zohar* [Tel Aviv: ʿam ʿoved, 2005], 19)

Seeing the act of Torah study as the most highly praised form of devotional activity places the Zohar squarely within the Talmudic tradition and at the same time provides a setting in which to go far beyond it. Here, unlike in the rabbinic sources, the *content* of the exegesis as well as the *process* is erotic in character. The Talmudic Rabbi Akiva, the greatest hero of the rabbinic romance with the text, was inspired by his great love of the Torah to derive "heaps and heaps of laws from the crowns on each of the letters." It was the rabbis' intense devotion to the text and to the *process* of Torah study that was so aptly described by the erotic metaphor. But the laws derived in the course of this passionate immersion in the text might deal with heave offerings and tithes or ritual defilement and ablutions; all of these were equally to be celebrated as resulting from the embrace of the Torah. That indeed is the genius of Rabbi Akiva's school of thought: *All* of the Torah, even the seemingly most mundane parts, belongs to the great mystical moment of Sinai, the day when God gave the Torah to Israel and proclaimed his love for her in the Song of Songs. But the authors of the Zohar crave more than this. The *content* as well as the *process* has to reveal the great secret of unity, not just the small secrets of one law or another. In the Zohar, the true subject matter that the Kabbalist finds in every verse is the *hieros gamos* itself, the eros that underlies and transforms the cosmos, the text, and the soul of the interpreter, all at once. In this sense, it may be said that Zoharic exegesis seeks to reread the entire Torah as an expanded version of Rabbi Akiva's Holy of Holies, the Song of Songs. It succeeds in doing so to a remarkable degree.

THE LOVE SONG OF THE MILLENNIUM: MEDIEVAL CHRISTIAN APOCALYPTIC AND THE SONG OF SONGS

E. Ann Matter

The Latin Middle Ages was a period of great Christian interest in the Song of Songs. Judging from the surviving texts, at least twenty Latin line-by-line expositions of Solomon's love songs were written between the seventh and the eleventh centuries, and over thirty survive from the twelfth century alone.[1] These are curious works of literature in a number of ways. For one thing, they were the product of an intellectual elite made up entirely of celibate men living in religious (usually monastic) communities. For another (and this is the reason that monks could have such an open interest in something as steamy as the Song of Songs), the treatises were developed out of a rhetorical system that assumed multiple layers of allegorical readings, one in which the poems of the Song of Songs were turned from human love songs into spiritual tales of at least three passionate links: one between divine love and the earthly institution of the church, another between God and the human soul, and third—the case we will explore in this essay—the passionate longing for the gathering in of the End Times, the end of the world promised when Jesus returns again.

Such multiple layers of allegory often overlapped and were intertwined to make one narrative, even if this made it a narrative with multiple and even contradictory meanings. This type of biblical interpretation required a type of rhetorical and allusive encounter with the text that was rejected by the literalist biblical commentators of the Protestant Reformation and that is still often misunderstood. I hope in this essay to show how and to what purpose this technique was employed by a true master of the genre. I will do this through an examination of a long and rhetorically virtuoso commentary on the Song of Songs written in Germany sometime after 1132 by the Benedictine monk Honorius Augustodunensis.[2]

Honorius goes through the eight chapters of the Song of Songs in a line-by-line commentary, which, as the two long introductory prologues explain, he proposes to explicate on different levels of allegory. Then, at the very end of his commentary, Honorius returns to the beginning of the Song and does it all over again, in a sense summarizing all that he has already written. I offer here a translation of this final synopsis, a text that, like most of Honorius's commentary, has never appeared in English. In it, the reader will note how Honorius, in typical medieval fashion, takes each moment of the literal text as having an allegorical significance. The letter is the husk; the kernel inside, which must be freed to the reader, is the Christian understanding of the Hebrew poem and therefore (for the denizens of this world) its true meaning. Such an interpretation may be at once shocking and very interesting to readers who love the Song of Songs and appreciate the diversity of its explications, but have never seen medieval Latin allegory in action. Honorius says:

> This book begins where humankind receives peace, that is, the grace of God. By "Let him kiss me" (1:1) the incarnation of Christ is indicated. Through this [kiss] peace is brought to men, peace that was lost by the first parents, peace for which the church always hopes, that is, Christ, the Word of God, the bridegroom of human nature is the true peace to which our human nature is united. And when God became man, then indeed man became God. Truly, by rising again, he gives back to the faithful the peace stolen by Victor Death, saying: "Peace be with you" (John 20:19). And this was the kiss of the mouth of God's peace given back by the Word of God (Christ), and since then our nature is made impassible and immortal in Christ, just as it had been created in the beginning. By "breasts," (1:1) we understand evangelical doctrine. By "unguents," the gift of the Holy Spirit. By "name poured out as oil," (1:2) is signified the new name of Christians which is put on through the holy oil in the baptism of Christians.
>
> By "draw me" (1:3) the Ascension of Christ is understood, through which the wished-for church is drawn into heaven. Thus follows "the odor of the unguents," (1:3, var.) which was the sweetness of the gifts of the Holy Spirit.
>
> "The king led me" (1:3) describes the conversion of the primitive churches, which he leads after the gift of the Holy Spirit. "I am

black" (1:4) signifies the tribulation of the primitive church, borne on account of the perfidious Jews. "Show me" (1:6) leads out of the narrow place signifying the depravity of the heretics. "If you do not know yourself" (1:7) shows the teachings of the apostles, which was to them as the tabernacle to the shepherds.

By "the nard," and "the little bundle of myrrh," and the "cluster of cypress" (1:11–13) are suggested the passion of Christ, and this is to be imitated through suffering. Thus for nard is understood the incarnation, for myrrh [is understood] the passion, for a bundle of cypress [is understood] the resurrection of Christ.

"Behold you are fair my friend" and the rest up to "on my bed" (1:14–15) expresses the praise of the faithful and the work of Christ for the primitive church and the action of grace by that same church through the gift of the Holy Spirit and the preaching of the church to the Gentiles.

Indeed, from "on my bed" up to "I will go to the mountain of myrrh" (3:1–4:6), we note the introduction of the church of the Gentiles, which was led by the apostles out of the desert of infidelity to the bed of Solomon, and is led to the banquet on the litter, and received by the daughters of Solomon, and praised by the magnificent king of peace.

From that same "I will go to the mountain of myrrh" up to "a garden enclosed" (4:6–4:12), the struggle of the church is signified, since it fought against Amana, Sanir, and Hermon, that is, against the princes of the peoples, who were leopards and lions, that is, fierce persecutors of the armies of the faithful and the suffering.

For that same "garden enclosed" up to "arise, north wind, and come, south wind" (4:6–4:16) through different types of aromatic herbs are understood different orders of the just, like different legions of martyrs fighting for Christ. "Rise, north wind" up to "I sleep" (4:16–5:2) expresses the affliction of the church, since it is afflicted, under the heretics, for the sake of faith. "I sleep" is understood as the peace and security of the church. "I rose to open" (5:5) signifies the church's preaching. "My soul melted" (5:6) is understood as the church penitent. "Of what sort is your beloved" up to "I went down to the nut grove" (5:9–6:10) is the church of the imperfect led by Christ to become the church of the perfect.

"I went down to the nut grove" to "come, my beloved" (6:10–8:14, var.) is the conversion of the synagogue, and his [Christ's?] struggle under Antichrist, that is, his order described. And so, to the end of the book is explained the calling of the unfaithful after Antichrist, and the rewarding of the faithful, and the separation of the good from the bad through the Last Judgment.

After this, the universal church, the bride of Christ, united by flesh with the Word of God, through her struggle will be crowned with glory and honor, and in the litter of glory [*in thalamo gloriae*], that is, in the manifest vision of God, will be united with [*copulabitur*, lit. "will copulate with"] her bridegroom. (PL 172: 494D–496C)

This pithy summary of the meaning of the Song of Songs (just two columns in the Patrologia Latina) is interesting in a number of ways. For one thing, it shows very well how the medieval Christian tradition of Song of Songs commentary is a "quest for narrative." The end purpose of this allegory of narrative is a type of symbolism that works through simile more than metaphor: "this is like this, and that is like that."[3] Here, Honorius plows through the text of the Song of Songs, beginning to end, identifying a few turning points, all in order to demonstrate that this book of the Bible is a story about God's succeeding dispensations among human beings. The narrative stretches from the "primitive church" to the "perfected church," from the Fall of humankind to the Judgment of the Second Coming, from Creation to Eschaton.

In doing so, Honorius in fact deviates from the carefully crafted allegories of his much longer commentary. This deviation is not in ultimate meaning, since this short interpretation does end up in the same place, at the End of Time. I want to show here how and why that point is reached.

Let me say first that the overall meaning Honorius gives the text is not in itself particularly original. In describing three ages of the church (a theme, incidentally, that he expands in the two prologues, which offer a sophisticated rhetorical theory of interpretation of the Hebrew Bible as a whole),[4] we can easily recognize three of the four senses of Scripture classically defined by the fifth-century author John Cassian: the allegorical (or Christological), the tropological (or moral), and the anagogical (the sense having to do with the End Times).[5] Honorius omits the literal sense and reads the Song allegorically as pertaining to Christ and the church. This is the level of interpretation that predominates in medieval Christian commentary on the Song, in which the Song is read as a sort of church history. According to the tropological or moral reading, the Song of Songs is a story of the love between Christ and the human soul. Finally, according to the anagogical sense, the text reveals the mysteries of the End Time, taking us, as Cassian put it in an allusion to Paul's letter to the Galatians, to "that Jerusalem who is the mother of us all."[6] This anagogical reading of the Song of Songs is worthy of closer investigation.

For the contemporary reader, the anagogical level of medieval Christian exegesis, with its concern for Last Things, may seem to be the least likely of an unlikely collection of possible meanings. An apocalyptic understanding of the Song of Songs, while never hidden or in any way occult, is an elusive element in the tradition of Christian interpretation. I can think of no single Christian commentary that programmatically sets out to interpret the poems as pertaining to Last Things or the end of the world. This fact may not initially seem surprising until one begins to note the many connections that can be made between this biblical love song and the dire predictions of the Last Judgment. For one thing, the Apocalypse, or the Revelation to John, the last book of the New Testament, culminates in the marriage of the Heavenly Jerusalem, decked as a bride, to her husband, the Lamb of God (Apocalypse 21:2–9). This passage is easily linked to the most common medieval Christian interpretation of the Song of Songs, the allegorical or ecclesiological level.

Furthermore, in Christian medieval exegetical thinking, there is a deep connection between Christ's union with the church and expectations of the End Time. Up to the twelfth century, an impressive number of Christian exegetes were drawn to and commented on both the Song of Songs and the Apocalypse. Even though not all of the commentaries are still extant, it is possible to put together an impressive list of medieval Christian exegetes from the fourth to the twelfth centuries who were drawn to these two books: Victorinus of Pettau, Apponius, Gregory of Elvira, Apringius of Beja, Justus of Urguel, the Venerable Bede, Beatus of Liebana, Alcuin, Haimo of Auxerre, Anselm of Laon, Bruno of Segni, and Rupert of Deutz.[7]

In spite of this connection between the Song of Songs and the Apocalypse, after the fourth-century rejection of chiliasm—the belief in Christ's return to earth to reign for the millennium—Christian commentary on the Apocalypse became decidedly unapocalyptic.[8] The shift, which began with Jerome's fourth-century editing of the first Latin Apocalypse commentary by Victorinus of Pettau, continued until the original and startlingly apocalyptic exegesis of the twelfth-century visionary Joachim of Fiore.[9] In this period, interpretation maintained an ecclesiological framework in which John's vision on Patmos was understood to reveal, under the veil of allegory, the church's history of trial and triumph. The exegetical *Tendenz* in medieval Christianity, in other words, linked the Song of

Songs and the Apocalypse to the church's ultimate marriage to Christ at the Last Judgment.

It is not surprising, therefore, that Honorius should make this exegetical and symbolic connection. How he did it, though, that is, his particular reading of the Song of Songs, is quite original and inventive. Honorius's reading also raises deeper questions about themes of Christian self-understanding and biblical revelation. In the two prologues that open his commentary, Honorius places the Song of Songs within the framework of universal history. The first of the prologues identifies four movements in the text; the second relates each of these to the periods of the history of the world. The entire enterprise is understood in a cosmological framework, since the four parts of the text are related to the four corners of the world, the four winds, the four humors, and the four types of human characters. Figure 1, a modern version of a chart found in many medieval manuscripts, shows how this cosmology was schematically represented.

This is, of course, a venerable way of looking at the relationship between inner microcosms and the huge, swirling macrocosm of the universe. This categorical view could also encompass other groups of four,

Medieval Cosmology

COLD	North Water Winter Phlegm Phlegmatic	MOISTURE
West Earth Autumn Black Bile Melancholic	Direction Element Season Humor Temperament	East Air Spring Blood Sanguine
DRYNESS	South Fire Summer Yellow bile Choleric	HEAT

Figure 1

such as the four evangelists (as often seen in medieval manuscript evangelists pages) and the four levels of interpretation of Scripture. Honorius applies this system to the identification of the four parts of the Song of Songs in a very original way. He sees in the Song of Songs four brides of Solomon: the daughter of the pharaoh, the daughter of the king of Babylon, the Shulamite, and the Mandrake. No other medieval Christian commentary divides the text this way or sees these four "brides" as protagonists. Yet Honorius does so on the basis his reading of the text itself. As he sees it, the first bride is the *amica*—my love—who comes in the chariots of the pharaoh (1:8); the second arrives as the south wind (4:16); the third is the "Sunamita" in the four-wheeled chariot of Aminadab (6:11–12); the fourth appears with the mere mention of the Mandrake. (7:11). These references, then, become the four brides. The four brides are interpolated into the fourfold cosmological scheme to show the connections between twelfth-century cosmological thought and Honorius's idiosyncratic reading of the Song of Songs. Figure 2 illustrates this system, which is at once cosmological, historical, and prophetic.

Three of Honorius's four brides are portrayed in a remarkable series of full-page illustrations found in a number of South German manuscripts.[10] Figures 3, 4, and 5 are taken from MS W29, a twelfth-century manuscript now in the Walters Art Museum, Baltimore. In this series of illustrations, the portrait of the first bride (the daughter of the pharaoh) is commonly portrayed as a representation of a bridegroom and a bride (Christ and Ecclesia) seated and embracing, a scene found in many medieval manuscripts of Latin Song of Songs texts and commentaries.[11] By contrast, the three other brides are depicted as true illustrations of Honorius's commentary. The images here are not exact as literal text-to-image representations of Honorius's allegories of the last three brides, but they clearly come out of Honorius's particular and peculiar vision of the Song of Songs.

For example, figure 3 shows the beginning of Honorius's book 2, in which the Filia Regis Babylonis, the King of Babylon's Daughter, arrives riding on a camel (or camels) and accompanied by three orders of prophets: philosophers (who lead the way), apostles, and martyrs (who follow her). At the top of the picture is a sun with the inscription "Meridies," "Midday, that is, the South," and the title "Regina Austri," the "Queen of the South."[12] Bride three, the Shulamite, comes from the West in a four-wheeled chariot, described by Honorius as the "quadrigas Aminadab," "the four-wheeled chariot of Aminadab." This seems to be a conflation between the Vulgate Latin Bible reading of Song of Songs 6:11

Honorius's Cosmological-Prophetic Division of the Song of Songs

	Filia Pharaonis Pharoah's Daughter	*Filia Regis Babylonis* King of Babylon's Daughter	*Sunamite* Sulamite	*Mandragora* Mandrake
The Bride	*Filia Pharaonis* Pharoah's Daughter	*Filia Regis Babylonis* King of Babylon's Daughter	*Sunamite* Sulamite	*Mandragora* Mandrake
How she comes	In a chariot	On a camel	*In quadrigas Aminadab* In the four-wheeled cart of Aminadab	By hand
From what direction	East	South	West	North
According to which dispensation	*Ante legem* before the Law	*Sub lege* under the Law	*Sub gratia* under Grace	*Sub Antichristum* under Antichrist
Accompanied by	Patriarchs	Prophets	Apostles	Antichrist
Age of man / world	*Puerilis* Infancy	*Juvenilis* Youth	*Senilis* Old Age	*Decrepitas* Decrepitude
Level of Allegorical Interpretation	*Historia* History or Letter	*Allegoria* (Christ and Church)	*Tropologia* (Christ and Soul)	*Anagogia* The End Times

Figure 2

235

Figure 3. *Filia Regis Babylonis*, the daughter of the king of Babylon, arrives from the South, riding on a camel (or camels) and accompanied by three orders of prophets. Baltimore, the Walters Art Museum MS W 29, f. 43v.

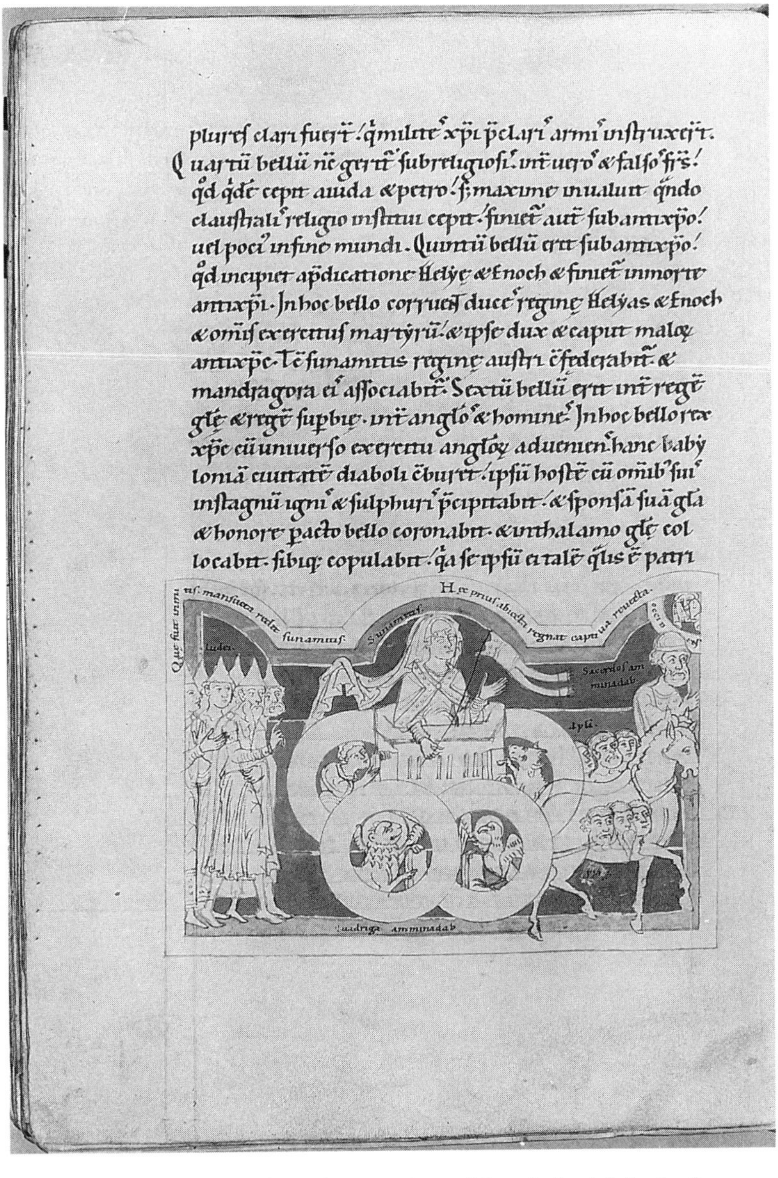

plurcs clari fucrit / qmilite xpi pclari armi instruxerit.
Quartu bellu ne gerat subreligiosi. unt uero a falso fri/
qd qde cepit auida & petro / si maxime inualuit qndo
claustrali religio institut cepit. finiet aut sub antixpo/
uel poca infine mundi. Quintu bellu erit sub antixpo/
qd incipiet apdicatione Helye & Enoch & finiet in morte
antixpi. Jnhoc bello corruet duce regine Helyas & Enoch
& omis exercitus martyru. & ipse dux & caput male
antixpe. Te sunamitis regine austri cofederabit. &
mandragora ei associabit. Sextu bellu erit int rege
gle & rege supbie. unt anglos & homines. Jnhoc bello rex
xpe cu uniuerso exercitu anglos aduenient hanc baby
lonia ciuitate diaboli cburet. ipsu hoste cu omib sui
instagnu igni & sulphuri pcipitabit. & sponsa sua gla
& honore pacto bello coronabit. & ur thalamo gle col
locabit. sibiq copulabit. qa se ipsu et tale qlis e patri

Figure 4. *Sunamita* comes from the West *in quadrigas Aminadab*, in the four-
wheeled chariot of Amanidab. Baltimore, the Walters Art Museum MS W 29, f. 89v.

237

Figure 5. *Mandragora*, the Mandrake, is pulled from the earth by Christ, who places his head on her body. Baltimore, the Walters Art Museum MS W 29, f. 103v.

("nescivi anima mea conturbavit me propter quadrigas Aminadab") and a figure named Abinadab who in 2 Samuel (Vulgate 2 Kings) 6:2–3 took the Ark of the Covenant out of his house in a new cart. In Honorius's interpretation of the four-wheeled cart, each wheel represents one of the evangelists, the authors of the four Gospels. A flattened representation of the symbol of each evangelist is found at the center of each wheel of the cart. The man who represents Matthew is seen at the top left, the lion of Mark at the bottom left, Luke's ox at the top right, and John's eagle at the right bottom.[13] The Shulamite rides triumphant in the cart of the Gospels, led by Aminadab, apostles, and prophets, and followed by the Jews.[14]

But it is the bride of the Last Times, the one who issues in Honorius's book 4 that I wish to examine more closely. In this last book, Honorius follows the same method as in the previous three by dividing the text into pericopes and then offering commentary at each of the four levels of interpretation. But now, throughout these four overlapping readings, Honorius is especially concerned about the Last Days, since the Mandrake—the ultimate bride of Christ—will be the manifestation of the church that ushers in the Second Coming.

Figure 5 shows this eschatological identification precisely. In a time sequence characteristic of medieval art in which two narrative moments happen in the same frame, the Mandrake is pulled from the earth by Christ, who places his own head on the Mandrake's headless body. Next to the open-mouthed dragon from which the Mandrake had been extracted, the severed head of the Antichrist rolls out of the picture's bottom frame. Christ the bridegroom stands accompanied by young men ("Adulescentule," on the far left), queens ("Regine," who help extract the Mandrake), and friends ("Amici," on the right). The text describes this as a moment of "decrepitude," the passing away of the time of earthly creation, and plunges deeply into Christian ideas of supercession over the Jews, as it explains:

> The Mandrake is a plant in the shape of a human body without a head, and it is understood to signify the multitude of the infidels. When he existed [on earth], Antichrist, the head of all evil, was Mandrake's head. But when the head of Mandrake was cut off, Antichrist was killed. After this killing, the bridegroom sees that the synagogue is the conversion of the infidel [now] without the head of Antichrist. But [the synagogue] is still lacking the head of Christ, hoping to associate herself in faith with Christ, and to take

on the head of Christ. The bridegroom says: "Come, my beloved, let us go out into the fields, let us linger in the villages." (7:11)

It is at this point that Christ gives the decapitated Mandrake his own head.

Who, then, is the Mandrake? The text explains that when the night of Antichrist is over, the bride and bridegroom go out into the fields to see if the vines have flowered (7:12). The vines, we are told, are Synagoga, who will burst into flower only with Christian faith; she will thus drink from the breast of her mother (the mother church) when she takes in the doctrine of both the old and the new covenants (PL 172:472C–D). According to the allegorical sense, Honorius explains, the breasts of the mother are two revelations of the divinity of Jesus: They refer first to his encounter with the elders in the Temple at the age of twelve (Luke 2:41–49) and then, at the beginning of his public ministry, to Jesus' preaching in the synagogue of Nazareth (Matthew 13:54–58, Mark 6:1–6, Luke 4:13–30). On both of these occasions, she (the mother, the church) shows the relationship between the old and new law through which Jesus will lead Synagoga into the true Judea, "the home of my mother" (8:2), and the true Jerusalem, "and into her room" (8:2, var.).

With this allegorical turn, Honorius shows that the calling of Synagoga, the church of the Jews, is the last stage of the preparation for the Eschaton. Honorius's understanding of the repeated verse, "I adjure you, daughters of Jerusalem, neither arouse nor cause to awaken the beloved until she wishes" (8:4, with variants at 2:7 and 3:5) signifies three ages of the church: the Ecclesia Primitiva, or Primitive Church, the Ecclesia Gentium, or Church of the Peoples ("the Gentiles" in a universal sense), and the Synagoga Conversa, the Converted Synagogue that will be the Church of the End Times. The Jews are implicated in the stories of the first and third churches, because although Honorius says that Christ first came for Synagoga, she refused him. As a result, the Gospel message went to the Gentiles. But, says Honorius, in the end, Synagoga will also become one of the brides of Christ when, in the form of the Mandrake, she loses the imposed head of the Antichrist and instead receives the head of Christ upon her body (PL 172:474D–475C).

"Under the apple tree I aroused you," says Song of Songs 8:5, and this, says Honorius, is where Synagoga will also be aroused—aroused to the true faith when she becomes the last stage of the church on earth. The apple tree of this passage is conflated with the most highly symbolic "tree" in Christian thought, the tree of the cross of Jesus. Synagoga slept under the apple tree, even though there Christ rose from the death on the tree. And this is the reason why, Honorius says, it was there that Synagoga was corrupted (8:5) when she cried out "Let his blood be upon us and our children" (Matthew 27:25). She was also violated when the law shifted from literal to spiritual (PL 172:481B). And also there is a third possibility—"the mother, that is the Jewish people, was violated when, because of the liberation [or vindication] of the cross, she was enslaved by Titus and Vespasian"[15]

This extended allegory emphasizes the traditional Christian supercessionary teaching that the Jewish people (the "mother" of Synagoga) falls short by ignoring the message of Jesus (when they slept under the tree of the cross) by seeing the law "corrupted" by the Christian insistence on the spiritual over the literal. As a result, they were historically cast out of their own "motherland" by the Romans. Later, Honorius offers the same point of view with regard to the Jews in his commentary on 8:10, "I am a wall and my breasts like towers / since I am made in his presence as if finding peace." "Judah [the Jews], will have no peace with Christ and man," says Honorius, "since he cried, 'Let his blood be upon us and our children' (Matthew 27:25). As a consequence, [Judah] serves all people under tribute [*sub tributo*], being dispersed over all the world, and all people demand recompense for the blood of Christ spilled at his hand. But after his conversion to Christ, he will have peace with all people" (PL 172:488C–D). Just as Judah (who stands for the Jews, and whom Honorius conflates with Synagoga) eventually finds acceptance in the communion of the church, he will find full peace when he rejoices with the angels before Christ, the Prince of Peace.

By this point, Honorius has moved from a traditional (if complicated) allegory to a prophetic stance. What will be the signs indicating that the end of the world is at hand? What will it take to bring Christ's Second Coming to pass? For Honorius Augustodunensis, this culminating event in history demands major changes in the world. On the tropological, level this entails the conversion of Christians to the virtues of the monastic life (cf. PL 172:476A–477A). On both the allegorical and anagogical levels, however, it requires the conversion of history—the final coming of Synagoga to Christianity. Thus, the personification of the Jewish people, long outside the Christian covenant, comes into the new law, and Synagoga becomes Ecclesia.

Why does Honorius worry so much about the conversion of the Jews? Why is this so crucial to his understanding of the Song of Songs as an apocalyptic text? Jeremy Cohen has recently studied Honorius's Song of Songs exegesis for clues about Christian attitudes toward Jewish communities in the twelfth century.[16] Concentrating on Honorius's book 3, the story of Solomon's wedding to the Shulamite who comes in the four-wheeled chariot of Aminadab, Cohen suggests that Honorius shows understanding, even sympathy, for these Jewish communities whom contemporary Christian scholars and exegetes may well have known. I am intrigued by this suggestion and find it in accord with what we know of other twelfth-century Christians. Cohen's reading of Bernard of Clairvaux shows that a Christian could base an argument against the persecution of Jews on the fact that Jews are necessary for God's plan for the world, even if the same Christian author repeats the ancient slander that Jews do behave badly and harm Christians through their usury.[17] Bernard McGinn has also characterized Honorius as the author of one of the more positive medieval Christian portraits of the Jews, pointing to the "optimistic implications" of Honorius's "unusual" eschatology.[18]

"Unusual" may be a good word to describe Honorius and his commentary on the Song of Songs, but of course, Christian eschatology had long linked the legend of the Antichrist and the Jews. For instance Hippolytus's *On the Antichrist* (ca. 200) describes the Jewish origins of the Antichrist,[19] and the Latin Tiburtine Sibyl, which McGinn has called "the earliest and most cogent proof of the revival of apocalypticism in the Christian Roman Empire of the fourth century,"[20] says specifically that just before the Antichrist arises from the tribe of Dan, "the Jews will be converted to the Lord, and his sepulcher will be glorified by all. In those days Judah will be saved and Israel will dwell with confidence."[21]

It is fair to say that both Bernard of Clairvaux, and, in a prime example, Honorius's commentary on the Song of Songs show a new emphasis on the conversion of the Jews as one of the signs of the Last Days. Other texts echo this idea; it is found, for example, in Otto of Freising's *The Deeds of Frederick Barbarosa*, in both Joachim of Fiore's Apocalypse commentary and his *Book of Figures*, and (perhaps most significantly) in the thirteenth-century Franciscan literature inspired by Joachim.[22] From this late-medieval period, the idea of the conversion of the Jews as a sign of the age of the Antichrist passed into Protestant Christianity, both in the Lutheran world that was directly influenced by the friars and in English millenarianism.[23] We can see it today in American fundamentalist dedication to Israel and the hope of some Christians for the building of the

Third Temple in Jerusalem.[24] It is strikingly (some would say shockingly) pronounced in the wildly popular *Left Behind* novels, Tim LaHaye and Jerry Jenkins's stories of the End Times.[25] Here, major characters include the converted Jews Chaim Rosenzweig and Tsion Ben-Judah. Given this *Nachleben*, perhaps Honorius's apocalyptic treatment of the Jews needs to be reevaluated and is not so positive or optimistic, but Honorius Augustodunensis is, nevertheless, an interesting turning point in Christian understanding of the Song of Songs. In his hands, the most beautiful love song of the Hebrew Bible becomes the love song of the millennium, a dramatic change with serious implications for the Christian view of the Jewish people, the people who gave us the song in the first place.

THE BODY OF THE TEXT AND THE TEXT OF THE BODY: MONASTIC READING AND ALLEGORICAL SUB/VERSIONS OF DESIRE

Mark S. Burrows

In his classic and still controversial study, *Love's Body*, Norman O. Brown suggested that:

> The reality is flesh. But flesh is a figure, the reality of which is yet to be unveiled. The reality of body is not given, but to be made real, to be realized; the body is to be built; to be built not with hands but by the spirit. It is the poetic body; the made body; Man makes himself, his own body, in the symbolic freedom of the imagination. The eternal body of Man is the Imagination, that is, God himself, the Divine Body, Jesus: we are his Members.[1]

Flesh as a figure, the realized body, the poetic body, the made body: These describe in a curiously apt manner the imagined world of much of the medieval Christian reading of the Song of Songs, particularly as it found expression within monastic circles. But what sort of imagination is this? Is it a spiritualizing—or "pious bias," to recall Ariel Bloch's vivid description—that obliterates the plain sense of this erotic text? That levels its erotic heights and turns from its sensuous depths? That translates—or, one might conclude, *mis*translates—eros by taming it of its wildness, subverting the physicality of desire in order to render it palatable to spiritual sensibilities? Such questions must arise to modern readers—and indeed, they have.

But is it necessarily the case that the spiritual reading of the Song, with its sublimation of the raw energy of sex into the conventions of monastic experience, is a final loss of erotic integrity? Or is it, as sublimation, an eroticizing of the spiritual, an erotic translation of the spirit into a key that only the body's passions can suggest? Bernard of Clairvaux does not follow the rabbinic tradition by speaking of the woman's breasts as Moses and Aaron. But he does, in a sumptuous passage of erotic insinuation, describe the outpouring of the spirit by interpreting the text "Your name is oil poured out" (1.2)—and he assumes that this is an outpouring of perfume upon the woman's breasts, one of which is the inward strengthening of virtues and the other the outward gift of service.[2] Surely this is not an image that would easily arouse even the more ardent among us. What Bernard does indeed accomplish with such an interpretive approach is the spiritualizing of the body and the eroticizing of the spiritual by which the monk discovers that his sexual fantasies are not an improper occasion for a flowering of the interior life. As he puts it in an outburst found in one of his last sermons: "O love! Precipitous, violent, burning, impetuous! I can think of nothing except for you; you reject everything else, you spurn all other things, and find contentment only with yourself. You confound order, put utility aside, ignore moderation."[3]

But what precisely is Bernard thinking about other than passionate love? What can he have in his mind other than the elevation of spirituality through the energies of erotic fantasy?

These are the questions I would like to explore with primary attention to the sermons of Bernard of Clairvaux, produced in fits and starts during the last two decades of his life (ca. 1135–1153). In this elaborate rhetorical commentary, Bernard develops a form of allegorical reading that serves him as a tool for the construction of monastic life, an approach to both text *and* body as a unified field of vision, a single arena of interpretation. Within these sermons, Bernard reads the biblical text as an occasion for the construction of monastic life. His habits as a reader actually served to establish the monastery as what Brian Stock calls a "textual community" where his confreres might learn to read for conversion—by which he meant the translation of the *littera* as found both in the body of the text and in the "text" of the body. He accomplishes this through a *somatic* reading, one that postulates how the text calls the reader to "make" the body by modulating the *littera* of unconstructed desires. Read in such a way, we begin to see Bernard's allegorical reading as a sublimation, yes, of the Song's plain sense, but not as a flight from the literal sense. On the contrary, this approach validates the erotic nature of the biblical text by transposing the melody of somatic experience into a new and—according to Bernard at least—"higher" (i.e., angelic) key.

Learning to read properly, to engage Scripture not on its "face," but in its depths, was for Bernard what monastic life was all about. It was a way of accommodating the bodily "dislocations" of monastic life: celibacy, in the first instance, and, second, the entrance into the monastery, which exiled the monk by "unhousing" him from his familiar world. The body thus represents a "primary text" for Bernard's fellow monks, and the biblical text—in this case, the erotic narrative of the Song of Songs— became in his hands a "body" to be read properly, to be "built" with meaning. Body as text and text as body: Monastic life depended upon learning to "realize" meaning within the framework of what might now be understood as a synoptic vision required of monastic readers. Allegory as an *interpreted* literal sense became a tool by which Bernard and his readers made the body or made meaning in and through the body, which remained the proper con-text for monastic conversion. Not only did Bernard insist that it was "possible for religious texts to have an erotic and lyrical sense without ceasing to be religious," as Burcht Pranger has recently suggested.[4] He also held that erotic texts could be spiritual without ceasing to be erotic. Quoting the book of Sirach repeatedly in his sermons on the Song, Bernard called his readers in the voice of God to "Come to me, all who desire me" ("transite ad me, omnes qui concupiscitis me.")[5] "Desire is endless,"[6] he insists, a claim he meant his fellow monks to discover not as an intellectual truth, but in tasting the strength of their bodily passions.

This understanding of desire is a crucial point in appreciating the somatic nature of Bernard's exegesis and the erotic locus in which he articulated this monastic exegesis. The *littera* of the textual body remained, even in its constructed form, just as the monk's own body remained the arena of monastic conversion. Here, the "made" sense, to borrow Norman O. Brown's felicitous insight, converts the literal sense such that the "accidents" remain even while the "substance" is changed. *Hoc est corpus meum*: allegory is the mode of this transubstantiation, and this occurs through the consecration of reading.

The grammar of desire that shapes Bernard's allegorical reading thus exemplifies what might be called a poetic dynamism, a lyric art of speaking shaped by a tensile mingling of conventions and inventions and an extravagance of metaphor. His intended readers, bound to the monastery as a single dwelling place in order to fulfill the monastic vow of stability (*stabilitas loci*), came to the text with a similar commitment: they made a lifelong choice to stay in one place, and, in entering a celibate life, to discover the experience of this body by dwelling in one text in a particular way until death. Monastery and Scripture alike become the habitable con-texts for this bodily exegesis, establishing an interpretive labyrinth in which the monk's conversion was more like a "wandering" within a bounded space than a mapped journey toward some distant, but observable goal.[7] "The fixed outlook of the surroundings, architectural as well as literary," Burcht Pranger reminds us, "allows an infinite number of configurations. . . . Rather than grasping the unfolding of a linear story, the [monastic] reader ought to be concerned with catching the sparks resulting from the confrontation between fast moving images and massive *loci* seemingly fixed forever."[8] The clear boundaries of the monastery, in other words, led the monk into an apparently unbounded wandering of the mind, into the dreamworld of Cistercian literary art, which Henri de Lubac has suggestively called a "broderie mystique."[9] In Bernard's rhetorical embellishing of this embroidery through his poetic sensibilities, his voice decorated the bare walls (*murus nudus*) and shaped the deep silences of Cistercian monastic houses. The extreme austerity of the monastery, in Etienne Gilson's view, established the locus for understanding Bernard's ornate imagination, an effusive style that flowers above all in the sermons.[10] Here, eros becomes a playful guide for the imagined life in the presumed absence of direct physical experience.

Monastery and biblical text function as an erotic labyrinth for Bernard and his readers. Those drawn to enter this world knew that the pleasure of this experience lay primarily in the wandering, in the certainty of losing one's way, even while knowing that there *was* a way out. Bernard applies other metaphors to make the same point. In one place, he speaks about the monk's encounter with the "face" of Scripture, which "inspires and entices [him] to read, so that he might find delight even in the hard work of investigating what is hidden and not grow weary in searching out difficult matters."[11] And as he elsewhere suggested, "I do not know why it is that what is more hidden is more pleasing, and we long more avidly for what is denied us" ("Nescio enimquo pacto quae plus latent, plus placent, et avidius inhiamus negatis").[12] Delight arises from the apparently infinite variety and complexity of exploratory paths, and the reader's enjoyment depends upon the difficulty encountered and the exertion this calls forth. The text as labyrinth, and even as wilderness, offers a mirror for the monk to find his "self"; the journey *is* the destiny, and exegesis becomes an invitation to "perform" the monastic life as if it were an erotic and apparently unbounded text of self-discovery. Thus, we hear him asking, "What boundary can be set for anyone who does seek?" This endless search, sharpened by the felt absences of the beloved (God) and the anguish this induced, was not only a quest for refuge in the monastic wilderness. It was, as well, a yearning for a deep human discovering, if in a spiritual key, of the melodies rising through the body's desires.

Examples of this carefully ordered "wandering" abound in Bernard's sermons on the Song of Songs. For the purposes of this study, I will explore one of these that is particularly revealing of Bernard's erotic reading habits. In sermons 15 and 16 on the Song of Songs, we encounter his labyrinthine style at its best, here in the form of an elaborate and rhetorically complex digression on the meaning of the number seven. To explore this question, Bernard draws upon an Old Testament text that at first glance might seem to us—as it apparently first did to him, and probably also to his hearers—as completely irrelevant to his running exposition of the Song. The text tells the strange story of Elisha's "healing" of the unnamed Shunammite woman's dead son (see 2 Kings 4): Elisha "got down, walked once to and from in the room, then got up again and bent over [the deceased son of the Shunammite woman]; the child [yawned] seven times, and then opened his eyes."[13]

Bernard uses this story to explain in an intricate rhetorical detour how the name of Jesus is a medicine for the monk's "spiritual maladies." This Old Testament text, which Bernard had already used in an earlier sermon on the Song (SCC 2), acquires a momentum demanding interpretation when placed within the monastic life, with its yearning for spiritual growth. That is, the complex layering of stories from the Old and New Testaments relates a common monastic experience (type) to its assumed precedent in the prophetic witness (antitype). The various details of this story from the Elisha cycle, which seemed to have no particular significance for the narrative—for example, the staff that could not effect a cure without the prophet's presence and the "seven yawns" by which the dead boy revived—offered a warrant, in Bernard's mind, to assume that they were included for some later use. In this case, he interprets these details typologically in order to ground monastic conversion through an intertextual cross-reference that was surprising precisely because it seemed uncontextual, even to him. He grounds this strategy in his bold claim (see SCC 79.i.1) that "love speaks everywhere" ("amor ubique loquitur"), and, on the basis of this conviction, reminds his audience that they were to find themselves everywhere in this love story, if they learned to read properly.

Thus far, then, we have a mimetic example of "layered" narrative, constructed on the foundation of Bernard's confidence that Old Testament narratives provided types of later events—both those of the New

Testament and those emerging in the continuing life of the church.[14] In this particular case, we find ourselves within an allegorical rereading of one narrative in terms of another. But before continuing on his interpretive wandering, Bernard pauses to offer his companions in the monastic journey an apology of their vocation as allegorical readers:

No one should either lament or be vexed if I show myself attentive in scrutinizing these matters [i.e., the significance of the number seven], for in them is to be found the storeroom of the Holy Spirit. I know that we live by these things, and I find in them the life of my spirit. And I must warn those whose genius flies ahead of me and in every sermon make demands of me prematurely rather than attentively comprehending the beginnings, that I am first of all indebted to the slow learners. But my purpose is not so much to explain words as to inspire hearts. I must both drink in and offer forth [this work], something I shall not accomplish rapidly but only by examining the matter diligently and offering frequent exhortation—though my hope in our consideration of these mysteries [*sacramentorum*] was that we would not have been detained at such lengths. I actually thought, I must confess, that one sermon would have sufficed, and that we might have passed quickly through that shadowy forest filled with hidden allegories and arrived after a day's journey perhaps on the open plains of the moral sense. We did not succeed. We have already been two days traveling and the end has yet to be reached. Looking into the distance we can see treetops and mountain peaks, but our eyes cannot penetrate the great valleys beneath us nor pierce the dense thickets. How, for instance, could it have been possible for me to have foreseen that, with the reference to Elisha's miracle, I should suddenly have thought of the call of the gentiles and the rejection of the Jews? And now that we have come upon it we must pause in considering this, and later return to what we have set aside, for what is this too but nourishment for our souls? Hounds and hunters often abandon the beast they have pursued and chase another that they have unexpectedly encountered.[15]

This remarkable digression amplifies not so much the particular rules as the underlying principles that shaped Bernard's subversive allegorical approach. In order to grasp how Bernard viewed allegory not as a separate *sense*, but as a particular way of *reading*—in this case, a conversion of the text's *littera* based upon monastic "bodybuilding"—a more careful consideration of these principles is warranted.

In a formal sense, Bernard's allegorical reading illustrates his conviction that the Holy Spirit "stores up treasures" in textual details, and by this he means those "hidden" under the *scripturae facies* (the "face" of Scripture, an unusual description of the literal sense).[16] As he insisted in one of the later sermons on the Song, "I admit that I have long been convinced that in the sacred and precious writings [Scripture] there is no slightest detail which is without significance."[17] This is a classic defense of allegorical reading, articulated already in late antiquity by Origen and his heirs. But in Bernard's hands it acquires a particular purpose: in scrutinizing textual details, he guides his readers into the strange labyrinth not only of the text but of monastic conversion. This journey into the interior darkness, beneath the surface of the letter, is a movement toward a goal at best dimly perceived. Here, we are in a culture of slow readers—or "mumblers,"[18] in Ivan Illich's vivid description—for whom the meaning of the *littera* was a sweet taste to be deliberately extracted by chewing it with the "teeth of the mind."[19] In a later sermon he returns to this theme, citing Paul's distinction of spirit and letter (2 Cor. 3.5) to clarify the apostle's claim that "the Spirit utters mysteries." As he here claims, the Holy Spirit gives life that is "understanding" (*intellectus*), and understanding

> does not remain outside, nor does it cling to the surface, nor run its finger over the exterior like a blind man, but it explores the depths and often raises precious stores of truth, bringing them away with great eagerness; and says to God with the prophet, "I will rejoice at your words like a man who finds great treasure." So indeed the kingdom of truth suffers violence, and the violent take it by storm.[20]

The biblical allusion from the Gospel text (Matt. 11.12) is not unimportant here, for it confirms Bernard's practice of biblical reading: not as a leisurely occupation for scholars, even though monastic culture depended upon the slow and meditative reading of the biblical text (*lectio divina*), but as a difficult and even "violent" struggle, one demanding that the reader search vigorously and patiently for what is hidden under the "face" or within the *littera* (i.e., the *intellectus*, or "understanding"). Monastic conversion happens in a strenuous act of reading, more like a "hunt" for necessary food than a sport for diversion.

Bernard notes how startled he also had been in discovering this cross-reference: Far from offering a sanctuary for monastic repose, this text provoked in Bernard the dramatic sense of the hunt—in this case, one leading into the untamed and foreboding woods where adventure and discovery, but also violence and danger, awaited. The discipline of lingering and pondering, on the one hand, and the tumult of searching and hunting, on the other, are the dialectic metaphors by which Bernard describes the texture of monastic reading. The biblical text becomes for a monastic reader under Bernard's tutelage "part of a spiral and circular process of writing and reading rather than telling a linear story."[21]

Bernard also insists that the very nature of this discovered truth, these "treasures" hidden in the depths, requires that he communicate this learning in an appropriate manner: not by a quick movement of insight, but through a deliberate process that slowly penetrates the text's veiled depths. That is why he often uses the traditional monastic image of *ruminatio* to explain the necessity for monks to "chew" the text slowly, not only for purposes of proper digestion, but in order to "taste" it fully: "Let us now chew, therefore, like 'clean animals,' what we have so greedily swallowed today from the Good Shepherd."[22]

Therefore, proper reading recovers the true meaning of the *littera* as an "interpreted" sense. Here we must consider a crucial detail from this description of the "hunt" for meaning: the reader moves *through* "the shadowy forest where allegories lurk unseen" *toward* the "open plain" of the moral sense. The end of reading, as the purpose of monastic conversion, is not the final arrival at a clarifying experience of ecstatic vision; such experience points the way toward the realization of the moral life, and, as I have suggested, this involves the strenuous task of constructing the monastic "body."

In one of the final sermons on the Song written at the end of his life, Bernard introduces the experience of mystical vision in aesthetic categories, asking "In what therefore does beauty of soul consist?" Answering his own question, he refutes the notion that this most intimate expression of monastic conversion—which "only the touch teaches, and only experience unfolds"[23]—leads the monk on a spiritual pilgrimage away from his body. In this case, one might well speak here of an erotics of reading, a feature that led Henri de Lubac to speak of "the wildness of the Cistercian literary paradise."[24] Allegory as a method, for Bernard, is a sublimation that sanctions the erotic. In a fascinating aside, Bernard comments that such an experience eventually "makes the body a mirror of the soul" ("mentis simulacrum corpus excipit"); as he goes on to say, this "touch" "spreads through the limbs and senses [*et diffundit per membra et sensus*] so that every action, every word, look, movement and even laugh (if there should be laughter) radiates gravity and is full of honor."[25] In other words, conversion constructs the monk's experience of his body, which Bernard understands as the soul's outward and sensual expression. The body is "a spirit clothed in flesh and living on the earth" (involutus came ac terrae incola spiritus) and as such, human beings must "strive to achieve gradually and little by little, through sensory knowledge" what the angels attained without bodily mediation.[26] The "soul's beauty" (animae decor) both depends upon the body and in turn yearns for bodily expression. In seeking conversion of life, the monk's allegorical reading struggles to construct an experience that emulates that of angelic bodies, and this occurs as this reader longs to discover an interior beauty concealed within the text's literal sense.

Finally, it is crucial to understand that Bernard's method, both of reading and of representing his discoveries, exemplifies his intention "not so much to explain words as to move hearts" (non verba pensanda sunt, sed affectus).[27] This is a theme that we find again and again in his sermons. At a later juncture, interpreting the refrain "He [the bridegroom] is mine, and I am his" (Song of Sol. 2.16), he insists that discovery of the meaning hidden in this text, the "secret" locked within its labyrinth, depends upon an "affective" understanding: "It is the affectus, not the intellectus, which has spoken [in this text], and it is spoken not for the intellect to grasp."[28] These affectus Bernard goes on to suggest, "have their own voice in which they disclose themselves even if they do not wish to do so."[29] This becomes Bernard's way of clarifying the mystical goal of Scripture. But it is not simply a placing of limits on the function of language. It is his affirmation of the affectus as the most sublime form of knowing—one that begins with the literal sense and returns to it in an apprehension that transcends the power of ordinary language. The allegorical reader as a hunter of the heart discovers not only within the text, but within himself the true meaning of the littera.

Bernard's somatic exegesis retains an intense engagement with the literal sense, leading him in a manner startling within the tradition of earlier monastic literature to emphasize "carnal love" (amor carnalis) as the inevitable starting place for monastic reading.[30] For those entering the Cistercian houses of Bernard's day, because of the constitutional rules prohibiting the entrance of children, the vow of conversio morum addressed the entering novices' sexual experience—and, indeed, its lingering life as memory. Conversion had to begin with what these adult monks knew when they arrived, and thus they had to begin reading by means of the first love that they knew "in the flesh." The monk's eventual conversion from the "letter" of carnal experience meant excluding what Bernard called a "life of the flesh" (*vita carnalis*) in order to love "better" (*amor rationalis*) until attaining perfection (*amor spiritualis*).[31] But this is to say that the conversion of the *vita carnalis* depends upon the progression of our loving, and this occurred through the exercise of monastic bodybuilding. It is this perfecting of a "secular" mode of living that restructured (or, in Janet Coleman's more severe reading, "cauterised") the memory that mature initiates brought with them into the monastery. Thus, monastic conversion as the central drama of Cistercian life became identified by Bernard with a way of *reading*. For Bernard's monks, therefore, the goal of conversion was not only to move beyond "material desires" but to progress still further beyond any use of "bodily likenesses."[32] But as we have seen, to arrive at this "place" purified of all metaphor, where the monk experienced his body in a manner freed of carnal lust, but not emptied of desire, brought him into proximity with the angelic beings, long understood as the goal and presumed destination of monastic life.[33] This required of the monk an ecstatic experience that Bernard described quite literally as a "going out of oneself" or self-transcendence in order to "escape far away and [find] *a refuge in the wilderness*."[34] Ironically, of course, this became for Bernard the ultimate way of finding oneself, of living peaceably within one's body and thus in harmony with others.

It is this description of mystical experience as an ecstatic refuge in the wilderness that brings us back to where we began: the *stabilitas* of monastery and of biblical text and the erotic manner in which the monastic reader dwells in both through the "poetic body." It is in this particular sense that we must understand Bernard's strong claim that love is the principle speaker in the Song. And just for this reason, he insists that this is not a language that all are able to hear, but remains the privileged guide of those seeking monastic conversion for whom such an eroticized spirituality serves as a countervailing force to "the confused world of non-monastic imagination."[35] The key to living this life, in other words, is *not* found in the externally perceptible order of the monastic regimen. It is hidden within the interior pattern of reading. Thus, allegorical reading is not only its interpretive key, it becomes the very substance of monastic conversion. Bernard did not call monks to such conversion in order to learn how to read; he taught them how to read in order to lead them toward this conversion: "Today let us read the book of experience" (Hodie legimus in libro experientiae).[36] Gregory the Great could earlier suggest that "it is in ourselves that we must transform what we have been reading."[37] Bernard reverses direction and suggests that the very texture of erotic reading becomes the path of conversion.

Bernard's allegorical reading is thus a method deliberately meant to subvert what he felt to be "mere" carnal love—not wrong in itself, but not sufficient to grasp the depths of human experience. It offered a clear defense of monastic life against "the world," but more importantly created an erotic language of spiritual experience as the hallmark of monastic profession. In this sense, it "makes" a reality, the "poetic body" of somatic experience, through constructing the meaning of the body. Bernard assumes, in other words, that he is not simply describing one way of understanding somatic reality; he is discovering its essential, if also hidden meaning. He is reading the true voice of its literal sense. It is not interpretation that he is after, but the construction of experience itself.

What does this deliberately sub/versive strategy of allegorical reading yield for modern readers? Perhaps little more than the offering of what Jon Whitman has called "the solace of fiction," which "tries to express a truth by departing from it in some way." Is this an anticipation of the postmodern turn, in which "the text [becomes] a readerly function and product"? Perhaps.

Whether or not this is so, we might—to return to the questions posed at the outset—consider all of this an intellectually quaint but finally irrelevant means of engaging the Song. But just at this point, Julia Kristeva offers another view, suggesting against the grain of modern worries that

> when boredom sets in at the sight of Bernard climbing the terraces that lead him to the pure love of God, let us not forget that within our own loves, in addition to and beyond desire and pleasure, we are caught within an alchemy of idealization, of whose twists and turns we are secularly ignorant. If we have difficulty loving, it is because we have difficulty idealizing—difficulty investing our narcissism in an other who is considered to have immeasurable value, thus guaranteeing our own potentiality for immoderation. And on the contrary, when we succeed in loving, is it not because someone . . . was able to withstand our unflagging power of distrust, hatred, and fear of delegating ourselves to an ideal otherness? Finally, are our own stages of affection for our loved ones so different from the ascent toward pure love that the twelfth-century Cistercian devoted to his ideal object, his God?[38]

THE FEMALE VOICE: HILDEGARD OF
BINGEN AND THE SONG OF SONGS

Margot Fassler

Hildegard of Bingen was deeply engaged with Scripture, and one of the ways to understand her thought is by tracing her treatment of particular figures from the Bible or especially important passages from favored sections of the text. How did she organize her commentaries—written, visual, and sonic? How did she take the common coin of theological understanding and turn it into a practiced, embodied knowing within communal action? These are the questions addressed here, and they are grappled with by focusing primarily upon this theologian/composer/poet's treatment of the Song of Songs.[1] Hildegard knew the book as a source of readings, and for singing on several feasts, but most particularly for the Feast of the Octave of the Assumption of the Virgin. According to a contemporary source,[2] the readings for this day were taken from the Song 6:9–8:10; the chants came from a variety of verses, some of which were fused to make a kind of *Songsprach*, as is the case with the the the following responsory.

> Vidi speciosam sicut columbam, descendentem desuper rivos aquarum, cuius inaestimabilis odor erat nimis in vestimentis ejus; et sicut dies verni circumdabant eam flores rosarum, et lilia convallium. Quae est ista quae ascendit per desertum sicut virgula fumi, ex aromatibus myrrhae et thuris?

> Respond: I saw her when, fair like a dove, she flew down over the rivers of waters. The priceless savor of her perfumes hung heavy in her garments. And about her it was as the flowers of roses in the spring of the year, and lilies of the valleys. Verse: Who is this that

cometh out of the wilderness like a pillar of smoke, perfumed with myrrh and frankincense?[3]

In Hildegard's region, this familiar text was associated with the Feast of the Assumption of the Virgin Mary, both at matins and as a processional piece.[4]

Rachel Fulton, Ann Matter, Barbara Haagh, and others have been particularly attentive to the ways in which the Song of Songs has been used in the medieval offices of Marian feasts to create a life for the Virgin Mary as the woman beloved of God and as a type of the church.[5] Hildegard comes at the relationship between human beings and God through many venues, but she always rooted her experience of human love in the church and in the cloister, the places she knew best.[6] The Song of Songs was available to her as a canonical framework for exploring relationships and expressing them in the terms of human love.[7] Within this framework Mary becomes a multilayered image of *ecclesia*, and Christ is the lover of this bride, whom he takes unto himself as he lifts Mary out of worldly life and into his eternal, heavenly embrace.[8] Hildegard transforms these common themes and infuses them with new life in her theological and poetic writings as she makes them crucial to her understanding of the central act of the Mass liturgy, moving from the consecration of the elements to the reception of Communion.

The shifts to the Eucharist that Hildegard offers in her interpretation of the Song of Songs should not surprise us. The Assumption of the Virgin Mary was not a favored topic with Hildegard, either in her theological treatises or in her poetry. Rather, her works are centered upon the Incarnation, and especially upon the Incarnation as a moment of change, both in history and in the individual soul. And so she relocates the language of love from the Assumption to the Eucharist, reshaping it in the process and offering a new world of interpretations whose powers work across the disciplines of theology, poetry, music, and drama.[9]

Hildegard uses the biblical language of embrace leading to intercourse and extended to conception adapted from the Song to refer to seen and unseen moments of change in body and soul. Different kinds of intercourse, mingling, or exchange are matched: the disobedient sexual action of the fall from grace in the Garden of Eden, the Annunciation that provoked conception without penetration, the transformation of the elements of the Eucharist in the Mass, and the new bridehood of virgins found in the history of the church and in Hildegard's own cloister. She can work with such complex imagery because her mode of exploration is so carefully constructed. She derives her essential understanding of the Song from the context of the Feast of the Assumption; subsequently, she both builds upon and transforms this understanding into a larger and more dramatic picture of God's encounter with human beings through the sacrament of Eucharist. This is laid out most fully in book 2 of her treatise *Scivias*, the text upon which this paper will focus. At the close, a brief examination of a set of poems Hildegard composed for the Feast of Saint Ursula will provide an example of her use of these themes in a liturgical context.

Scivias, Book 2, Vision 6: A Visual Introduction

Hildegard's first major treatise, *Scivias* (Know the ways of the Lord), was written when she was in her forties; it was some ten years in the making. Among the most controversial aspects of the treatise are the illuminations that survived the Middle Ages in the Rupertsberg manuscript, which was unfortunately lost in World War II.[10] The opening image painted for *Scivias* 2:6 contains two zones, each of which portrays the crowned *sponsa* who represents the church. Her character relates as well to her hand-maidens, the consecrated virgins, who support the figure of Ecclesia in a unique, God-given way. At the top, Christ on the cross is labeled with a key text: "And I heard the voice from Heaven saying to Him: 'May she, O Son, be your Bride for the restoration of My people; may she be a mother to them, regenerating souls through the salvation of the Spirit and water.'"[11] Images of the crucified Christ, with the Virgin Mary on his right and John the Evangelist on his left, are prominent in medieval missals, as they are in sacramentaries; introduce the canon, the long prayer said by the priest at the time of consecration of the elements. This aspect of the Mass liturgy seemed to interest Hildegard most as a theologian.[12] The canon begins "Te igitur, clementissime Pater . . . supplices rogamus," "Most merciful Father . . . we humbly ask you," with the initial "T" replaced by a crucifix.[13]

This program was readily adapted, as Lieselotte Saurma-Jeltsch shows in her discussion of the image in *Scivias*, to incorporate elements of other iconographic ideas, including depictions of the personified church collecting the sacramental water and wine flowing from Christ's side.[14] In the *Scivias* image the church is pictured twice: in the upper zone, the new bride stands to the side of her spouse, collecting in a chalice water and blood from his breast, rather than from his side;[15] in the lower zone, she prays at the altar as streams of light enfold the chalice and host. In this lower zone, she gestures to icons of four miracles of restoration: the birth, passion and burial, resurrection, and ascension of Christ—all of which "shine brightly in the sacrament of the altar."[16] The body and blood of Christ form the dowry of the bride, and she is open and gazing upward, ready to receive the gift; she approaches, even touches, the altar table, which is enfolded in cloth and forms the *thalamus* or bridal bedchamber for incarnate action.[17]

Hildegard's Eucharistic Theology and the Song of Songs

In *Scivias*, book 2, vision 6, the act of consecration on the altar becomes the new joining of the Song of Songs' *sponsus* and *sponsa*, a re-creation of the coupling of Adam and Eve in a wholesome freshness not tainted by sin. The imagistic pouring out of the fluids from Christ's breast into the cup held by Ecclesia is sexual; it suggests a reworking of human intercourse that leads to life and regeneration, rather than to sin and death. The fluid of salvation is a new, life-giving liquid, flowing from the verdant tree in the center into the church that it will regenerate. There are two streams, one of blood and water running into the chalice, the other, water alone, flowing across Ecclesia's brow, no doubt in allusion to baptism, a sacrament Hildegard discusses elsewhere in her treatise. Hildegard says of the action on the altar: "The Church in the voice of the priest seeks her dowry, which is the body and the poured-out blood of My Son, in order to be fit for blessed childbearing in saving souls; for when that precious blood was poured out she was increased by a great multitude of peoples."[18]

This new liquid, a life-begetting force, impregnates the ecclesial body that brings forth the saved who feed upon the blood of the Christ.[19] This action takes place at the altar, which is filled with a calm light that at first seems to be far different from the burning heat of carnal intercourse. But when the actual transformation of the host occurs, the light turns to fire. As elsewhere, Hildegard plays here with the sense of heat and warmth she so frequently associates with intercourse:[20]

And when the Gospel of peace has been recited and the offering to be consecrated has been placed upon the altar, and the priest sings the praise of Almighty God, "Holy, Holy, Holy, Lord God of Hosts," which begins the mystery of the sacred rites, Heaven is suddenly opened and a fiery and inestimable brilliance descends over that offering. For when the fresh and living breath of the royal kiss has been given,[21] and the fruit of noble life, which is to be sanctified and purified, has been put as a stone into God's wall, and the messenger of truth utters the sweet sound of the threefold invocation of the Lord of Hosts in praise of the Creator of all and thus begins the mystery of the shining dawn, the Incarnation of the Son of God in the Virgin; then suddenly the glorious tabernacle opens on the mystery of the sacrament, and an inconceivably calm and lofty brilliance shines down. And it irradiates [the offering] completely with light, as the sun illuminates anything its rays shine through; in the power of the Father the holy heat so strikes the sparkling circle of that oblation that the radiant splendor wholly enters into the thing it falls upon.[22]

This incarnate action is the framework for the coming together of *sponsus* and *sponsa* at the table; it is there that their love will be made manifest to the community, and its product, the host, tasted.[23] The body and the blood of the host are created by the action of both church and Holy Spirit together. Just as Mary's willing body joined with the Holy Spirit's fire to make the *sponsus* "in the fullness of time," so the new Adam "is born" through the procreative action of the sacrament of the Mass. Like the quickening of the womb itself, this Eucharistic action happens in an instant. With the sweet tastes of the Song of Songs in mind, Hildegard describes the elements of bread and wine as formed through divine heat:

That oblation, by the power of God, is invisibly borne on high and brought back again in an instant, and so warmed by the heat of the Divine Majesty that it becomes the body and blood of God's Only-Begotten. People do not perceive this mystery with their bodily sense; it is as if someone encased a precious unguent in simple bread and dropped a sapphire into wine, and I then changed them into a sweet taste, so that in your mouth, O human, you could not taste the unguent in the bread or the sapphire in the wine, but only the sweetness—as my son is sweet and mild.[24]

The elements are the incarnate *sponsus*, ready to feed his bride with the kiss of his mouth and with the sweetness of his wine. Hildegard employs a direct quotation from the Song, which is then extended into the language of a love feast, accounting for the fountainlike breasts of Christ in the image discussed above: "For the Son of God, fulfilling the precepts of His Father, offered Himself for people's salvation and gave His body and blood to be eaten and drunk for their sanctification, as the

Bridegroom declares to his friends in the Song of Songs, saying, 'Eat, my friends; drink, and be inebriated, my dearly beloved.'"[25]

How is this invitation to be comprehended? "Be inebriated with love, you who are so dear to Me, and flow with brooks of Scripture so that you will know best how to break away from carnal desires; and then I will awake in you splendid virtues pleasing to Me and give you the blood of my Only-Begotten."[26]

This Incarnation, so quick and sparkling, has a long afterlife and begets other actions of its type. The consecrated elements make possible the taking of the *sponsus*'s flesh; this then unleashes the procreative power within those impregnated by the host's elements, for they in turn will now be part of the saving vine branch that sways in the history of salvation, as told in the Gospel parable of the vine: "For as wine flows out of the vine, so My Son went forth from My heart; and My Only-Begotten too was the true Vine, and many branches went forth from Him, for in Him the faithful have been planted who through His Incarnation are fruitful in good works. . . . 'A cluster of grapes of Cyprus is my beloved to me in the vineyards of Engedi.'"[27]

The wine is the blood daily consecrated in the action of the altar. The liquid imagery led Hildegard to ponder the *sponsus* as a woman, that is, as a *sponsa* who will offer her liquid to feed those she loves.[28] The creator God genders the *sponsus* female. Hildegard becomes his mouthpiece, reminding us that literal interpretation of the Song or any binary opposition of male and female images is limited: "But I, Who am the Beginning and the End, again say to you, O human, that My noble Son is the flower of roses and lilies of the valley, born of the chaste Virgin who brought Him forth in wholeness . . . and they who now faithfully receive His flesh and blood will be so sweetly enlivened that they will never be despised or rejected."[29]

If Christ is the liquid, the church has the breasts through which it flows. Hildegard discusses this image with Song of Songs 8:1 in mind:

> "Who shall give you to me for my brother, sucking the breasts of my mother, that I may find you out of doors and kiss you, and no one will despise me?" What does this mean? . . . [The church says:] You, whom I name my brother because of Your Incarnation, and Who sucks the mercy and truth that nourish humanity from the Divinity, which is my mother in my creation . . . You Who are the Living Bread and the fountain of living water make her fully abound in the sacrament of Your body and blood.[30]

The church offers the breasts that flow with the beloved's own life-giving wine; through the kiss of the Song, she takes him into herself: "And thus I may kiss You, for You were incarnate for my salvation, and You now make me a sharer in your body and blood."[31] The taking of the sacramental kiss at the time of Communion is radiant with the Divine "heat," as Hildegard has God explain through her words:

> Now therefore, O human, as you see, when the sacrifice has been offered at the altar and the priest begins to invoke Me in those words appointed for him by the Holy Spirit, verily I say to you that I am there in My burning heat, and with full will I perfect that sacrament. How? To effect this mystery I extend over this offering My ardent charity at the moment when the priest invokes Me and remembers that My Son blessed bread and wine in the agony of His Passion as the sacrament of His body and blood, giving them to His disciples that they might do the same for the salvation of the people.[32]

Here we return to the illumination that governs this section of the treatise, the church standing by the bridegroom on the cross and receiving the dowry of his life: "And the Church stood by My Only-Begotten in that place and received her wedding gifts; and these must now be celebrated by the children of the Church."[33] The new flesh and blood of the altar is a miracle, like the begetting of children, and leads to the blood imagery associated with the holy joining of the virgin Ursula to her *sponsus*, the Lamb of the apocalyptic end of time.[34]

Saint Ursula: Archetypal Virgin Martyr and Bride of Christ

The love feast that Hildegard spreads before our eyes in the *Scivias* is a banquet for the daily needs of those who strive on earth. But it is also a banquet for the saints who feed and drink joyfully and whose miraculous deeds inspire those not yet saintly. Quotations from the Song are prominent in several of Hildegard's song texts, but none is developed on the grand scale we find in the chants for Saint Ursula and her companions. As in the *Scivias*, she uses Song of Songs texts to explore the sacrament of the table, but now she extends those texts to celebrate the lives of the martyred virgins. Apart from those works dedicated to the Virgin Mary, the chants for Saint Ursula are Hildegard's fullest song complex; it comprises responsories, an antiphon, a set of antiphons for Lauds that includes two extra pieces for other hours, a sequence for the Mass, and an

Office hymn. The entire set of chant texts is bound together by Song of Songs imagery, much of which recalls the themes encountered in *Scivias* as described above. The chants offer both narrative progression and a hearkening back to preestablished imagery. In the narrative, Ursula moves from love and the wedding feast to the sacrifice of death, which provides a kind of sacramental consummation: her blood is not that of the hymen in intercourse, but that of the slain virgin, mingling with that of her Lover's liquid life. He is the Lamb who was slain, whose life forces join with hers in his high court, at the sonorous apex of the church.

Hildegard's focus on Ursula and her companions was rooted in the history of her own region. Bodies assumed to be those of the virgins were uncovered near Cologne in the mid-twelfth century, and the remains of men were believed to have been found with them.[35] Elizabeth of Schönau wrote to Hildegard about this discovery; Elizabeth's life of Ursula and her companions emphasized the mixed character of the company, thus explaining the newly uncovered relics. Hildegard's own hagiographical exercise defends this position and helps us to date the songs after 1156, the date of the discovery of the particular group of relics alluded to in Hildegard's chants for the Feast of Saint Ursula and her Companions. With so many virgins and companions, the discovery provided relics for many churches and monastic foundations; the eagerness for Office music for this group of saints is tied to their recently elevated cult, and we may suppose that Hildegard's own church received one of the widely dispersed relics from the dig and that her work may have been composed for its reception.[36]

The story was well-suited to Hildegard's interest in the importance of sacrifice, both of the Mass and of the cloistered life. Ursula was a fourth-century queen of Britain who renounced her betrothed to join with other virgins in a life consecrated to God. Legend has it that the virgins were wont to sail and to swim near their boat, but one day a sudden gale blew the entire company off to the Continent. There the virgins became famous as agents of religious conversion, but their triumphant progress was cut short by Attila the Hun and his soldiers; encountering them near Cologne, he slaughtered them all, Ursula and eleven thousand virgins. They had been asked to submit or die, and only the latter course proved acceptable to them. Hildegard's texts refer to male companions, that is, to defenders who died with the virgins they sought to care for and protect. She offered her chants as worthy companions to new texts by Elizabeth of Schönau and others. The poems Hildegard wrote for the Feast of

Saint Ursula and her Companions complete the stories that were circulating, but also relate the martyrs' sacrifice to the sacrifice of the Mass.

The first responsory and antiphon are appropriate for the First Vespers of the feast; the second responsory would have been used at Matins; the five Lauds antiphons make an appropriate set for the Psalms of Lauds, with "Et ideo puelle iste" serving for the Benedictus at this hour; "Deus enim rorem" might have been used for the little hours, including that of Terce, which preceded Mass; and the last of the eight psalter antiphons for the Second Vespers.[37] The hymn is a mighty work, and it could have served at any of the Office hours; the sequence would have graced the Mass, set in its traditional place before the reading of the Gospel.

The texts reveal that the plan—if it can be called such—was to offer both a narrative and a time for reflection, with steady repetition of the most important images, especially that of blood. This is a feast venerating martyrs of the church, but in this case the martyred were also a group of virgins. As I discuss the pieces in quasi-liturgical order here, my goal is to emphasize allusions to the Song of Songs and to demonstrate ways in which these allusions in the poetry join the pieces to the liturgical commentary of *Scivias* 2, with the images and their theological context forming a useful decoder for a difficult group of song texts.

"Spiritui sancto" sets the stage for Ursula's fateful journey to the continent, making her an Abraham who takes a flock—in this case, of doves, the *columbae* of the Song of Songs—to a new land.[38] The metaphors of doves (and turtledoves) and shepherds, mingled in the Song (1:6–14), are found here as this new Abraham, Ursula, takes her flock to lie with the Lamb. The refrain of the responsory points to the new joining at the end of the journey: "For the sake of the Lamb's embrace she tore herself away from betrothal to a man."[39] The virginal army with golden locks takes Hildegard by surprise: "Whoever heard such things?" she queries. Hildegard both alludes to and defends the way her nuns dressed on major feast days, in elaborate robes, with jewels, crowns, and loosely flowing hair—a practice criticized in her own time.[40] Through a group of holy women from the historic past, women who reflect her community's own experience of cloister and church, Hildegard plays with favored images relating to love and the sacrament.

The second piece, "O rubor sanguinis," was likely conceived as the antiphon for the Magnificat, the Gospel sung at Vespers.[41] The antiphon would be well suited to Luke 1: 46–55, a text alluded to in the responsory discussed above. Here, the lowly have been elevated as the imagery of blood that begets and makes new resonates powerfully with "Abraham's seed forever." Blood streaming down recalls the illumination opening *Scivias* 2.6. In the poetry, the blood that makes the procreative action of Communion and that streams from on high includes the blood of the martyred virgins, who have been taken up to join the beloved. These are innocents: The shower of blood they create as they flow is unblasted by the serpent's breath. Like Mary, they have achieved productivity without physical intercourse, a productivity that here depends upon oblique allusion to the Mass liturgy as explored in Hildegard's theology. The text of this antiphon makes a fascinating parallel with "O cruor sanguinis," an antiphon for the Son.[42] In this poem, the Son is suspended on high, and his blood causes the elements to cry out. His blood also becomes an unguent for the sick and wounded, a notion that connects the Ursula antiphon to Hildegard's *Ordo virtutum*.[43]

In the responsory "Favus distillans," Ursula is seen as a woman who has had a dream in which Christ becomes her lover, causing her to reject her human spouse for union with the Godhead. Both the opening of the poem and the subsequent verses place Ursula in the context of the Song of Songs and treat her as the *sponsa*. Her spouse is the paschal victim, the Agnus Dei. From the grove of her sweet lover, Ursula moves to the court of the Lamb and then, more locally, to the dawn of monastic song and the morning liturgy, taking Hildegard and her community of nuns into this kaleidoscope of the grandiose and the intimate, the general and the particular: "Response: A dripping honeycomb was Ursula the virgin, who yearned to embrace the Lamb of God, honey and milk beneath her tongue. For she gathered to herself a fruitful garden and the choicest flowers in a flock of virgins.[44] Verse: So rejoice, daughter of Zion, in the most noble dawn."

The Lauds antiphons tell the story of Ursula and the virgins. The set begins with praise ringing out as God gives them the great kiss of welcome. The people follow, welcoming the saints into their regions, with monks joining the women to protect and nurture them. *Osculum* is a rare word in the Vulgate Bible. Hildegard no doubt uses it at the opening of her set of antiphons to allude to the opening of the Song of Songs, "Let him kiss me with the kisses of his mouth!" A kiss then sets the stage for a journey of these "young maidens" who run, inspired, toward the King's embrace; he is both the life-giving wind that blows them and the leader of the men who care for them.[45] The implicit parallels between Hildegard's understanding of love offered by humans to God and returned by God to them is sustained by the opening of the Song. However, this biblical beginning undergirds not only the Ursula texts, but her liturgical poetry as a whole. The richly laden opening of the Song depicts the creative power of desire and union in the context of royal nuptial imagery, blended with the wine and oil of the love feast:

> Let him kiss me with the kiss of his mouth: for thy breasts are better than wine, smelling sweet of the best ointments. Thy name is as oil poured out: therefore young maidens have loved thee. Draw me: we will run after thee to the odour of thy ointments. The king hath brought me into his storerooms: we will be glad and rejoice in thee, remembering thy breasts more than wine: the righteous love thee. (Song 1:1–3)

The emphasis on sweet smells and the male provider leads to further speculation upon the masculine role as protector and caregiver. In the context of the liturgical life of the nuns, we think of the importance of the priest as the one who consecrates and serves the love feast to which they are called regularly.[46] Hildegard's favored term for speaking about the priest is *pigmentarius*, or spice merchant: One finds this word in *Scivias* 2.5, as well as in her responsory for John the Evangelist, the saint associated in the medieval liturgy with the celebration of the priesthood.[47] In the Song of Songs, the perfumer draws the beloved to the bedchamber of Solomon, which was for Hildegard the altar of the King who "makes church" and who is intimate with the daughters of Sion:[48]

> 3:6–11. Who is she that goeth up by the desert, as a pillar of smoke of aromatical spices, of myrrh, and frankincense, and of all the powders of the perfumer [*pigmentarii*]? Behold threescore valiant ones of the most valiant of Israel, surrounded the bed of Solomon? All holding swords, and most expert in war: every man's sword upon his thigh, because of fears in the night. King Solomon hath made him a litter of the wood of Libanus: The pillars thereof he made of silver, the seat of gold, the going up of purple: the midst he covered with charity for the daughters of Jerusalem. Go forth, ye daughters of Sion, and see king Solomon in the diadem, wherewith his mother crowned him in the day of his espousals, and in the day of the joy of his heart.
> 5:12–16. His eyes as doves upon brooks of waters, which are washed with milk, and sit beside the plentiful streams. His cheeks are as beds of aromatical spices set by the perfumers [*a pigmentariis*]. His lips are as lilies dropping choice myrrh. His hands are turned and as of gold, full of hyacinths. His belly as of ivory, set with

sapphires. His legs as pillars of marble, that are set upon bases of gold. His form as of Libanus, excellent as the cedars. His throat most sweet, and he is all lovely: such is my beloved, and he is my friend, O ye daughters of Jerusalem.

The sparkling jewels we find in the treasure trove of these passages, along with ivory and the gold, evoke the heavenly Jerusalem; the daughters of Sion are its high priestesses who minister to Solomon, the type of Christ. That they see him in the crown or diadem helps explain Hildegard's steady connection of the woman saints she describes and their work of church building with imagery of jewels and crowns.[49] The hymn "Cum vox sanguinis," "With the voice of blood," is carefully drawn through First Testament references to sacrifice and to several types of Christ's priesthood: Abel, Abraham, and Moses.[50] The virgins are incorporated into the stock Marian image of the burning bush unharmed by flame (Exodus 3:2), which is then joined with the glistening, bejeweled walls forming the body of the great lover and high priest, the Christ/Solomon. He lies with the virgins as they taste the triumphant banquet, as their voices cry out for others to join them: "The bush that Moses saw in flames, burning but not consumed, signifies this flock, this root of healing in the human stock that God modeled from clay to live without coupling. Clear rang their voices in a cry of fine gold, topaz and sapphire set in rings of gold." Hildegard moves swiftly from one realm to the other; the upward motion in the poetry is as swift as her sudden rising through the tessitura of varied modal realms in the characteristic leaps of fourths and fifths that Audrey Davidson has called the "thumbprint" of her melodic style.[51]

In the final verses of the sequence "O ecclesia" Ursula becomes the church as she is the bride of the Lamb, with the favored poetic structures of the Song of Songs: "Ecclesia! your eyes are like sapphires, your ears like Mount Bethel, your nose like a mountain of incense and myrrh, your voice like the sound of many waters." Ursula and her companions discover a new Cana in their own wedding feast, and their blood's wine is a drink of special savor.[52] The language of desire and union continues in the second responsory, which draws heavily upon the Song of Songs. The participation of Ursula in the Song imagery takes her to the lush garden of the altar and the love feast of the Eucharistic meal, offering Hildegard and her nuns a strong sense of ecclesial partnership with all who tend the garden. These images bring new figures to the Garden of the Fall, reshaping the ancient sin of lust and carnal joining with the virgins who come to the altar for a new coupling with the God-man. Hildegard's view takes us beyond the Song of Songs to the Song of the Virgins who praise the Lamb in the book of Revelation, which offers a picture of the Eucharistic sacrifice at the end of time. Thus she joins of the two canonical songs that had special appeal for her as an artist.

Like all medieval exegetes, Hildegard was accustomed to lying between the breasts of scriptural and liturgical images, nurtured by one verse and then another, drinking from several streams of words. To find her using disparate metaphors is not to be wondered at, but rather expected. The liturgy was her food; the singing of the office and regular participation in the Eucharist sustained her and gave her a sense of what life was about. The Song of Songs, as she came to expound it, is the link between her theological treatise *Scivias* and the liturgical texts she composed for singing at the Mass and office. From the Song's font of imagery, she presented the Eucharist as a love feast with an incarnational heart and the Christ who hosts the supper as masculine and feminine. The garden of the altar gives a second chance to those who have suffered the Fall. They too can enter the love orchard of the King. Through the biblical text and her explanations of it, Hildegard transforms the monastery liturgy into an earthly paradise, sustaining the lives of nuns who ventured into a special relationship with God, whose Son was their *sponsus* and their Lamb.

THE HARLOT AND THE GIANT:
DANTE AND THE SONG OF SONGS

Lino Pertile

In his treatise the *Monarchy*, Dante argues against those who maintained that the foundation of faith consists in the traditions of the church. He distinguishes three stages in the history of Scripture: before the church (i.e. the Old and the New Testament), with the church (the early fathers), and after the church (the *decretales*). In defining the first stage, the stage *ante Ecclesiam*, Dante states that "this is what the Church says speaking to her bridegroom: 'Draw me after thee.'"[1] The standard footnote tells us that this sentence—"Trahe me post te" in the Vulgate's Latin—is a quotation from the third verse of the Song of Songs. But what is a verse from Solomon's wedding song doing in the middle of Dante's controversy with the Decretalists? We will see later how that same verse comes to underlie, significantly, the main action of the griffin in Dante's earthly Paradise (*Purgatorio* 32). Meanwhile, however, it is important to contextualize Dante's citation of the Song of Songs within the historical and theological discourse of the *Monarchy*.

Dante's division of the history of Scripture in three stages is an open allusion to the allegorical-historical interpretation of the Song of Songs that, during the previous three centuries or so, had been gaining currency in connection with the power struggle between papacy and empire.[2] Here are two examples of this kind of reading, the first taken from the twelfth-century exegete Honorius Augustodunensis and the second from a contemporary of Dante, Giles of Rome.

Honorius Augustodunensis views the Song allegorically, as both describing a historical event and foreshadowing nothing less than the history of the world. He divides the biblical book into four parts, each

corresponding to a different phase in salvation history and each represented by a different hypostasis of the bride of the Song. The first phase,
the phase *ante legem*, covers the period from the Creation to Moses: Here,
the bride is the daughter of the pharaoh who comes from the east in a
chariot. The second, the phase *sub lege*, goes from Moses to Christ: The
bride is now the daughter of the king of Babylon, and she comes from
the south on a camel. The third is the phase *sub gratia*, beginning with
Christ and continuing into Honorius's own day: The bride is the Sunamita, and she comes from the west in the four-wheeled cart of Aminadab.
The fourth and final stage is the future phase of the Antichrist, and the
bride comes from the north as the mandrake that is picked by hand.
These four phases are also meant to represent the four periods in the life
of any individual human being, as well as the four ages of the world:
puerilis, juvenilis, senilis, and *decrepita*. They correspond to the Scripture's
four orders of meaning: *historia, allegoria, tropologia*, and *anagoge*.[3]

The hermeneutic scheme adopted by Giles of Rome in his commentary on the Song of Songs is much simpler than Honorius's and much
closer to Dante's. I should say first that Giles's commentary follows an
Aristotelian approach, and for this reason it was traditionally attributed
to Saint Thomas, among whose exegetical works it was still printed in
the nineteenth century. Giles divides the Song into three parts, corresponding to three historical phases. The first goes from Adam to the
Redemption and is the phase of the synagogue or the primitive church;
the second is the phase of the church of the Gentiles, during which almost
all the peoples of the world are progressively converted; the final is the
phase yet to come, when the Jews, too, will be converted to Christ and
the world will end. To sum up, the Song of Songs, says Giles, describes
the mutual desires of the church and Christ according to what the church
was, is, and will be like in her primitive, middle, and final states.

Although Honorius's exegetical scheme is perhaps unusually complex
and Giles's unusually Aristotelian in its approach, these two examples
give a good idea of what for us is a remarkable hermeneutic procedure—
one, however, that was widespread in the late Middle Ages and indeed
that was adopted by Dante himself. The Song of Songs was an ideal
ground for this kind of hermeneutics: The vagueness and weakness of
the historical and literal foundations of the text allowed for the development of an almost limitless polysemy. Moreover, each one of the Song's
words and sentences offered scope for the endless exercise of intertextuality involving not only the Old and the New Testaments, but also the

works of the fathers of the church. It was a massive tradition that permeated the culture of Europe at a time when the European nations were
beginning to write in their new vernacular tongues. In Italy, it was particularly dear to the Franciscan spiritual milieu, the Joachimites, the mystics,
the apocalyptics, and generally to the Christian thinkers who yearned for
a return of the church to her pristine purity. Indeed, the Song of Songs
was often read and commented on in association with the book of Revelation, with which it made an almost inseparable prophetic unit.[4] This
tradition was upheld in Florence by the Franciscans of Santa Croce, especially after Pietro di Giovanni Olivi lectured in their midst from 1287 to
1289.[5] This, very briefly, is the fairly well known background to Dante's
quotation of the Song in the *Monarchy*.

What has not been recognized, however, is that the Song of Songs,
with all the exegetical literature it spawned in the late Middle Ages, is
also responsible for one of the most astonishing passages in Dante's *Divine
Comedy*, the section occupying the last six cantos of the *Purgatorio* and
describing the earthly Paradise.[6] As a major example of the intertextual
evidence that has brought me to this conclusion, I will consider only the
sequence describing the appearance of the harlot and the giant (*Purg.*
32.148–60) with which the pageant of the church comes to its conclusion.
My intention is to make two points. First, the structure and imagery of
this final sequence is based, to a large extent, on the commentary tradition
on the Song of Songs; second, what stimulated Dante's work as a poet
was not his ultimate biblical source, but the intermediate elaborations of
it that shaped his culture.

Let me first summarize the context of the scene. Standing by the small
river that runs through the earthly Paradise, Dante, the pilgrim, has been
talking to the lovely Matelda, who stands on the far bank, when suddenly
he sees a phantasmagoric procession coming slowly toward him from the
east on the other side of the stream: first, seven treelike golden candle-
sticks, followed by twenty-four venerable old men dressed in white; then
a two-wheeled triumphal chariot drawn by a griffin and accompanied by
a winged animal on each of its four corners, with seven nymphs by its
two wheels. Following the chariot are two old men, then four, and finally
a single old man. As the chariot reaches the spot directly opposite Dante
on the other bank of the river, it comes to an abrupt halt at the sound of
a thunderclap. With this, canto 29 ends. Now a veiled lady appears standing on the chariot as angels sing and scatter lilies. Dante knows instinc-
tively that this veiled figure is Beatrice. In a state of great emotional
turmoil, he turns to Virgil, only to discover that his beloved master is no

longer there. What immediately follows is anything but the lover's reunion we had anticipated. Instead, Beatrice scolds Dante at great length
and vehemently, and only after he has publicly repented does Matelda
draw him across the water to where the griffin stands on the other side
of the river (cantos 30 and 31). The griffin draws the chariot to an extremely tall tree, which uniquely in this luxuriant garden appears to be
totally barren. Once he ties the chariot to it, however, the tree is instantly
covered with new leaves and flowers. At this point, the griffin and the
procession's old men vanish into the heavens, while Beatrice, Dante, and
the seven nymphs remain by the tree—with the empty chariot still
attached to it (canto 32.1–108).

Descending through the branches of the tree, an eagle (32.115) breaks
some of its bark, leaves, and flowers and violently strikes the chariot; a
fox (32.119) begins to attack the chariot, but Beatrice turns her away; the
eagle comes down again and leaves on the chariot some of her feathers
(32.126); a dragon rises from the ground underneath, drives his tail
through the chariot, and carries away part of its flooring (32.130–35); the
plumage, left behind by the eagle, spreads over what is left of the vehicle,
covering even its wheels and shaft (32.136–40); the chariot is transformed
into a living monster with seven heads, three on the shaft with two horns
each and four on the corners with one horn each (32.142–47); upon this
chariot/monster sits a harlot, and standing next to her is a giant. The two
kiss each other repeatedly (32.148–53); the harlot looks lasciviously
toward Dante, whereupon the giant lashes her from head to toe; then he
unties the chariot-monster from the tree and drags it away into the forest
with the harlot still sitting on it (32.154–60). Thus ends *Purgatorio* 32.

The dramatic sequence I want to focus on is the last moment in this
enigmatic chain of events, starting from when the harlot appears, sitting
on the chariot-monster:

> Sicura, quasi rocca in alto monte,
> seder sovresso una puttana sciolta
> m'apparve con le ciglia intorno pronte;
> e come perché non li fosse tolta,
> vidi di costa a lei dritto un gigante;
> e basciavansi insieme alcuna volta.
> Ma perché l'occhio cupido e vagante
> a me rivolse, quel feroce drudo
> la flagellò dal capo infin le piante;
> poi, di sospetto pieno e d'ira crudo,

disciolse il mostro, e trassel per la selva,
tanto che sol di lei mi fece scudo
a la puttana e a la nova belva. (32.148–60)[7]

Firm as a rock upon a mountain high,
Seated upon it, there appeared to me
A shameless whore, with eyes swift glancing round,
And, as if not to have her taken from him,
Upright beside her I beheld a giant;
And ever and anon they kissed each other.
But because she her wanton, roving eye
Turned upon me, her angry paramour
Did scourge her from her head unto her feet.
Then full of jealousy, and fierce with wrath,
He loosed the monster, and across the forest
Dragged it so far, he made of that alone
A shield unto the whore and the strange beast.

All the commentators observe that this scene is derived from Revelation 17:1–5:

> Then one of the seven angels . . . came and said to me: "Come, I will show you the judgment of the great harlot who is seated upon many waters with whom the kings of the earth have committed fornication, and with the wine of whose fornication the dwellers on earth have become drunk." . . . I saw a woman sitting on a scarlet beast which . . . had seven heads and ten horns. . . . and on her forehead was written a name of mystery: "Babylon the great, mother of harlots and of earth's abomination."[8]

At first sight, this seems to be a good fit. In the literature and art of Europe from the eleventh to the thirteenth century, there are countless illustrations of and variations on the apocalyptic theme of the seven-headed monster. The image of the Whore of Babylon, the *meretrix magna*, was quite commonly used in Dante's times as a symbol of an utterly corrupted church. Religious polemicists, heretics, followers of Joachim of Fiore, Franciscan spirituals, and other radical critics of ecclesiastical degradation exploited it unsparingly.[9] Two centuries later, Protestant writers and preachers would readily appropriate it as a powerful emblem in their fierce attacks on a church that they felt had become unworthy of her mission. For Dante, too, the harlot clearly represents the antithesis of Beatrice, whom she replaces on the chariot-monster.

Nonetheless, many questions remain. What about the giant and the kissing? What about the lashing of the harlot and the dragging away of the chariot-monster? Again, it is generally agreed that this is an allegory of the obscene affair between the papacy and the house of France, which culminated in the removal of the papal court to Avignon under Clement V in 1309. And so it may be. But what about the remarkable imagery? We are referred back again to the book of Revelation, with its heavy hints of fornicating kings and general abomination. However, we can be much more precise with regard to the richly dynamic significance of Dante's invention.

Even a superficial glance at the action, so carefully constructed by the poet, will suggest that there must be a pattern and a meaning to what Dante says is happening before his eyes. We have seen how the griffin drew the chariot to the tree and, after Beatrice alighted, tied it to the trunk. Now we see that the giant unties the chariot-monster from the same tree and drags it away with the harlot still on it. There are therefore three perfectly antithetical sets of figures in the sequence: the chariot-monster, the giant, and the harlot are the polar opposites respectively of the triumphal chariot, the griffin, and Beatrice. The exegetical tradition has never had any hesitation in explaining the antitheses of triumphal chariot and chariot-monster and of Beatrice and the harlot. However, it has seldom noticed and never satisfactorily explained the antithesis of the griffin and the giant, and this difficulty has in turn impaired our full appreciation of the whole sequence. We are told that Dante chose the griffin because the mythical bird is an "animal binato" (*Purg*. 32.47)—a "twofold creature" in Longfellow's translation—half lion and half eagle and therefore a perfect symbol of Christ in his human and divine natures.[10] But what about the giant? How can a giant be the antithesis of a Christ-griffin? What is the connection? Where does the giant come from? Is he Dante's own creation?

The first giant of the Bible is Nimrod, or Nembroth, king of Babylon, whom the Vulgate calls a "mighty hunter before the Lord" (Genesis 10:8), but who was known as the "giant hunter" in the old Latin translation of the Bible, the *Vetus latina*. Through Augustine's quotation of it,[11] it was established throughout the Middle Ages, despite the triumph of Jerome's Vulgate. This giant is Dante's Nembrotto, the architect of the Tower of Babel, responsible for the confusion of languages, who is seen in *Inferno* 31.67–82 to be a mighty and irascible fool, incapable of uttering a meaningful sound. Nimrod cannot be associated with our giant, however, because although he is undoubtedly wicked and cruel, he is also articulate and fully aware of what he is doing. The question we must ask ourselves is: Is there some other equally powerful creature, possibly a "good" giant, of which the "bad" giant in Dante's *Purgatorio* could be the antithesis?

The answer is yes. As patristic writers often point out, a good giant does exist in the Bible.[12] We find him in Psalm 18 (19 in the modern version), which, in Augustine's estimate, is an allegory of Christ, a glorious hymn of joy in praise of the Lord's justice.[13] Here are its first six verses:

The heavens show forth the glory of God;
　　and the firmament declares the work of His hands.
Day unto day utters the word,
　　and night unto night proclaims knowledge.
There is no speech, nor are there words,
　　where their voices are not heard.
Their sound has gone forth into all the earth,
　　and their words unto the ends of the world.
　　In the sun he has set His tabernacle,
He comes forth like a bridegroom out of his chamber;
　　He has rejoiced as a giant to run his way,
his rising is from the end of heaven,
　　and his circuit even to the height of it;
　　and there is no one that can hide from His heat.

The verse, crucial for us, is the sixth, which begins "In the sun he has set"—in Latin, "In sole posuit tabernaculum suum; Et ipse tanquam sponsus procedens de thalamo suo. Exultavit ut gigas ad currendam viam." Here, then, is the giant we were looking for. As will presently become apparent, this verse is quoted time and again in all sorts of writings throughout the Middle Ages, for the giant of the psalm was identified with the bridegroom of the Song (2:8) who runs toward his bride.[14] It is precisely on account of this that Christian writers can speak of a "good" giant, often contrasting him with the "bad" Nembroth.

Writing of Nembroth, Saint Ambrose stresses that he is black and adverse to light, more akin to the night than to the day; as a hunter, he says, Nembroth lives in the forests among wild animals and beasts.[15] On the contrary, the good giant of Psalm 18 comes forth from heaven and is as immaculate as pure, dazzling light. Saint Augustine never tires of referring to this figure, as in his commentary on the psalm: "*Et ipse tanquam sponsus procedens de thalamo suo.* He came forth from the Virgin's womb, where God contracted with human nature as it were the union [*copulatus est*] of bridegroom and bride."[16]

In the second discourse on the same text, he expands on this likeness further:

> When the Word was made flesh, He found as a bridegroom His nuptial chamber in the Virgin's womb. Thence He came forth, united to a human nature, as from a chamber of surpassing purity, humble below all in His mercy, strong above all in His majesty. This is how the giant has rejoiced to run His way, *gigas exsultavit ad currendam viam*: He was born, grew up, taught, suffered, rose again, ascended; He ran his course, He did not loiter upon it. This same bridegroom who accomplished all these things, He it is who has set His tabernacle, the Church, in the sun, in full view of all men.[17]

Among Christian writers, the good giant of Psalm 18 is, without any doubt, Jesus Christ, understood specifically in his twin nature, human and divine. Indeed, whenever it is quoted, the verse from the psalm is related to or associated with the mystery of the Incarnation. Take a typical and probably very influential example from Saint Augustine's *Confessions*:

> You seek the happy life in the region of death; it is not there. How can there be a happy life where there is not even life? He who for us is life itself descended here and endured our death and slew it by the abundance of his life. In a thunderous voice he called us to return to him, at that secret place where he came forth to us. First he came into the Virgin's womb where the human creation was married to him, so that mortal flesh should not for ever be mortal. Coming forth from thence "as a bridegroom from his marriage bed, he bounded like a giant to run his course [*velut sponsus procedens de thalamo suo exultavit ut gigans ad currendam viam*]."[18]

The figure of Christ as giant became integrated into the church liturgy to the point that it appears, for instance, in a Christmas hymn to Mary, probably by Venantius Fortunatus, where it is said: "tanquam sponsus thalamo procedit ab alvo exultatque gigans Christus eundo viam [As a bridegroom from his nuptial chamber, He comes forth from the womb, and He leaps, the giant Christ, as He goes along His way]."[19]

Even more clearly, Bruno of Asti writes in his commentary on the Psalms: "Coming forth as a bridegroom from his nuptial chamber, that is, from the Virgin's womb, where that inexpressible union took place, where divine and human natures were inexpressibly united. . . . But why is it said "as a giant"? As a giant he was made lord, for he is strong and invincible. Moreover, the giants, too, were reputed to be of twin nature."[20]

Similarly, Rupert de Deutz, in his commentary on the Gospel of John, talking about Christ's twin natures, writes:

> We do not worship a recently made Lord, as Cerynth, Marcion, Ebion, and all the other Antichrists have falsely asserted. What they said, that before Mary Christ did not exist, is a lie. Christ, who now is man till the end of time, was Lord at the beginning and before all time. He was not in the totality, in which He is now, that is, flesh and Word, but He was just Word. Now he is one giant of twin substance, and one person of double operation; in the beginning however, He was one person of one substance and one operation.[21]

Likewise Saint Thomas Aquinas in his commentary on Psalm 18: "*Ipse tamquam Sponsus procedens de thalamo suo*: the marriage bed is the Virgin's womb, whence He came forth as a bridegroom, for in that perpetual union he married human nature."[22]

For our purposes, what is most interesting is the association made at the very beginning of this tradition between Christ the giant as *sponsus procedens de thalamo*, "as a bridegroom from his marriage bed," and the bridegroom of the Song of Songs, as we will shortly see.

These few examples suffice to show that a giant was well established in the Scriptures and in the liturgy of the medieval church. Indeed, the medieval figure of the Antichrist is based *e contrario* on that of the "good" giant with whom it shares his twin nature, both human and divine. Thus, writing in 1300, John of Paris states that the Antichrist "will say he is the sun of justice and a giant of twin substance [*gemine substantie*], namely, the divine and the human."[23] And the same formula is repeated in a commentary on the Apocalypse attributed to Saint Thomas.[24] Having clarified this point, everything in the puzzling sequence of the whore and the giant becomes clear and meaningful.

Dante's giant performs four actions: First, he exchanges kisses with the harlot; second, he flagellates the harlot from head to toe; third, he unties the chariot-monster from the newly flowered tree; and fourth, he drags the chariot-monster away into the forest with the harlot still on it. These four actions are all intertextually inspired, again *e contrario*, by the commentary tradition of the Song of Songs.

First, the kiss, or rather, the kissing. Dante's text says: "e basciavansi insieme alcuna volta." This is not, as it is usually said, Dante's own reworking of the Apocalypse's allusion to the harlot fornicating with the kings of the earth. Quite obviously, Dante's true model is the opening sentence of the Song of Songs: "Osculetur me osculo oris sui," "Let him kiss me with the kiss of his mouth."

That of the Song was perhaps the most famous kiss in the culture of the Middle Ages. In the manuscripts of the Song of Solomon, we find it often illustrated inside the letter "O" of the first word of the text: "Osculetur." For instance, in a twelfth-century manuscript of Saint Beda's commentary on the Song, now in Cambridge (King's College, MS 19 f 12v), Christ and the church are depicted as a man and a woman sitting side by side and kissing; in another twelfth-century manuscript, now in Valenciennes (Bibliothèque Municipale, MS 10, f. 113), the same couple is seen kissing in a standing position.

The kissing between the harlot and the giant in Dante is the perverse parody—the antithetical figure—of this sacred biblical kiss. The enormous diffusion of the first line of the Song and the strength of its iconographic tradition free me from having to offer any further evidence on this point. Quite simply, it does not seem possible that anyone in the early fourteenth century could portray Christ and the church, or their antitheses, in a kissing position without implicitly alluding to the biblical kiss.

The interpreters of the Song, beginning at least with Origen,[25] explain the form "Osculetur me osculo," or "osculis," by observing that the bride does not wish any more to be greeted just by the bridegroom's heralds and servants, nor does she want any more to receive his gifts through intermediaries. She yearns now to be visited by the bridegroom in person, to be kissed directly with the kiss of his mouth. This sacred kiss heralds the Incarnation; it seals the reconciliation between God and his church; it reopens the gates of Heaven ending five thousand years of exile. This same kiss is understood to be a prefiguration of the Eucharist as the perfect joining of Christ with the purified soul.[26] Given the existence of this model, the first action performed by the harlot and the giant in Dante's scene must be understood as a dark parody, a willful, diabolical perversion of the original sacred text. Indeed, it is the most blasphemous deed portrayed in the *Comedy*.

After the exchange of kisses, the other three actions performed by Dante's giant are the flagellation of the harlot and the untying and dragging away of the chariot-monster into the forest. Leaving aside for the time being the flagellation, let us attend to the other two actions. Dante's text says, "disciolse il mostro e trassel per la selva" (He loosed the monster, and across the forest / Dragged it [32.158–59]). Loosening and dragging conspire to undo the earlier work of the griffin, who first drew the chariot and then tied it to the tree:

E vòlto al temo ch'elli avea tirato,
trasselo al piè de la vedova frasca,
e quel di lei a lei lasciò legato.

And turning to the pole which he had dragged,
He drew it close beneath the widowed bough,
And what was of it unto it left bound. (32.49–51)

Here the word that is crucial for my argument is "trasse," "he drew,"
a verb that, not by chance, appears in both sections of Dante's narrative:
"trasselo al piè de la vedova frasca" (32.50) and "trassel per la selva"
(32.158). The same verb is also the first word of the much-quoted third
verse of the Song of Songs, which, in the traditional punctuation, reads:
"Trahe me post te, curremus In odorem unguentorum tuorum," "Draw
me after thee, Let's run after the fragrance of your perfumes." As we
have already seen, Dante quotes this verse in his *Monarchy* in connection
with the historic subdivision of the Song. Moreover, if we examine the
Song's exegetical tradition, we discover something vital to my argument,
for this particular verse is regularly cited and explained with intertextual
reference to the giant of Psalm 18.[27] In other words, Christ, the bridegroom of the Song, is viewed as the giant who comes to earth to draw
allegorically the church, morally the individual soul, to heaven.

Thus, the exegetic tradition of the Song links together Dante's two
texts, providing the political thinker of the *Monarchy* with a seminal point
for his historical and political argument while also inspiring the poet of
the *Purgatorio* with the key image for his fantastic reworking. In the
Purgatorio, Dante applies the pattern of Song 1:3 twice: first, positively,
to the griffin's action, and then, negatively, to the giant's. This reading is
not based on guesswork; it is the exegetic tradition that authorizes it. In
fact, this reading is so rich that it also reveals the source for the giant's
flagellation of the harlot, the only action in the sequence without apparent
model in the Song.

The most significant, though not unique text that compels us to connect Dante's episode to the Song is Saint Bernard's commentary on the
Song of Songs. The relevant passage is found in the twenty-first sermon,
the first that Bernard devotes entirely to the third verse of the Song. Here
we read:

Let her say then: "Draw me after you: we shall run in the odor of
your ointments." Where is the wonder that she needs drawing who
chases after a giant, striving to catch him as he goes "leaping on the

mountains, bounding over the hills"? "His word runs swiftly." She is not able to match his running, cannot compete in swiftness with him "who exults like a giant to run his race"; it is beyond her own strength, so she asks to be drawn. "I am tired," she says, "I grow weak; do not desert me, draw me after you or I shall begin to stray after strange lovers, I shall be running aimlessly. Draw me after you, for it is better that I be drawn by you, that you use any force you please against me, terrifying me with threats or harassing me with scourges [*exercendo flagellis*], rather than spare my lukewarmness and abandon me to false security [*securam*]. Draw me even against my will, and make me docile; draw me despite my indolence and make me run."[28]

In this passage, we not only have the usual identification of the giant of the psalm with the bridegroom of the Song, but also the bride, who is beseeching Christ, at once giant and bridegroom, to draw her, indeed to drag her—as the giant does with the harlot in Dante—even against her will, even by means of threats (*minis*) and flagellations (*flagellis*), rather than abandon her in the tepidity of her false security: "exercendo flagellis," exactly Dante's "la flagellò"; "securam," exactly as Dante depicts his harlot from the very opening word of his portrait: "Sicura, quasi rocca in alto monte."

A little further on in the same sermon, Saint Bernard comes again to talk of the *sponsa*'s spiritual condition, and, insisting on her readiness to accept *flagella*, makes her say:

"It is me that you must correct, my Bridegroom" she says, "me that you must test, put on trial and draw after you, because I am ready for the lash [*flagella*] and strong enough to persevere. . . . Let mercy but return and we shall run again. You with your giant's power can run with your own strength; we can run only when your ointments breathe their scent."

Dante's poetic construction is a dramatic adaptation of Bernard's passionate meditation on the Song, except that Dante's visionary energy transforms the saint's words into visible actions and objects. Whereas Bernard narrates in one and the same passage both the desires and fears of his *sponsa*, Dante polarizes this psychological conflict by splitting it into two events, the second of which is a negative copy of the first. Thus, Bernard's interpretation of the Song is principally moral and spiritual; Dante's representation is mainly allegorical, even if, as Beatrice later says

(*Purg.* 33.72), the pilgrim and we readers are expected to understand it morally.

We must therefore conclude that Dante's violent sequence of the harlot and the giant is deliberately set in symmetrical opposition to the earlier scene where the griffin gently draws the chariot, with Beatrice on it, and ties it to the tree. Both episodes are conceived and artistically constructed on the dramatic pattern provided by the commentary tradition on the Song of Songs. The subtext of the earlier episode leading to the flowering of the sacred tree is the Song as an allegory of love; the subtext of the latter episode, leading to the kidnapping of the chariot, is the Song, as well, but now as political allegory.[29] This in no way precludes the Apocalypse from being part of the textual equation, it only shows how Dante transformed and renewed his sources by threading into the suggestive and highly dynamic narrative of the Song the popular and powerful, but static image of the whore of Babylon.

I have suggested elsewhere that this is only one of many instances in which the Song emerges as a powerful inspiration in Dante's construction of earthly Paradise.[30] The biblical poem's influence should not be surprising. The drama of the Song of Songs provided Dante with a polysemous narrative pattern in which his autobiographical and theological concerns, his personal anxieties and social/historical beliefs, were already synthesized in one integrated system. It is characteristic of him that in constructing his earthly Paradise, he dared to emulate that sacred, all-encompassing system.

PART SIX

Reimagining the Song

IN THE ABSENCE OF LOVE

Carey Ellen Walsh

As is true of no other Scripture, I find myself compelled to return to the Song of Songs time and again. A return to a text as rich as this one can only be stimulating, for rereading is its own reward. And yet, coming back to the Song brings me something more—an infusion of joy. In afterlife, the Song has a formidable presence: It lingers in the present, gathering up the past of its origins and thus ensuring its own future. The Song is robustly alive in every rereading.

As other essays in this collection will show, the Song has always been a source for exegetical invention. I am not the only reader who has kept returning to this delicious, delightful scene or who has been caught up in the multiple meanings that keep emerging from it. This multiplicity brings about a dynamic encounter between text and reader and, for me transforms my sense of what language *does*. The Song, a text about human desire, ignites my desire for more interpretation and impels me to think about the link between desire *and* interpretation. To this end, I have sought the aid of psychoanalytic and literary theory to shed light on reading as encounter. Perhaps I did so because I also wanted to account for that infusion of joy I experience each time I return to the Song.

The book's power is not merely a question of rhetoric. Literary convention, technique, and polish are only part of its brilliance: Even taken together, these features do not account for the reader's joy. Rather, joy comes out of the relationship the reader develops with the text. This is *attraction*—not voyeurism, at least in my reading. I am not merely looking at the two lovers, but am drawn into the process of desire itself. I am helped in understanding this experience by psychoanalyst Jacques Lacan, whose exploration of the interstices of desire, language, and reading has illuminated the Song for me. For Lacan, language is so communal that the distinction between the reader and the writer is blurred. Reader and writer both—all of us, in fact—are caught up in the web of language.[1] Whereas other perspectives offer insight into the minds of the Song's characters or its author(s), Lacan's psychoanalytic perspective is instead concerned to treat the text itself as analysand, to discern how it expresses desire. Lacan once stated that desire itself is interpretation; so let it be that for us with this Song.

Before proceeding to an examination of the Song's imagery, I want briefly to sketch Lacan's view of the connection between language and desire. To begin with, Lacan shares Freud's belief in radical heteronomy, that is, a description of a thing is not the thing itself.[2] Language therefore is not simply referential, not a vehicle to represent a reality that is already there. Instead, it helps to create reality. The idea of any clean separation between, say, a text and the world behind it is, from a Lacanian standpoint, an illusion. In fact, language contributes to the making of the world. For instance, a child initially has no choice but to mediate her experience of the world through inherited language. Early childhood experience is quite relevant in any discussion of desire, because desire and language arise simultaneously in human development. Since desire begins in the separation of the child from the mother, Lacan argues that *want* is the occasion for language: for cries, gestures, and, eventually, words.[3] Because the pleasure of union is temporarily lost, separation begets desire, which begets the onset of language.[4] Separation, and the pain that goes with it, together urge the child toward efforts at communication. A baby will have a need, say, of hunger, which will then be satisfied by the mother. Adult sexual desire is forever marked by this initial experience of satisfaction. At first, desire for food is pure instinctual need "without psychic mediation."[5] However, when need later arises, instinctive drive takes on a memory trace of pleasure that dates from earlier satisfaction. This trace includes the satisfaction of the need, the presence and power of the mother, and the pleasure of love and reassurance. What happens at this point is crucial for Lacan, for now an other, that is the mother, is linked to the child's desire. So, too, is language, since the child will try to enunciate what she wants, namely, that extra trace, that love beyond the milk. Adults spend lifetimes trying to articulate just that—the love beyond the milk—and invariably sense that they come away empty-mouthed. Desire becomes ardent out of "Lack"; it is fanned by the presence of something indescribable. So, when Lacan speaks of Lack or absence, he does not mean nothingness. Absence is heavy, its weight substantial; language, however, cannot convey it.

Human sexual desire in the Song of Songs is recounted from the perspectives of its two lovers and of the "daughters of Jerusalem," those bystanders who behold the spectacle of want (1:5; 2:7; 3:5; 5:8, 16; 8:4). Speech about desire is used in a variety of ways. In *Exquisite Desire: Religion, Erotics, and the Song of Songs*, I note four ways in which speech articulates desire. First, there is aesthetic appreciation, in which the speaker celebrates the attractiveness of the other. Second, there is subjective want, in which the speaker reveals the psychophysical effects of desire upon himself or herself; she proclaims, for instance, "I am faint with love" (2:5; 5:8), or "You have ravished my heart" (4:9). In the third place, we find overt depictions of sexual arousal: "my head is wet with dew" (5:2); "my hands dripped with myrrh" (5:4). Finally, the text cautions about the extreme power of desire, for example, "do not awaken love until it is ready" (8:4); "love is strong as death, passion fierce as the grave" (8:6); "many waters cannot quench love, neither can waters drown it" (8:7). It occurs to me now that the delectable elements in the Song need further exploration. In this essay, I want to address two questions: How is absence paradoxically present throughout the Song, and why does its imagery revolve so insistently around oral delights.[6]

Desire grows in a hyperenchanted garden, a microcosm in which imagery is rich and lush. The lovers discuss their yearning amid the bounty of animals and plants, fruits and nuts. Lacan enables us to view this setting for desire as more than what it might appear otherwise: utopian fabrication or romantic idealization. To assume a utopia at work here would reduce the figurative language to a code needing to be deciphered, one that points either to the text's alleged author or to that author's ordinary world. Through such a reading, the lushness of the lovers' garden would become no more than regular agrarian life augmented by a surfeit of fruit, wine, and lovemaking. To assume the world of the Song is an idealization born of love implies that the couple's view of their world is distorted and merely temporary. Neither assumption does justice to the figurative language of the Song; both reflect condescension on the interpreter's part. Instead, let us assume that the Song's language has a real referent that is neither utopian nor idealized, but rather that the Song signifies something, rather than nothing.[7]

Lack

Although throughout the Song the lovers speak of reuniting, although they recall previous intimate encounters, they remain separated. They are desperate for one another: "Upon my bed at night I sought him whom my soul loves; I sought him but found him not" (3:1). The temporary loss of their intimacy fuels their desire to make love; it also excites the reader. It is virtually impossible to remain an innocent bystander to the Song. Separation is a necessary literary contrivance: Desire itself, rather than consummation, drives the poem. The language of desire, then, substitutes for consummation, and hence the theme of the Song, as of all love poetry, is truly sexual desire, not sex. This is Lacan's point: Language is our effort to draw near what we do not have.

The lovers are kept apart through several means. There is evidence of some social oppression or disapproval, as when the city guards beat the woman (5:7) and when the two lovers fear to share a kiss in public (8:1). In addition, the very language the lovers use to describe one another reinforces the sense of distance and barrier between them. The man views the woman as being largely inaccessible. In his descriptions, she is well guarded behind towers and by armies (4:4; 6:4); she is sequestered in the dens of wild animals (4:8) or kept far off in foreign countries (4:8, 15; 7:4). He cannot attain her. By contrast, the woman views the man as elusive. She searches ardently, but he is not in the pasture (1:8), not in the street (3:2); he is always just beyond the door (5:6), outside the window (2:9), or seen on the horizon, skipping off like the timorous gazelle that he is (2:17; 8:14). They express their desire for intimacy, yet the very images they use are distancing. They create one another through words, yet the more they say, the farther apart they become.

Everything in the Song is predicated upon Lack. The lengthy speeches, the hyperabundance of imagery, all point to what is not there. It is only in the absence of lovemaking that the lovers make love. As Lacan argues, speech about desire functions ironically as a substitute for the desire itself. All language does this; it makes a "presence out of absence."[8] Just as desire arises out of Lack, so, for Lacan, language is always about loss. The moment we utter our desire, we manifest the absence of the desired object. Thus, when the woman of the Song of Songs speaks about "my beloved," she draws our attention to the man who is not there. All of the detailed depictions of the lover's physical beauty fail to conjure him up. Indeed, words about his black hair, bright eyes, and column-hard thighs (5:11–12, 15) are poor substitutes for the beloved's body; they do not capture the human lover at all. What we have instead of two lovers, in fact, is a heap of dismantled body parts. Because the lover is not captured by details or by looking—by what Lacan calls the "scopic drive"—we know something else remains, something unspoken, unseen.

Lack accounts for the poignancy in descriptions of desire, the little wince of pain that comes with the recognition that desire is the substitute for the thing desired. Lack is vital to desire; it maintains a status, becomes a presence in the absence of the thing sought. Even the greatest eloquence fails to turn the signifier into the signified.

Lack in the Song does not merely turn on the fact that the lovers remain separate from each other; it is a condition of the poem's figurative language, as well. Imagery *plays* with the Lack of precision; it does not correct for it. The very potency of a metaphor, as Paul Ricoeur has noted, rests on its similarity and difference in analogy.[9] As we saw, the Song champions the man's thighs as "alabaster columns" (5:15). They are as firm and majestic as columns, yet of course are not columns at all. His eyes are "doves bathed in milk" (5:12). They are bright, soft, but they are not birds. Metaphor always maintains the tension of absence within its comparisons. Curiously, even when we recognize that there are no columns or doves here, we are nonetheless not left with "nothing." The absence of the descriptor demonstrates a palpable presence in the described.

Lack is present in small details. The woman's wistful memory of her lover's embrace—"O, that his left hand were under my head and his right hand embraced me" (e.g. 2:6)—is used as a refrain, with his loss recalled by the e/vocative "O." There are descriptions of Lack within the self, rather than of the other: The lovers describe themselves as "faint with love," "ravished" by a look, in a dreamy state, or drunk on love. Lack is also manifest in descriptions of the day breathing and the shadows fleeing, of the windows open, the streets empty, and the animals scurrying. These images help to convey the fleetingness of desire, the Lack that fuels it.

The overtly sexual passage about the bolted door being opened conveys the restless quest of desire for fulfillment. Note the woman's frantic—and failed—attempt to let her lover in:

I slept, but my heart was awake.
Listen! My beloved is knocking.
"Open to me, my sister, my love,
My dove, my perfect one;
For my head is wet with dew,
My locks with the drops of the night."

My beloved thrust his hand into the opening,
And my inmost being yearned for him.

I arose to open to my beloved,
And my hands dripped with myrrh,
My fingers with liquid myrrh,
Upon the handles of the bolt.
I opened to my beloved,
But my beloved had turned and he was gone.
My soul failed me when he spoke.
I sought him but did not find him,
I called him but he gave no answer. (5:2, 4–6)

There can be no doubt that the imperative "open," repeated four times, makes its point. The woman is aroused and longs for the intimate presence of her lover. This description is so vivid and successfully erotic that it is easy to overlook what else an opening signifies, namely, a space where there hadn't been one before. Physiological arousal lays bare the woman's yearning for what she does not have in herself, for what eludes her own grasp. She is, in other words, open to her lover, and yet "he is gone." This is the only time in the Song when the lovers even come close to uniting, as they try to get this "door" unlocked. The arousal is for naught: She cannot, he cannot, we cannot—in short, the Song cannot—open the door of desire.

Could this attempt at union be merely wish fulfillment, a fantasy that does not come true? Perhaps the woman is in some type of dreamscape, or, given her arousal, in the midst of a wet dream. She tells us "I slept, but my heart was awake" (5:2): She is neither conscious nor unconscious here. She thinks she hears him knocking at the door to her chamber; she hears him calling. Wet with anticipation, she rushes to let him into her room, but just as she opens the door "My beloved had turned and was gone." This liminal space between sleep and wakefulness permeates the poem. Even desire itself, in the Song's refrain, is presented as sleeping: "Do not stir up or awaken love until it is ready" (e.g. 2:7; 3:5; 8:4). The Song's refrain, its leitmotif, testifies to the Lack within desire; we are not allowed to forget that love, for all the times it is mentioned, is absent. It is asleep, not present.

The recurring image of sleep, with its echoes of absence, is not the poem's most pronounced articulation of Lack, however. The most profound absence of all, of course, is death, which appears in what is perhaps the Song's most famous verse: "Love is as strong as death / Passion fierce as the grave"(8:6). This verse is usually understood as a superlative, to mean that love is stronger than death. In the Hebrew, however, it is clearly a simile. Love does not conquer death, it shares its strength. Desire is partly about self-transcendence, as boundaries give way, as self is propelled beyond itself toward the other. Passion shares with the grave the loss of self, the annihilation of individual identity. In desire, too, we long to lose ourselves in the other. Desire and death both have the force to void the self.

These articulations of absence occur throughout the Song. They are neither accidental nor artificial, precisely because they express a semantic meaning about desire. It is Lacan (along with other postmodernists) who encourages us to pay attention to the silences within language, to note its essential indeterminacy. We can better glimpse desire's expression, just as Elijah glimpsed God—not in the stuff of wind, earthquake, or fire, but in palpable absence, in the sound of sheer silence (I Kings 19:11–12). Lacan's psychoanalytic perspective allows us to see the Lack within desire; through this lens the Song's imagery and its paradox of Lack and lushness begin to make sense.

The Flamboyance of Fruit

I have said that the setting of the Song is a hyperenchanted garden, one abounding with fruits and flowers. Why might this be so? As a way to address this question, I turn now to a discussion of fruit metaphors and ask how desire can be both chaste and voluptuous. The lovers use wide-ranging metaphors to depict one another, as well as to express their own individual longing. Their metaphorical lexicon includes plants (vines and palms), animals (foxes and gazelles), spices (myrrh, frankincense, and cinnamon), and architecture (walls and towers). The richness of these metaphors expresses the superabundance of the lovers' desire. The lovers draw from the world around them; little of the created order is left out. The lovers' world is incandescent; senses are first teased, then fed.

For instance, the man refers to his beloved as "O Delectable One!" (7:6). This favored endearment for the beloved suggests the erotic intensity of the man's desire. He treats the woman as a food to be consumed, a delectation, full of flavor and juice. The implication of oral sex is unmistakable, yet the work of metaphor is indirect and all the more provocative for being so.

Indeed, this provocation begins at the very outset of the poem. The song opens with a kiss, or, at least, the desire for one: "Let him kiss me with the kisses of his mouth! / For your love is better than wine" (1:2). This yearning is decidedly oral, and the imagery that opens the song is overdetermined: Kisses by their very nature are always the gift of some-one else's mouth. Throughout the Song, wine overflows its containers, mouths release their juices, lips kiss, tongues taste—all as expression of sexual desire (2:3; 4:10–11; 5:1, 16; 7:2, 6, 9). Oral pleasures are stimulated during arousal; the psychoanalyst will tell you that this is so because pleasures recall the primary desire for the mother's breast.

Lacan accounts for the surplus element in oral pleasure, the "enjoy-ment *plus*," as Dor describes it.[10] Whereas Freud focused on the "oral" element of pleasure, Lacan focuses on "pleasure" itself. *Jouissance*—roughly, "enjoyment"—suggests the surplus of emotion that goes beyond mere sexual release. [11] I want to suggest that the Song's fruit imagery is its primary means of expressing *jouissance*. Although oral pleasure might be signaled through any number of metaphors, fruit, especially when ripe and bursting with juice, is particularly evocative. Its heady ripeness, intoxicating tastes and scents allure us. When eating fruit, only a delicate skin separates us from juicy enjoyment. Also, the delectation of fruit is as old as Eden: In Robert Alter's translation, "the woman saw that the tree was good for eating and that it was lust to the eyes and the tree was lovely to look at, and she took of its fruit and ate, and she also gave to her man, and he ate" (Gen. 3:16). For the Song's lovers, fruit and wine signify abundant enjoyment. The poem's sustained celebration of fruit is an Israelite way of depicting *jouissance*, a pleasure greater than enjoy-ment, a deep relish.

There is an additional move to be made here, from the eating of the fruit to the delectation of the text. We can link the request that opens the Song—for a kiss "from the kisses of his mouth"—to modes of reading. In reading aloud, as the ancients did, mouths move, caress the language. We can think of reading as kissing a text, of reading aloud as kissing with joyful abandon. Lips are moistened by saliva; they dance as they articulate the lovers' delight in each other. The very reading of this poem, in other words, requires our own orality. This orality is arousing: In reading, our "hearts are awake" as well. As readers, then, we take our cue from these lovers and experience our own *jouissance*, the infusion or perk of joy with which I began. Lacan's theory, like the Song's practice, illumines this facet of desire, and, more importantly, gives us permission to watch for it.

Fruit becomes particularly intoxicating when it becomes wine. Thus, in the Song, we move from devouring the beloved to drinking her: "Your navel is a rounded bowl / That never Lacks mixed wine" (7:2). Metaphor transforms the woman's body into a chalice, from which the lover has clearly sipped often. We wonder if she is always wet for him, if her taste is musky, like a mulled wine. A simile would reduce the range of reference, because it does the work for the reader and therefore limits the likeness. If, for instance, the man had said, "Your navel is *like* a rounded bowl that never lacks mixed wine," we would have been reminded of the pottery of banquet tables, we would have been led to think that she, the woman, was well-made, round and inviting to the touch. We might have thought that she was fortifying to a lover. Simile enforces similitude, whereas metaphor allows for a host of associations, holding in tension similarity and difference. When the woman's navel is described as a full drinking bowl, the imagination is given license to rove. It wanders from intoxication to wetness, from a spicy taste to the dark fragrance of must, from a man's knowing kiss to a woman's shudders of delight.

In these descriptions of desire and delight, mouths bathe in sweetness and overflow with intoxicating liquids. Orality is heightened, as the woman's own taste is further detailed: *She* is delicious. And what he has been feeding on in love renders his mouth, his words, sweet. His tongue has delighted in, partaken of, the delicacies of her body: "Your lips distill nectar, my bride, / Honey and milk are under your tongue" (4:11). "Honey" in ancient Israel could mean many things: the product of bees, of grapes, or of dates. In 7:7–9, the man describes the woman herself as a date palm tree he desires to climb, expresses his hope that its juice be in her mouth, which makes the metaphor especially evocative. Milk, in turn, would have carried similar associations to the ones we have now: mother, nurse, comfort, nourishment. Taken together, however, milk and honey have become a strong biblical trope, as they recall descriptions of Canaan's Promised Land famously flowing with milk and honey. It was the hope of oral satisfaction that lured the murmuring Israelites toward their destination. The phrase "milk and honey" is shorthand for the lush Promised Land. But in the Song, the phrase is recontextualized: The political becomes intensely personal and erotic. "Milk and honey" resituate a national hope for the land of Israel within the lover's body, as though to say, "*Here* is your Promised Land!" This daring, even outrageous metaphor transfers a cherished religious trope to a woman's mouth. Her open mouth becomes a national mandate. The shock value is similar to a Christian asserting, "This is my body" in an erotic context.

The allure of milk and honey in the Song is coupled with the intoxicating properties of wine. Throughout the Song, grapes, vineyards, and chalices overflow as the viticultural world of ancient Israel becomes a metaphor for the woman herself. Her vulva, like a cluster of grapes, is tender, ripening, dark, drooping, tartly sweet; it comes alive in the Song's predominant metaphor. All of this is sexual desire, pricked by Lack, full of *jouissance*. The Song's language about desire is a fine balancing act between Lack and flamboyance.

The Ark's Empty Mercy Seat

With Lacan, we can see that the figurative imagery of the Song does not simply represent desire. It also *simulates* the tension built into desire—a longing fueled by Lack but marked by *jouissance*. This tension entices the reader into his or her own encounter with desire. Lacan would contend that I keep returning to this Song because it simultaneously whets my readerly pleasure *and* keeps me from attaining satisfaction. Before Lacan, of course, Freud discussed this notion in his description of the "Fort/Da" game. He watched his baby nephew throw a wooden spool and say "Fort" (German for "there"), and then retrieve it and say "Da" ("here"). In Freud's view, the importance of this game was the baby's gradual learning how to cope with loss, and in particular, to cope with the loss of the mother's presence. The baby learned that, just as the spool could be reclaimed, so, too, would the mother return after an absence. This is the lesson about absence and joy, about the loss of a loved one and the pleasure of reunion. Anxiety or longing becomes relief at return, but what transpires here is more than just relief. It is *jouissance*, the extra element, the *plus*. The child giggles and throws the spool again. He enjoys this game; the torture becomes the delight of it.

The Song plays a version of the "Fort/Da" game with us, except now the stakes are much higher. The dialectic of desire—union, loss, return, joy—is rehearsed over and over again. Its descriptions of human desire do not merely fill a void into which the lover disappears, as if the poetry were merely a way to kill time until he returns. Instead, it testifies to missed pleasure and, through the heady use of lush, fruit-laden, wine-filled imagery, to *jouissance*. It does this so well that only a superlative—the Song *of Songs*—could serve as the book's title. Desire is metonymic, reaching out to a host of possible satisfactions, but never securing the single one to satisfy it fully. The reader keeps returning to this song of all songs to learn how to trust that absence is only temporary and that relish is permissible. The language of Lack draws us in, exposes our own Lack; the language of voluptuousness keeps us there, stimulating our own hope, our own memory of *jouissance*, as something that can be enjoyed again, with one's lover, in lush creation—and in texts as lush as this one.

Lacan helps us see closely how desire conveyed in language enacts the reader's own desire. He suggests how the ineffable is written within language itself. Lacan maintains that ineffability enhances, rather than confounds literary description; it is not something to be vanquished through interpretation. It is not only postmodern thinkers who stress the indeterminacy of language, of texts such as the Song. The rabbis viewed the Torah as "black fire on white fire": It is a text that always exceeds interpretation, that can never be resolved. The text is alive, its meaning always tantalizingly beyond the interpreter.

This is nowhere more evident than in the Bible, whose goal is to maintain the ineffability of its central character, God. The absence of this Other, with a big "O," fuels the biblical quest. The Bible *is* desire—it is interpreting the ineffable through language, a task surely as bold as it is unending. Scripture makes a presence out of absence. It isn't God who created out of nothing, it is the biblical authors. By practicing the speech of desire on the absent lover in the Song, the woman and the reader both learn to accept Lack as part of desire's structure, as part of life's sense of loss. That absent lover does not represent God as he does in allegorical readings of the text. Instead, he becomes a suggestive metonym for desire's loss of any object. God is not the Song's male lover; he is the lover's *absence*.

Finally, our application of Lacan elucidates what Rabbi Akiba meant when he daringly proclaimed the Song of Songs to be the Bible's Holy of Holies, its inner sanctum. Akiba's was an elliptical theology, even subtler, even more negative than Elijah's, which could situate God only in absence, "in the sound of sheer of silence" (1 Kings 19:12). Akiba's view preserves the ineffability of God. It seeks out the quiet clearing in the thicket of words. His own metaphor also works well in Lacan's world of discourse. The Holy of Holies is the inner sanctum of God's house, the place of his absent presence. Tellingly, to reach deep in Scripture for a description of that most sacred of rooms is to come to the Ark of the Covenant's empty Mercy Seat, where absence marks divine presence. So, too, with the Song of Songs, the Bible's Holy of Holies.

SONG? SONGS? *WHOSE* SONG?:
REFLECTIONS OF A RADICAL READER

Carole R. Fontaine

On radical readers reading. . . .

As a classically trained biblical scholar suspicious of the current penchant for autobiographical criticism, with its elevation of the interpreter
to the level of the text, it is with chagrin that I find myself embarking
here on this kind of essay—and for the *second* time, no less.[1] Yet despite
my scruples, it strikes me as important to reflect on how and why one
comes to any reading, be it radical or otherwise. After all, we read in
company, and when we read in good company, our readings grow and
change, though never so as to achieve a final resolution. In this respect,
reading itself is not unlike the elusive "plot" of the Song.[2] Furthermore,
reading the Song is a lifelong event, and as scholar Athalya Brenner said
in her own autobiographical work on the Song, by sharing what matters
to us with other readers, we are able to see it more clearly, differently,
and can then keep our unique perspective from mattering "too much."[3]
In a postmodern critical climate where the eternal verities that used to be
proclaimed by all senior scholars have been silenced by assaults on meaning, the autobiographical critical choice represents a different strategy. If
all is relative, then one can speak only with the certainty that bias *will* be
present, for how can we read except through the lens of bias and personal
experience? The rest is silence, and silence, which presumes consent to
the status quo, has never been a particular friend to women of faith.

I refer to *radical* reading and readers in my title because my first reading of the Song as a Southern Baptist youngster in a racist South constituted a highly radical act for my community of faith. Raising questions
about the Song proved to be a decisive moment in my textual consciousness. Not only did the community frown on my reading the book at

294

all—*so* different from the typical attitude toward daily Bible reading, a staple of Protestant piety—but what I read (the King James Version, of course) was a first step into textual criticism and concern about what translations bring in and leave out. A baby Bible geek was born in that reading, and my current resistance to silencing the Song in liturgy, preaching, and theology derives from that very primary insight.

Why Protestants Don't Read the Song

Along with other texts of wisdom literature, the Song is largely neglected in Protestant churches, especially conservative ones, in favor of primary focus on the Hebrew prophets. The prophetic teachings on economics and rich-poor relations seem to be steadily ignored by most churches— they certainly do not seem to have had much effect on Christian praxis. Still, since the prophets are understood to refer unambiguously to the coming of Jesus as the Christ, they feed the theological streams of Christian triumph over Judaism, deep wells of hate that in turn provide the ubiquitous groundwaters of anti-Judaism and its practical cousin, anti-Semitism. Put another way, the prophets, with their relentless characterization of sin in the pornographic terms of erring wife stripped naked before her lovers,[4] are seen to be legitimate, while the Song, which takes a rather different approach to the same marital metaphor, is most decidedly *not*.

It is not only the Song's frank enjoyment of sexuality that lessens its vitality and even visibility in Protestant worship and theology; it is also the historical associations that have accrued to it. The Song is somehow conceived of as the natural property of those embodied *others*, the Catholics, whose pernicious distortion of biblical truth has been roundly rejected. The poem is all of a piece with the scents and sounds, the movements, sacraments, and sculptures that render Catholicism so foreign to fundamentalist Protestant sensibilities. Naturally, the kind of Christians who have female saints and even an important role for the Mother of God *would* be the sort to indulge themselves in the Song's riot of earthy, concrete imagery. If my Protestants realized (which they probably did not) that the Song was read in connection with the celebration of the Blessed Virgin Mother, it would scarcely have been considered a Good Thing. As long as salvation is understood to be personal, individual, and utterly otherworldly, then a biblical book that barely mentions God and offers nary a glimpse of a pale, spiritual heaven will hardly be loved for its uninhibited celebration of heterosexual love or for its disclosure of a sexuality that seems to know nothing of original sin.

As a feminist critic with much to say about the distortion of sexuality that has been perpetuated by all churches, I view the Song in terms antithetical to those of the Southern Baptists with whom I first learned to read the Bible. The Song is a biblical corrective to the patriarchal denigration of women, their bodies, their capacities, and their loves. Thus it seems to me to be a place in the Scripture where the sickness appears next to its cure. Like stinging nettles that grow next to burdock root, which is the well-known folk cure for their sting, the Song lives alongside the books of the prophets, offering a reminder of other biblical perspectives on human love—ones that do not equate it with moral corruption inevitably associated with women.

Song? What Songs?

Given my comments above, it will come as no surprise that it was *not* the Southern Baptist church that introduced me to reading the Song. Committed, faithful little thing that I was, I naturally read the Bible willingly and compulsively, as directed. This meant daily readings of the Gospels and an occasional Psalm; the latter was left up to one's personal taste. Certainly, no one ever passed out a list of the parts of the Hebrew Bible that *ought* to be read frequently, but the Psalms were packaged with the New Testament in those tiny pocket editions awarded to children who had excellent Sunday school attendance. Therefore, I naturally assumed they were of equal authority to the Gospel.

But a funny thing happened to me on the way to becoming an adult: I began to take notice of the upsurge in violence and despair as my neighborhood moved into the throes of multicultural evolution. White neighbors fled when African-Americans moved close by; later, African-Americans tried to leave (not always successfully) when the neighborhood "went Haitian." As always, at least in the experience of this woman, the greatest danger was from the corrupt police (white) and the KKK (*very* white). Quite frankly, the prostitutes and heroin addicts had better excuses for their behavior and were far less frightening than the upstanding white folks who were the arbiters of morality in the South of the early 1960s. It was not a comfortable situation to be the only white family in the midst of this socio-economically inspired struggle between white and black racisms. Both groups felt themselves without ally in our Florida world: The Haitians were too dark; the Cubans too light; the Jews too rich; the cops simply too violent ever to be trusted. During the worst of the gun battles, riots,[5] or hurricane-inspired looting, I quickly determined that windows were dangerous things to look out of, and the closet in our little home was clearly the most sheltered location available to a child with good survival instincts.

The closet was a shelter that could house only one child sitting on the floor, and was not a) well ventilated or b) particularly interesting. It was there, however, and had to be made to serve. Other than typical closet odds and ends, it housed only three items to cheer the avid reader: an enormous unabridged *Webster's Dictionary*, a *Child's Treasury of Best-Loved Folktales of the World*, and the King James Bible. Reading the Scripture in tandem with folklore and against the background of gunfire turned out to be a signal act in my forming critical consciousness about texts. It was clear that certain patterns repeated themselves, whether the stories were secular or sacred. That was interesting, and in some ways, very counter-fundamentalist—wasn't *our* Bible the be-All and end-All of the Greatest Story Ever Told? So, where did this Wotan or Balder come from? Or that tree with the funny name, Yggdrasill? And the females! Goddesses starting wars between Greece and Troy, giving wisdom to Athens, and olives, too! (By contrast, the women in the Bible mostly seemed to be wives and mothers without much character development.) There was a world "out there" that suddenly, felicitously, widened in the stifling, "in here" of the closet.

I must confess, Gentle Reader, that I did not find the Song on my own during my closeted Bible-reading, Sunday-school-going days.[6] Had it not been for Leviticus, which is now also among my well-loved books, I might have come to it. With plenty of closet time on my hands, I decided that I would read the Bible from cover to cover and started at the beginning. I weathered all those "begats" (so odd, too, with no women helping), and even found the "how to build a desert sanctuary" section of Exodus of moderate interest. But when I got to Leviticus, I found . . . well, the folktales of the world were *way* more interesting! So, I returned to the Gospels and Epistles, and with the help of C. S. Lewis and *The Chronicles of Narnia*, did very well, or so I thought at the time.

During the lulls in the neighborhood agonies, we all went about our daily tasks and employments, one of which was, naturally, watching television. One particular Western—like *Shane* or *Gunsmoke*, but neither of those—featured a gorgeous male hero stranded with a missionary's daughter around some isolated campfire.[7] In what was racy dialogue for the time, the gunslinger teased the Christian with the knowledge of biblical texts he had gained in jail during one of his many incarcerations. She harrumphed in response, but was clearly impressed—*until* he began to quote from the Song and elicit her maidenly fears.

I listened and watched with interest. I actually knew a lot more about folks who saw the inside of jails than I did about missionaries and their sexual codes, but I was utterly astonished to learn that love poetry existed in the Bible! *Where?*!! Why had no one ever told me about this, or even hinted at it? This was my first outrage at the gap between the church and its sacred text. Empowered, I marched to my closet Bible and began to search the table of contents: ah-hah! It *was* there and *not* an invention of Hollywood! I devoured it in one sitting—not hard, it's only eight chapters, and it wasn't the least like Leviticus. I was amazed; I had finally found a place where a female character was at least as interesting as a Greek goddess or a Hibernian warrior queen.

But there was strangeness, too, abounding in this little book. I was used to the ever-so-helpful red letters for the *ipsissima verba* of Jesus, which in reality allowed readers to ignore everything that was not found in red. After all, whose speech could dare trump the Master's? The very first line of the Song, with the KJV's kinky use of typeface, made me pause: "The Song *of* Songs, which *is* Solomon's."

Even as a youngling in a closet, I knew that italics carried *meaning*, though I did not know then to call them morphemes. But what was the meaning of this special usage here, I asked myself. Was the Song Solomon's, or was it not? Was it supposed to be Song or *Songs*? What and where exactly were those *other* Songs to which this title seemed to allude? That italicized "of" left me wondering what was going on. Having no answer and no footnotes, I read bravely on: "Let him kiss me with the kisses *of* his mouth: for thy love *is* better than wine."

More questions! Did Solomon have some sort of kiss that *wasn't* from his mouth? *Was* his love better than wine, or was it not? It sounded like the speaker was making some affirmation against type: a flat assertion that, whatever others might think, this poet believed Solomon's love was indeed better than wine. Fair enough; it seems I was somehow in the middle of a dialogue of different views, even though I could not tell who was speaking or who in addition to me was listening. Then I read: "I *am* black, but comely, O ye daughters of Jerusalem, as the tents of Kedar, as the curtains of Solomon. Look not upon me, because I *am* black, because the sun hath looked upon me: my mother's children were angry with me;

they made me the keeper of the vineyards; *but* mine own vineyard have I not kept."

OK, now *this* made sense. "Darkness" was nothing to be happy about—I knew *that* from daily observation we when all boarded the public bus.[8] Where I lived, everybody knew that some people were *too* dark, and if darker than a brown paper bag, would never be allowed to work in white stores or businesses. Yet that darkness, in my childish opinion, had no real effect on "beautiful": I saw that reality clearly every day, too. Women, exquisite in their dusky skin, flashing dark eyes, and braver than any soldier—these were all around me, gorgeously so, although scorned by white folks.[9] I could imagine Celestine or Jackie, wreathed in white gardenias and night-blooming jasmine, saying clearly and in truth, "No, but I *am* beautiful, no matter what they say." I immediately parsed the "daughters of Jerusalem" as the ruling class, with their own self-referential standards of beauty. My neighborhood did not yet know that black was beautiful, nor did we know, prior to Thurgood Marshall's challenge to segregation in schools, that African American children readily internalized the culture's view of them as "lesser" from the earliest age, although we may have had our suspicions. It turned out that the little ones knew very well that the white dolly was the nice one and the black dolly was bad. Yet there it was: Before there was Black Power or the defiant Afro haircut instead of straightening, there was the Song, calling out to a racist culture that cherished its Bible that blackness did not rule out the presence of beauty. I was glad.

But the questions about the italics and the identity of the speakers worried at me as I read on; I did not understand what was being emphasized. As a result, I became the bane of all Sunday-school teachers: I asked what the text meant. The response recalled the scene in *Oliver!* where the orphan asks for more porridge; my questions were met with astonishment and disapproval. How much of their dismissal was a cover for their ignorance, I do not know. First, what on earth was a youngster doing reading the Song? Where were her parents? Had a schoolteacher, perhaps, or a liberal librarian pointed me to this book? My teachers were interested to know where I had even learned of its existence, much less been encouraged to take it seriously. (I never confessed that I learned of the Song from television.) My questions made their way up through the hierarchy, but no one, not even our pastor, could answer me. I was secretly shocked and disgusted. How could I trust them on all the other things they told me the Bible was saying if they could not answer a straightforward question about a little, out of the way book?

As it turned out, anyone with elementary knowledge of first-year Hebrew can explain the matter simply and easily. I wonder now why our pastor could not, he who called himself "Doctor." The King James Version, with nice attention to syntax, routinely italicized those words supplied in English to make sense of the Hebrew constructions. This included construct chains that indicate possession (Song *of* Songs: the "of" is absent in Hebrew), that supply existential verbs ("is," "am," etc.), or that fill in ellipses in the translator's move from bare-bones Hebrew to fulsome English. This orthographic convention appeared in many of the KJV's earlier editions of the last century, and it was one of precisely that vintage that I was reading. Even children can be careful readers and raise valid questions. That the "experts" could not help me suggested *not* that my questions were invalid, but that I needed to become my own expert. On such tiny incidents of reading are literary-critical careers built.

Some Content May Be Unsuitable for Younger Audiences

As I experienced critical crisis by the very existence of my unanswered questions, reading the Song also brought a biblical, textual critique to my denomination's view of sexuality—no doubt the reason that its reading was largely forbidden. From the earliest times in Sunday school, when we were separated into male and female groups for Bible study, the message to the girls was relentless. Even the *names* of our after school religious education groups told us how it was supposed to be: The boys went to "the Royal Ambassadors"; the girls went to "'the Girl's Auxiliary." The boys were encouraged to become warriors for the Lord: missionaries, pastors, community leaders who would enforce Baptist values. The girls, on the other hand, were "auxiliary," a theological afterthought, and we were to progress through the ranks of "maiden" and "lady-in-waiting" all the way to "queen with a scepter."[10] No text was ever heard in our all-girl class that did not subtly or openly endorse our future. We were to be "fine Christian girls" who would marry "fine Christian men" and, yes, produce "fine Christian children," where the prefix "fine Christian" clearly meant "fundamentalist Baptist." Our destiny was to be "fine Christian mothers." We were here on earth only to be like Ruth and Esther, building up the house of the New Israel, and we were never, *ever* allowed to forget that.

Hence our teachers inculcated the fetish of religious and sexual purity whenever they could: We prayed heartily and with genuine concern for girls who dated Catholic boys; we guarded our technical virginity, await-ing the time when it would suddenly be converted by a white dress into neutral marital acquiescence to the necessary unpleasantness of mating in order to get our babies. We firmly refused to go to slumber parties if boys were part of the hosting family; we never played cards or went to swim parties if boys were going to be there. Although we secretly danced to *American Bandstand* while experimenting with lipstick and nail polish, we never let on. In fact, all signs of deviance from the fundamentalist code were expunged by Sunday morning: No crimson threads or heated glances for us, thank you. We were "fine Christian girls" (you could tell by the little white gloves and flat-heeled shoes). Swathed in poodle skirts, the "maidens" never imagined a world of thongs.

But, amazingly, there was the Song. I confess that I unleashed it on our unsuspecting class of "maidens" as we sat beneath our Auxiliary flag. which bore the legend:

J = Jesus first
O = Others second
Y = You last

Though I did not know who the Shulamite was, I could tell she was dancing, just like David in that little festival of the Ark incident. The young Baptist "maidens" in my class were delighted by this forbidden knowledge and eager to access this dimension of a biblical female's char-acter—after all, she was in the *Bible* dancing, wasn't she?[11] Revolution was at hand! If we entertained the concept that males and females might dance as an authorized way of making a joyful noise to the Lord—well, what next, wondered the adults charged with our indoctrination. Dogs and cats living openly together? Jews or Catholics marrying the *real* Christians? Lordy!

Next in my course in subversion through Bible reading came the whole content area of "desire." It certainly *seemed* like the couple in the Song weren't married: They had as hard a time finding sheltered space and time for a little hanky-panky as any Baptist girl at a drive-in movie with her fine Christian boyfriend. It didn't sound like the Beloved thought her joy was the J-O-Y equation we had learned from our flag. (Onward, Christian automatons!) Nor did the couple *ever* talk about hav-ing children; it was almost as though that project were *not* the main function and meaning of their longing for each other. This also was news to the "maidens," even though they had no specific dispute with the future laid out for them, except with respect to fashion and fun.

Finally, the Song disclosed a whole new aspect of female voice, at least to me. We were used to barren women behind the flap of the tent, daughters bartered away into marriage with strangers or given to mobs for purposes of gang rape, or the faithful standing at the foot of the Cross. We were most certainly *not* used to a female who spoke her own desire, even against her male relatives' attempts at obstruction, or that the content of that desire should be for a *man* and not a baby!! *Double*-good golly! This last bit really took the rag off the bush, because the desirable Shulamite was looking for neither economic security nor a personal form of devotion to the Lord. A whole new concept of female religious subjectivity struck this little fox in the Baptist vineyards,[12] though such terms had not even been dreamed yet in the fundamentalist world of the 1960s. Indeed, at that time, the Song proved its contention that there *was* indeed something as strong as death, as relentless as the grave of racism and poverty in which I was mired, and love was its name.

In Case of Emergency, Read Song

If the Song, as discovered by an underage radical reader, set the "maidens" longing for the lover's scepter, it raised particular concern for little me waiting out danger in my closet. By this time, I had read enough to become concerned about the Epistles' view of sexuality. Jesus was a Good Guy, but Saint Paul's teachings on prostitution in the New Testament were chilling. The whores living next door—perky Haitians, black as the tents of Kedar—were always in danger due to their line of work. Like the Song's Beloved, they were beaten by the "watchmen," the cops on patrol, for being out at night doing the nasty. Their "brothers" certainly bartered away their sexuality for personal gain and met any challenge to their male honor with swift abuse.[13] Rather than visit a doctor or a policeman when assaulted, these girls visited The Woman, a voodoo priestess who lived down the street. No church wanted these daughters of poverty; no social worker came looking for the throwaway fourteen-year-olds trapped in poverty and vice. It seemed to me, looking cautiously out my window, that Saint Paul got it all backwards: It was the men who were abhorrent sinners, not the little girls they defiled. These were black and beautiful, alright, but the church did not seem to have much place for them. And if that was not bad enough, the Bible suggested they were "joined" and part of the body of every man who had bought them, irredeemably linked to the men who violated and then abused them. Could these women ever be part of the body of Christ, the living church, with such a background? Would anyone ever care about saving *them*?[14]

In our world of open vice and the victimization of girls and women, the voice of the Lover rang out like that of a Savior offering rescue: *Come away*!! Come out from those tight spots that hold you enslaved; come away from the predetermined life of lessened personhood; O beautiful dove, come away! Just over the horizon, high on a mountaintop, the gazelles of the Song waited for us, suggesting escape and loving acceptance. When the voice of love is heard—or even imagined—it changes the landscape forever.[15]

Out of the Closet and Into the World: Why Protestants Need the Song

Many years later, any debt the cosmos owed me for putting up with Southern Baptist "readings" of the Bible was paid in full when I enrolled in a graduate class on the Song taught by the eminent wisdom and psalms scholar Roland E. Murphy, a Roman Catholic of the Carmelite order. In that context, I was invited—nay, *required*—to read in company, because Roland assigned each of us a commentator in a foreign language whose work we would present in our own journal of readings, translations, and essays. Encouraged, I brought to class not only my French scholar in love with love, but my own artistic self, as well. I had color-coded my Bible, highlighting plants and animals, dividing them by hue into loose and intuitive categories such as "fragrant," "medicinally active," "beautiful," "food," and "wild," "tame," and "threat." "What is *this*?" the dear monk wanted to know, eyeing the mélange of colors. "Is this supposed to mean something?" Roland asked when he looked at my work. "I don't know yet," I told him, and he joked, "Well, let me know when you find out! I just saw *The Muppets* in color last night for the first time, and this reminds me of that: It's all green and purple! No one ever put color in their journal before. This is a first for me, just like *The Muppets*."

This, I reminded myself, was the man chastised by the Vatican for suggesting the Song might be about human sexuality; this was the brave exile, the mendicant monk first packed off to remote Palestine for archeological excavation and then cast adrift in the Methodist wilds of Duke Divinity School. This was a man who was both rooted and in progress, and I blessed the kind fates that sent me his way.

Much is made by scholars of God's absence in the Song. Roland acknowledged the observation, but contended that it missed the point, namely, that relationship of any kind ought to be a theological category for the Sacred.[16] How could I disagree? Apart from the injunction to "set me as a seal upon your heart" in 8:6, which may include an allusion to God's name, religious orthodoxy in the Song yields the stage to other discourse entirely. The Song's conversation with the reader concerns a partnership in eros, rather than subjugation to social codes and expectations. The beloved asks him to set her as a seal upon her heart; this is an invitation not a command. It pierces the veil of religious language more powerfully to me than any other speech in the Bible.

We read the Song and say, "The Sacred is here." The Song speaks of a salvation in *this* world. If not now, then in some future, the reader knows she will be seen truly and welcomed in her loveliness. Reading the Song teaches faithful women about the power of choice, pleasure, and delight in the Other. The harmony of the sexes as embodied in the loving couple,[17] the concord between species and Earth, people and land—these are all marks of the Sacred Presence,[18] even though the Sacred chooses to disclose its power not in burning bushes but in the flashing flames of love.

In one of my last exchanges with Roland Murphy regarding an essay I was writing about the violent watchmen, brothers and veils in the Song, my teacher shared his dismay that I was highlighting these notes of violence in a critique of the Song. Yes, he said, the brothers *are* imbeciles and there is no defending them, but the watchmen and the veil are simply part of the culture and not necessarily evocative of violence. Elsewhere in print, he had viewed the suspected rape scene with the watchmen (5:2–7) as a dream sequence, because its aftermath plays no role in the subsequent chapters. To allege such shadows in the Song, he opined, was to deface it.

I disagreed: Even in our own day, the repression of a violent event is too often a female response to an attack. The veil, I suggested, required discussion in the context of cultures that veil women; we could not think of its removal as anything but an act of aggression designed to inspire terror and enforce control. Further, the *need* to be veiled speaks of a desire to force women to internalize the patriarchal code. I suggested that interpreters' normalization of the violent watchmen, conniving brothers, and lost veil is in some ways more troubling than the appearance of such motifs within the text itself; I argued that the theological use of the Song might be enlarged by attention to the actual conditions of female love and desire in the culture that authored it. If the experts shirk the hard questions, what will happen to the "ordinary" readers who depend, in some measure, upon their expertise? Roland and I agreed that interpretive context is extremely important: I observed that Catholic women had no problem appropriating the goddess imagery behind the Song as a "type" of the Virgin Mother. On the other hand, Protestant women encountering the same imagery were distressed by it—they simply had no way of understanding female sacrality. We agreed at the end of our exchange that questions are good, that no reading is final, and that Lacan and archaeology might indeed have something major to contribute along the way.

Protestants, especially conservative ones, *must* read the Song,[19] hear it in their hymns, embody it in their worship, dance it in their aisles,[20] know it in their hearts. In a world where women and girls are still pawns whose sexuality is bartered away by men for their own purposes, the Song is a harsh critic of the status quo, religious or secular. It presents an internal hermeneutic on sexuality that needs to be fore-grounded in any biblical ethics of sexuality and in any use of the marriage metaphor. Furthermore, it speaks to universal human experiences of desire and love. If we cannot love this Earth and all the creatures that inhabit it—whom we *can* see—how shall we learn to fall in love with a God whom we do *not* see? That the churches have always offered Christ the Redeemer to the soul in the form of a bridegroom is no mistaken allegory, but a deep, accrued insight. Should we be surprised? Of course not. It *is* the Song *of* Songs.

HONEY AND MILK UNDERNEATH YOUR TONGUE: CHANTING A PROMISED LAND

Jacqueline Osherow

When I think now of my introduction to the Song of Songs—at Jewish summer camp, at fifteen, when they were looking for volunteers to chant it—I can't decide whether to emphasize that it was a fluke or one of those moments in life for which we Ashkenazic Jewish reserve the untranslatable Yiddish word *beshert*, which means a host of untranslatable Yiddish things, including, as I'm using it here: "profoundly and irrevocably predestined." Perhaps I will reveal a bit too much about myself if I tell you that, for me, they are precisely the same thing—the fluke and the *beshert*—the accidental and the predestined. Why should my first encounter with the Song of Songs be any different?

All I can tell you is that even now—thirty years later—*Shir Hashirim*, and I do think of it as *Shir Hashirim*—remains for me very much as it was then, something inextricable from the chanting of it, a series of unspeakably exquisite sounds, some of which I even understood, coming, miraculously and astonishingly, out of my own mouth. It is lovely in English, but I have no patience for it—except perhaps for that dear slight mistranslation "how beautiful are thy feet in sandals" (this is one of my goals in life, to be told, before I die, how beautiful are my feet in sandals) and "your nose is like the tower of Lebanon facing toward Damascus," which can conjure up in me, even now, unmixed affection for my—with any luck—soon to be ex-husband. The first thing that I have to admit to you—shocking as it is—is that I still prefer the Song of Songs as I first experienced it. Even though my biblical Hebrew has significantly improved since I was fifteen years old, and I probably understand the Song's vocabulary infinitely better than I did then, *Shir Hashirim* remains for me, above all, not just something chanted, but a beautiful something I only partly understand.

Why is this shocking? I am one of those annoyingly cerebral poets, perhaps overinfluenced by what a teacher once said to me at an impressionable age: "some people think poetry is above making sense; I don't think so." I too, on the whole, don't think so. I believe that, however many meanings may inhere in a line of poetry, there should be some clear, specific meaning available from its surface. But whenever I teach the Song of Songs in my Hebrew Bible as Literature class—and I could regale you with lots of stories about teaching the Hebrew Bible as literature in Utah—I always quake in fear that some student will ask me what certain passages are supposed to mean. Because frankly, I haven't got a clue. *It means just what you think it means* is what I'm tempted to reply, and please don't report me to the pornography czar. (We do, in Utah, have a pornography czar; I guess the powers that be want to keep our attention focused on our fabulous deserts and mountains.)

There is, I think, some truth to what I think of telling my students about meaning in the Song of Songs. It dares us to believe it means what we suspect it means. This may well be the secret of its erotic power, the way it forces us to engage our own erotic imaginations.

I've been reading and rereading *Shir Hashirim* in preparation for the writing of this essay, but it was only a few weeks ago, when I was preparing to chant chapters 4 and 5 in synagogue for the intermediate Sabbath of Passover (I always get this gig; not too many people have this particular skill in Salt Lake City) that I started genuinely to have any real thoughts. Somehow, I get the meaning of the text only when I'm chanting it. Here, let me tell you my newest revelation: I was chanting *dvash vᵊhalav tachat lᵊshonech*—"honey amd milk underneath your tongue." This is easy Hebrew—everybody who's ever been to Hebrew school knows what *dvash* and *chalav* are—the honey and milk that are everywhere in the Torah, flowing through God's Promised Land. I remember understanding this verse of *Shir Hashirim* with shock and pleasure when I first chanted chapter 4—an easy one—at summer camp. *Honey and milk underneath your tongue.* I'm not sure I'd yet engaged in what we then referred to as French kissing, but while I understood that it was a widespread practice, not limited by the borders of France, I had certainly never expected to find it in my Hebrew Bible. I mean, I knew that people "knew" each other in there, but I certainly never dreamed that they French kissed. I was supposed to chant *this* at the beginning of Friday night services?

Clearly, in poetry, you could get away with things; this was an enterprise worth pursuing. In any case, here I was, a couple of weeks ago, practicing my chanting, and when I got to *dvash vᵊhalav tachat lᵊshonech,* with its charged and droll implications of the Promised Land being located "beneath your tongue," I suddenly thought of three of my favorite lines in Donne:

> License my roving hands and let them go
> Before, behind, between, above, below.
> Oh, my America, my newfound land.

The brilliant little thief, I thought to myself, the adorable genius: He stole that from *dvash vᵊhalav tachat lᵊshonech*—the essential thrill and joke at the same time: Who needs a promised land, when I've got your body? The Reverend Dr. Donne just lifted it from *Shir Hashirim,* chapter 4, and used—always a timely devil, our Mr. Donne—America in place of the Holy Land. Brilliant. Indeed, something of an improvement, since America was, to the likes of Donne, at least, virgin territory, involving perpetual discovery. . . . Good for him. I can do the same thing with— what?—one of the moons of Jupiter? The best gelateria in Florence? Well, I'll work on it—but the point is that chanting *Shir Hashirim* makes me notice things about the poem that I simply don't notice when I'm merely reading it. That Donne was indebted to the Song of Songs is of course nothing new, but this particular bit of pilfering intrigues me.

But chanting, I'm always first overwhelmed by the beauty of the sounds and then made aware that the sounds are having a directed effect: They are producing and conveying an elaborate array of multiple meanings. This begins with the poem's first three words: *Shir hashirim asher,* literally: "the Song of Songs that." But listen to it: *Shir*—"song"; *hashirim*—"the songs"; *asher*—"that". The word *shir* ("song") morphs into *asher* ("that") so that listening to the three words *Shir hashirim asher,* one hears, as the poem opens: "Song! Hah! Songs! Aah! Song!" As if the text itself wants to make sure that we understand what we're in for. And then *shirim* ("songs") morphs into *Shᵊlomo*—as if Solomon is the song, in the same way the lovers and the language of this poem are perpetually confused with one another. The same sort of thing happens in the next line: *shemen turak shᵊmecha.* "Oil" (*shemen*) contains the syllable *shem* ("name") of *shᵊmecha* ("your name"), so that "your" very "name" is invested with the power to anoint. It's not the lover's body here, but the lover's "name"—the sounds that represent that body—that has this erotic and kingmaking power. So the poem opens by insisting on the potency of language, even as it demands something physical—the "kisses of his mouth." The physicality of the demand is extreme: not just "let him kiss me" but "let him kiss me with the kisses of his mouth." The language absolutely insists on the physical at the same time that it underscores the potency of poetry itself. And the poem's limitless force comes through its capacity to convey evanescent and intangible meanings. The poem's power, its insatiability, the way it, like the lovers it describes, must contain and do everything at once, doesn't just describe, but replicates the unbounded power of the erotic. The syllables of the song perpetually enact what they convey: Everything is both itself and something else. Everything is fluid. Boundaries are perpetually abolished.

And, for me, the chanter, it is most profoundly through sound that they are abolished. The singer is so sure of her poem's power that, again by way of an undermining set of syllables, she can minimize it. She sings *nazkirah dodecha miyayin mesharim 'ahevucha*. The King James Version renders this: "we will remember thy love more than wine: the upright love thee." But *mesharim 'ahevucha*—which does mean "the upright love thee"—can easily, indeed must almost necessarily, be read another way. The sentence itself has already set up the grammatical reading of *mi* or *me*—literally "from " and "from the " as "more than" in the word *miyayin*, "more than wine." *Sharim* can mean "those that sing" or "them singing" and isn't at all far from *shirim* (songs). So *nazkirah dodecha miyayin mesharim 'ahevucha*—at least when I hear it coming from my mouth—means something like "We will remember your love more than wine, more than the singing of your love" or "more than the songs of loving you" or "more than the act of singing of loving you." What's remarkable about the line is that the poem is in the act of immortalizing the memory of love; we know this from Shakespeare and Spenser, who are constantly claiming that they will bring their lovers (albeit anonymous) immortality through their poems. But the singer here is making the opposite claim: that even the mere memory of the love is greater than the poem that attempts to contain it. The poem absolutely insists on its inability to achieve what it has set out to do. The sounds of *Shir Hashirim* simultaneously acknowledge the poem's limitations and explode them. The poem insists on the power of memory: *nazkirah dodecha*—we will remember your love—but underplays its own power—more than the singing of it. Maybe she's trying to tantalize us, to excite our imaginations by telling us we're not getting it all.

But at the same time, a phrase in the previous line reads *'alomot ahevucha*, literally "the maidens love you," but *'olamot* means "worlds" and "eternities"—"the eternities love you." One phrase gives while the other takes away. And the poem gets carried away with itself in precisely the way that the lovers get carried away with themselves. The—let's call them roving—syllables that perpetually enact the transformation of one thing into another are meant to mimic the way sexual ecstasy confuses and fuses the physical and the emotional.

Shir Hashirim, more than any other text with which I'm familiar, both exploits and celebrates the capacity of language to locate and inhabit the place where the tangible and the intangible fuse. There is a reason that anyone can read anything in the Song of Songs. It's there.

So when I think of my fifteen-year-old self being given the opportunity to hear this—and to hear it coming out of my mouth—I think, whether it was fluke or *beshert*, it was, undoubtedly *mazel*, luck, of the greatest sort. What this experience taught me is both what poetry is and that it was by birthright, by heritage, and the power of its holy tongue—a tongue beneath which I could find infinite quantities of milk and honey—undeniably mine. It is the language (the same word, in Hebrew, as tongue) that is the Promised Land.

Think of the education I received, as I chanted, in the nature of metaphor and simile; I think it's Robert Alter who points out that *Shir Hashirim* contains more usages of the word *dome*—"is like"—than the rest of the Holy Scriptures put together. I haven't counted; I take his word for it. But the word *dome* in Hebrew is profoundly charged. It is the verb form of the noun *dᵊmut*—"likeness"—which appears when God announces his plan to create man: *naʿaseh ʾadam bᵊtzalmenu, bidᵊmutenu*: "we will create man in our image, in our likeness." Poetic similes are likenesses, then, in the way that we are likenesses of God.

But, as everyone knows, they aren't actual likenesses of anything. I have a friend—an ABD in physics from Berkeley, now an algebra teacher in the Salt Lake City public schools—who, when leading children's services in our synagogue, brought in a felt board on the day Song of Songs was chanted. She placed on it an empty pink felt head. She then proceeded to read from chapter 4: "Your eyes are doves," she read, and put two white felt doves where the eyes belong. "Your hair is like a flock of goats coming down Mount Gilead." So she put little felt goats from the crown down along the sides of the face. "Your lips are scarlet threads"—on came the scarlet threads. The children, needless to say, found this hilarious. Poetry, the physicist manqué explained to the children, is not about literal description, it's about engaging the ear and the imagination.

Nothing replicates the effect of poetry; only it can do what it does. And *Shir Hashirim* profoundly revels in this fact. It is, of course, always about itself and the miraculous way it achieves its pyrotechnics. The line that perhaps best embodies this (at least in my admittedly somewhat unhinged reading), is the eleventh verse of the first chapter: *torei zahav na'aseh lach 'im nᵊkudot hacasef.* The King James Version translates this as "we will make thee borders of gold with studs of silver"; the Artscroll Version prefers "circlets of gold with points of silver"; but every time I chant the line, I think: *torei zahav* (Torahs of gold ") *na'aseh lach* (we will make you) *'im nᵊkudot hacasef* ("with silver vowels.") The "silver vowels" aren't even a pun. *Nᵊkudot*—translated in this context as "points"—is the very word used for "vowels" in the Hebrew language, because of the little points used to represent them in writing. As for "Torahs of gold"— well, it's a tad irreverent, I suppose, but they don't exist as anything but an intention, promise, a longing: "We will make them" is an expression of the unbounded possibilities that their erotic adventure represents; the lover/singer is talking simultaneously about the poem he's engaged in writing and their erotic encounter.

His *na'aseh*—"we will make," when he is after all, an individual speaker—is reminiscent of "God's *na'aseh*, we will make," the very first *na'aseh* in the Torah, a verse I've already quoted: *na'aseh 'adam bᵊtzalmenu, bidᵊmutenu,*" "we will make man in our image, in our likeness." Much speculation has been generated by God's *na'aseh*, his "we will make." (Whom, after all, can the sole inhabitant of the universe be addressing?). But its meaning to me—and, I'd wager, given the use of it here, to the singer of Song of Songs—is obvious from the verse of Genesis that comes after: *Vayivr'a 'elohim 'et ha'adam bᵊtzalmo, bᵊtzelem 'elohim bar'a 'oto, zachar unᵊkevah bar'a 'otam,* "And God created man in His image, in the image of God He created them, male and female He created them." Clearly the image of God *is* male and female, and God is addressing his *na'aseh*—his "we will make"—to his female other half.

The singer of *Shir Hashirim* is doing precisely the same thing with his *na'aseh*: speaking to his female other half, and, through the use of this verb, making their union—and the poem that describes it—yet another embodiment of God's image. But the word *tor*—of *torei zahav*, my "Torahs of gold"—also means "turtle dove," as in the next chapter: *kol hator nishᵊm'a bᵊ'artzeinu,* "the voice of the turtle is heard in our land." The poet/lover's handiwork is now likened to the music of the natural world, specifically, the song that heralds spring. *Tor* is also a verb, meaning "to follow, to travel, to pursue"; I've seen it translated "explore," as in Numbers 15:39: *lo taturu 'acharei lᵊvavᵊchem*—"you shall not follow after/ explore your own hearts." *Torei zahav* could be understood to mean something like "explorations of gold," so that the poem becomes a kind of erotic map that the lovers both create and follow. On that path, they'll discover everything: birdsong, jewelry, motion, and poetry. When we return to the surface meaning of the line, the "circlets of gold studded with silver," we see that erotic love and the poem are simultaneous gifts the lovers are both composing and bestowing. It's amusing that the King James Version uses the mistranslation "border," because it is precisely borders that this language is abolishing: particularly the one between the poem and the eroticism it describes.

The gold and silver that first appear here in *Shir Hashirim* return throughout the text in the lovers' descriptions of one another and the sites of their coming together—further fusing the language of this poem with its subject. When the female speaker says: *yadav gᵊlilei zahav mᵊmula'im batarshish*, which the King James Version tames by translating it "his hands are gold rings set with beryl," she is not actually describing the hands themselves, but the way she responds to them. *Gᵊlilei zahav* are not "golden rings." They're "golden cylinders," "golden rolls," "golden phalanxes," even "golden geography"—*galil* is Hebrew for "Galilee." Clearly, the speaker is describing the effect of her lover's hands on her body: It's as if what she feels when he touches her inheres in his hands. (Chana and Ariel Bloch ingeniously capture this by using the word "scepters.") These hands are moving, rolling; they are whole phalanxes and they are finally fused with the regions in herself that they locate. But at the same time, a person writes with the hand: The golden Torah is linked to the golden hand that writes it, and both are indistinguishable from the eroticism that has set them in motion.

Similar kinds of interconnections are established with *'apiryon ʿasa lo hamelech shᵊlomo meiʿatzei halᵊvanon: ʿamudav ʿasa cesef rᵊfidato zahav mercavo 'argaman, tocho ratzuf 'ahava mibᵊnot yᵊrushalayim* (3:9, 10). I would translate this—with a glance into a number of warring translations: "King Solomon made himself a palanquin/chariot/canopy/pavillion from the trees of Lebanon; its pillars he made silver with bases of gold, its couch purple, its midst paved with love from the daughters of Jerusalem." The gold pillars with silver bases are like the golden Torahs with their silver vowels . . . but the confusion within this structure between actual materials and metaphoric ones—what does it mean for a place to be paved with love?—further invites us to realize that the words are meant to set us moving. That's the reason I'm attached to the translations that insist that this structure is also a mode of transport, a palanquin, most likely, though the King James Version uses "chariot"—because it is both a site of lovemaking and itself a thing in motion, like the text that contains it. Solomon's making of it—the word *'asa*, "he made," appears twice—furthers the connection between the palanquin and the text, which, of course, is attributed in its first line to Solomon.

That this contraption is made of the trees of Lebanon enables me to introduce what I think is the most evocative and far-reaching use of sound in the poem: the triumvirate of words—two of which are used again and again—*l³vanon, l³vana, l³vona*—*l³vanon* is "Lebanon," *l³vana* is "moon," and *l³vona* is "frankincense," and all of them contain the word *lev*, "heart," and *lavan*, the "white" that both contrasts with the "black" of "black but comely" of the poem's fifth line and unites with it to describe writing. *L³vanon*/Lebanon is of course a specific earthly location; *l³vana*/moon is a celestial one—and *l³vona*/frankincense appears as a tree (*'atzai l³vona*) as defining a hillside (*givat l³vona*), and as burning insense (*miḳuteret mor ul³vona*) and so is partly of the earth, partly of the air. But my fifteen-year-old's confusion, my thinking I was reading about the moon when I was reading about frankincense, and constantly reading one of these words instead of another, was undeniably both accident and *beshert*. The sonic blurring among *l³vanon, l³vana,* and *l³vona* is surely intentional and meant to confuse and fuse the earthly, the celestial, and their perfumed meeting place, which is, surely, the poem itself. That *l³vanon—Lebanon*—is evoked as the origin of cedars (themselves both aromatic and solid), the source of precious water (*nozlim mil³vanon*) and the site of love (*'iti mil³vanon cala, 'iti mil³vanon tavoi*, "with me, from Lebanon, bride, with me from Lebanon, you'll come") makes it all by itself far-reaching. When it is mixed up with the moon, its reach vastly widens: *Mi z'ot hanishḳafah c³mo shachar, yafa cal³vona, bara cachamah 'ayumah canid³galot*, "Who is this, looking forth as the dawn, beautiful as the moon, "Who is this, that looking forth as the morning, clear as the sun, and terrible as"—thank God for Ariel and Chana Bloch—"the stars in their courses?" (6:10). The lover is every imaginable kind of celestial light: moon, sun, dawn, star. . . . The text insists on including every possibility, just as the poet insists, by likening love to *l³vana, l³vona,* and *l³vanon*, on evoking every region of the universe: the earth, the heavens, and the perfumed air that mediates them, all starting out from *lev*, "heart." The lover is himself likened to *l³vanon* : *Mareihu cal³vanon bachur ca'arazim*, "his countenance is like Lebanon, a youth like cedars."

The lover is thus made of the same material as Solomon's palanquin. The lovers/their love/the site of their love and the poem are all made of the same stuff, as well as the same sounds. His countenance is like *l^əva-naon*; hers like *l^əvana*. They, too, are variants on the same sounds, each starting out from the "heart."

When Shulamit is burning her frankincense, she is rising from the desert: *mi z'ot 'olah min hamidbar . . . m^əkuteret mor ul^əvonah*, "Who is this rising from the desert—burning myrrh and frankincense" (3:6) The word *midbar*, "desert," is also used in the poem for speech: *mid^əbarech naveh*, "your speech is comely" (4:3). She is herself *sh^əchorah v^ən'ava*, "black and comely." The comely lover rises out of the poet's comely speech. I suddenly wonder whether these people could possibly ever have existed outside of language. And I think to myself: You fool! Haven't you seen Janine's felt board? Of course they couldn't exist outside of language? How would they get around on legs like pillars of marble, set upon sockets of fine gold?

I used to be jealous of musicians when I read Pater's statement that music is the highest art because in it, form is indistinguishable from content. What the Song of Songs demonstrates is that poetry can achieve that same indivisibility. Not only does the poetic hold wildly varied elements together, it interchanges them through the sheer force of its sounds. The exhilaration set off by a poem that insists on including every aspect of the known world: architecture, landscape, animals, plants, arts and crafts—is achieved through the music that makes them so effortlessly not only belong together, but be one another. My confusion as I chanted turned out to be an introduction to poetic meaning of the most profound sort. Singing this song, I found out what poetry was capable of . . . and what can I tell you? I wanted to do that. Because I knew that the things I really cared to get at couldn't be approached any other way.

"WHERE HAS YOUR BELOVED GONE?": THE SONG OF SONGS IN CONTEMPORARY ISRAELI POETRY

Lesleigh Cushing Stahlberg

In an essay in this volume, Ellen Davis contests the predominant scholarly understanding that the Song of Songs gained its place within the canon entirely because the rabbis *mis*read the book, taking it not as a poem about human love, but as pertaining rather to the love of God and Israel. She contends that this scholarly view represents a misunderstanding, that in fact "the Song was correctly understood by those who accorded it a place among Israel's Scriptures."[1] Thus, in Davis's view, the Song "really is, in large part, about the love that obtains between God and Israel—or, more broadly, between God and humanity."[2] To read it only as a poem about human desire therefore is to misread it. Taking a divergent position, André LaCocque contends that while the Song may be about the love that obtains between God and Israel, it subverts the biblical understanding of the relationship between God and Israel because it "defigurativizes" the language of the prophets. Nonetheless, in this transposition, the erotic poem does not become wholly anthropocentric: LaCocque identifies in the Song "a dialectical quality," a "simultaneous play with flesh and spirit."[3] Arguably, it was this complex interplay of human elements with divine ones that drove the rabbis who fixed the canon to set the Song of Songs as the Holy of Holies of the Hebrew Bible.

As many of the works in this volume suggest, this interplay has also captured the imagination of generations of readers. We have seen a range of interpreters—from ancient rabbis, Jewish mystics, and medieval Christians to contemporary translators, feminists, and poets—grapple with the relationship between flesh and spirit in the Song. Some have asserted that the Song is to be taken literally, as a poem of the carnal; others, that it should be understood allegorically, as spiritual. Still others assert that the poem must always be understood as simultaneously literal and metaphorical. As I turn my attention from the ground already covered in this volume to a new matter—the poetic afterlife of the Song—it is this last possibility that most interests me.

The afterlife of the Song of Songs is rich indeed, and one could certainly write volumes on its place in literature, music, and art. Here, I will consider the Song as it recurs in the recent work of two contemporary Israeli poets: Admiel Kosman and Yehuda Amichai. Both Kosman and Amichai steep their poetry in biblical imagery, with which their upbringings made them intimate. However, Kosman's reworking of the Bible is often an inversion of it; Amichai's almost always a subversion.

One might describe their poems as midrashic—or at least, they share with the *Song of Songs Rabbah* "midrashic preservation of the binocular vision, the seeing both the *pᵊshat* (literal) and *sod* (allegorical) levels of meaning at the same time."[4] In the midrash on the Song, "when these [levels of meaning] are placed side by side then we have the exploration of human sexual desire and spiritual desire and the correlation of God's kiss and mouth and breath and word with the human word and breath."[5] In rather different ways, and to different ends, the same is true of the poems we will consider here.

Although these works are quite new (most have been published in English since 2000), all bear the weight of the last century. They are at once a response to the Bible and to the Holocaust, to the Promised Land of the Torah and the modern nation of Israel, to human meddling in history and divine intervention in human affairs. Thus the poems' connections to their biblical urtext has as much to do with allusion as affinity: All the poems draw phrases and images from the Song of Songs, but—more significantly—all negotiate between the disparate realms of flesh and spirit, just like the Song itself.

Moreover, both Kosman and Amichai's poems raise questions of how to read not only the Song of Songs, but the poems themselves. As these varied poems rooted in the Bible suggest, to read the Song only on its literal level is to misapprehend it. To use LaCocque's terminology, then, this contemporary Israeli poetry "defigurativizes" biblical language. It reenacts the very maneuvers LaCocque sees the Song itself as making.

In a first move, he claims, the author of the Song defigurativizes the language that the prophets typically use in describing the vertical relationship between God and Israel. In other words, she restores eros to the horizontal plane of love, where it is naturally enjoyed between lovers. It is on this plane that her refiguration must be read, for, in a second move, the author extols physical love, which she clothes in metaphors drawn from the realms of nature, courtship, luxury, and eroticism—all of which the prophets and sages by and large found objectionable. In summary, LaCocque says, language has come full circle. It begins on the horizontal plane of daily parlance, where the prophets found it in the first place; it moves then to the vertical plane via a radical, ad hoc metaphorization; finally, it returns to the horizontal by means of a poetic reclamation and refiguration.[6]

In the case of the modern poems, of course, there is an added layer. They defigurativize the language of the Song, which is itself a defigurativization of the language of the prophets. They take the Song, which shifts from human to divine to human, and emphasize its human aspects. The poetry I consider lifts words and images from ancient Israel and sets them down in the modern nation, gaining meaning through the dislocation. Often the new meaning has as much to do with the dis-figuring of the human-divine aspect of the biblical Song as with the transposition to a modern setting, and this is the most compelling aspect of this new round of "poetic reclamation and refiguration."

Our first poem, by Admiel Kosman, is only loosely intertextual. The only explicit—and unambiguous—allusion to the biblical text is its title: "The Song of Songs." A few isolated words are pulled from the Bible; a few phrases suggest its urtext. "Whither does one go" recalls the "whither has your beloved gone" of Song 6:1. The speaker's timid query, "How is love in the south? Do explain, how is she in the north?" is a distant echo of the woman's assertive cry, "Awake, O north wind, Come O south wind!" (4:6). And yet this poem is, ostensibly, another Song of Songs:

How does it work in love, do explain, how does it work?
How is love in the south? Do explain, and how is she in the north?
Please tell how she is in the villages, in the suburbs, in the city?
Whence and whither does one go, and how does one exit? And
    what does one breathe,
get up, go, lie down? Do explain to us, please
we, the new neighbours above, we do not know.

How does it work in love, do explain, how is it in the cold?
In the heat? How does it come with the air? From where does it
    enter in the morning,
evening, noon? And what does one breathe? From
which part of the city? And how does one do it with two hands?
    From which

part of the poem? Do explain to us, please,
we, the new neighbours above, we do not know.[7]

The tone of the poem is at once playful and earnest, reflecting a naï-
veté absent in the biblical Song. There, the lovers know precisely how
love works: Their problem is ensuring that they are able to work their
love again. Here, however, the question is how one enacts the Song of
Songs. We have the necessary ingredients, the new neighbors seem to ask,
but how exactly do we make love? Their problem, of course, is the opposite of the one ascribed to the rabbis: They are taking the biblical Song at
the literal level (*pᵊshat*) only. They want the Song to explain how they
should admit love into their bed. More absurdly, they want the Song to
be a sex manual; they want it to teach them where and how to place their
hands.

Like the rabbis (as understood by contemporary academics) or the
contemporary academics (as understood by Davis), the neighbours are
*mis*readers of the poem. They do not understand that the Song *must* be
read on multiple levels simultaneously. In this respect, the poem is both
whimsical and cautionary. It gently teases the neighbors while warning
its own readers about the complexities of the act of reading. Reading
well, as LaCocque would have it, is a dialectical process: It demands a
willingness to engage multiple meanings at once.

In "A New Commentary with God's Help," another poem with subtle
resonances of the Song, Kosman speaks to the importance of reading on
different levels at once. The poem is a commentary on a woman's breasts,
which are not the "two fawns, twins of a gazelle" (Song 4:5), "clusters of
fruit" (7:7, 7:8), or "towers" (8:10) of the Song, but rather are "leaves, with
clear light between branches" (l.7).[8] The speaker asserts:

I'm writing now, with God's help, a new commentary on your
    breasts.
A dear and blessed composition. . . .
A lovely *midrash*, an ancient compilation, delicate and soft, between
    my two lips is bound." (ll. 1–3)

This composition he presents "by way of hint, literal sense, and homiletics
and hidden meaning" (l. 4)—the four levels of scriptural meaning (*pᵊshat*,
remez, *dᵊrash*, and *sod*). Kosman is not only a poet, but a professor of
Talmud. His life's work is uncovering the interplay of meanings in traditional Jewish texts. Thus, his poem, a midrash both on the woman's
breasts and on the Song, aspires to engage different levels simultaneously,
like the Song itself.

To read these levels simultaneously requires sophistication. In the poem cycle "The Bible and You, The Bible and You, and Other Midrashim," Yehuda Amichai warns against conflating the levels of meaning. Part 18 of the poem outlines the perils of reading the metaphorical literally:

The singer of the Song of Songs sought his beloved so long and
    hard
that he lost his mind and went looking for her with a simile map
and fell in love with the images he himself had imagined.
He went down to Egypt, for he had written "to a mare among
    Pharaoh's chariots
I compare thee," and he went up to Gilead to see her flowing hair,
for he had written "Thy hair is like a flock of goats flowing down
Mount Gilead," and he went up to the Tower of David, for it says
"Like the tower of David is thy neck," and he got as far as Lebanon
    and found
no peace, for it says "Thy nose is like the Tower of Lebanon that
    looks
out toward Damascus," and he wept by the waterfalls
of Ein Gedi, for he had written "Many waters cannot extinguish
this love," and he went looking for doves in Bet Guvrin
and got all the way to Venice, for he had written "My dove in the
    clefts of the rock."
And he dashed off to the desert, for it says "Who is that rising
from the desert like pillars of smoke." And the Bedouin thought
he was one of the crazy prophets, and he thought
he was King Solomon. And he is still wandering, a fugitive and a
    vagabond
with the mark of Love on his forehead. And sometimes he happens
    upon
the loves of other couples in other times; he even got as far as our
    home
with its broken roof on the border between Jerusalem
and Jerusalem. And we never even saw him because we
were in each other's arms. He is still wandering, shouting
"You are beautiful, my bride," as if from within a deep sack
of oblivion. And whoever wrote "Love is as fierce as death"—
he understood his own simile only at the end,
understood and loved and died.[9]

Here, in a rather different way than in Kosman's "Song of Songs," the literal level of the text is rendered meaningless. The poem indicates the words of the Song are merely words—products of the author's mind— and do not point to a physical world beyond the text: In this telling, the singer of the Song *imagined* a series of images (l. 3). When he sought these images, he failed to look for the woman whom they describe. Instead, he set off in search of the vehicle, rather than the tenor, of his own metaphors. In this respect, the literal level effaces the metaphorical, and the result is catastrophic. The singer's misapprehension of his own poem led to his decline. First, he lost his mind (l. 2), and was mistaken for "one of the crazy prophets" (l. 16). Next, he lost his identity, believing "he was King Solomon" (l. 17), to whom he ascribed his own poem. Devoid of sanity and self, he became, like Cain, a marked wanderer—"a fugitive and a vagabond"—who could find no peace (ll. 17–18). Finally, however, he "understood his own simile," (l. 25) and corrected his misreading. At the end of his life, at last, he "understood and loved and died" (l. 26).

The hermeneutics here are complex. The poem suggests that we cannot read the Song literally: We must understand it metaphorically. The metaphorical level, however, does not push us beyond the text to a spiritual level, as Davis would have it. Rather, a proper awareness of the figurative points us not to the divine, but back to the human. Here, Amichai lines up with LaCocque, who sees the Song as a refutation of the earlier biblical texts to which it responds. It takes the praise and devotion directed at God in the Bible and transfers it to a human.[10] According the LaCocque, in transposing desire from the vertical axis (God-human) to the horizontal one (human-human) the Song subverts the biblical tradition.[11] Likewise Amichai, whose poetry is marked by an insistence on reversing the place of the finite and the infinite, on placing "the human before the divine."[12] In this poem, he strips the Song of allegory: The images do not point to the divine. The poem seems to say, contra Davis, that the Song really is *not*, in large part, about the love that obtains between God and Israel. It is about human love, and a misunderstood human love, at that.

One can push the poem so that it yields a spiritual meaning, and to do so is to become immersed in Amichai's own complex theology.[13] Raised an Orthodox Jew, Amichai struggled relentlessly with the idea of God. Many of his poems suggest that, while God had once existed, he was no longer present to his chosen people. Others go so far as to say that God had never existed at all. He responded to the traditional Jewish credo "'Ani ma'amin" (I believe) with a poem called "Ha'ani lo ha'amin sheli"

(My "I don't believe").[14] His constant wrestling with the im/possibility of God was always articulated in the language of the tradition, however:[15] Amichai's poems draw from the Bible, the prayer book, the Talmud. Amichai's Song of Songs was the Song as understood by the rabbis. In their reading, God is the beloved and Israel the lover. If these values are transposed into Amichai's poem, Israel the lover has created God the beloved, and has "[fallen] in love with the images he had imagined" (l. 3). The quest for the beloved will always be futile, because the beloved is but a figment, a manifestation of the lover's own desire.

This highly unorthodox perspective recurs throughout Amichai's poetry. Amichai's God is often a human creation, and Amichai's vertical axis often positions humans above God. Responding once again to "'Ani ma'amin," the creed based on Maimonides' thirteen principles of faith, Amichai opened a poem in his final collection with a direct invocation of the prayer's beginning: "I believe with perfect faith." This poem, part 3 of "Gods Change, Prayers Are Here to Stay," begins:

> I declare with perfect faith
> that prayer preceded God. Prayer created God
> God created human beings,
> human beings create prayers
> that create the God that creates human beings.[16]

Contrary to the narrative of Genesis, God did not speak the world into being: Prayers spoke God into being.

God is not always a human product, however. In other instances, God is not only distinct from humans, but wholly inaccessible to them. This elusive God is a recurring figure in Amichai's poetry. Chana Bloch has noted that "the God in these poems, who at times seems no more than a figure of speech, deeply embedded in the language, makes his presence strongly felt even in his absence."[17] Two other poems in *Open Closed Open* culminate in descriptions of a God who cannot be found by those who think themselves his chosen people. Part 23 of "Gods Change, Prayers Are Here to Stay" is a lament:

> From the crematoria of Auschwitz, black smoke rises—
> a sign the conclave of God has not yet chosen
> the Chosen People.
> After Auschwitz, no theology:
> the numbers on the forearms
> of the inmates of extermination

are the telephone numbers of God,
numbers that do not answer
and now are disconnected, one by one.[18]

God here is unreachable. Even those people who thought they were his have no access to him: The numbers on their arms are reminders of his pervasive absence. To invoke LaCocque's image of axis once again: The orientation of the axis may in fact be less significant than the recognition that the human and the divine are at opposing poles.

As Part 5 of "Gods Change" attests, God is at a great distance from people:

When God packed up and left the country, he left the Torah
with the Jews. They have been looking for Him ever since,
shouting, "Hey you forgot something, you forgot,"
and other people think shouting is the prayer of the Jews.
Since then, they've been combing the Bible for hints of his
    whereabouts,
as it says: "Seek ye the Lord while He may be found, call ye
upon Him while He is near." But He is far away.[19]

The great gulf between humans and God is insurmountable. Like the singer of the Song of Songs in the poem with which we began our discussion of Amichai, the Israelites turn to the Bible as a road map. Having misplaced their God, they seek him through Scripture. What they do not seem to understand is that he will not be found. The point is underscored in "Jewish Travel: Change is God and Death is His Prophet":

That's why
. . . [the Jews] call their God *Maḳom*, "Place."
And now that they have returned to their place, the Lord has taken
    up
wandering to different places, and His name will no longer be Place
but Places, Lord of the Places.[20]

The people have returned to Israel, but the Lord has become the itinerant wanderer. No amount of seeking will reveal his location.

This message is consonant with much of Amichai's work. There are physical remnants of God's presence—these are as disparate as numbers tattooed on arms and the Holy Bible—but God himself is far away. The poems show Amichai's theology at work. He is on a quest for "a God he stopped believing in long ago."[21] That he does not believe in God is not to say there is no God, however. Rather, the cause for unbelief is not the nonexistence of God, but his pervasive nonpresence.

In light of this perceived absence, the Song of Songs is a perfect scripture for Amichai: It expresses continual longing for an unattainable beloved. In Davis's view, the Song "returns us to Eden with the intent of imaginatively healing the ruptures that occur there: between man and woman, between humanity and God, between human and nonhuman creation."[22] For Amichai, by contrast, it is a reminder of the continued rupture between humanity and God. The Song is about memory of union; much of Amichai's poetry about God explores a relationship that exists only in memory. It laments the loss of a moment long ago when God was active in history. The questions that punctuate the Song—Have you seen the one I love? (3:3); Where has your beloved gone? (6:1)—are questions to be posed on the vertical axis. These are the questions we ask of a silent God.

These are questions Amichai asked—overtly and obliquely— throughout his life. Consider, finally, his selective use of the Bible in poem 29 of his 1978 collection, *Time*:

> From the Scroll of Esther, I filtered out the sediment
> Of vulgar joy, and from the Book of Jeremiah
> The wailing of pain in your guts. And from
> The Song of Songs, the endless search
> Of love, and from Genesis
> The dreams and Cain, and from Ecclesiastes
> The despair, and from the Book of Job, Job.
> And from the leftovers, I pasted together a new Bible for myself.
> I live censored, pasted, limited, in peace.
>
> One woman asked me yesterday in a dark
> Street about the health of another woman
> Who died before her time, or anybody's time.
> In great weariness I answered:
> She's fine, she's fine.[23]

Faced with untimely death, with the sorrow of outliving, Amichai finds no solace in Scripture. Or at least, not in Scripture as we know it. Rather, he censors the canon, cuts and pastes himself a new one. In his filtering, Amichai creates a human Bible, one that deals with desire and joy, pain and despair, only on the horizontal axis. There would seem to be no room for God in this work, certainly not for a God who allows those too young to die. And so, when Amichai includes the Song of Songs in his new Bible, one assumes that it is to be understood exclusively as a song of human love.

However, Amichai characterizes the Song as "an endless search of love," and the adjective gives us pause: why "endless"? Many of Amichai's poems are love poems: Love comes easily to this writer. At least, human love does. But does the endlessness of the search imply a vertical axis, a quest for "the God of his unbelief"? Haunted by this God he no longer believes in, Amichai cannot abandon the "endless search of love" for him.

The issue of God's absence, his unattainability, surfaces again in our last poem. Were a current Israeli newspaper and a Song of Songs concordance to couple, the offspring might closely resemble Kosman's, "I Told the Jerusalem City Watchman." Sprinkled amid modern terms such as "walkie-talkie," "photo," "identity document," "cordless or mobile phone," and "barbed wire," we find abundant words from the Song: "Jerusalem," "city," "watchman," "guard," "mountain," "land," "gate," "heart," "beloved," "bed," "walls," and "listen." Kosman makes the Song contemporary, transposing its images onto the physical and political landscape of modern Jerusalem. This move is enabled by a literal understanding of the biblical poem: Its specific signs are understood to have concrete referents. In this account, then, it is the watchmen at the city walls who threaten to keep the couple apart: The lover cannot procure the documents he needs in order to gain access to his beloved. Kosman conceals the identities of the lovers—are they Jews? Arabs? A combination?—and focuses on the obstacles between them. From behind the barbed wire at the outskirts of the city, the lover speculates about his "beauty / sleeping now" (ll. 42–43) behind the walls, "already dripping with frankincense / and myrrh" (ll. 53–54).

> I told the Jerusalem city watchman that my beloved lives here.
> But I didn't have any proof. I forgot everything,
> my name and my place of origin,
> the name of my mountainous country
> and the site of the distant and foreign land
> from which I came to the gates of the city
> where she rests
> in tranquility,
> my beloved!
>
> I told the Jerusalem city watchman that my beloved lives here.
> The Jerusalem city watchman consulted, on his walkie-talkie,

the guard outside the Gate of Water, but
oh no! I wasn't carrying my papers!
I had only two tablets,
two tablets of a loving heart,
of a loving heart, very heavy,
made of marble.

What am I to do?
Please tell me, my watchmen,
good watchmen, guards, defenders of the city,
good old boys.
I didn't have a photo in my pocket,
nor a paper document,

only iron certificates,
certificates in stone,
crumbling historical limestone documents.

Watchmen! Guards of the Western Wall!
My watchmen! Guards of the city
where she rests now
in her bed
in tranquility
my beloved!

You, you—watchmen devoted to your task,
deployed now at the portals in the walls.
Listen, listen,
I'm calling on you for help
from the outskirts of the city.

Could you please
just wake her
up—just for a minute—
my beauty—

my beauty
sleeping now
in tranquility
inside my city, mine,
in her bed?

Please, one of you guards of the city of Jerusalem,
Call to her! Wake her up! With a cordless or a mobile phone!
Watchers of the city, heroes and soldiers!
Please, please, call to her
to come to me right now.

Perhaps she's ready?
Perhaps she's already dripping with frankincense
and myrrh?

And wrapped—
for me alone—
in a night-
gown?

Perhaps I'll see
her,
now?
Perhaps she'll lift her glance
to me—

from behind barbed wire?[24]

At first glance, it seems that Kosman uses imagery from the Song of Songs and layers a political dimension rather than a religious one onto the poem about lovers desiring union. (In the modern Jerusalem, where Kosman's poem is set, the political and the religious are, of course, inextricable.) On the literal level, the barriers between the lovers—watchmen, walls, distance—are physical, just as they are in a literal understanding of the Song. And more than the other poems we will consider here, the imagery conspires to keep us at the literal level. It is mired in the quotidian details of the modern Jerusalemite: struggles with guards, checkpoints, papers, documents. That this poem might have to do with a life beyond this one, with the relationship between God and humans, seems remote.

When we recall, however, the acute awareness of the layered meanings of texts evident in Kosman's "A New Commentary with God's Help," we are prompted to reconsider the poem. It is a concrete image that cues us to the possibility of a spiritual resonance. Speaking to the Jerusalem city watchmen, the lover realizes with a start, "Oh no! I wasn't carrying my papers!" (l. 13) In place of the documents he needs to enter the city, he has instead "only two tablets, / two tablets of a loving heart" (ll. 14–15).

These *shᵊnei luchot* recall, of course, the tablets of the law that Moses carried to the people Israel. God himself decreed that his people set upon their hearts the commandments (Deut. 6:6), and the imagery here marries the tablets to the heart as in Deuteronomy. The command is God's way of ensuring that his people not forget the law. The irony here, of course, is that despite carrying tablets on/of the heart, the lover cannot remember. The mnemonic device, the inscription of God's word onto the self, has a Lethean effect, however: The lover no longer remembers who he is. He tells the Jerusalem city watchman that his "beloved lives here," but he can offer no proof: He has forgotten "everything, his "name and place of origin" as well as "the name of [his] mountainous country . . . from which [he] came to the gates of the city" (ll. 2–6).

The temporary amnesia, the loss of identity, means that the speaker is denied access not only to the literal beloved, the woman who "rests / in tranquility," his "beloved" (ll. 7–9), but to two figurative beloveds, as well. The first is the gated city itself, which the speaker describes in the same possessive terms he uses for the woman he loves:

> my beauty
> sleeping now
> in tranquility
> inside my city, mine,
> in her bed?

The woman is his; the city is his. And yet he can enter neither. Moreover, that he is barred from the woman and the city alike means that he is also kept from a third beloved: God.

The city—ostensibly *his* city—is not any city at all, but Jerusalem, the city of God (cf. Pss. 46, 48, 87). The physical obstacles that result from the political situation therefore have religious implications: A man who cannot enter Jerusalem cannot encounter his God. The inaccessible beloved is arguably the Beloved, who cannot hear the cries (prayers?) of the lover beyond the wall. The only hope of connection is through chance: the speaker wonders, "Perhaps she'll lift her glance / to me— / from behind barbed wire?" (ll. 62–64). Unlike in the Song of Songs, the beloved here—as the woman, the city, the divine—is oblivious to the lover's desire for connection. This poem about the frustrations of living in a fortified city thus can also be seen as articulating the frustrations of dealing with an absent God.

Like the Song of Songs, then, the poem can also be iconic. As Davis explains, "The icon is a window opening between two worlds: the world of history and ordinary sense perception, on the one hand, and on the other, the transcendent realm we designate as 'heaven,' 'eternal life,' 'the kingdom of God.'"[25] Kosman's walkie-talkie, photo document, cordless phone, and barbed wire belong to the world of ordinary sense perception. Likewise, the inaccessible modern city of Jerusalem. However, when we understand Jerusalem also to be the Jerusalem of the Song and of the Psalms, we see that the ordinary woman whom the watchmen will not rouse also points to another world. When Jerusalem becomes the city of God, it is the Lord who sleeps through the cries of the lover. Suddenly, Kosman's poem—like Amichai's—belongs equally to the transcendent realm as to the world of history.

Davis characterized the debate over the nature of the Song thus: "Where LaCocque hears deliberate irreverence, rebellion against the tradition, I hear adoration—that is, prayer—in a distinctly traditional mode."[26] We can hear in the poems of Admiel Kosman and Yehuda Amichai deliberate rebellion that makes use of (though not without irony) the scriptural legacy. Amichai in particular offers prayer in a traditional mode, as does Davis's Song. His rebellion lies in the fact that he offers prayers to a God who may have abandoned his people. Kosman's God is the God of Jerusalem, a remote God sequestered behind city walls. The pleas of his people do not reach him. The poems remain in a traditional mode because they have not banished God. Their rebellion lies in the fact that they suggest that God has vanished.

And yet, both poets continue to speak to their elusive God. As post-Holocaust prophets of a new Israel, their cry is different from their biblical predecessors'. They do not insist, as Jeremiah did, "I will not mention Him, / No more will I speak His name" (Jer. 20:9) because they feel too strongly the pull to speak of God to which the agonized prophet succumbed. Jeremiah gave in: his word "was like a raging fire in my heart, / Shut up in my bones; I could not hold it in, I was helpless" (Jer. 20:9). So, too, Amichai and Kosman: their God, though absent, continues to assert himself on their speech. He is gone, but he will not leave them alone.

Ultimately, then, the dialectic quality of these poems is as complex as that of their inspiration. Like their biblical parent text, the modern-day songs can be heard to speak at once of flesh and spirit, continuing the "midrashic preservation of the binocular vision." We cannot eliminate the possibility that, like the Song, they maneuver simultaneously along the divine-human vertical axis and the human-human horizontal axes. And, perhaps in their greatest affinity with the Song, they are ambiguous in their relationship to tradition. They use the familiar language of the Bible to address a God who has become unfamiliar. The once intimate beloved has become foreign, remote; the lover seeks her in earnest. While they are certainly skeptical and sometimes ironic, these contemporary poems ask a genuine question: Where has the beloved gone?

NOTES

"All That You Say, I Will Do" / Ellen F. Davis

1. Karl Barth, *The Word of God and the Word of Man*, trans. Douglas Horton (New York: Harper and Bros., 1957), 92.

2. See Walter Brueggemann's comment on the Psalms and other texts that reflect liturgical affirmations of God's power: "The new tales based in the credibility of concreteness lead to a different world." *Israel's Praise: Doxology against Idolatry and Ideology* (Philadelphia: Fortress Press, 1988), 86.

3. The Hebrew records variant readings, both with or without "to me."

Beginning with Ruth / Ellen F. Davis

1. Ellen F. Davis and Margaret Adams Parker, *Who Are You, My Daughter?: Reading Ruth through Image and Text* (Louisville: Westminster John Knox, 2003).

2. Ronald Knox, *On Englishing the Bible* (London: Burns Oates, 1949), 94.

3. I consulted the New Revised Standard Version; the New Jewish Publication Society's *JPS Hebrew-English Tanakh: The Traditional Hebrew Text and the New JPS Translation*, 2d. ed. (Philadelphia: Jewish Publication Society, 2003); Richard Elliott Friedman, *Commentary on the Torah* (San Francisco: HarperCollins, 2001; and Everett Fox, *The Five Books of Moses* (New York: Schocken, 1995).

4. See page 5 above.

5. "Knows" is singular in Hebrew and deliberately so in English.

6. See both the New Revised Standard Version and the Jewish Publication Society translation.

7. It is likely that Proverbs reflects the social situation in the *post*monarchic (postexilic) period, when for a second time Israel-Judah found itself without king and temple and a centralized social structure.

8. Since the ordering of the Writings, the third part of the Jewish canon, varies to some degree, Ruth sometimes but not always follows Proverbs directly.

9. George Steiner, *Real Presences*, the Leslie Stephen Memorial Lecture, November 1, 1985 (Cambridge: Cambridge University Press, 1986), 18.

10. Hannah and Abigail both refer to themselves thus in speaking to Eli and David, respectively (1 Sam. 1:16, 1 Sam. 25:24, 25, etc.).

Subverting the Biblical World / André LaCoque

1. Phyllis Bird, "Images of Women in the Old Testament," in *The Bible and Liberation: Political and Social Hermeneutics*, ed. Norman K. Gottwald, (Maryknoll, N.Y.: Orbis Books, 1983), 260.

2. Carol L. Meyers, "The Roots of Restriction: Women in the Early Israel," in *The Bible and Liberation*, 295.

3. Ibid., 302.

4. Oswald Loretz, "The Theme of the Ruth Story," in *CBQ* 22 (1960): 391–99.

5. Most probably, the author of Ruth was a woman. The whole story imposes a shift of perspective from male to female. From beginning to end, the author sheds a positive light upon women, while the males remain largely anonymous. In the case of Boaz, the best man of his generation, the male responds to the extraordinary that is embodied in the female characters. Boaz never steps onto the center stage. His part in the narrative never sidetracks the feminine complex Naomi/Ruth. The story is not Boaz's, but Ruth's and Naomi's. Obed is "son to Naomi." For all practical purposes, Boaz disappears after begetting a son. The Midrash concludes that he died during the wedding night. On this, see my *The Feminine Unconventional: Four Subversive Figures in Israel's Tradition*, Overtures in Biblical Theology (Minneapolis: Fortress Press, 1990) and my commentary on Ruth from the same press (2004).

6. For a full discussion of the "setting in life" of Ruth, see my Ruth commentary.

7. Furthermore, "So-and-so" is under no legal obligation to Ruth the Moabite. Boaz goes beyond the demands of Torah, a step that the Talmud calls going *liphᵊnim mishurat haddīn*.

8. *Megillat Pesharim*.

9. Concerning the Baal Peor event of Numbers 25: Because it would have been improper for women to meet travelers in the desert, the Talmud finds only the Moabite males to be guilty of an offense to Israel. This argument is untenable in regard to the biblical tradition, however.

10. So say *Yebamot* 47b; *Ruth Rabbah* 1.4.

11. Nelson Glueck, *Hesed in the Bible* (Cincinnati: Hebrew Union Press, 1967).

12. Significantly, the story ends with a genealogy.

13. Søren Kierkegaard's "teleological suspension of the ethical" comes to mind. See my discussion of this point in *Thinking Biblically* (with Paul Ricoeur), chapter 2 on Exodus 20:13. (Chicago: University of Chicago Press, 1998).

14. Harold Fisch, "Ruth and the Structure of Covenant History," in *VT* 32, no. 4 (1982): 431.

15. In a similar way, another biblical heroine, Esther, is the redemptive recapitulation of 1 Samuel 15 and Judith of Genesis 34, to take only examples of females.

16. See Eliahu ki Tob, *Midrash Sepher Hattorah*; *Ruth Rabbah* 8.1.

17. Joseph Blenkinsopp, *Isaiah 1–39: A New Translation with Introduction and Commentary*, Anchor Bible 19a. (New York: Doubleday, 2000), 364.

The Book of Ruth as Comedy / Nehama Aschkenasy

1. See E. F. Campbell's introduction to the Anchor Bible edition of *Ruth* (Garden City, N.Y.: Doubleday, 1975), 5, 6–9.

2. I choose to hypothesize about Aristotle's view of comedy on the basis of his theory of tragedy as presented in the *Poetics*; see Aristotle, *The Poetics*, in *Aristotle on Poetry and Style*, trans. G. M. A. Gruss, (New York: Bobbs Merrill, 1958), 5–100. All references to the *Poetics* here are to this edition. I have also adopted some of the views offered by scholars who have attempted to reconstruct Aristotle's definition of comedy from the *Poetics* and the *Tractatus coislinianus*, attributed to Aristotle. See Richard Janko, *Aristotle on Comedy: Towards a Reconstruction of Poetics II* (Berkeley: University of California Press, 1984) and Dana F. Sutton, *The Catharsis of Comedy* (Boston: Rowman and Littlefield, 1984).

3. Northrop Frye, *Anatomy of Criticism* (Princeton: Princeton University Press, 1957), 163, 178. See especially Frye's theory of comedy in the chapter "The Mythos of Spring: Comedy," 163–86.

4. Dorothea Krook, *Elements of Tragedy* (New Haven: Yale University Press, 1969), 8–18.

5. Frye, *Anatomy*, 218.

6. Henri Bergson, "Laughter," in *Comedy*, ed. Wylie Sypher (Garden City, N.Y.: Doubleday, 1956), 121.

7. Northrop Frye, *A Natural Perspective: The Development of Shakespearean Comedy and Romance* (New York: Columbia University Press, 1965), 73.

8. Frye, *Anatomy*, 171; see also Caesar J. Barber, *Shakespeare's Festive Comedy* (Princeton: Princeton University Press, 1959), 15, 36.

9. On the affinities between these stories in terms of their genealogical links, literary motifs, and cultural practices, see Harold Fisch, "Ruth and the Structure of Covenantal History," *Vetus Testamentum*, 32, no. 4 (1982): 425–37, also Nehama Aschkenasy, *Eve's Journey: Feminine Images in Hebraic Literary Tradition* (Philadelphia: University of Pennsylvania Press, 1986), 85–88.

10. See Robert S. Miola, "Roman Comedy," in *Shakespearean Comedy*, ed. Alexander Leggatt (Cambridge: Cambridge University Press, 2002), 22.

11. See Krook, "The Scheme of Tragedy," in *Elements of Tragedy*, 8–34.

12. See Nehama Aschkenasy, "Language as Female Empowerment in Ruth," in *Reading Ruth: Contemporary Women Reclaim a Sacred Text*, ed. Judith A. Kates

and Gail Twersky-Reimer (New York: Ballantine, 1994), 111–24; see also my *Woman at the Window: Feminine Images in Hebraic Literary Tradition* (Detroit: Wayne State University Press, 1998), 146–56.

13. With regard to Orpah, who leaves the story early on, we may say that her synecdochic name is the first hint of the comic in the story, for we will now forever see her not as a full human being, but as a "back of the neck" (*oreph*) disappearing into the horizon. And indeed, tradition related Orpah's name to her actions. Even earlier, Naomi's sons' rhyming names, Machlon and Kilyon, with the macabre meaning "illness" and "demise," introduce a shade of black humor to the story. For more on Orpah's name, see Campbell's introduction to the Anchor Bible edition of Ruth, 55.

14. See Miola, "Roman Comedy," 18; also, John Creaser, "Forms of Confusion," in *Shakespearean Comedy*, 82.

15. Bergson, "Laughter," 79–86.

16. Frye, *Anatomy*, 172–75.

17. Ibid., 173.

18. Ibid., 172.

19. The three citations are from Bergson, "Laughter," 111, 135, and 93 respectively.

20. Creaser, "Forms of Confusion," 82–83.

21. Frye, *Anatomy*, 165.

22. On the festive ending of comedy, see Frye, *A Natural Perspective*, 128–30.

23. Shimon Levy studies the theatrical aspects of Ruth and its potential for stage performance, but does not go into genre analysis. Although his chapter on Ruth paraphrases a famous Shakespearean title, he does not recognize the comedic elements of the tale. See "Ruth: The Shrew-ing of the Tame," in *The Bible as Theatre* (Brighton: Sussex Academic Press, 2000), 82–103.

24. See Sigmund Freud, *Jokes and Their Relation to the Unconscious*, trans. James Strachey (New York: Norton, 1963).

25. See Mikhail Bakhtin, *Rabelais and His World*, trans. Helene Iswolsky (Cambridge, Mass.: MIT Press, 1968) and *The Dialogic Imagination*, trans. Caryl Emerson and Michael Holquist (Austin: University of Texas Press, 1981).

26. On this aspect of Ruth, see E. F. Campbell's comments on Ruth in the Anchor Bible edition, 26.

Transfigured Night / Judith Kates

1. Translations of *Ruth Rabbah* are from *Midrash Rabbah*, trans. L. Rabinowitz (London: Soncino Press, 1983).

2. Phrases taken from *The Reason of Church Government* and *Paradise Lost* 1.

3. Avivah Zornberg "The Concealed Alternative," in *Reading Ruth: Contemporary Women Reclaim a Sacred Story*, ed. Judith A. Kates and Gail Twersky Reimer (New York: Ballantine, 1994). All subsequent references to Zornberg come from this essay.

Dark Ladies and Redemptive Compassion / Nehemia Polen

1. Outside the land of Israel, Shavuot is observed as a two-day festival, and Ruth is read before Torah on the second day, but the basic point is the same.

2. Translations of biblical verses are based on Jewish Publication Society 1999 translation.

3. Rolf Rendtorff, *Canon and Theology*, trans. and ed. Margaret Kohl (Edinburgh: T and T Clark, 1993), 53.

4. Ibid., 60.

5. The quote follows the version found in *Bereshit Rabbah*, 3 vols., ed. Julius Theodor and Chanock Albeck (Jerusalem: Warhmann, 1965), 2:1031.

6. Ibid., 2:537–38.

7. See Rashi's comment on the passage; see also Shabbat 113b.

8. Zohar 1:187b–188b.

9. This Zohar builds upon an enigmatic Talmudic passage in Sanhedrin 107a.

10. Tikva Frymer-Kensky, *Reading the Women of the Bible* (New York: Schocken, 2002), 263.

11. Gershom Scholem *The Messianic Idea in Judaism and Other Essays on Jewish Spirituality* (New York: Schocken, 1971).

12. Gershom Scholem, *Sabbatai Sevi: The Mystical Messiah* (Princeton: Princeton University Press, 1973), p. 810.

13. Rabbi Zadok ha-Kohen of Lublin, *Sefer Tzidkat ha-Tzadik* (Jerusalem: 'A' Publishers, 1968), p. 68.

14. Ellen Davis reminds us that Elijah alludes to the "still small voice." Ruth can be thought of as the still small voice in the canon.

Ruth amid the Gentiles / Peter S. Hawkins

1. *The Complete Poems of John Keats* (New York: Modern Library, 1994).

2. "The seventh stanza of Keats' 'Ode to a Nightingale' [is] famous for an unexpected allusion to the Book of Ruth and for a peculiar resistance to criticism." Andrew J. Kappel, "The Immortality of the Natural: Keats' 'Ode to a Nightingale,'" *ELH* 54, no. 2 (Summer, 1978), 270. Helen Vendler's magisterial reading of the poem in *The Odes of John Keats* (Cambridge, Mass.: The Belknap Press of Harvard University Press, 1983), 77–109, shows no interest in the difference between the situation of Keats's Ruth and the Bible's account.

3. All citations of the Bible are from *The New Oxford Annotated Bible, NRSV with Apocrypha*, 3rd ed. (Oxford: Oxford University Press, 2001).

4. Julia Kristeva, in *Strangers to Ourselves*, trans. Leon S. Roudiez (New York: Columbia University Press, 1991), says of David's dubious Moabite lineage, "[David's] ancestor Ruth the foreigner is there to remind those unable to read that the divine revelation often requires a lapse, the acceptance of radical otherness, the recognition of a foreignness that one might have tended at the very first to

consider the most degraded. This was not an encouragement to deviate or prose-lytize but an invitation to consider the fertility of the other. Such indeed is the role of Ruth—the outsider, the foreigner, the excluded" (75).

5. For a superb study of Matthew's genealogy, see Raymond E. Brown, *The Birth of the Messiah: A Commentary on the Infancy Narratives in Matthew and Luke* (Garden City, N.Y.: Doubleday, 1977), 57–95.

6. All citations of the *Commedia* are from *Dante Alighieri, The Divine Comedy*, trans. with a commentary, by Charles S. Singleton, Bollingen Series 80, 3 vols. of text and 3 of commentary (Princeton: Princeton University Press, 1970–75). For a discussion of the Hebrew women as "types of the Church," see Giuseppe C. Di Scipio, "The Hebrew Women in the Heavenly Rose," DSARTS 101 (1983): 111–21, esp. 118–19.

7. John Chrysostom, "Homilies on the Gospel of Saint Matthew," in *A Select Library of the Christian Church: Nicene and Post-Nicene Fathers*, ed. Philip Schaff, first series (New York: The Christian Literature Company, 1886–1890), vol. 10, Homily 3: "It is then for this reason that both Joseph has his genealogy traced, and the Virgin betrothed to him. For even if he, who was both a just and won-drous man, required many things, in order that he should receive that which had come to pass; an angel, and the vision in dreams, and the testimony of the proph-ets; how could the Jews, being of so unfriendly spirit towards Him, have admit-ted this idea into their minds? For the strangeness and novelty thereof would be sure greatly to disturb them, and the fact that they had never so much as heard of such a thing having happened in the time of the forbearers" (15).

8. Jerome, cited in Thomas Aquinas, *Catena Aurea: Commentary on the Four Gospels Collected out of the Fathers*, vol. 1, part 1, Saint Matthew (1842; Albany, N.Y.: Preserving Christian Publications, Inc., 1998), 19–20.

9. Chrysostom, "Homilies," 15–16.

10. Ibid., 16.

11. Ambrose, *Exposition on Luke 3*, cited by Aquinas, *Catena Aurea*, 21–22 and found in its entirety in PL 15, cols. 1589A–1612C. For a contemporary con-sideration of Ambrose's "revelry" in the impropriety of Jesus' foremothers, see F. Scott Spencer, *Dancing Girls, Loose Ladies, and Women of the Cloth: The Women in Jesus' Life* (New York: Continuum, 2004), 24–36.

12. Chrysostom, "Homilies," 17.

13. In addition to the medieval sources mentioned in my text, I want to draw attention to other allegorical readings, e.g. the extensive *Commentarium in librum Ruth* attributed to Rabanus Maurus (PL 108. cols. 1199C–1222B), Peter Damian's *Epistola XIV ad sorores sua Rodelindam et Sufficiam* (PL 144. cols. 0489C–0497A), and Petrus Riga's "Biblia Versificata" on the book of Ruth in *Aurora, A Verse Commentary on the Bible*, ed. Paul E. Beichner, C.S.C. part 1 (Notre Dame, Ind.: University of Notre Dame Press, 1965), 244–46.

14. *Glossa ordinaria*, Walafrid Strabo, Patrologia Latina. 113, cols. 0531D–0537A. English based on a translation by Nancy Sullas.

15. Ibid.

16. Hugh of Saint Victor, sermon 56, "De anima obediente," PL, vol. 177, cols. 1064C–1067A. English based on Latin translation by Nancy Sullas.

17. www.catholicliturgy.com/index.cfm/FuseAction/TextContents/Index/4/SubIndex/6 6/TextIndex/12, last accessed September 28, 2005.

18. Phyllis Trible, *God and the Rhetoric of Sexuality* (Philadelphia: Fortress Press, 1978), 173. Kristeva refers to the same rabbinic tradition: "One cannot help emphasize, as several commentators have done, that Ruth's merit will be more sound than that of Abraham, and therefore worthy of a *perfect* reward. Could this be because Abraham left his father's house in answer to a call from God, while Ruth the foreigner did it on her own initiative?" *Strangers to Ourselves*, 73.

19. Ann Belford Ulanov, *The Female Ancestors of Christ* (Boston: Shambala, 1993), 54.

20. Ibid., p. 64.

21. Trible, *God and the Rhetoric of Sexuality*, 196.

22. Ulanov, *The Female Ancestors of Christ*, 90.

23. Joan D. Chittister, *The Story of Ruth: Twelve Moments in Every Woman's Life* (Grand Rapids, Mich.: William B. Eerdmans, 2000), 89.

24. Victor Hugo, *Selected Poems of Victor Hugo: Bilingual Edition*, ed. E. H. and A. M. Blackmore (Chicago: University of Chicago Press, 2001).

Ruth Speaks in Yiddish / Kathryn Hellerstein

1. Erich Auerbach, *Mimesis: The Representation of Reality in Western Literature*, trans. Willard R. Trask (Princeton: Princeton University Press, 1953), 11.

2. Ruth 1:8–9, *The Holy Scriptures According to the Masoretic Text* (Philadelphia: Jewish Publication Society, 1955), 2:1943.

3. Roza Yakubovitsh, *Rut*, in *Mayne gezangen* (Warsaw: Tsentrale Yidishe Bibliotek un Prese Arkhiv, 1924), 39–40. Translated by Kathryn Hellerstein. All translations are by Kathryn Hellerstein, unless otherwise noted.

4. Ibid., 39, ll. 1–8.

5. Ibid., ll. 9–14.

6. Ibid., ll. 15–21

7. Ibid., 40, ll. 22–27.

8. Meyer Waxman, *A History of Jewish Literature* (1933; New York: Thomas Yoseloff, 1960) 2:634–35. Also, Jerold C. Frakes, *Early Yiddish Texts, 1100–1750* (New York: Oxford University Press, 2004), 540–42.

9. Jacob ben Isaac Ashkenazi of Yanow, *Tsenerene*, in *Tz'enah Ur'enah: The Classic Anthology of Torah Lore and Midrashic Comment*, trans. Miriam Stark Zakon (Brooklyn: Mesorah Publications, in conjunction with Jerusalem: Hillel Press, 1984), 3:859.

10. Ibid., 3:866.

11. Ibid., 3:867.

12. Ibid.

13. Ibid.

14. Ibid., 3:868.

15. Ibid., 3:872.

16. I. L. Peretz, "What Our Literature Needs," trans. Nathan Halpern, in *Voices from the Yiddish: Essays, Memoirs, Diaries,* ed. Irving Howe and Eliezer Greenberg (Ann Arbor: University of Michigan Press, 1972), 31, 25, 26, 31.

17. David G. Roskies and Leonard Wolf, introduction to *The World According to Itzik: Selected Poetry and Prose,* trans. Leonard Wolf, ed. Leonard Wolf and David Roskies (New Haven: Yale University Press, 2002), xx.

18. Ibid., xxi–xxii.

19. Itsik Manger, *Rut,* in *Medresh Itsik,* ed. Khone Shmeruk (Jerusalem: Hebrew University Press, 1984), 108.

20. Alexander Spieglblatt, *Bloe vinklen: Itsik Manger—lebn, lid, un balade* (Tel Aviv: I. L. Peretz Farlag, 2002), 415. Spieglblatt notes that Manger used to memorize his poems and wonders why, if two-thirds of the Ruth manuscript was lost during his travels in North Africa, Manger did not simply transcribe the lost poems from memory, once he was in London.

21. Itsik Manger, *Rut,* in *Medresh Itsik,* 107–24. According to Shmeruk, two translations of selections from the *Rut* poems have appeared in English: "At the Crossroad (Naomi and her Daughter-in-law)," in *Onions, Cucumbers, and Plums,* no. 26. and "Orpah and Ruth," in *The Golden Peacock,* trans. Samuel Leftwich, 557. The *Rut* poems were not included in Manger, *The World According to Itzik.*

22. Itsik Manger, "Nomi zogt 'got fun avrom,'" in *Rut, Medresh Itsik,* 109–10, ll. 1–8.

23. "Gott fun avrohom," *The Complete Artscroll Siddur,* trans. Rabib Nosson Scherman, ed. Rabbi Nosson Schermann and Rabbi Meir Zlotowitz (Brooklyn: ArtScroll, Mesorah, 2000), 620–21.

24. Manger, "Nomi zogt got fun avrom," 110, ll. 33–36.

25. Manger, "Nomi ken nisht shlofn," *Rut,* in *Medresh Itsik,* 113, ll. 17–24.

26. Ibid., 114, ll. 33–40.

27. Manger, "Orpe ken nisht shlofn," *Rut,* in *Medresh Itsik,* 115–16, ll. 21–28).

28. Ibid., 116, ll. 21–32.

29. Ibid., 116, ll. 33–36.

30. Manger, "Afn sheydveg," *Rut,* in *Medresh Itsik,* 121, ll. 1–12.

31. Manger, "Orpe gezegnt zikh," ibid., 123–24, ll. 1–24.

32. Manger, "Nomi ken nisht shlofn," 114, ll. 37–40.

33. Manger, "Nomi farlozt dos dorf," 120, ll. 29–32.

34. Ibid., ll. 25–28.

35. See Spiegelblatt, *Bloe vinklen,* 414–20, for another account of this same idea. Also, see Roskies and Wolf, introduction to *The World According to Itzik,* xxi.

Printing the Story / Margaret Adams Parker

1. Paper was invented in China around 100 CE, and prints were made there centuries earlier than in the West. Mayor A. Hyatt, *Prints and People* (Princeton: Princeton University Press, 1971), 1–4.

2. James Snyder, *Northern Renaissance Art: Painting, Sculpture, the Graphic Arts from 1350 to 1575* (Englewood Cliffs, N.J.: Prentice-Hall, 1985), 270–71.

3. I have omitted, as not within the purview of this essay, another category: images where the artist uses the biblical images to treat issues unrelated to the text. One example of this is George Segal's 1978 bronze sculpture *In Memory of May 4, 1970: Kent State—Abraham and Isaac*. Although the text of Genesis 22 is printed out on a wall beside the sculpture, Segal's statements make clear that he was using the biblical text to explore the morality of the Vietnam War: "Doesn't a father have to stop and think about declaring war and sending his son out to be killed?" Sam Hunter and Don Hawthorne, *George Segal* (New York: Arthur A Bartley, 1998), 102.

4. Paper began to be massed produced in Europe in the early fifteenth century. Allan Shestak, *Fifteenth-Century Engravings of Northern Europe* (Washington, D.C.: National Gallery of Art, 1967), introduction, 1.

5. Hence Martin Luther's complaint about friars who sit "all day in the church to sell souvenirs and little picture to pilgrims." Hyatt, *Prints and People*, 11–13.

6. Richard S. Field, *Fifteenth-Century Woodcuts and Metalcuts* (Washington, D.C.: National Gallery of Art, 1965), note for woodcut 8.

7. Ibid., notes for woodcuts 174 and 210.

8. Shestak, *Fifteenth-Century Engravings*, note for engraving 38.

9. Snyder, *Northern Renaissance Art*, 268–71.

10. There were even earlier versions where the woodcut illustrations were accompanied by handwritten texts. Arthur M. Hind, *An Introduction to a History of Woodcut, Vol. I.* (New York: Dover, 1963), 130–34.

11. James Strachan. *Early Bible Illustrations* (Cambridge: Cambridge University Press, 1957), 8.

12. Ibid., 12.

13. Ibid., 11.

14. Hind, *Introduction to a History of Woodcut*, 30.

15. Shestak, *Fifteenth-Century Engravings*, introduction, 6.

16. Eamon Duffy, *The Stripping of the Altars* (New Haven: Yale University Press, 1992), 155.

17. Feya Anzelewsky, *The Drawings and Graphic Work of Dürer* (London: Hamlyn Publishing Group, 1970), 34.

18. Writing about a later generation of Dutch artists, Hidde Hoeckstra mentions "the prevailing view that everyone should identify with the Prodigal Son." Hidde Hoeckstra, *Rembrandt and the Bible* (Weert, Netherlands: Magna Books, 1990), 337.

19. Rembrandt's large and magnificent prints of *Christ Presented to the People* and *The Three Crosses* are an exception to his almost exclusive reliance on etching; he executed these plates entirely in drypoint, a medium in which the artist draws with a bare needle on copper. As with engraving, the drypoint line is made without acid, but where the engraved line is precise and cold, the drypoint line is ragged, rich, and warm.

20. I mention nine works on the Prodigal Son by Rembrandt, fully aware that scholars constantly debate which works are by his hand and which by his pupils or assistants. Since the production by others in Rembrandt's studio consistently reflects the master's style *and* his chosen subject matter, any reattributions should not diminish my claim that the Prodigal Son was a major subject for the artist.

21. Kenneth Clark, *An Introduction to Rembrandt* (New York: Harper and Row, 1979), 137.

22. Ibid., 136.

23. John Booty's words, written about twentieth-century religious art, are equally apt here: "the finest examples . . . are revelatory," and "the spectator becomes a participant not only in the work of art, but in the meaning, the essence the work reveals." John Booty, "Concerning Twentieth Century Faith Statements in Art," *Reformed Liturgy and Music* 23, no. 3 (Summer 1989): 116–19.

24. Wood engraving is a relief technique developed in the nineteenth century. The wood engraver carves a block composed of end-grain wood. Despite its name, this is relatively free of grain; it allows the artist to manipulate special engraving tools with fluid, supple movements.

25. Moser's engravings for this project were carved in resingrave, a synthetic product that can be used in place of end-grain wood.

26. In a collagraph, shapes and objects are attached to the plate (as in a collage), inked, and printed on an etching press. The resulting print often has an embossed surface.

27. Ellen F. Davis and Margaret Adams Parker, *Who Are You, My Daughter? Reading Ruth through Image and Text* (Louisville, Ky.: Westminster John Knox Press, 2003), 83–84, and Ellen F. Davis, *Proverbs, Ecclesiastes, and Song of Songs* (Louisville, Ky.: Westminster John Knox Press, 2000), 153.

Translating Eros / Chana Bloch

1. Unless otherwise indicated, all quotations from the Song are from Ariel Bloch and Chana Bloch, trans. *The Song of Songs: A New Translation* (New York: Random House, 1995; Modern Library Classic paperback, 2006).

2. Marvin H. Pope, *Song of Songs: A New Translation with Introduction and Commentary*, vol. 7c of *The Anchor Bible* (Garden City, N.Y.: Doubleday, 1977), 471, paraphrasing Midrash Rabbah.

3. Ibid., 593, 617–20.

4. *Shorerekh'aggan aggan ha-sahar* means literally "your navel is the bowl/basin/cup of the moon." Most translators take "the moon" here as a metaphor suggesting roundness—e.g. "Your navel is a rounded bowl" (RSV)—but the phrase "cup of the moon" may be understood simply as a possessive. Bloch and Bloch, *The Song of Songs*, 200–201.

5. We explain our procedures in detail in our introductory essay, "About the Translation," and in the extensive commentary to our translation.

6. *Dodim* occurs once more in the Song, in the phrase *shikhru dodim*, "get drunk on love" (5:1). The Septuagint, Vulgate, KJV, RSV and other translations read *dodim* here as a plural noun in synonymous parallelism with "friends." Ariel Bloch comments: "One can see why this reading was preferred by those to whom the notion of getting drunk on love may have been too blatantly erotic. But it is an interpretation with a very low degree of plausibility." Bloch and Bloch, *The Song of Songs*, 179.

7. Ibid., 166–68. Although the word *tsammah* appears three times in the Song, in 4:1, 4:3 and 6:7, the context in each case does not provide sufficient evidence to establish its meaning. Ariel Bloch's reasoning depends on a careful reading of *galli tsammatekh*, "expose your hair," in Isaiah 47:2–3, the only other passage in the Hebrew Bible where *tsammah* occurs.

8. Harold N. Moldenke and Alma M. Moldenke, *Plants of the Bible* (1952; rpt., New York: Dover Publications, 1986), 184–88.

9. Pope, *Song of Songs*, 552, 584–92; Robert Gordis, *The Song of Songs and Lamentations: A Study, Modern Translation, and Commentary* (New York: Jewish Theological Seminary, 1954).

10. This psalm is a portion of the Hallel recited at the Passover Seder; the phrase appears as well in the Song of Hannah (1 Sam. 2:8).

11. Verse 6:12, generally considered the most difficult verse in the Song, has received a wide range of interpretations and emendations and has at times been omitted as untranslatable. Our translation is based on the Masoretic text, with a single crucial emendation at the end. Bloch and Bloch, 192–95.

"I Am Black and Beautiful" / André LaCoque

1. André LaCocque, *Romance, She Wrote: A Hermeneutical Essay on Song of Songs* (Harrisburg, Pa.: Trinity Press International, 1998).

2. Tremper Longman III, *Song of Songs*, The New International Commentary on the Old Testament (Grand Rapids, Mich.: Eerdmans, 2001).

3. Francis Landy, *Paradoxes of Paradise: Identity and Difference in the Song of Songs* (Sheffield: Almond Press, 1983), 17. To "cock a snook" in American English is to thumb one's nose.

4. Karl Kerenyi, *Umgang mit dem Göttlichen* (Göttingen: Vandenhoeck & Ruprecht, 1955), 20.

5. LaCocque *Romance*, 190–91.

6. The Cushite period in Egypt ran from 711 to ca. 593, but Cush had ongoing preeminence even after that era. See Herodotus 3.26–30.

7. Compare Song 1.8.

8. L. Köhler and W. Baumgartner, eds. *Lexicon in Veteris Testamenti Libros* (Leiden: Brill, 1953), 609b (after G. R. Driver's "Studies in the Vocabulary of the Old Testament," *JTS* 34 [1933]: 380–81.)

9. Marvin H. Pope, *Song of Songs: A New Translation with Introduction and Commentary*, vol. 7c of The Anchor Bible (Garden City, N.Y.: Doubleday, 1977), 323.

10. On *notérah 'eth ha-kerâmîm*, Pope rightly refers to Isaiah 27:2–3, where God is the *nôṣér* of his *kèrèm* ("I, the Lord, am its keeper" [the root is akin to *ntr*]), that is, the keeper of Israel. The idea of using this text in the Canticle is the same as the one just reviewed. But the insistence of Song of Songs here on the verb *nâtar* (see also 8:11–12) should not be ignored. It stands in a play of words with the preceding verb, *ḥary*, because *natar* means "to be angry" or "to keep or bear a grudge" (see Lev. 19:18: *lo thittor 'eth beney 'ammèka*, "you shall not bear a grudge against any of your people"). Incidentally, one reads in *Babli Ketuboth* 37a, *menâtera naphᶜsha*, "she kept herself," that is, her purity.

11. LaCocque, *Romance*, 73.

12. Frank Kermode, *The Classic: Literary Images of Permanence and Change* (Cambridge, Mass.: Harvard University Press, 1983), 15–16.

Reading the Song Iconographically / Ellen F. Davis

1. Hermann Gunkel, *The Legends of Genesis: The Biblical Saga and History*, trans. W. H. Carruth (1901; New York: Schocken, 1964).

2. André LaCocque, *Romance, She Wrote: A Hermeneutical Essay on Song of Songs* (Harrisburg, Pa.: Trinity Press International, 1998).

3. Marvin Pope, *Song of Songs: A New Translation with Introduction and Commentary*, vol. 7c of The Anchor Bible (Garden City, N.Y.: Doubleday, 1977).

4. David J. A. Clines, "Why Is There a Song of Songs, and What Does It Do to You If You Read It?" in *Interested Parties: The Ideology of Writers and Readers of the Hebrew Bible*, Journal for the Study of the Old Testament supp. series 205 (Sheffield: Sheffield Academic Press, 1995), 94–121.

5. Fiona Black, "Unlikely Bedfellows: Allegorical and Feminist Readings of Song of Songs 7.1–8," in *The Song of Songs: A Feminist Companion to the Bible*, second series, ed. Athalya Brenner and Carole R. Fontaine (Sheffield: Sheffield Academic Press, 2000), 104–29.

6. Marcia Falk, *Love Lyrics from the Bible: A Translation and Literary Study of the Song of Songs* (Sheffield: The Almond Press, 1982); Ariel Bloch and Chana Bloch, *The Song of Songs: A New Translation with an Introduction and Commentary* (New York: Random House, 1995).

7. I say that I am "almost alone," because Sister Edmée, SLG (Oxford University) also treats the Song as a mystical text about the love between God and

humanity. She does not share my view that the Song is also a celebration of human love. See Sister Edmée, SLG, "The Song of Songs and the Cutting of Roots," *Anglican Theological Review* 80, no. 4 (Fall 1998): 547–61, and "On Interpreting the Song of Songs," *Fairacres Chronicle* 26, no. 1 (Spring 1993): 16–25.

8. Ellen F. Davis, *Proverbs, Ecclesiastes, and the Song of Songs*, Westminster Bible Companion (Louisville: Westminster John Knox, 2000).

9. LaCocque argues strongly for female authorship of the Song; I treat it as a possibility. However, since I think female authorship is more likely here than with other biblical books, in the interest of balance, I adopt the feminine pronoun in reference to the author.

10. Harold Fisch, *Poetry with a Purpose: Biblical Poetics and Interpretation* (Bloomington: Indiana University Press, 1988), 80–103.

11. Andrew Louth observes: "The Scriptures tell the story of God's way of leading men back into unity, and the way *has* to be from the fragmented to the unified. The history of the Old Testament fashions a matrix, a kaleidoscope, which shares in our fragmentedness and yet harks forward to the One 'in quo omnia constant.'" *Discerning the Mystery: An Essay in the Nature of Theology* (Oxford: Clarendon Press, 1983), 130.

12. *Mishnah Yadayim* 3:5.

13. Michael V. Fox, *The Song of Songs and the Ancient Egyptian Love Songs* (Madison: University of Wisconsin Press, 1985).

14. All translations are my own, unless otherwise indicated.

15. While I recognize that "whole-being" is poetically awkward, I use it in order to avoid the dichotomy between the physical and the spiritual that the common (and in some ways good) translation "soul" may evoke. The Hebrew word *nefesh* denotes an animate creature, human or nonhuman, in its totality. It literally means "throat," through which one breathes and eats. It is therefore evident that any translation that allows physical being to be overlooked—or even accorded second place—is inadequate, and especially so in the context of the Song.

16. I am persuaded to adopt this translation (over the traditional "apple") by the argument of Ariel and Chana Bloch, *The Song of Songs*, 149.

17. Tremper Longman III emphasizes the note of yearning in his *Songs of Songs*, The New International Commentary on the Old Testament (Grand Rapids: Eerdmans, 2001).

18. André LaCocque, *Romance, She Wrote*, 117.

19. Phyllis Trible, *God and the Rhetoric of Sexuality* (Philadelphia: Fortress, 1978), 159–60.

20. It was Michael Fox who first drew my attention to this with his argument that the biblical lovers go much further than their Egyptian counterparts in using metaphors to construct an imaginative world. See his "Love, Passion and Perception in Israelite and Egyptian Love Poetry," *JBL* 102, no. 2 (1983), 227.

21. *Tosefta Sanhedrin* 12:10 (also *Baba Sanhedrin* 101a).

22. Andrew Louth, *Discerning the Mystery*, 91.

23. Vladimir Lossky, drawing on the thought of Basil the Great and Ignatius of Antioch, observes that there is "'a margin of silence' which belongs to the words of Scripture and which cannot be picked up by the ears of those who are outside" (cited by Louth, ibid.).

Unresolved and Unresolveable / Marc Brettler

I would like to thank the participants of the Song of Songs conference and especially Peter Hawkins, its convener, for the stimulation they offered.

1. Joseph Qafikh, *The Five Scrolls*, in Hebrew (Jerusalem: The Society for the Preservation of Yemenite Manuscripts, 1962), 26. On the attribution of this commentary to Sa'adiya, see 9–11. More broadly, on the interpretation of the Bible in the Gaonic period, see Robert Brody, *The Geonim and the Shaping of Medieval Jewish Culture* (New Haven: Yale University Press, 1998), 300–15. The first part of this statement is widely quoted. See, for example, Daniel Boyarin, "The Song of Songs: Lock or Key? Intertextuality, Allegory and Midrash," in *The Book and the Text: The Bible and Literary Theory*, ed. Regina Schwartz (Oxford: Balckwell, 1990), 214–30. Translations from Hebrew sources and the Song of Songs are my own; translations from other biblical books typically follow *Tanakh: A New Translation of the Holy Scriptures according to the Traditional Hebrew Text* (Philadelphia: Jewish Publication Society, 1985).

2. Quotations from Ibn Ezra are from the standard rabbinic Bible.

3. See, in addition to the commentaries ad loc., Ludwig Koehler and Walter Baumgartner, *The Hebrew and Aramaic Lexicon of the Old Testament*, 5 vols. (Leiden: Brill, 1994–2000), 1:80.

4. For the date of the Song, see esp. Michael V. Fox, *The Song of Songs and the Ancient Egyptian Love Songs* (Madison: University of Wisconsin Press, 1985), 186–90

5. Ibid., 187.

6. For the distribution of *sh*, see Koehler and Baumgartner, *Hebrew and Aramaic Lexicon*, 4:1365; see also W. Randall Garr, *Dialect Geography of Syria-Palestine 1000–586 B.C.E.* (Philadelphia: University of Pennsylvania Press, 1985), 85–87.

7. See the discussion in Hans-Joachim Kraus, *Psalms 1–59*, Continental Bible Commentary Series (Minneapolis: Augsburg, 1988), 22–23.

8. The Hebrew text contains seven references, but 1:5 should most likely be emended.

9. See the commentaries ad loc.

10. See the commentaries on the verses noted below.

11. See the detailed discussion in Roland E. Murphy, *The Song of Songs* (Minneapolis: Fortress, 1990), 191–92 and note the observation of Fox in *The Song of Songs*, 171, "We certainly should not try to hang too much theological weight on this very uncertain reference to God."

12. See the summary of John Barton, "The Significance of a Fixed Canon of the Hebrew Bible," in *Hebrew Bible/Old Testament: The History of Its Interpretation I/1; Antiquity*, ed. Magne Sæbø, (Göttingen: Vandenoeck & Ruprecht, 1996), 67–83, and, more recently, Philip R. Davies, *Scribes and Schools: The Canonization of the Hebrew Scriptures* (Louisville: Westminster John Knox, 1998).

13. For an exploration of this issue, see Magne Sæbø, "On the Canonicity of the Song of Songs," in *Texts, Temples, and Traditions: A Tribute to Menahem Haran*, ed. Michael V. Fox et al. (Winona Lake, Ind.: Eisenbrauns, 1996), 267–77.

14. Carey Ellen Walsh, *Exquisite Desire: Religion, the Erotic, and the Song of Songs* (Minneapolis: Fortress, 2000), xi.

15. On the force of this word, see Carol Meyers, *Discovering Eve: Ancient Israelite Women in Context* (New York: Oxford University Press, 1998), 110–11.

16. The translation of *tapuach* is debated, since it is uncertain when apples were introduced to the area; see the commentaries. Among those defending "apple" is Michael Zohary, *Plants of the Bible* (Cambridge: Cambridge University Press, 1982), 70.

17. On the history of interpretation of the Song, see Marvin Pope, *Song of Songs: A New Translation with Introduction and Commentary*, vol. 7c of The Anchor Bible (Garden City, N.Y.: Doubleday, 1977), 89–229; interesting observations on the allegorization of the Song are in Fiona C. Black, "Unlikely Bedfellows: Allegorical and Feminist Readings of Song of Songs 7.1–8," in *The Song of Songs*, ed. Athalya Brenner and Carole R. Fontaine, *A Feminist Companion to the Bible*, second series (Sheffield: Sheffield Academic Press, 2000), 104–29.

18. Many of these issues are discussed in relation to Judges in Marc Zvi Brettler, *The Book of Judges*, Old Testament Readings (London: Routledge, 2002).

19. These terms have been borrowed from Daniel Grossberg, Centripetal and Centrifugal Structures in Biblical Poetry, Society of Biblical Literature Monograph Series 39 (Atlanta, Ga.: Scholars Press, 1989); note esp. his discussion of the Song on 55–81.

20. Brettler, *The Book of Judges*, 103–16; Mignon R. Jacobs, *The Conceptual Coherence of the Book of Micah*, Journal for the Study of the Old Testament Supplement 322 (Sheffield: Sheffield Academic Press, 2001).

21. Brettler, *The Book of Judges*, 10–12.

22. J. Cheryl Exum, "A Literary and Structural Analysis of the Song of Songs," *Zeitschrift für die Alttestamentliche Wissenschaft* 85 (1973): 47–79. The chart reproduced below is on 77. She now views the arrangement of the Song of Songs differently. See *The Song of Songs: A Commentary* (Louisville, Ky.: Westminster John Knox, 2005).

23. Ibid., 78.

24. See William H. Shea, "The Chiastic Structure of the Song of Songs," *Zeitschrift für die Alttestamentliche Wissenschaft* 92 (1980): 378–96, and David A. Dorsey, "Literary Structuring in the Song of Songs," *Journal for the Study of the Old Testament* 46 (1990): 81–96.

25. J. Cheryl Exum, e-mail communication.

26. The literature on chiasmus is vast; see esp. John W. Welch, ed., *Chiasmus in Antiquity: Structures, Analyses, Exegesis* (Provo, Utah: Research Reprint Edition, 1999), and John W. Welch and Daniel B. McKinlay, eds., *Chaismus Bibliography* (Provo, Utah: Research Reprint Edition, 1999).

27. Brettler, *Judges*, 12.

28. Ibid., 11 and 118 n. 6.

29. Shea, "The Chiastic Structure of the Song of Songs," 378.

30. Dorsey, "Literary Structuring in the Song of Songs."

31. Ibid., 93–94.

32. See the similar critique in Tremper Longman III, *Song of Songs* (Grand Rapids, Mich.: Eerdmans, 2001), 56.

33. In fact, there are more than three proposed structures—see, in addition to those already mentioned, Edwin C. Webster, "Pattern in the Song of Songs," *Journal for the Study of the Old Testament* 22 (1982): 73–93.

34. Indeed, this is the main case of chiasmus adduced in a work that popularized the notion for biblical scholars; see J. P. Fokkelman, *Narrative Art in Genesis: Specimens of Stylistic and Structural Analysis* (Assen: Van Gorcum, 1975), 35.

35. Roland E. Murphy, "The Unity of the Song of Songs," *Vetus Testamentum* 29 (1979): 436–43.

36. Ibid., 443.

37. Fox, *The Song of Songs*, 220; see also 218–26.

38. Murphy, "The Unity of the Song of Songs," 436–37.

39. For *mah* as a negation, see Paul Joüon and T. Muraoka, *A Grammar of Biblical Hebrew*, Subsidia Bilica 14 (Rome: Pontifical Biblical Institute, 1991), sec. 144h; for *'im* as a negation in oaths, see secs. 165–66.

40. For example, Murphy, "The Unity of the Song of Songs," 438.

41. On the general variation between these forms, see Joüon and Muraoka, *A Grammar of Biblical Hebrew*, sec. 62g.

42. Rhyme is not a regular feature of biblical poetry, but it does occur, perhaps as a variant of alliteration; see Wilfred G. E. Watson, *Classical Hebrew Poetry: A Guide to Its Techniques*, Journal for the Study of the Old Testament Supplement 26 (Sheffield: JSOT Press, 1986), 229–34. There is a significant debate concerning meter and rhythm in biblical texts; see the summary in Watson, *Classical Hebrew Poetry*, 87–113. Insistence on the presence of meter in biblical poetry is often associated with the Cross-Freedman School; see the helpful summary by David Noel Freedman, "Prolegomenon" in George Buchanan Gray, *The Forms of Hebrew Poetry* (Hoboken, N.J.: Ktav, 1972), viii–lvi. This perspective is critiqued throughout James L. Kugel, *The Idea of Biblical Poetry: Parallelism and Its History* (New Haven: Yale University Press, 1981).

43. Many biblical books show clear cases of reworking and of various types of editorial activity, so it is incorrect to read a biblical work such as the Song with the assumption that it must be a unified whole.

44. Among recent scholars, the anthology or collection model is accepted by Marcia Falk in *Love Lyrics from the Bible: A Translation and Literary Study of the Song of Songs* (Sheffield: Almond, 1982), 62–70, and Othmar Keel, *The Song of Songs*, Continental Commentary Series (Minneapolis, Fortress, 1994), 62–67. For earlier scholars who suggested that the Song is an anthology, see Exum, "A Literary and Structural Analysis of the Song of Songs," 48, n. 6. There are, of course, different types of anthologies with different structures and degrees of coherence; see the discussion concerning Jewish anthologies in *Prooftexts* 17 (1997) and 19 (1999).

45. The change in scholarly attitudes toward editors and redaction in general is one of the most remarkable changes in biblical scholarship from the early to the late twentieth century. The newer attitude is captured in John Barton, *Reading the Old Testament: Method in Biblical Study* (Louisville: Westminster John Knox, 1996), 45–60.

46. Ariel Bloch and Chana Bloch, *The Song of Songs: A New Translation with an Introduction and Commentary* (New York: Random House, 1995), 19.

47. Ibid., 20.

48. On the waṣfs, see Falk, *Love Lyrics from the Bible*, 80–88, Athalya Brenner, ed., *A Feminist Companion to the Song of Songs*, Feminist Companion to the Bible 1 (Sheffield: Sheffield Academic Press, 1993), 214–57, and Fiona C. Black, "Beauty or the Beast? The Grotesque Body in the Song of Songs," *Biblical Interpretation* 8 (2000): 302–23.

49. The meaning of both *pelakh* and *tzammah* is debated; see the commentaries.

50. The issue of plot in the Song is generally ignored; for an exception, see Yair Mazor, "The Song of Songs or the Story of Stories? 'The Song of Songs': Between Genre and Unity," *Scandinavian Journal of the Old Testament* 1 (1990): 1–29.

51. See Robert C. Culley, *Oral Formulaic Language in the Biblical Psalms* (Toronto: University of Toronto Press, 1967). For a summary of oral poetry and a discussion of oral variants, see Watson, *Classical Hebrew Poetry*, 66–83, and more recently, Alan Dundes, *Holy Writ as Oral Writ: The Bible as Folklore* (Lanham: Rowman & Littlefield, 1999).

52. This is done, for example, in Bloch and Bloch, *The Song of Songs*.

53. Brenner, ed., *A Feminist Companion to the Song of Songs*, 58–97.

54. Athalya Brenner and F. van Dijk-Hemmes, *On Gendering Texts: Female and Male Voices in the Hebrew Bible*, Biblical Interpretation Series 1 (Leiden: Brill, 1996).

55. It is translated as S. D. Goitein, "The Song of Songs: A Female Composition," in Brenner, ed., *A Feminist Companion to the Song of Songs*, 58–66.

56. Ibid., 59.

57. Ibid., 58–59.

58. Ibid., 88–89. Many of the arguments adduced here by Brenner, along with other arguments for possible female authorship for parts of the Song, are summarized in Brenner and van Dijk-Hemmes, *On Gendering Texts*, 82–90.

59. Ibid., p. 91.

60. Walsh, *Exquisite Desire*, 139.

61. André LaCocque, *Romance, She Wrote: A Hermeneutical Essay on Song of Songs* (Harrisburg, Pa.: Trinity Press International, 1998), esp. 39–53.

62. Compare Aaron Demsky, "Education in the Biblical Period," *Encyclopaedia Judaica* (Jerusalem: Keter, 1971), 6:382–98, with David W. Jamieson-Drake, *Scribes and Schools in Monarchic Judah: A Socio-Archeological Approach*, The Social World of Biblical Antiquity 9, Journal for the Study of the Old Testament Supplement 109 (Sheffield: Almond Press, 1991). A sober middle position is found in Menaham Haran, "On the Diffusion of Literacy and Schools in Ancient Israel," *Supplements to Vetus Testamentum* 40 (1988): 81–95.

63. David J. A. Clines, *Interested Parties: The Ideology of Writers and Readers of the Hebrew Bible*, Journal for the Study of the Old Testament Supplement sup. series 205 (Sheffield: Sheffield Academic Press, 1995), 94–121, esp. 102–6.

64. Jack M. Sasson, "A Major Contribution to Song of Songs Scholarship," *Journal of the American Oriental Society* 107 (1987): 735.

65. See esp. Keel, *The Song of Songs*, 198–205.

66. One of the few scholars who comments on this violence is J. Cheryl Exum, "Ten Things Every Feminist Should Know About the Song of Songs," in Brenner and Fontaine, eds., *The Song of Songs*, 30–31.

67. See paradigm 20 in Joüon and Muraoka, *A Grammar of Biblical Hebrew*.

68. Daniel Grossberg, "Two Kinds of Sexual Relationships in the Hebrew Bible," *Hebrew Studies* 35 (1994): 7–25.

69. For one perspective, see Deborah Tannen, *Gender and Discourse* (Oxford: Oxford University Press, 1996).

70. See Mary R. Lefkowitz, "Did Ancient Women Write Novels," in *"Women Like This": New Perspectives on Jewish Women in the Greco-Roman World*, ed. Amy-Jill Levine, Society of Biblical Literature, Early Judaism and Its Literature 1 (Atlanta: Scholars Press, 1991), 199–219, and Ross S. Kraemer, "Women's Authorship of Jewish and Christian Literature in the Greco-Roman Period," ibid., 221–42.

71. Kraemer, "Women's Authorship," esp. 235.

72. On this familial unit, see Paula McNutt, *Reconstructing the Society of Ancient Israel* (Louisville: Westminster John Knox, 1999), 87–94.

73. They are mentioned in 1:5, 2:7, 3:5, 10, 5:8, 16, and 8:4; for attempts to identify them, see the commentaries to 1:5.

74. The best treatment of the women of Ruth is Danna Nolan Fewell and David Miller Gunn, *Compromising Redemption: Relating Characters in the Book of Ruth* (Louisville: Westminster John Knox, 1990).

75. See the similarly nuanced approach in Exum, "Ten Things that Every Feminist Should Know," 28–29.

76. This is especially true of Bloch and Bloch, *The Song of Songs*, which shows keen poetic sensitivity.

77. For English, see the rich list of words in John Ayto, *The Oxford Dictionary of Slang* (Oxford: Oxford University Press, 1998), 64–87.

78. See the discussion of ʿ*agavim* in Moshe Greenberg, *Ezekiel 21–37*, The Anchor Bible 22A (Garden City, N.Y.: Doubleday, 1997), 686.

79. The most complete exploration, frequently emphasizing how much we do not know, is Athalya Brenner, *The Intercourse of Knowledge: On Gendering Desire and 'Sexuality' in the Hebrew Bible*, Biblical Interpretation 26 (Leiden: Brill, 1997).

80. For a comparative study of images of fruit and their relation to sexuality, see W. G. Lambert, "Devotion: The Languages of Religion and Love," in *Figurative Language in the Ancient Near East*, ed. M. Mindlin et al. (London: School of Oriental and African Studies, 1987), 25–39.

81. Fellatio was practiced in ancient Mesopotamia; see Gwendolyn Leick, *Sex and Eroticism in Mesopotamian Literature* (London: Routledge, 1994), 151.

82. The semantically close *zerʿa*, "seed," certainly can do so, as in the phrase *shikhvat zarʿa* of Leviticus 15:16 and elsewhere.

83. For the English usage, see J. E. Lighter, ed., *Random House Historical Dictionary of American Slang* (New York: Random House, 1997), 372–81.

84. Similar themes are explored in J. Cheryl Exum, "In the Eye of the Beholder: Wishing, Dreaming, and *Double Entendre* in the Songs of Songs," in *The Labor of Reading: Desire, Alienation, and Biblical Interpretation*, ed. Fiona Black et al. (Atlanta: Society of Biblical Literature, 1999), 71–87.

85. For example, 1 Samuel 23:6.

86. Murphy, in his version of *The Song of Songs* (Minneapolis: Fortress, 1990), translates this as "flee"; Pope, in his *Song of Songs* translates it as "bolt," and Fox, in his *The Song of Songs* translates it as "bolt away."

87. Quoted in Pope, *Song of Songs*, 79.

88. In a note, however, the Blochs observe that the verb typically expresses separation; see Bloch and Bloch, *The Song of Songs*, 221.

89. Ibid.

90. Tentatively, this is claimed in Murphy, *The Song of Songs*, 139, 142; note the English term "cleavage."

91. See the similar suggestions of Fox in, *The Song of Songs*, 177, and Murphy, *The Song of Songs*, 200.

92. Marc Brettler, "Sensual or Sublime: On Teaching the Song of Songs," in *Approaches to Teaching the Hebrew Bible as Literature in Translation*, ed. Barry N. Olshen and Yael S. Feldman (New York: The Modern Language Association, 1989), 133–35.

93. See Koehler and Baumgartner, *Hebrew and Aramaic Lexicon*, 2:387.

94. Note the translation of Pope 1975, 501, "hole."

95. Both connotations are attested with the root *hmh*; see Koehler and Baumgartner, *Hebrew and Aramaic Lexicon*, 1:250.

Entering the Holy of Holies / Judith A. Kates

1. Translation modified as quoted in Marc Hirshman, "Love and Holiness: The Midrash on Song of Songs and Origen's Homilies" in *A Rivalry of Genius: Jewish and Christian Biblical Interpretation in Late Antiquity* (Albany: SUNY Press, 1996), 83.

2. Ibid.

3. *B. Pes* 21b, *b. Men* 29b

4. Ariel Bloch and Chana Bloch, *The Song of Songs: A New Translation* (Random House, 1995). All subsequent quotations of the Bloch translation are from this edition.

5. *Song of Songs Rabbah*, trans. Maurice Simon, in *Midrash Rabbah* ed. H. Freedman and Maurice Simon (London: Soncino Press, 1983), 1.10:1

6. Ibid., 1.10:2

7. I am indebted for this point to Daniel Boyarin, "The Song of Songs, Lock or Key: The Holy Song as a Mashal" in *Intertextuality and the Reading of Midrash* (Bloomington: Indiana University Press, 1990), 110.

8. Ibid. See also Daniel Boyarin, "Two Introductions to Midrash Shir haShirim" (Hebrew), *Tarbitz* 56 (1987).

9. Boyarin, "The Song of Songs, Lock or Key," 110.

10. Ibid.

11. Ibid.

12. Ibid., 105.

13. *Song of Songs Rabbah* 1.1:8. Translation from Boyarin, *Intertextuality*, 105–6.

14. Ibid., 2.14:2. Translation from Boyarin, *Intertextuality*, 111.

15. *Mekhilta d'Rabbi Ishmael*, Beshallach, 3. Translation from Boyarin, *Intertextuality*, 111.

16. *Song of Songs Rabbah*, trans. Maurice Simon, 1.1:8.

17. Ibid., 1.2:3.

18. Ibid., 2.16:1.

19. Ibid., 3.11: 2.

20. I am indebted to Prof. Nehemiah Polen of Hebrew College in my discussion of this midrash.

The Love Song of the Millennium / E. Ann Matter

1. For a list of at least some of these texts, see E. Ann Matter, *The Voice of My Beloved: The Song of Songs in Western Medieval Christianity* (Philadelphia: University of Pennsylvania Press, 1990), 204–10.

2. Honorius Augustodunensis, *Expositio in Cantica Canticorum* Patralogia Latina 172: 347–496 (hereafter PL). My translations. For the dating, see Valerie I. J. Flint, "The Commentaries of Honorius Augustodunensis on the Song of

Songs," *RB* 84 (1974) 196–211. Honorius is also the author of a shorter commentary on this text, probably written in England earlier in his career: The Seal of Blessed Mary, PL 172: 495–513; for an English translation see Amelia Carr, *The Seal of Blessed Mary by Honorius Augustodunensis* (Toronto: Peregrina Publishing, 1991).

3. I am grateful to Sara Japhet for helping me to see this essential literary function of medieval Christian exegesis.

4. Matter, *The Voice of My Beloved*, 49–85.

5. John Cassian, *Collationes* XIV.8, Sources Chrètiennes 54, ed. E. Pichery (Paris, 1958), 150. For the fourfold method and Song of Songs commentary, see Matter, *The Voice of My Beloved*, 54–58.

6. "Civitas dei illa caelestis, 'quae est mater omnium nostrum.'" Cassian, *Collationes* XIV.8, ed. Pichery, 190.

7. The following medieval Christian authors have a commentary on either the Song of Songs or the Apocalypse and are said by contemporary witnesses also to have written on the other book: Victorinus of Pettau, *In Apocalypsin*, ed. J. Haussleiter, CSEL 49 (Vienna, 1916) and the new edition of M. Dulaey in SC 423 (Paris, 1997); Apponius, *In Canticum Canticorum*, ed. B. de Vregille, and L. Neyrand, CCSL 19 (Turnholt: Brepols, 1986, republished in SC 420, 421, 430, Paris, 1997–1998), also ed. Hildegard König (Freiburg: Herder, 1992); Gregory of Elvira, *Epithalamium, sive explanatio in Canticis Canticorum*, ed. V. Bulhart, in CCSL 69 (Turnholt: Brepols, 1967), also ed. Eva Schulz-Flügel (Freiburg: Herder, 1994); Apringius of Beja, *Tractatus in Apocalipsin*, ed. M. Férotin (Paris, 1900), also ed. A. C. Vega ([Escorial]: Typis Augustinianis Monasterii Escurialensis, 1940) and ed. Alberto del Campo Hernandez (Estella: Editorio Verbo Divino, 1991); Justus of Urguel, *In Cantica Canticorum explanatio mystica*, PL 67: 963–94; and Beatus of Liebana, *Commentarius in Apocalipsin*, ed. E. Romero-Pose (Rome: Typis officinae polygraphicae, 1985). The following authors have extant commentaries on both texts attributed to them: Bede, *In Apocalypsin* and *In Cantica Canticorum*, ed. D. Hurst, in CCSL 199B (Turnholt: Brepols, 1985); Alcuin, *Compendium in Canticum Canticorum*, PL 100: 639–66 and *Commentariorum in Apocalypsin libri quinque*, PL 100: 1085–1156; Haimo of Auxerre, *Commentarium in Cantica Canticorum*, PL 117: 295–358 and *Expositionis in Apocalypsin B. Joannis libri septem*, PL 117: 937–1220; Anselm of Laon, *Enarrationes in Cantica Canticorum*, PL 162: 1187–1228 and *Ennarationes in Apocalypsin*, PL 162: 1499–1586; Bruno of Segni, *Expositio in Cantica Canticorum*, PL 164: 1233–1288 and *Expositio in Apocalypsin*, PL 165: 603–736; Rupert of Deutz, *Commentaria in Canticum Canticorum*, ed. Hrabanus Haacke, CCCM 26 (Turnholt: Brepols, 1974) and *Commentaria in Apocalypsim*, PL 169: 825–1214.

8. See E. Ann Matter, "The Apocalypse in Early Medieval Exegesis," in *The Apocalypse in the Middle Ages*, ed. Richard K. Emmerson and Barnard McGinn (Ithaca: Cornell University Press, 1992), 38–50 for a more detailed discussion of this shift and the unapocalyptic nature of early medieval Apocalypse exegesis.

9. Many of Joachim's works are not in modern editions, but see *Liber figurarum*, ed. L. Tondelli, M. Reeves and B. Hirsch-Reich (Turin: Società editrice internazionale, 1953) and *Abbot Joachim of Fiore: Liber de concordia Noui ac Veteris Testamenti*, ed. E. Randolph Daniel (Philadelphia: American Philosophical Society, 1983), as well as the selected English translations of Bernard McGinn in *Apocalyptic Spirituality* (New York: Paulist Press, 1979), 97–148, and *Visions of the End: Apocalyptic Traditions in the Middle Ages* (1979; New York: Columbia University Press, 1998), 126–41. There is more literature on the (heterodox) Franciscan followers of Joachim than on the Calabrian Cistercian himself, but see Randolph Daniel, "Joachim of Fiore: Patterns of History in the Apocalypse," in *The Apocalypse in the Middle Ages*, ed. Emmerson and McGinn, 72–88.

10. See Michael Curschmann, "Imagined Exegesis: Text and Picture in the Exegetical Works of Rupert of Deutz, Honorius Augustodunensis, and Gerhoch of Reichersberg," *Traditio* 44 (1988): 145–69. There are eight known extant manuscripts of Honorius's works that reproduce this iconographic scheme. Six are from the second half of the twelfth century: Munich, Bayerische Staatsbibliothek Clm. 4550, Clm. 5118, and Clm. 18125; Vienna, Österreichische Nationalbibliothek lat. 942; Baltimore, the Walters Art Museum MS W 29; and Augsburg, Universitätsbibliothek I 2 2 13. The other two are from the fourteenth century: Saint Florian XI, 80, and Saint Paul in Lavanthal 44/1, formerly 25.3.5.

11. See Matter, *The Voice of My Beloved*, 102, 105, for two twelfth-century examples of this artistic motif.

12. Baltimore, the Walters Art Museum MS W 29, f. 43v.

13. In Christian art and textual interpretation, the four evangelists are portrayed with these symbols from the fourth century on. These are, of course, the four beasts of the visions of Ezekiel (1:1–14 and 10:1–22) and Daniel (7:1–8), as retold in the Christian biblical book of the Apocalypse or the Revelation to John (4:7). See the explanation of Jerome in his preface to the *Commentary on Matthew*, Nicene and Post Nicene Fathers 2, 6.1036–37.

14. Baltimore, the Walters Art Museum MS W 29, f. 89v. This image has also been discussed by Jeremy Cohen in "The Salvation of Israel in Honorius of Augustodunensis' Song of Songs Commentary," a lecture delivered to the Department of Religious Studies of the University of Pennsylvania, February 2002.

15. "Vel genitrix, videlicet Judaica gens est violata, quando ob vindictam crucis a Tito et Vespasiano est captivata" (PL 172: 4 81C).

16. Jeremy Cohen, "*Synagoga Conversa*: Honorius Augustodenensis, the Song of Songs, and Christianity's 'Eschatological Jew,'" *Speculum* 79 (2004): 309–40.

17. From Bernard's Letter 363; see Jeremy Cohen, *Living Letters of the Law: Ideas of the Jew in Medieval Christianity* (Berkeley: University of California Press, 1999), 243.

18. Bernard McGinn, *Antichrist: Two Thousand Years of the Human Fascination with Evil* (San Francisco: HarperSan Francisco, 1994), 118.

19. Ibid., 60–61.

20. McGinn, *Visions of the End*, 43.
21. Ibid., p. 49.
22. Ibid., 118, 134, 138, and 191 (the fascinating case of Roger Bacon's writings on the coming "angelic pope").
23. McGinn, *Antichrist*, 217–18. For the Lutheran adaptation of Franciscan Joachite ideas, see David Todd Heffner, " 'Eyn Wunderliche Weyssagung von der Babstums': Medieval Prophecy into Reformation Polemic," Ph.D. diss., University of Pennsylvania, 1991.
24. Lawrence Wright, "Letter from Jerusalem: Forcing the End," *The New Yorker*, July 20, 1998, 42–53.
25. Tim LaHaye and Jerry Jenkins, *Left Behind: A Novel of the Earth's Last Days* (Wheaton, Ill.: Tyndale House Publishers, 1995) and sequels. Twelve volumes have appeared to date, with the twelfth and final novel appearing in March of 2004. For plot summaries, see www.leftbehind.com (last accessed 4/25/2006).

Monastic Reading and Allegorical Sub/Versions of Desire / Mark S. Burrows

1. Norman O. Brown, *Love's Body* (New York: Random House, 1966), 225–26.
2. Sermon 18.1 on The Song of Songs, *Sermones super Cantica Canticorum*, ed. J. Leclerq, C. H. Talbot, H. M. Rochais, hereafter SCC, in *Sanctus Bernardi opera*, vols. 1–2 (Rome: Editiones Cistercienses, 1957). All translations are my own based on this edition and cited by sermon number and notation.
3. SCC 79.i.1.
4. M. B. Pranger, *Bernard of Clairvaux and the Shape of Monastic Thought: Broken Dreams* (Leiden: E. J. Brill, 1994), 141. He is arguing here in direct opposition to Etienne Gilson's view, as expressed in *La théologie mystique de Saint Bernard* (Paris: J. Vrin, 1947), 192–215.
5. SCC 79.i.2; here, citing Sirach 24.26.
6. SCC 84.1.
7. Here, the contrast to the admonition found in Benedict's *Rule* reminds us of the cultural distance that separated Bernard's "textual community" from the early forms of monastic life envisioned by the founding father. See *Rule*, ch. 6, "Restraint of Speech": "We absolutely condemn in all places any vulgarity and gossip and talk leading to laughter. "
8. See Pranger, *Bernard of Clairvaux*, 91.
9. Henri de Lubac, *Exégèse médiévale: Les quatre senses de l'écriture*, part 1, vol. 2 (Paris: Desclée de Brouwer, 1959), 582.
10. Gilson, *La théologie mystique*, 80–81. Pranger comments quite critically on this insight and the manner in which Gilson reformulates Bernard's thought into a "respectable philosophical theology" that dismisses the power and genius of his literary achievement. See Pranger, *Bernard of Clairvaux*, 226–27.
11. SCC 1.iii.5.

12. SCC 67.v.7. Such claims, reminiscent of Augustine's celebrated defense of "difficult" biblical texts, underscore the pleasure that the interpreter derives precisely because of the text's ambiguities, its openness to the "work" of reading.

13. Bernard drew upon the same narrative in his first sermon from the series *De resurrectione*. For further discussion of this text, see Pranger, *Bernard of Clairvaux*, 293–313. The citation Bernard used, based upon the Vulgate, is different in important details from modern renditions based upon an older Hebrew text.

14. The classic study of this principle is A. C. Charity, *Events and their Afterlife: The Dialectics of Christian Typology in the Bible and Dante* (Cambridge: Cambridge University Press, 1966).

15. SCC 16.i.l.

16. SCC 1.iii.5. Bernard's use of this text suggests a biblical text he often turned to in describing what the search for God was like: "Seek [God's] face always" (Ps. 104.4). The "face," whether of Scripture or of God, was a partial revealing, not a complete concealment; as such, the literal sense as the "face" of Scripture was crucial in the process of the revelation of meaning.

17. SCC 72.iii.6.

18. See Ivan Illich, *In the Vineyard of the Text: A Commentary to Hugh's Didascalicon* (Chicago: University of Chicago Press, 1996), 54–57.

19. See especially SCC 7.iv.6.

20. SCC 73.i.2.

21. Illich, *In the Vineyard of the Text*, 54.

22. SCC 53.iv.9. See also SCC 7.iv.5, where Bernard explains what Benedict meant in exhorting monks to "sing wisely" (see *Rule*, ch. 19, "The Discipline of Psalmody"); in this passage, Bernard reminds his brothers that they are to "chew" the Psalms with "the teeth of their minds" in order to extract the "sweet taste" held in the words: "Tantum illum terere non negligat fidelis et prudens anima quibusdam dentibus intelligentiae suae, ne si forte integrum flutiat, et non mansum, frustretur palatum sapore desiderabili, et dulciori super mel et favum." For further discussion of this point in relation to Bernard, see Adriaan H Bredero, *Bernard of Clairvaux: Between Cult and History* (Grand Rapids, MI: Eerdmans, 1993), 194–95, and, in terms of monastic practices generally, see Jean Leclercq, *The Love of Learning and the Desire for God*, trans. Catharine Misrahi (New York: Fordham University Press, 1982),72–73.

23. SCC 1.vi.11.

24. See Pranger, *Bernard of Clairvaux*, esp. 6–7.

25. SCC 85.iv.11. The wondering about laughter—a striking point for an abbot to make—is a reflection on Benedict's admonition against laughter; see *Rule* ch. 6, and above, n. 7.

26. SCC 5.i.4.

27. SCC 79.i.1.

28. SCC 67.ii.3.

29. Ibid.

30. A point worth further exploration is the frequency with which Bernard speaks affirmatively about *desiderium*, often using derivations of *concupiens* or verb forms of *concupiscere* to underscore the strength of this attribute. In the penultimate sermon, in fact, Bernard draws upon Psalm 44.12 to suggest how God loves us: "The King shall desire your beauty" ("Concupiscet . . . rex decorem tuum"). This usage is particularly noticeable in Bernard's final sermons on the Song; see especially SCC 79–85.

31. SCC 20, especially at vv. 6–9.

32. SCC 52.iii.5: "Not to be gripped during life by material desires is a mark of human virtue, but to gaze without using bodily likenesses [*corporum vero similtudinibus speculando non involvi*] is the sign of angelic purity. Each, however, is a divine gift, each is a going out of oneself, each a transcending of self, but in one one goes much farther than in the other." The eventual goal of monastic conversion, as Bernard understood it, was to be like the angels—which is to say, living in "spiritual bodies" and thus unaffected by material desires or cares. He earlier discussed the nature of angels' perception and its difference from bodied creatures; see SCC 5.i.4.

33. See, for example, SCC 72.iii.6, where Bernard interprets "aspiring" as a word that signified "a marvelous richness and power of the spirit, to be manifested on that day when not only our hearts but also our bodies [*cum non solum corda, sed et corpora*] will become spiritual after their own fashion, and will be inebriated with the wealth of the house of the Lord and drink of the river of his pleasures."

34. SCC 52.iii.53; the biblical reference here is to Ps. 55.8.

35. Pranger, *Bernard of Clairvaux*, 154.

36. SCC 3.i.l.

37. Gregory the Great, *Moralia in Job*, ed. Robert Gillet, trans. André de Gaudemaris, bk. 1, ch. 29; in Sources chrétiennes, vol. 32 (Paris: Éditions du Cerf, 1975), 161–62.

38. Julia Kristeva, *Tales of Love*, trans. Leon S. Roudiez (New York: Columbia University Press, 1987), 169.

The Female Voice / Margot Fassler

1. This paper is part of a larger study of Hildegard's exploration of the Song of Songs. An earlier one is focused on the poetry and music for the Ursula chants and on her play *Ordo virtutum*. See "Music for the Love Feast: Hildegard of Bingen and the *Song of Songs*," in *Women's Voices across Musical Worlds*, ed. Jane Bernstein (Boston: Northeastern University Press, 2004), pp. 92–117. Latin texts are from the Vulgate; translations are taken from the Douai-Rheims Bible.

2. *Engleberg 103*. With Tova Choate, Iris Mueller, and others, I am preparing a paper on this noted antiphoner that has been ascribed to the Disibodenberg, the Benedictine monastery in which Hildegard was formed and from which her

community split off around 1150, building their own church dedicated to Saint Rupert.

3. Text for a Great Responsory of Matins associated with the Feast of the Assumption. As the first responsory for the feast, the chant set the tone for the whole Office, which is entirely based on the Song of Songs. For the manuscript tradition, see R.-J. Hesbert, ed., *Corpus antiphonalium officii*, 4 (Rome: Herder, 1970), 461, resp. 7878. Readers may also refer to the Cantus on-line database for further study, http://publish.uwo.ca/~cantus/. For discussion of the Office of the Assumption, see Rachel Fulton, "'Quae est ista quae ascendit sicut aurora consurgens?': The Song of Songs as the Historia for the Office of the Assumption," *Mediaeval Studies* 60 (1998): 55–122, and her "Mimetic Devotion, Marian Exegesis, and the Historical Sense of the Song of Songs," *Viator* 27 (1996): 86–116.

4. Another source for incipits of Office chants in Hildegard's region can be found on-line through the Cantus project and in hard copy in Hartmut Möller, *The Zwiefalten Antiphoner, Karlsruhe, Badische Landesbibliothek, Aug. perg. LX*, a Cantus index, project director Ruth Steiner Musicological Studies, LV/5, The Institute of Medieval Music (Ottawa: Institute of Medieval Music, 1996). Möller's introduction is a useful overview of the sources connected with the Hirsau reform movement and can be supplemented by the discussion by Felix Heinzer in "Der Hirsauer *Liber ordinarius*," *Revue Bénédictine* 102 (1992).

5. In addition to Rachel Fulton's articles cited above, and her book *From Judgment to Passion : Devotion to Christ and the Virgin Mary, 800–1200* (New York: Columbia University Press, 2002), see also the study of medieval commentaries on the Song of Songs by E. Ann Matter, *The Voice of My Beloved: The Song of Songs in Western Medieval Christianity* (Philadelphia: University of Pennsylvania Press, 1990) and Barbara Haagh-Huglo's study of the Cambrai *Recollectio*, "The Celebration of the 'Recollectio Festorum Beatae Mariae Virginis', 1457–1987," *Studia Musicologica Academiae Scientiarum Hungaricae* 3 (1988): 361–73.

6. For an introduction to this topic of Hildegard's interpersonal relationships, see Barbara Newman's essays on Hildegard's life in *The Voice of the Living Light: Hildegard of Bingen and Her World*, ed. Barbara Newman (Berkeley: University of California Press, 2000), 12; Peter Dronke, "Hildegard of Bingen," in his *Women Writers of the Middle Ages* (Oxford: Oxford University Press, 1981), 144–201; Sabina Flanigan, *Hildegard of Bingen, 1098–1179: A Visionary Life*, rev. ed (London: Routledge, 1998); and Edward Peter Nolan, *Cry Out and Write: A Feminine Poetics of Revelation* (New York: Continuum, 1994). In his provocative and elegant study *Music, Body, and Desire in Medieval Culture: Hildegard of Bingen to Chaucer* (Stanford: Stanford University Press, 2001), Bruce Holsinger interrelates Hildegard's understanding of "musical pleasure and musical violence" (101). My own "Music for the Love Feast" (note 1) notes the importance of Hildegard's play as a way of building corporate understanding of Eucharist.

7. Barbara Newman speaks in her magisterial *Sister of Wisdom: St. Hildegard's Theology of the Feminine*, 2d ed. (Berkeley: University of California Press, 1997) about Hildegard's lack of attention to the Song of Songs. Newman is correct:

other books are cited far more frequently. But the way Hildegard ties the Song to the sacrament of the Eucharist and then uses it in several modes of interpretation gives it special importance in her thought.

8. For an introduction to Hildegard's Mariology, see Barbara Newman, *Sister of Wisdom*, my essay, "Composer and Dramatist: 'Melodious Singing and the Freshness of Remorse,'" in *Voice of the Living Light*, 149–75; and Margot Schmidt, "Maria: 'materia aurea' in der Kirche nach Hildegard von Bingen," in *Hildegard von Bingen: Prophetin durch die Zeiten*, ed. Edeltraud Forster (Freiburg im Breisgau, 1997), 262–83.

9. In "Music for the Love Feast" I interpret Hildegard's play *Ordo virtutum* as a communal exercise that was followed by Mass and included the reception of communion.

10. What remains today is a black-and-white photocopy made in 1927, which is now studied in conjunction with a hand-made and hand-painted copy made by the nuns of Eibingen between 1927 and 1933, based directly on their work with the original. For two viewpoints regarding the illuminated *Scivias* and its date and apparent dependence on Hildegard herself, see especially Lieselotte E. Saurma-Jeltsch, *Die Miniaturen im "Liber Scivias" der Hildegard von Bingen: Die Wucht der Vision und die Ordnung der Bilder* (Wiesbaden: Reichert, 1998) and Madeline Caviness, "Artist: 'To See, Hear, and Know All at Once,'" in *Voice of the Living Light*, 110–24. Caviness, who sees the work of Hildegard herself in the paintings, says (111): "tragically, the Rupertsberg *Scivias* disappeared from Dresden during World War II, leaving us with black-and-white photographs and a handmade replica in full color from which to judge the qualities of the original. I find it of some comfort that the last scholars to claim Hildegard's participation in the design of these pictures were German graduate students who had access to the original manuscript."

11. All English quotations are from Hildegard of Bingen's *Scivias*, trans. Mother Columba Hart and Jane Bishop (New York: Paulist Press, 1990). The critical edition in Latin is by Adelgundis Führkötter and Angela Carlevaris, vols. 43–43a of the *Corpus Christianorum continuatio medievalis* (Turnhout: Brepols, 1978). The label for the illumination of Christ on the cross is found in Hildegard's opening vision for *Scivias* 2, 6 (237) and can be seen as well on the replica of the painting, as is discussed below.

12. For the development of this aspect of sacramentaries from the eighth through the thirteenth centuries see Rudolf Suntrup, "*Te igitur*-Initialen und Kanonbilder in mittelalterlichen Sakramentarhandschriften Roma," in *Text und Bild*, ed. C. Meier and U. Ruberg (Wiesbaden: Reichert, 1980); for a brief introduction to the tradition in missals, with discussion of later devotional practices as well, see Michal Albaric, "Décors et images des missels de rite latin," in *L'illustration: Essais d'iconographie; actes du Séminaire CNRS Paris, 1993–1994*, ed. Maria Teresa Caracciolo (Paris: Klincksieck, 1999), 91–101.

13. The words at this most mystical point of the liturgy were said silently in the Middle Ages while the Sanctus was being sung, as Hildegard knew full well

from her own observations. The "Benedictus" of the Sanctus was not sung until after the elevation of the elements. The opening part of the "Te igitur" below demonstrates the relationship established in the prayer between Christ and the church, a relationship that underlies Hildegard's entire exploration of the mystery and the place of the virgins within the church as models for a new kind of intimacy: "Wherefore, we humbly pray and beseech Thee, most merciful Father, though Jesus Christ Thy Son, Our Lord, to receive and to bless these gifts, these presents, these holy unspotted sacrifices, which we offer up to Thee, in the first place, for Thy holy Catholic Church, that it may please Thee to grant her peace, to guard, unite, and guide her, throughout the world."

14. See Saurma-Jeltsch, *Die Miniaturen*, pp. 112–21.

15. For exploration of images of the Christ who nurses, see Carolyn Walker Bynum, *Jesus as Mother* (Berkeley: University of California Press, 1982).

16. *Scivias*, 2.6, 17, 246.

17. The bridal bed of Christ and his bride, the church, is discussed in Hildegard's exegesis on the Song of Songs as found in this same passage of the treatise.

18. *Scivias*, 2.6, 6, 241.

19. Hildegard's image of the blood from the side of the Christ "sprinkling" his bride is clearly sexual, for it impregnates the bride: "That when blood flowed from the wounded side of My Son, at once salvation of souls came into being; for the glory from which the Devil and his followers were driven out was given to humanity when My Only-Begotten suffered temporal death on the cross, despoiled Hell and led the faithful souls to Heaven. Therefore, in His disciples and their sincere followers faith began to increase and strengthen, so that they became heirs of the celestial Kingdom. Hence that image raises herself upward so that she is sprinkled by the blood from His side; and thus, by the will of the Heavenly Father, she is joined with Him in happy betrothal." *Scivias*, 2.6, 1, 238.

20. Hildegard speaks most graphically of human intercourse in *Scivias* 1, 2. In this vision, she employs many ideas borrowed from classical antiquity and kept current throughout the Middle Ages, including the image of plow and soil for man and woman and the importance of the man's "heat" for the quickening of the womb. For this see especially 1, 2, 19–20, from which the following passages are taken: "When a male is at the age of strength, so that his veins are full of blood, then he is fertile in his semen . . . let not a man emit his semen in excessive lust before the years of his strength; for if he tries to sow his seed in the eagerness of lust before that seed has enough heat to coagulate properly, it is proof that he is sinning" (82).

21. The royal kiss is that of Song 1:1.

22. *Scivias*, 2.6, 11, 243.

23. Ibid., 243–44: "The Bride of My Son offers the gift of bread and wine on My altar with a most devoted purpose. How? To remind Me in faithful memory by the hand of the priest that in this same oblation I delivered up the body and blood of My Son. How? Because the sufferings of My Only-Begotten are seen

perpetually in the secret places of Heaven; and thus that oblation is united to My Son in My ardent heat in a profoundly miraculous way and becomes most truly His body and blood. And thence the Church is quickened with blessed strength." 24. Ibid., 13, 245. The sapphire is found infrequently in the Bible, and only once in the Song (5:14) as part of an extended description by the woman of her beloved: Among other attributes, he has a "belly as of ivory, set with sapphires." The only place in the Vulgate where sapphires and unguent are both present is Exodus 39, wherein the beauties of the Tabernacle as finished by Aaron and his sons are described.

25. Song 5:1; *Scivias*, 2.6, 20–21, 248–49.

26. *Scivias*, 2.6, 21, 249.

27. Song 1:13; *Scivias*, 2.6, 28–29, 255. Here Hildegard joins the imagery of the Song with that of John 15:5–9, which is another statement of love, and one that shaped Hildegard's sense of true fruitfulness. "I am the vine; you the branches: he that abideth in me, and I in him, the same beareth much fruit: for without me you can do nothing. If any one abide not in me, he shall be cast forth as a branch, and shall wither, and they shall gather him up, and cast him into the fire, and he burneth. If you abide in me, and my words abide in you, you shall ask whatever you will, and it shall be done unto you. In this is my Father glorified; that you bring forth very much fruit, and become my disciples. As the Father hath loved me, I also have loved you. Abide in my love."

28. See discussion of Christ's breasts above.

29. *Scivias*, 2, 6.34, 259.

30. Ibid., 35, 259.

31. Ibid., 259–60.

32. Ibid., 36, 260.

33. Ibid., 38, 261.

34. For the final parallel between the flesh of conception and the flesh of the sacrament, see Ibid., 43, 262–63.

35. See Anne Clark's discussion in Elizabeth of Schönau, *The Complete Works*, translated and introduced by Anne L. Clark, preface by Barbara Newman (New York: Paulist Press, 2000).

36. In addition to the correspondence between Elizabeth of Schönau and Hildegard regarding Saint Ursula, there is also a sorrowful letter from an abbess of the monastery at Cologne dedicated to St. Ursula and near to the supposed site of the martyrdom. The letter reveals great personal intimacy between these two figures; see *The Letters of Hildegard of Bingen*, vol. 2, trans. Jospeph L. Baird and Radd K. Ehrman (New York: Oxford University Press, 1998), 104.

37. All the chant texts are readily available in Barbara Newman's edition of Hildegard's *Symphonia*, 2d ed. (Ithaca: Cornell University Press, 1998). Newman provides two translations, one poetic and the other literal.

38. There is reference here to Genesis 12:1–3, which in its turn was picked up in the great Marian canticle, the Magnificat. "And the Lord said to Abram:

Go forth out of thy country, and from thy kindred, and out of thy father's house, and come into the land which I shall shew thee. And I will make of thee a great nation, and I will bless thee, and magnify thy name, and thou shalt be blessed. I will bless them that bless thee, and curse them that curse thee, and in thee shall all the kindred of the earth be blessed." Resonating phrases from Luke 1:46–55: "My soul doth magnify the Lord . . . for behold from henceforth all generations shall call be blessed. . . . And his mercy is from generation unto generations, to them that fear him. . . . He hath received Israel his servant, being mindful of his mercy: As he spoke to our fathers, to Abraham and to his seed for ever."

39. *Symphonia*, 230–331. "Et etiam propter amplexionem Agni desponsationem viri sibi abstraxit." The verb *amplexor* is used of the *sponsus*'s embrace in Song 2:6 and 8:3, forming a kind of refrain there, as well: in Song 2:6, "His left hand is under my head, and his right hand shall embrace me."

40. See Guibert of Gembloux, Letter 38 in *Epistolae*, ed. Albert Derolez, et al., CCCM 66–66a (Turnhout: Brepols, 1988–89), 375. Tenxwind of Andernach's famous criticism of Hildegard and her nuns and Hildegard's response have been much studied; see, for example, John Van Engen, "Abbess: 'Mother and Teacher,'" in *Voice of the Living Light* (n. 6), 30–51, and especially 36–37. Van Engen says of Hildegard's justification for the way her nuns dressed en route to church on major feast days: "Virgins, she explained, were not subject to a man, unlike their married counterparts, so the full vitality of each of their selves as manifest in their hair (their 'greenness') remained within their own wills. They might choose to cover their hair in humility or to uncover it when they went as brides to meet their Spouse." Van Engen suggests in passing that the practice of particularly lavish dress and flowing hair may have been deemed appropriate for the reception of communion (37). I think he is correct in this assumption, and that Hildegard's own theology provides the context for this understanding.

41. In their performance of this chant, the group Anonymous IV has interpreted the piece this way, singing it before and after the intoned Magnificat. See *Hildegard von Bingen, 11,000 Virgins: Chants for the Feast of St. Ursula*, Harmonia Mundi 907200, track 15. Barbara Newman suggests the same use, *Symphonia*, 309.

42. For discussion, see Newman, *Symphonia*, 269–70.

43. See my "Music for the Love Feast" (n. 1).

44. Compare with Song 4:11: "Thy lips, my spouse, are as a dropping honeycomb, honey and milk are under thy tongue," as well as with Genesis 1:10–12, especially provocative in the Latin: "Et vocavit Deus aridam terram congregationesque aquarum appellavit maria. Et vidit Deus quod esset bonum. Et ait: germinet terra herbam virentem et facientem semen et lignum pomiferum faciens fructum iusta genus suum, cuius semen in semetipso sit super terra. Et factum est ita," "And God called the dry land, Earth; and the gathering together of the waters, he called Seas. And God saw that it was good. And he said: Let the earth bring forth the green herb, and such as may seed, and the fruit tree yielding fruit

after its kind, which may have seed in itself upon the earth. And it was done." The "most noble dawn" of the responsory is part of a large thematic complex that operates throughout Hildegard's liturgical poetry, stressing the coming of the light and the kindling of fire and the monastic love song of greeting offering by those wise virgins who have longed for the bridegroom throughout a long night. For discussion of this theme, see my "Composer and Dramatist" (n. 8), and also my "Hildegard and the Dawn Song of Lauds: An Introduction to Benedictine Psalmody," in *Psalms in Community: Jewish and Christian Textual, Liturgical, and Artistic Traditions*, ed. Harold W. Attridge and Margot E. Fassler (Atlanta: Society of Biblical Literature, 2003), 215–39.

45. The wondrous kiss of Hildegard's opening psalter antiphon is a kiss of peace, which resonates with liturgical action and takes the practiced singer to Psalm 84 in the Vulgate (85 in the Hebrew Psalter), a text that personifies virtues much as Hildegard does in her play and that fructifies the result of the kiss: Ps. 84:10–13: "Surely his salvation is near to them that fear him: that glory may dwell in our land. Mercy and truth have met each other: justice and peace have kissed. Truth is sprung out of the earth: and justice hath looked down from heaven. For the Lord will give goodness: and our earth shall yield her fruit."

46. In her sequence for her first patron, Disibod, Hildegard calls on his ability to protect those who sing God's praise. See *Symphonia*, 188–89, strophe 5a.

47. See "O dulcis electe" in *Symphonia*, 168–69, and Newman's commentary on the text, 287–88.

48. The point is made elegantly in her sequence for Saint Maximin, a fourth-century bishop, whom Hildegard connects to Solomon. In her sequence for this saint, she speaks of the perfumers, the *pigmentarii*, as those who offer sacrifices in the Temple, here making a connection with the Eucharistic sacrifice as well: "O pigmentarii, qui estis in suavissima viriditate hortorum regis, ascendentes in altum quando sanctum sacrificium in arietibus perfectistis," "O spice-dealers! you who dwell in the sweetest foliage of the King's gardens, mounting on high when you have accomplished the holy sacrifices with rams." For the full text, translation, and notes, see *Symphonia*, 212–15 and 302–3. For further commentary on the typology of the sequence, see Christopher Page, *Sequences and Hymns* (Lustleigh: Antico, 1983).

49. When describing the saints who sing on high in the heavenly Jerusalem in the sequence for the patron of her own monastery, Saint Rupert, Hildegard says "Hear, O crowned ones, O radiant-gowned ones" (see *Symphonia*, 197). In an unpublished paper written for one of my seminars, Isabelle Fabre discussed the importance and meanings of crown imagery in Hildegard's liturgical poetry. Of course, there is reference here to the liturgical vestments of the Rupertsburg nuns as they welcomed the bridegroom in their own Eucharistic feasts.

50. *Symphonia*, 244–47. For a succinct discussion of the typology operating in this text see Newman's notes, 312–14.

51. See her paper in Audrey E. Davidson, ed., *Ordo virtutum of Hildegard of Bingen: Critical Studies* (Kalamazoo: Western Michigan University Press, 1992)

52. This sequence is transcribed and analyzed in my "Music for the Love Feast," n. 2.

53. This paragraph is directly borrowed from my essay "Music for the Love Feast" (n. 1), 97.

The Harlot and the Giant / Lino Pertile

1. Dante Alighieri, *Monarchy* 3.3.12, ed. and trans. Prue Shaw (Cambridge: Cambridge University Press, 1996), 67. Dante quotes the version of the Song, very common in the Middle Ages, in which the comma was placed after, not before "post me."

2. The main studies on the commentary tradition of the Song of Songs in the Middle Ages are Friedrich Ohly, *Hohelied-Studien: Grundzüge einer Geschichte der Hoheliedauslegung des Abenlandes bis um 1200* (Wiesbaden: Franz Steiner Verlag, 1958); Helmut Riedlinger, *Die Makellosigkeit der Kirche in den lateinischen Hoheliedkommentaren des Mittelalters*, Beiträge zur Geschichte der Philosophie und Theologie des Mittelalters 38, no. 3 (Münster: West Aschendorff, 1958); Rosemarie Herde, "Das Hohelied in der lateinischen Literatur des Mittelalters bis zum 12. Jahrhundert," *Studi Medievali* 3a, series, 8 (1967): 957–1073; Ann W. Astell, *The Song of Songs in the Middle Ages* (Ithaca: Cornell University Press, 1990); and E. Ann Matter, *The Voice of My Beloved: The Song of Songs in Medieval Christianity* (Philadelphia: University of Pennsylvania Press, 1990).

3. An excellent synthesis of Honorius's commentary can be read in Matter, *The Voice of My Beloved*, 49–85. My summary refers to Honorius's first prologue (Patrologia Latina, henceforth PL, 172: 347–53).

4. See Matter, *The Voice of My Beloved*, 106. See also the lists, albeit incomplete, of the commentaries on the Song and Apocalypse in Conrad Spicq, *Esquisse d'une histoire de l'exégèse latine au Moyen Age* (Paris: Vrin, 1944), 397, 400.

5. See Raoul Manselli, *La "Lectura super Apocalypsim" di Pietro di Giovanni Olivi: Ricerche sull'escatologismo medievale* (Rome: Istituto Storico Italiano per il Medio Evo, 1955) and David Burr, *Olivi's Peaceable Kingdom: A Reading of the Apocalypse Commentary* (Philadelphia: University of Pennsylvania Press, 1993), which has an ample and up-to-date bibliography. Olivi's commentary on the Song, of which there are various manuscripts in Italy, is little known, even to scholars of the Bible in the Middle Ages; it can be read among the works attributed to Saint Bonaventure in *Sancti Bonaventurae . . . operum . . . supplementum*, ed. Benedetto Bonelli (Trent: J. B. Monauni, 1772–74), vol. 1, 52–281. But see now the recent text and Italian translation by Francesca Borzumato (Casale Monferrato: Piemme, 2001).

6. See Lino Pertile, *La puttana e il gigante: Dal Cantico dei cantici al Paradiso Terrestre di Dante* (Ravenna: Longo, 1998). The present contribution is an abbreviated translation of chapter 9, 203–25. See also Paul Priest, "Dante and the 'Song of Songs,'" *Studi Danteschi* 49 (1972): 79–113, and Johan Chydenius, *The*

Typological Problem in Dante (Helsingfors: Societas Scientiarum Fennica, 1958), 110–48.

7. All citations of the *Commedia* in Italian are taken from the Petrocchi text. I am quoting the English, here and elsewhere, from the translation of Henry Wadsworth Longfellow, the most literal that I know.

8. I am citing the Douay Rheims version of the Bible in English. The Vulgate to which I refer is from the Deutsche Bibelgesellschaft Stuttgart edition (1983).

9. Dante himself uses it in *Inferno* 19.106–11.

10. Peter Armour recently challenged this interpretation in his *Dante's Griffin and the History of the World* (Oxford: Clarendon Press, 1989). For Armour, the griffin should be understood as a symbol of Rome's binary imperium.

11. Saint Augustine, *De civitate Dei* 16, chapters 3, 4, and 10.

12. See, for example, Cassiodorus, *Expositio psalmorum*, ed. Marc Adriaen, Corpus Christianorum Series Latina (henceforth CCSL) 97, psalm 32, l. 295; Beda Venerabilis, *In principium Genesis*, ed. Charles W. Jones, CCSL 118A, book 2, chap. 6, l. 998.

13. *Saint Augustine on the Psalms*, trans. Scholastica Corrigan and Felicitas Corrigan, Ancient Christian Writers, Westminster, Md.: Newman Press, 1960), 1, 182.

14. See Saint Ambrose, *De interpellatione Iob and David*, 4, 1, 3 (PL, 14: 812).

15. Saint Ambrose, *De Noe et arca*, 34, 128 (PL 14, cc. 436–38).

16. *Saint Augustine on the Psalms*, 1, 178.

17. Ibid., 189.

18. Augustine, *Confessions* 4.12, 18–19, trans. Henry Chadwick (Oxford: Oxford University Press, 1991), 64.

19. *Venanti Honori Clementiani Fortunati . . . Opera poetica*, ed. F. Leo, Monumenta Germaniae Historica, Auctorum antiquissimorum, 4, 1 (Berlin: Weidmann, 1881) 372, "Carminum spuriorum appendix, I: *In laudem sanctae Mariae*," my translation.

20. *Expositio in psalmos*, 18 (PL 164: 758), my translation.

21. *Ruperti Tuitientis commentaria in evangelium Sancti Johannis*, ed. Hrabanus Haacke, Corpus Christianorum Continuatio Mediaevalis (henceforth CCCM) 9, book 1, 1, 10–19 (PL 169: 207), my translation.

22. *Divi Thomae Aquinatis doctoris angelici . . . opera: Editio altera veneta* (Venice: Simon Occhi, 1775), vol. 1, 259, my translation. See also Alain de Lille, *Liber in distinctionibus*, PL 210: 803.

23. John of Paris's *Tractatus de Antichristo et eius temporibus* can be read in *Abbas Joachim Magnus propheta* (Venice: per Bernardinum Benalium, [1516]), cc. xliiii^r–li^v; the passage (quoted also in Armour, 230) is to be found on c. xlvi^r.

24. *Divi Thomae Aquinatis* in *Beati Ioannis Apocalypsim expositio* (Florence: apud Laurentium Torrentinum, 1549), 415.

25. See *Commentarium in Cantica Canticorum*, in *Origenes Werke*, ed. Willem A. Baehrens, vol. 8 (Leipzig: J. C. Hinrichs, 1925), 89.

26. See, for example, Saint Ambrose, *De sacramentis*, 5, 2, 5–6 (PL 16: 447). The kiss of the Song is often interpreted as a symbol of the Eucharist. In the liturgy of the Mass, when he kisses the altar, the priest is said to be symbolically kissing Christ. Pope Innocent III explicitly connects this ritual with the first line of the Song (*De sacro altaris mysterio*, 2, 15, PL 217: 807; see also Saint Bernard, *Sermones super Cantica Canticorum*, 1,1). On the relationship between the Song and Christian liturgy, see Jean Daniélou, *Bible et liturgie* (Paris: Éditions du Cerf, 1951), 32–33, and for a more specific discussion, Jean Daniélou, "Eucharistie et Cantique des Cantiques," *Irénikon* 33 (1950): 257–77.

27. See Saint Ambrose, *De Isaac*, 3, 10 (PL 14: 532); Gregory the Great, PL 76: 1954, a passage that reappears, almost verbatim, in Paterius, *Liber de expositione veteris et novi testamenti de diversis libris S. Gregorii M. concinatus*, PL 79: 907, Beda, *In Cantica Canticorum*, 4, l. 132 (ed. David Hurst, CCSL 119B), *In primam partem Samuhelis*, 1, line 705 (ed. David Hurst, CCSL 119), *In Lucae evangelium*, 1, l. 583 (ed. David Hurst, CCSL 120), etc.; Cassiodorus, *Commentarium in Cantica Canticorum*, PL 70: 1064; Peter Damian, *Sermones*, 20, 2 (ed. Johannes Lucchesi, CCCM 57); Guillaume de Saint-Thierry, *Exposé sur le Cantique des Cantiques*, sec. 150, 316–21, ed. Jean Marie Déchanet, trans. Pierre Dumontier (Paris: Éditions du Cerf, 1962).

28. *Sermones super Cantica Canticorum*, ed. Jean Leclercq, Charles H. Talbot, and Henri M. Rochais (Rome: Editiones Cistercienses, 1957), vol. 1,. 127 (trans. Kilian Walsh [Kalamazoo, Mich.: Cistercian Publications, 1983], 10–11). Dante could have read this passage in Hugh of Saint Cher's commentary on the Song, *Hugonis de Sancto Charo opera omnia*, (Venice: Pezzana, 1732), vol. 3, f. 107, which is partly copied verbatim from Saint Bernard's *Sermones*. Another possible source for Dante could have been the *De laudibus B. Mariae Virginis*, a work attributed to Albert the Great, in which some of Bernard's most memorable sentences reappear, but now in praise of the Virgin Mary: see *De laudibus B. Mariae*, 12, 2, 12, in *Opera omnia*, ed. Auguste Borgnet (Paris: Vivès, 1890–99), vol. 36, 643.

29. See Ian Stuart Robinson, "Political Allegory in the Biblical Exegesis of Bruno of Segni," *Recherches de Théologie ancienne et médiévale* 41 (1974): 5–37; Silvia Cantelli, "Il commento al Cantico dei cantici di Giovanni da Mantova," *Studi Medievali*, series 3, 26 (1985): 101–84.

30. See my *La puttana e il gigante*.

In the Absence of Love / Carey Ellen Walsh

1. Elizabeth Wright, *Psychoanalytic Criticism: A Reappraisal* (New York: Routledge, 1998), 112.

2. The Bible and Culture Collective, *The Postmodern Bible* (New Haven: Yale University Press, 1995), 200.

3. Joël Dor, *Introduction to the Reading of Lacan: The Unconscious Structured Like a Language* (New York: Other, 1998), 182.

4. Lacan in fact differs from Freud in that he views the Oedipal complex as a linguistic, rather than sexual event.

5. Dor, *Introduction*, 182.

6. Carey Ellen Walsh, *Exquisite Desire: Religion, Erotics, and the Song of Songs* (Minneapolis: Fortress, 2000).

7. Lacan uses Saussure's distinction between the signifier and the signified. For our purposes here, it should simply be noted that language is a convention: The terms themselves bear no necessary connection to an outside referent. For a thorough and clear explication of his use of Saussure, please see Dor, *Introduction*.

8. Jacques Lacan, *Écrits: A Selection*, trans. Alan Sheridan (New York: W. W. Norton, 1977), 65.

9. See especially his exhaustive study *The Rule of Metaphor: Multi-Disciplinary Studies of the Creation of Meaning in Language*, trans. Robert Czerny (Toronto: University of Toronto Press, 1977).

10. Dor, *Introduction*, 192.

11. Jacques Lacan, "On Jouissance," in *On Feminine Sexuality: The Limits of Love and Knowledge; The Seminar of Jacques Lacan*, book 20, trans. Bruce Fink (New York: W. W. Norton, 1998), 3.

Song? Songs? Whose Song? / Carol R. Fontaine

1. See my "The Voice of the Turtle: Now It's *MY* Song of Songs," in *The Song of Songs: A Feminist Companion to the Bible*, 2d series, ed. Athalya Brenner and Carole R. Fontaine (Sheffield, UK: Sheffield Academic Press, 2000), 169–85.

2. See André LaCocque, "I Am Black and Beautiful," in this volume. Most interpreters do not find any plot line at all in the Song.

3. Athalya Brenner, "'My' Song of Songs," in *The Song of Songs: A Feminist Companion to the Bible*, 154–68.

4. Much has been written on this topic; for an entry point into the feminist analysis of this metaphor, see Renita Weems, *Battered Love: Marriage, Sex, and Violence in the Hebrew Prophets* (Minneapolis: Fortress, 1995).

5. If your mom has not been gassed by the National Guard while standing in her very own garden, then you have *not* had the "American experience" as it is lived by those on the underside of the land of opportunity.

6. These ended, not through my teenage disinterest, but due to my involvement with the civil rights movement.

7. It was the show that had the major hunk, shirtless, stuck in quicksand with a Native American enemy—a scene that sets hearts a flutter and voices to whisper, *even* in Sunday school.

8. I was the only one at my stop who was allowed to board the bus at the front door. Nevertheless, I marched to the back and took the last "white" seats before the "colored" section, because the people up front were just so mean to my neighbors in the back. I used to sit in the "colored seats," but it caused unwelcome comment with which, at age ten, I was unable to cope.

9. The white men scorned them only by day, except on Sunday mornings, which were a very busy time for the girls.

10. There were many ranks of princess and queen; I never made it past lady-in-waiting, despite my exceptional memory for Bible verses—the effect of asking uncomfortable questions, no doubt.

11. Our teacher told us, in flustered heat, "It's *not* dancing, it's what it leads to!" This only egged us on to inquire further about the teleology of dancing to "jungle music."

12. Did I take a certain delight in this? I confess I did: I was never slated for a "fine Christian" anything, because I lived among African Americans and Haitians, had contact with Jewish families for whom my parents worked, and my best friend was Catholic—horrors! (Hence, my scholarly interest in the concept of social uncleanness.)

13. To be fair, they also provided a modicum of protection from abusive tricks, because abusing one of their girls was taken as a personal insult to her male owner.

14. My mother, no fan of the streetwalkers or dealers, routinely gave them water to drink along with her own take on a moral homily: "Nobody should have to sleep with that many white men! You do all the work, and your pimp takes all your money! You better get off the street, or you'll be dead in two years, like all the rest!"

15. Yes, Gentle Reader, I am painfully aware that this plays into the fantasy of "rescue" and "escape" that women are conditioned to long for as a remedy to their lot. Ultimately, it's not.

16. One of my former students had done a lay congregational Bible training event at which Roland was the featured speaker, and the topic was the Song. "By the time he was finished," she said, "we all just wanted to run out, grab our husbands, and have sex. Lots of it! What an exciting speaker!" Yes; very true.

17. Even if this harmony is a disjunctive fantasy of male authorship, it still has meaning for readers and theology.

18. See my " 'Go Forth into the Fields': An Earth-Centered Reading of the Song of Songs," in *The Earth Story in Wisdom Traditions*, ed. Norman C. Habel and Shirley Wurst, The Earth Bible 3 (Sheffield, UK: Sheffield Academic Press, 2001), 126–42.

19. To date, I have heard only two persons (other than Father Roland Murphy—*not* a Protestant) use the Song in preaching, and both of us, Mark Burrows and I are talking to you here in this volume.

20. For an example of use of the Song in ecologically focused Protestant worship, see my "The Song of Life," in *Seven Songs of Creation: Liturgies Celebrating and Healing Earth*, ed. Norman Habel (Cleveland: Pilgrim Press, 2004), 107–123.

"Where Has Your Beloved Gone?" / Lesleigh Cushing Stahlberg

1. Ellen F. Davis, "Reading the Song Iconographically," 173.
2. Ibid.

NOTES TO PAGES 315–328

3. André LaCocque, "I Am Black and Beautiful," 163.

4. Steven Kepnes, "Song Of Songs Rabba and the Mind-Body Problem," *Scriptural Reasoning* 3, no. 2 (August 2003).

5. Ibid.

6. LaCocque, "I Am Black and Beautiful," 163.

7. Admiel Kosman, "The Song of Songs," trans. Varda Koch Ocker, *European Judaism* 36, no. 2 (Autumn 2003): 147.

8. Admiel Kosman, "A New Commentary with God's Help," trans. Varda Kocher, *European Judaism* 36, no. 2 (Autumn 2003): 149.

9. Yehuda Amichai, *Open Closed Open*, trans. Chana Bloch and Chana Kronfeld (New York: Harcourt, 2000), 27.

10. LaCocque, "I Am Black and Beautiful," 163.

11. Ibid.

12. Chana Kronfeld, "'The Wisdom of Camouflage': Between Rhetoric and Philosophy in Amichai's Poetic System," *Prooftexts: A Journal of Jewish Literary History* 3 (September 10, 1990): 474.

13. Or, as Bloch and Kronfeld have it, his "counter-theology."

14. One is reminded here of Yiddish poet Jacob Glatstein's declaration "The God of my unbelief is magnificent."

15. For a discussion of Amichai's reworking of classical sources, see Nili Scharf Gold, "A Burning Bush or a Fire of Thorns: Toward a Revisionary Reading of Amichai's Poetry" *Prooftexts* 14 (1994): 49–69.

16. Amichai, *Open Closed Open*, 40

17. Chana Bloch, "Wrestling with the Angel of History: The Poetry of Yehuda Amichai" *Judaism* 45 (Summer 1996); 299.

18. Amichai, *Open Closed Open*, 47–48.

19. Ibid., 40–41.

20. Ibid., 118.

21. Chana Bloch and Chana Kronfeld, "Amichai's Counter-Theology: Opening *Open Closed Open*," *Judaism* 49, no. 2 (Spring 2000): 154.

22. Davis, "Reading the Song Iconographically," 000.

23. Yehuda Amichai, "29," in *Yehuda Amichai: A Life of Poetry, 1948–1994*, trans. Benjamin Harshav and Barbara Harshav (New York: HarperCollins, 1994), 276.

24. Admiel Kosman, "I Told the City Watchman," trans. Lisa Katz, *The Drunken Boat* (Spring 2002).

25. Davis, "Reading the Song Iconographically," 176.

26. Ibid., 174.

CONTRIBUTORS

Nehama Aschkenasy is professor of Comparative Literature at the University of Connecticut and Director of the Center for Judaic and Middle Eastern studies of its Stamford campus. She has published three books, *Biblical Patterns in Modern Literature*, the award-winning *Eve's Journey: Feminine Images in Hebraic Literary Tradition,* and *Woman at the Window*, as well as numerous book chapters and articles, and guest-edited a dedicated volume of the *AJS Review* titled *Recreating the Canon: The Biblical Presence in Modern Hebrew Literature and Culture.*

Chana Bloch is a poet, translator, scholar, and teacher. Among her published works are three books of poems, including *Mrs. Dumpty*, a critical study of George Herbert, and five books of translation from Hebrew poetry, ancient and contemporary. Bloch lives in Berkeley, California, and is emerita professor of English and former director of the Creative Writing Program at Mills College.

Marc Brettler is Dora Golding Professor of Biblical Studies in the Department of Near Eastern and Judaic Studies at Brandeis University. His main areas of research are religious metaphors and the Bible, biblical historical texts, and women and the Bible. He is author of *The Book of Judges: Old Testament Readings*, *The Creation of History in Ancient Israel*, and *How to Read the Bible*, and coeditor of *The Jewish Study Bible*.

Mark Burrows is professor of the history of Christianity at Andover Newton Theological School. A historian of medieval and early modern Christianity, Burrows in his research and teaching explores a spectrum of issues—mystical texts and visionary literature of the Middle Ages, with special interest in Julian of Norwich and late medieval England; Dante and medieval poetry; and the monastic writings of the early Cistercians.

Ellen F. Davis is professor of Bible and Practical Theology at Duke Divinity School. She is the author of *Proverbs, Ecclesiastes, and the Songs of Songs, Getting Involved with God: Rediscovering the Old Testament,* and *Wondrous Death: Preaching the Old Testament.* Her current work is on an agrarian reading of the Hebrew Bible.

Margot Fassler is Robert Tangeman Professor of Music History and Liturgy at Yale University. Her special fields of study are medieval and American sacred music and the liturgy of the Latin Middle Ages. Her subspecialties are liturgical drama of the Middle Ages and Mariology. Her book *Gothic Song: Victorine Sequences and Augustinian Reform in Twelfth-Century Paris* has received awards from both the American Musicological Society and the Medieval Academy of America.

Carole R. Fontaine is Taylor Professor of Biblical Theology and History at Andover Newton Theological School. A feminist scholar in biblical wisdom traditions and author of *Smooth Words: Women, Proverbs and Performance in Biblical Wisdom,* Fontaine is also a human-rights activist and a member of the board of interfaith NGOs.

Arthur Green, rector of Hebrew College's Rabbinical School and Irving Brudnick Professor of Philosophy and Religion, is recognized as one of the world's preeminent authorities on Jewish thought and spirituality. His most recent books include *Ehyeh: A Kabbalah for Tomorrow* and *A Guide to the Zohar.*

Peter S. Hawkins is professor of religion and Director of the Luce Program in Scripture and Literary Arts at Boston University. Hawkins's work has long centered on Dante, most recently in *Dante: A Brief History; Dante's Testaments: Essays on Scriptural Imagination,* winner of a 2001 AAR Book Prize; and in *The Poets' Dante: Twentieth-Century Reflections,* coedited with Rachel Jacoff. He has also published books on twentieth-century fiction, utopia, and the language of ineffability. His essays have dealt with such topics as memory and memorials, the NAMES Project Quilt, televangelism, and scriptural interpretation.

Kathryn Hellerstein is the Ruth Meltzer Senior Lecturer in Yiddish and Jewish Studies at the University of Pennsylvania. A poet and a translator as well as a scholar of Yiddish poetry, she is the author of *In New York: A Selection,* a translation and study of Moyshe-Leyb Halpern's poems, and of *Paper Bridges: Selected Poems of Kadya Molodowsky*. She is also coeditor of *Jewish American Literature: A Norton Anthology*.

Judith A. Kates is professor of Jewish women's studies at Hebrew College. A noted expert in the field, Kates is coeditor of *Beginning Anew: A Woman's Companion to the High Holy Days* and *Reading Ruth: Contemporary Women Reclaim a Sacred Story*.

Andre Lacocque is professor emeritus of Old Testament at the Chicago Theological Seminary. He is the author of many books, including *Romance She Wrote: A Hermeneutical Essay on Song of Songs, Jonah: A Psycho-Religious Approach to the Prophet*, and *Thinking Biblically: Exegetical and Hermeneutical Studies*.

E. Ann Matter holds the William R. Kenan Jr. Chair of Religious Studies and is Associate Dean for Arts and Letters at the University of Pennsylvania. Matter is a widely published scholar whose work encompasses studies of women in early modern Italy as well as the history of the interpretation of the Bible from the Middle Ages to the present. She is the author of *The Voice of My Beloved: The Song of Songs in Western Medieval Christianity* and the coeditor of *Creative Women in Medieval and Early Modern Italy: A Religious and Artistic Renaissance* and of *The Liturgy of the Medieval Church*.

Jacqueline Osherow is Distinguished Professor of English at the University of Utah, where her teaching focuses on poetry, the Hebrew Bible, and literature. An award-winning poet, Osherow has published five volumes of her own work: *Dead Men's Praise, With a Moon in Transit, Conversations with Survivors, Looking for Angels*, and *The Hoopoe's Crown*. Her poetry has appeared in *Ploughshares*, the *New Republic*, the *New Yorker*, and the *Paris Review*.

Margaret Adams Parker is an adjunct instructor at Virginia Theological Seminary. A sculptor as well as a printmaker, she sculpted *Reconciliation* for Duke Divinity School, and her *MARY* is in parishes around the country.

Lino Pertile is professor of Italian and director of the Italian graduate program at Harvard University. His interests include Dante, the Latin Middle Ages, and Renaissance literature in France and Italy. He is the author of *La punta del disio. Semantica del desiderio nella "Commedia"* and *La puttana e il gigante. Dal Cantico dei Cantici al Paradiso terrestre di Dante* and editor of *The Cambridge History of Italian Literature* and of *The New Italian Novel*.

Nehemia Polen is professor of Jewish Thought and director of the Hasidic Text Institute at Hebrew College. His edited and annotated translation of Malkah Shapiro's memoir, *The Rebbe's Daughter: Memoir of a Hasidic Childhood*, received the 2002 National Jewish Book Award. He is also the author of *The Holy Fire: The Teachings of Rabbi Kalonymus Shapia, the Rebbe of the Warsaw Ghetto*.

Lesleigh Cushing Stahlberg is assistant professor of religion and Jewish studies at Colgate University. Her teaching and research center on the literary afterlife of the Hebrew Bible.

Carey Ellen Walsh is professor of Hebrew Scriptures at Walsh University. She is the author of *Exquisite Desire: Religion, the Erotic, and the Song of Songs* and *The Fruit of the Vine: Viticulture in Ancient Israel*.

INDEX

INDEX OF SCRIPTURAL
CITATIONS

INDEX OF SCRIPTURAL CITATIONS